Borderblur Poetics

Borderblur Poetics

Intermedia and
Avant-Gardism
in Canada,
1963-1988

ERIC SCHMALTZ

© 2023 Eric Schmaltz

University of Calgary Press
2500 University Drive NW
Calgary, Alberta
Canada T2N 1N4
press.ucalgary.ca

All rights reserved.

This book is available in an Open Access digital format published under a CC-BY-NCND 4.0 Creative Commons license. The publisher should be contacted for any commercial use which falls outside the terms of that license.

LIBRARY AND ARCHIVES CANADA CATALOGUING IN PUBLICATION

Title: Borderblur poetics : intermedia and avant-gardism in Canada, 1963-1988 / Eric Schmaltz.
Names: Schmaltz, Eric, 1988- author.
Description: Includes bibliographical references and index.
Identifiers: Canadiana (print) 20230440819 | Canadiana (ebook) 20230440878 | ISBN 9781773854564 (hardcover) | ISBN 9781773854571 (softcover) | ISBN 9781773854595 (PDF) | ISBN 9781773854601 (EPUB) | ISBN 9781773854588 (Open Access PDF)
Subjects: LCSH: Experimental poetry—20th century—History and criticism. | LCSH: Canadian poetry—20th century—History and criticism. | CSH: Canadian poetry (English)—20th century—History and criticism
Classification: LCC PS8145.B67 S36 2023 | DDC C811/.5409—dc23

The University of Calgary Press acknowledges the support of the Government of Alberta through the Alberta Media Fund for our publications. We acknowledge the financial support of the Government of Canada. We acknowledge the financial support of the Canada Council for the Arts for our publishing program.

Copyediting by Ryan Perks
Front cover art: *CRACK* by Brian Dedora, 1978.
Back cover photo: Photograph of bpNichol and bill bissett at Writing in Our Time in Vancouver, 1979. From the private archive of bill bissett, used with his permission.
Cover design, page design, and typesetting by Melina Cusano

For Douglas...

Table of Contents

List of Figures	ix
Acknowledgements	xi
Introduction	1
Canons and Controversies: Literary Traditions and Intermediality in Canada	6
Bordering the Book: Critical Parameters	22
From Here to There: A Brief Chapter Outline	28
Chapter One: Bordering the Blur	31
In Search of Experience: Borderblur Poetics in Canada	35
Dropping Off the Borders: An International Network of Alternative Poetics	46
Intermedial Poesis in the Electric Age	51
"Fuck the Avant-Garde": Borderblur and Theories of the Avant-Garde	57
Chapter Two: Concrete Poetry	69
Beginning Again: A Confluence of Encounters	73
Canadian Concrete Poetry and the Electric Age	77
Against Manipulation: Advertising and Consumer Culture	80
Breaking the Typing Machines	89
(Moving) Images: Film, Television, Photography	103
Chapter Three: Sound Poetry	119
Questioning the Cadence: Sound, Nation, Affect	123
A Network of Sonic Affiliations	126
Language and Sound in the Electronic Age	139
Affect and Extension: Listening to Canadian Sound Poetry	147

Chapter Four: Kinetic Poetry 165
    Toward a Theory of Kinetic Poetics 169
    Kinetic Art and Literature: Borderblur's Kinetic Context 177
    Kinetics and Poetics in Canada 185
    Extending the Codex 191
    Games and Puzzles 199
    Immersive and Environmental Works 207

Coda: Intermedial Poetry in Canada Today 217

Notes 227

Bibliography 249

Index 273

List of Figures

0.1	Front cover of *Ganglia*, no. 1, published January 1965.	11
0.2	Front cover of Judith Copithorne's magazine *Returning*, no. 1, published 1972.	13
0.3	"What Is Can Lit?" by bpNichol, 1973.	16
0.4	"What Is Can Lit?" by bpNichol, 1973.	17
1.1	Front cover of *grOnk*, no. 1, published January 1967.	42
1.2	Excerpt from *END OF AUGUST GIANT grOnk MAILOUT*, published 1969.	49
2.1	"Blues" by bpNichol, from *As Elected: Selected Writing*, 1981.	83
2.2	Excerpt from *Touch* by David UU, 1967.	87
2.3	Untitled collage from *pass th food release th spirit book* by bill bissett, 1973.	90
2.4	Untitled collage from *pass th food release th spirit book* by bill bissett, 1973.	91
2.5	"The Plastic Typewriter, 12" by Paul Dutton (text sourced from the traditional Black US gospel song "Certainly, Lord").	97
2.6	Excerpt from *Release* by Judith Copithorne, 1969.	101
2.7	Excerpt from Shaunt Basmajian's "Personal Traumas," 1980.	104
2.8	Untitled collage from bill bissett's *Stardust*, 1975.	107
2.9	Untitled collage from bill bissett's *Stardust*, 1975	109
2.10	*CRACK* by Brian Dedora, 1978.	117

3.1	Liner notes to Penn Kemp's *Ear Rings*, 1987.	134
3.2	Excerpts from score for "ABCD" by Susan McMaster for First Draft, 1987.	156
4.1	"Like an Eddy" by Earle Birney, 1969.	190
4.2	Excerpt from "SCREAM (How To)" from *The Scream: First Draft, The Third Annual Group Show* by First Draft, 1984.	197
4.3	Front cover of *WAR*, vol. 1, by John Riddell, 1981.	200
4.4	The assembled text from John Riddell's *WAR*, vol. 1, assembled by the author in his home.	202
4.5	Installation photograph of *The Imagination of Aldo Breun* by Michael Dean, November 1981.	210
4.6	Installation photograph of *The Imagination of Aldo Breun* by Michael Dean, November 1981.	210

Acknowledgements

While this book traces the emergence and proliferation of a loose coterie of poets in Canada who sought to transgress the borders between literature and art, between national and international communities, and between art and life, this book also, in its own way, is the culmination—the blurring together—of multiple career stages, geographies, coteries, mentorships, and conditions of labour that I have had the privilege of experiencing in my life thus far. I wish to express my sincerest gratitude to the following persons, institutions, and various programs of support; each has come together to make this book possible.

What I am now calling *Borderblur Poetics: Intermedia and Avant-Gardism in Canada, 1963–1988* began in the Department of English at York University. Stephen Cain, chair of my dissertation committee, supported this project at its most nascent stages and saw it through to the very end. His commitment to academic rigour and open exploration gave me the necessary resources and space I needed to become the scholar and poet I am today. Also on my committee was Andy Weaver, among the kindest and most generous thinkers about poetry and poetics, and Lily Cho, whose considerations encouraged me to look more deeply at my work. I am grateful for their assessments of my research. While labouring as a graduate student at York, my work was also buttressed by the generous support and insights of various York faculty members, each of whom, in their own ways, inadvertently or not, shaped what this book has become. In particular, I wish to thank Marcus Boon, Marc Couroux, Marie-Christine Leps, Thomas Loebel, Susan Warwick, Allan Weiss, and Robert Zacharias. Thank you, too, to my external examiner, Peter Jaeger.

I rewrote a significant portion of this book during a Social Sciences and Humanities Research Council Postdoctoral Fellowship in the Department of English at the University of Pennsylvania. Thanks to Charles Bernstein for his support during this time. I also extend a heartfelt thanks to my dearest friends Martine Tchitcihe and Benjamin Sieff, who showed me such gracious hospitality while living in Philadelphia.

I must also thank poets David Aylward, bill bissett, Judith Copithorne, Michael Dean, Brian Dedora, Claude Dupuis, Paul Dutton, Penn Kemp, Susan McMaster, Andrew McClure, Colin Morton, Gerry Shikatani, and George Swede, and the stewards who care for the works of certain poets discussed here, including Eleanor Nichol, Madame Justice Wailan Low, Adrienne Copithorne, and Ingrid Harris. I am honoured to have their support and trust as I engage with the legacy of this work.

Thank you to the staff at the Thomas Fisher Rare Book Library at the University of Toronto for their assistance in accessing materials in their collections, especially John Shoesmith; likewise, thanks to Anna St. Onge for her assistance in the Clara Thomas Archives and Special Collections at York University. Additional thanks to Tony Power and David Kloepfer at Simon Fraser University Library Special Collections and Rare Books, Sara Viinalass-Smith of Library and Archives Canada, and Claire Sutton at the Ottawa City Archives.

Thanks also to friends and colleagues who supported this project with their time, resources, and attention, especially Patty Argydes, Derek Beaulieu, Gary Barwin, MLA Chernoff, Igor Djordjevic, Kit Dobson, Christopher Doody, Gregory Fast, Ryan Fitzpatrick, Deanna Fong, Kristina Getz, Beatriz Hausner, Karl Jirgens, Max Karpinski, Kyle Kinaschuk, Zane Koss, Aaron Kreuter, Mat Laporte, Jeremy Lucyk, Shannon Maguire, Donato Mancini, Philip A. Miletic, Jay Millar, Julia Polyck-O'Neill, Kate Siklosi, Dani Spinosa, Divya Victor, and Stephen Voyce.

Thanks, too, to my esteemed colleagues Charles Bernstein, Gregory Betts, Suzanne Zelazo, and Myra Bloom for their supportive words that accompanied this book into the world.

It has been a privilege to work with the University of Calgary Press, whose staff treats projects like these with the utmost care and dedication. Thank you to everybody at the press for your patience with me, for supporting this project, and for all the hard work done on its behalf—especially Alison Cobra, Melina Cusano, Helen Hajnoczky, Ryan Perks, and Brian Scrivener.

The work in this book benefited immensely from the significant support of the Social Sciences and Humanities Research Council (SSHRC) in the form of an SSHRC Postdoctoral Fellowship and a Joseph-Armand Bombardier Canada Doctoral Scholarship. I also wish to acknowledge the support of the Ontario Graduate Scholarship Program and York University's Linda Heather Lamont-Stewart Fellowship in Canadian Studies, Clara Thomas Doctoral

Scholarship in Canadian Studies, and Provost Dissertation Scholarship. I am grateful, too, to the coordinators of York's CUPE 3903 Contract Faculty Research Grant.

Thanks to *FORUM*, *Canadian Poetry*, and *Jacket2* for providing publication venues for certain sections of this work.

Finally, my deepest thanks to Alysha Dawn Puopolo. None of this would be possible without her tireless support and patience, which buoyed me during moments of struggle and permitted me the opportunity to dedicate many long hours, days, weeks, months, and years to this work.

But there is always an avant-garde, in the sense that someone, somewhere is always trying to do something which adds to the possibilities for everybody.

—Dick Higgins (1981)

Introduction

literature doesn't mean long live the empire; literature is words
—bill bissett (2 July 1967)

"This is the death of the poem as I have faithfully reported it, November 29, 1966, as I have faithfully reported it, this is the death of the poem" intones Canadian poet bpNichol one day after the Dominion Day celebrations marking Canada's centennial year. Addressing a national television audience, Nichol reads these lines with poets bill bissett and Phyllis Webb, who chant the words "obituary" and "mortuary" alongside him.[1] This poem was published in January 1967 in issue 1 of Nichol's mimeographed publication *grOnk*; it declares that "THE POEM IS DEAD," signifying, for Nichol, the potential for poetry's rebirth.[2] After the poets conclude their chant, the camera cuts from a close-up of bissett to a shot of all three poets sitting at the studio table. Webb instructs bissett, who wears a grotesque mask with a knife protruding from his neck, to "Take off your mask, bill, and join the group," and in doing so, as scholar Katherine McLeod recognizes, Webb "symbolically unmasks the strange identity of the new Canadian avant-garde" for the literary public.[3] Announcing poetry's demise and subsequent regeneration, this episode marks a meeting between Canada's literary public and an emergent generation of avant-garde writers who proclaim a poetics that secedes from established literary traditions. Nichol and bissett televise the advent of an expansive, liberated intermedial poetic they call *borderblur*. Taking borderblur as its subject, this book combines archival research, historical analysis, canon intervention, and literary criticism to trace the poetic's emergence and proliferation as a significant but underexamined node of avant-garde activity in Canada.

Nichol and bissett delivered this performance at the youthful ages of twenty-two and twenty-seven, respectively, on the CBC program *Extension: Here, Now, and Then*; the show was hosted by Webb, a well-known Canadian poet and public intellectual. Airing during Canada's centennial celebrations, in the summer of 1967, *Extension* featured the nation's established literati alongside some more emergent personalities.[4] Each episode was "an experiment in the staging of poetry in distinct contexts and manners, with poetry presented through film, theatrical readings, conversations at a table and even at a piano."[5] As avant-garde writers who experiment with language and media, Nichol and bissett were well-suited to a multimedia presentation of poetry. With cameras directed at them on a sound stage, a reel-to-reel tape player in the foreground, books, magazines, and papers spread across the table, and their drawings and poems tacked on to the walls, the studio space reproduces the distinctive multimedia characteristics of their work. They sip coffee and smoke cigarettes while Webb guides them through a conversation that touches on such topics as the influence of Allen Ginsberg's Beat poetry and lifestyle, the rock 'n' roll of Mick Jagger, the protest songs of Bob Dylan, and the jazz of Vancouver's Gerry Walker, all while weaving in discussion of their poetries' polyphonic qualities, the destabilization of Western reading practices, diverse uses of media, and implicit forms of social engagement. For Canada, the 1967 centennial signifies a historical turning point, a coming-of-age moment for the country and its cultural identity. I imagine that viewers who tuned in for *Extension*'s investigation of the nation's poetry one day after Dominion Day might have been perplexed by Nichol's poetic eulogy, bissett's grotesque disguise, and their discussions of new music, intoxication, and alternative lifestyles. While the show was meant to take the pulse of Canadian letters, Nichol and bissett ultimately offer their viewers evidence of an emergent poetic milieu distinguished from Canada's existing national literature by its playfulness, penchant for experimentation, and internationalist attitude.

Regarding nation and literature, Nichol and bissett discuss the ideas that inform their poetics within the context of an emergent sense of the world, unbound by electronic media and untethered from a particular nationalist ideology. At the time, this unbound sense of the world is described by renowned Canadian media critic Marshall McLuhan, who in *The Gutenberg*

Galaxy: The Making of Typographic Man (1962) first identifies this period as the *electric age* (more commonly known as the electronic or information age), wherein electronic media—radio, television, film, computers, and so on—accelerated the possibilities for information consumption and communication. "Now, in the electric age," McLuhan writes, "the very instantaneous nature of co-existence among our technological instruments has created a crisis quite new in human history. Our extended faculties and senses now constitute a single field of experience which demands that they become collectively conscious."[6] And in turn, the conditions of this age inspired a shrinking sense of the planet he referred to as the *global village*, a term he advanced in *The Gutenberg Galaxy* and recapitulated with more nuance in *Understanding Media: The Extensions of Man* (1964).[7] Nichol and bissett, it seems, had absorbed this sense of the world by 1967. bissett explains to Webb that their poetry emerges from "not having the margins, not having the borders. . . . Not being limited to a sentence construction or an idea."[8] By invoking "borders," bissett draws attention to the intermedial characteristics of his and Nichol's poetics while implicitly undercutting the nationalist ethos of the government-funded television show. For poets like bissett and Nichol, poesis occurs when poetry is enmeshed with other media, including song, image, movement, sculpture, painting, drawing, print, and more.

Given Webb's penchant for innovative and avant-garde poetic forms, it is hardly surprising that she pushes deeper into the fray.[9] She asks them, "is there any real point to trying to affix a label to a kind of poetry?" Nichol responds by explaining that "there's an Englishman who just called it borderblur." Webb chuckles at this, perhaps already familiar with British poet and theologian Dom Sylvester Houédard (also known as dsh), who coined the term. Nichol explains that borderblur reaches into "all the areas, crossing over into all the arts" to, in effect, dissolve boundaries between linguistic, visual, sonic, and performative modes of creative expression.[10] It may at first seem ironic that Nichol connects his and bissett's practices to the terminology of an Englishman, one who might conjure visions of Canada's ongoing colonial legacy. However, borderblur, as Nichol describes it, refuses traditional poetry's conventions, and it undermines the conceptual solidity of national borders. bissett agrees with Nichol and earlier in the episode locates their work within a global movement, suggesting that the point of borderblur is "to drop off the borders," like those poets, he notes, publishing in Brazil, Belgium, England, Holland, Japan, and Scotland. "It's not just a Canadian trip," he contends.¹¹ With this list of nations home to kindred avant-garde practitioners, bissett is likely thinking of the global currents of concrete poetry, which were being recognized in international anthologies at the time. This includes Emmett Williams's *An Anthology of Concrete Poetry* (1967), which was published by Dick Higgins's then New York–based Something Else Press and featured Nichol's concrete poem "eyes."¹² bissett further emphasizes his suspicions of nationalism by pointing out that "literature doesn't mean long live the empire; literature is words."¹³ While it's difficult to know exactly what bissett means here, I do not read this as an apolitical statement severing poetry from its social or political contexts; rather, by pledging a primary allegiance to words, bissett signals his rejection of the colonial spectre that looms over Canadian literary culture through the importation of its literary tradition and standardized use of British spelling and syntax. Instead, he imagines language to be part of a greater artistic force that does not require falling into the standards of conventional English, and through which he can reject singular notions of national literary hegemony and its "early fantasies of homogeneity."¹⁴ By invoking borderblur, both poets articulate their poetics as distinctive and formally inventive and locate their work within a broader international network of avant-garde practitioners. This book examines how this strain of avant-garde activity complicates long-standing narratives describing Canadian poetry as an expression of Canadian national identity.

I reflect upon this episode of *Extension* for the ways it highlights three central considerations of this study. Firstly, it tidily introduces the terminology that animates this project: *poetry, nation, media,* and *avant-gardism.* Working through these interlocking terms in chapter 1, I take up the idea of borderblur to theorize it as a poetic that allows me to understand the central characteristics and concerns that emerged under its immediate usage, and also how that idea formulated a network of like-minded poets in Canada in the second half of the twentieth century. This is important to note since borderblur is no longer really a term in vogue. Few poets today would use it to describe their work—they would likely prefer terms like multimedia or hybrid—even though many still fold poetry into other artistic modes; included in that group could be Jordan Abel, Oana Avasilichioaei, Gary Barwin, Derek Beaulieu, Stephen Cain, Wayde Compton, Adeena Karasick, Kaie Kellough, M. NourbeSe Philip, Jordan Scott, Kate Siklosi, Dani Spinosa, Matthew James Weigel, and many others. Borderblur emerges and proliferates within a specific context in the mid- to late twentieth century. Secondly, this episode of *Extension* introduces one of the main contentions that this study investigates. bissett's statement against borders highlights how these poets used the term "borderblur" to not only distinguish their poetic work but to announce their cosmopolitan outlook. As they note, the poets borrowed the term from British poet Houédard, thereby positioning themselves as Canadians who, by virtue of their poetic and its connection to an international context, complicate notions of poetry as an expression of national identity. Finally, but most importantly, the episode introduces the relationship between two of this book's principal figures—bissett and Nichol—and the contextual environment within which they created and published. I position them as two main actors whose poetries embody a set of common presumptions around which many other poets gathered in Canada. Some of these like-minded writers and artists include David Aylward, Shaunt Basmajian, Martina Clinton, Judith Copithorne, Brian Dedora, Paul Dutton, Roy Kiyooka, Steve McCaffery, Susan McMaster, Penn Kemp, John Riddell, Ann Rosenberg, Gerry Shikatani, David UU, and others—all of whom make an appearance in this book because of their shared interest in dissolving boundaries that separate creative fields, and because certain facets of their poetic outputs can be understood as representative of borderblur. To locate poets under a single banner may be more expedient than necessarily precise, but they are united by a network of small presses, little magazines, and performance spaces that distinguished them from the majority of the writers in Canada at that time, and, more concretely, they developed their work in proximity to Nichol and bissett, either through publication, friendship, performance, collaboration, or financial support. Taken together, they form an avant-garde network of affiliation that developed an alternative vision for poetry and its production in Canada, one that exceeds the traditional, page-based work that dominated the literary mainstream during the second half of the twentieth century. This book begins to tell the story of how this network of Canadian poets came to be connected by a shared poetics.

In the works of the poets examined in this study, I find indications that they imagined themselves to be working with a dynamic cosmopolitan outlook as the complexities of emergent electronic media and international relations formed their sense of poetry at home. But what specific conditions gave rise to this explosion of intermedial creativity in a Canadian literary context? If borderblur did not actively nurture the dominant national literary discourse, to what conversations and contexts does it contribute? How did borderblur intervene into the imaginative process of national identity formation? If borderblur is conceived as a cosmopolitan alternative to the dominant nationalist literature, what conditions have since arisen to welcome some of these poets into the fold of the Canadian literary canon? How does the legacy of borderblur live on in Canadian literature today? These are the questions that animate this study.

As cultural actors sought to modernize Canada's national and cultural identity in both the lead-up to 1967 and the years since, it seems that Nichol and bissett had already realized literary critic Jahan Ramazani's claim that "even a 'national poet' turns out, on closer inspection, to also be a transnational poet."[15] With that said, this book does not necessarily adopt a transnational critical approach. Rather, it maps the emergence and proliferation of borderblur poetics in Canada in the mid- to late twentieth century as the formation of a literary identity that is aesthetically diverse, internationalist, and intermedial. Borderblur is profitably recognized as a Canadian literary avant-garde "paratradition," a term used by scholar Gregory Betts to describe avant-garde literature, and which I invoke here to account for borderblur's Canadian context and its deviation from the national literary matrix. Despite borderblur's rootedness in the counterculture, as a description "paratradition" is preferable to "countertradition," since this latter term might suggest a persistent opposition to literary hegemony.[16] Given the poetic's propensity for aesthetic openness, to suggest that borderblur poets were explicitly nationalist, transnationalist, or anti-nationalist would be antithetical to their work. Just as they resisted aesthetic foreclosure, political circumscription risks over-generalization and does not account for the way their relationship to nationalism may shift over time and across contexts. Regardless of what this means for each poet's relationship to nationalism, I argue in this book that they created an intermedial literary paratradition that eschewed a distinctive nationalistic agenda and instead formed an active branch of an international avant-garde network that was entangled with the emergent conditions of their time.

Canons and Controversies: Literary Traditions and Intermediality in Canada

In the following chapters, I examine three manifestations of this Canadian literary paratradition by focusing on concrete poetry, sound poetry, and kinetic poetry, each of which can be neatly located under an umbrella term advanced by Fluxus artist Dick Higgins—namely, *intermedia*, which describes a broad range of creative work that falls "between media."[17] Originally published in 1966 in the *Something Else Newsletter*, Higgins offered "intermedia" as a term for engaging with works that fuse multiple art forms in such a way that it's difficult to distinguish them from one another. These kinds of works prompt critics and audiences to reconsider the conventional "separation between media [that] arose in the Renaissance,"[18] and to effectively unsettle the conventions of genre, literary practice, and the discourse of analysis. When Higgins began to take stock of his own avant-garde milieu, "intermedia" was an effective term that captured a broad range of practices happening across Europe, North America, South America, parts of Asia, and elsewhere. Reflecting on the mid-1960s when he first offered the term, he writes, "The world was filled at that time with concrete poems, happenings, sound poetry, environments, and other more or less novel developments."[19] This description corresponds to much of the work examined here.[20] In the context of this study, *intermedial* works create meaning and effect through the inseparable combination of language with other media, as implied by Nichol's definition of borderblur above. In the contemporary context, we might draw parallels between intermedia and the concept of *multimodal communication*, which recognizes, as leading scholars Gunther Kress and Carey Jewitt point out, that "*language is partial*"[21] to the pursuit of meaning-making, and this is true, too, for the poets discussed in this book. While I find *multimodality* to be a useful term for retroactively theorizing borderblur as a poetic, since it emphasizes that language is not the only means of communicating, *intermedia* is more directly applicable to the works that this book examines. Given the close temporal proximity between Higgins and the poets discussed in this book, as well as the network of avant-garde practitioners that they shared, intermedia as a term embodies both aesthetic principles of borderblur and gestures toward the cosmopolitan scene they were responding to. We shall see, too, the subtle and not-so-subtle ways that the term directly informed certain facets of avant-garde practices and communities in Canada. There was the formation in 1967 of the Intermedia Society, for example—an artist-run space in Vancouver dedicated to the exploration of emergent media by a variety of creative practitioners, including poets such as Copithorne, whose work is discussed in chapter 2. The term also places media near the centre of this book's discussion, an especially important point since the work of media theorists such as McLuhan (discussed below) were touchstones for situating borderblur as a practice in Canada. This is important to recognize because many of the books, poems, games, installations, and ephemera examined in this study are representative of borderblur in that they rely on the fusion of language with other media. Higgins's definition of intermedia is echoed by Nichol's fundamental argument, made in 1967, that "we have reached a point where people have finally come to see that language means communication and that communication does not necessarily mean language."[22] For Nichol, like Higgins, writing and art making occurs through interactions between language, image, sound, gesture, space, and so on. Thus, I recognize that the poets that I have here gathered under the umbrella term "borderblur" often embrace intermediality and all it offers. Though concrete, sound, and kinetic poetry have substantial, and at times overlapping, histories and meanings, each form sees specific combinations of language with other media. These forms distinguish borderblur poetics as a Canadian paratradition, since they are generally acknowledged as unconventional and certainly not mainstream. Concrete, sound, and kinetic poetry will be more thoroughly defined in each respective chapter, but for now, these three terms bear some cursory definition to understand what distinguishes this poetry from the singular media of Canada's dominant national literature.

Concrete poetry, sometimes also referred to as visual poetry, describes a poetic form that fuses literary and visual arts by combining language with non-linguistic elements. Concrete poems are often recognized for the ways that words and individual letters form shapes, patterns, and images through the poet's intentional arrangement of language and attention to related materials such as typeface, colour, graphics, and page layout and size. Sound poetry is a form that seizes upon the historically oral and aural aspects of poetry by bridging literature with auditory practices such as music, chant, and sound art. Sound poetry is often intended for performance and utilizes language and language's elemental parts—such as phonemes and morphemes—to create dramatic and often chant- or song-like poems. Kinetic poetry, meanwhile, as a pre-digital form, is significantly under-theorized in the Canadian context. While concrete and sound poetry, respectively, engage the optic and sonic realms of the human sensorium, kinetic poetry is holistic by comparison and incorporates body movement and gesture, feeling, and sensation. The kinetic poems examined in this book often require a more fulsome engagement with the audience's body in the process of meaning-making, as exhibited in flipbooks, immersive installations, and interactive and game-based works. Chapters 2–5 address each term's history and theorization in more detail, but it is significant to note, for now, that this book attends specifically to their manifestation under the aegis of borderblur poetics in the early 1960s and its proliferation in Canada through to the late 1980s.

As is well established in Canadian literary scholarship, there was a flurry of activity in the years before and after 1967 that effectively consolidated a distinguished national literature in Canada that largely excluded concrete, sonic, and kinetic poetries. These activities are recapitulated in Nick Mount's *Arrival: The Story of CanLit* (2017), which describes the establishment of Canadian literary hegemony, or as he calls it, the "CanLit Boom." Convinced that postwar affluence encouraged Canadian cultural development, Mount traces the emergence of Canadian literature as a distinctive part of Canadian public and private life. The period, according to Mount, begins in 1959 and concludes in 1974, and he narrates the emergence of such renowned Canadian literary personalities as Margaret Atwood and Michael Ondaatje; the rise of Canadian literary grant and prize culture as distributed by national institutions such as the Canada Council for the Arts; the establishment of Canadian literary presses like McClelland and Stewart, Anansi, and Coach House; the flourishing of new bookstores; and the arrival of an affluent Canadian reading public. *Arrival* has been criticized for its lack of diverse representation, which results from Mount's focus on a narrow canon of authors who assumed powerful cultural positions during the boom. In his review of the book, literary critic Paul Barrett, for example, finds fault in *Arrival* because its "cast of characters are exceptionally white in a way that is not truly reflective of the CanLit community."[23] Mount omitted, for example, indispensable writers such as Maria Campbell and Austin Clarke.

Though it might not call for the sort of urgent correction Barrett advocates, the fact is that avant-garde writers of the borderblur paratradition are similarly given only slight acknowledgement in *Arrival*. Though no single book of criticism could achieve encyclopedic completeness, such omissions and under-representations combine to produce an uneven account of the Canadian literatures that emerged during the postwar era. While Mount briefly attends to bissett and Nichol in his narration of the Canadian literary establishment, his predominant focus on traditional literary expression at the expense of intermedial forms of expression directs readers' attention away from many writers who were captivated by the possibilities of borderblur, some of whom were women and feminists like Judith Copithorne,

Penn Kemp, Susan McMaster, and Ann Rosenberg, as well as writers with compound identities such as Armenian Canadian Shaunt Basmajian and Japanese Canadian Gerry Shikatani. Within the existing scholarship, these writers remain under-acknowledged or ignored altogether. This book seeks to remedy this issue by writing these figures more forcefully into the narrative of borderblur's proliferation, thereby providing a critical aperture just wide enough that I hope other scholars and readers will continue to gaze. In 1964, Copithorne, for example, arguably produced the first concrete poem among the borderblur poets, published in *blewointment*, with her hand-drawn mixture of text and image. Soon after, *blewointment* featured an increasing number of related works (a significant point first publicly recognized by Betts in his 2021 book *Finding Nothing: The Vangardes, 1959–1975*). Likewise, Rosenberg's semi-erotic novel *The Bee Book* (1981)—which blends concrete poetry with prose narrative—has been overlooked by scholars, despite W. H. New's comparison between Rosenberg and the celebrated Québécois writer Nicole Brossard.[24] With its attention to these important figures, this study, generates a more diverse account of avant-gardism in Canada in the mid- to late twentieth century.

The beginnings of this thriving avant-garde literary culture can be seen, for example, in the network of little magazines and small presses that promoted borderblur poetics in Canada and brought scores of intermedial works into circulation. These venues and their publications gave writers an opportunity to combine and experiment with media and materials and write about taboo subjects while reaching a small but receptive audience. For example, bissett began publishing *blewointment* magazine in Vancouver; it ran from 1963 to 1977 (Blew Ointment Press operated from 1968 until approximately 1984) and inaugurated borderblur as a recognizable paratradition by featuring concrete poetry, lyric poetry, pattern poetry, collages, drawings, found materials, and more. Nichol, who lived in Vancouver during the early days of *blewointment*, relocated to Toronto and brought the publication's spirit with him. He then started Ganglia Press, which produced *Ganglia* magazine (active from 1965 to 1967), jointly edited and published with Toronto poet David Aylward, to initially feature some of the writers Nichol knew out West, notably George Bowering, Copithorne, and bissett. Its related outgrowth, *grOnk*, was published starting in 1967 and, formalizing its interests in international borderblur, called for "manuscripts concerned with concrete kinetic and related borderblur poetry."[25]

Figure 0.1: Front cover of *Ganglia*, no. 1, published January 1965.

These endeavours inspired other small presses and magazines and in this way helped to form a significant network of avant-garde literatures. A prolific publisher in his own right, David UU founded and operated Fleye Press (1966–70), Divine Order of the Lodge (1971–5), Derwyddon Press (1976–81), and Silver Birch Press (1987–94), alongside his work with Nichol on *grOnk*; in a flurry, Copithorne released three issues of *Returning* magazine from July 1972 until May 1973; bissett, with poets Patrick Lane, Seymour Mayne, and Jim Brown, founded Very Stone House in 1965; in 1970, Steve McCaffery began publishing a handful of works under the moniker of Anonbeyond Press; Michael Dean started Wild Press; Richard Truhlar and John Riddell co-founded Phenomenon Press and *Kontakte* magazine in 1975; in the same year, Truhlar founded the Kontakte Writers in Performance series, which featured readings and performances by Canadian and international writers and ran for a total of ten years; seeking opportunities to publish literature in more varied media in 1979, Dean, Brian Dedora, Paul Dutton, McCaffery, Nichol, Riddell, Truhlar, and Steven Ross Smith began publishing Underwhich Editions; and so on and so on.[26] Another significant venue for borderblur poetry was Toronto-based Coach House Press, where Nichol worked in various capacities and edited notable works like Copithorne's *A Light Character* (1985) and Rosenberg's *The Bee Book*. Coach House was also the publisher of the first anthology of women's poetry in Canada, according to Kemp, who edited it in the summer of 1973 (issued as *IS*).[27] None of these forums were exclusively dedicated to borderblur poetics; at times, they featured "trad" poetries, as the poets liked to call them (that is, traditional free verse poetry). However, they were essential venues for showcasing intermedial works in their magazines, books, chapbooks, broadsides, pamphlets, cassettes, vinyl records, floppy disks, games, and microfiche. With their support for an alternative intermedial poetic, these forums provide significant evidence of a thriving and dynamic paratradition that tested the limits of conventional poetry and publishing while seeking more expansive forms of poetic expression.[28]

These kinds of activities emerged because the poets mentioned above could not see themselves reflected in the efforts of established publishers, award juries, or other cultural leaders who endeavoured to articulate a Canadian literary identity during Mount's "CanLit Boom." This was the main objective, for example, of McClelland and Stewart's (hereafter M&S) New Canadian Library series (NCL). Under the general editorship of literary

Figure 0.2: Front cover of Judith Copithorne's magazine *Returning*, no. 1, published 1972.

critic Malcolm Ross, M&S published 152 volumes under its Main Series between its founding in 1958 and the end of Ross's editorial tenure in 1978, according to Janet B. Friskney. Ross and Jack McClelland, who handled the series as M&S's publisher, believed that the books published and reprinted in the series represented a Canadian literary tradition. This tradition includes Stephen Leacock, Mordecai Richler, Susanna Moodie, Catherine Parr Traill, Robertson Davies, Frederick Philip Grove, Leonard Cohen, and many other well-known, oft-studied Canadian writers. Despite Canadian publishing historian Friskney's claim that the NCL "had no claims to canonical status at any point,"[29] it laid a substantial amount of groundwork for the creation of a Canadian literary canon. These titles, many of which are still reprinted, anthologized, enjoyed, and taught today, consequently shaped the public's imagination of life and literature in Canada.

The NCL is predominantly comprised of fiction; as a whole, the series is somewhat homogenous and reflects a largely realist orientation. In aesthetic terms, any poetry in the series represents traditional poesis with few to no traces of intermediality. *Poetry of the Mid-Century, 1940–1960*, published as part of the Original Series in 1966 and edited by Romantic literature scholar Milton Wilson, includes poets Earle Birney, Irving Layton, P. K. Page, Leonard Cohen, Margaret Avison, Jay Macpherson, Raymond Souster, Alden Nowlan, James Reaney, and Kenneth McRobbie. Though some of these poets, like Birney and Avison, would come to briefly flirt with borderblur, this volume articulates a vision of Canadian poetry as predominantly "trad." Another anthology included in the NCL, *Poetry of Contemporary Canada, 1960–1970*, published in 1972 and edited by Eli Mandel, represents a slight evolution, including as it does Cohen alongside Al Purdy, John Newlove, Milton Acorn, Joe Rosenblatt, Margaret Atwood, Michael Ondaatje, George Bowering, Gwendolyn MacEwen, and, perhaps surprisingly, bissett. His included poems, however, are only representative of his distinctive orthography (with some play with margin indents), not his intermedial work.[30] Published one year before and five years after Canada's centennial year, neither of these volumes adequately reflect the avant-garde literature that emerged in the 1960s.

As editor and publisher, respectively, of the NCL, Ross and McClelland had somewhat divergent views on the merit of unconventional texts. Friskney explains that Cohen's amphetamine-fuelled postmodern novel *Beautiful Losers*, for example, was despised by Ross but adored by McClelland. Their correspondence on the subject, as summarized by Friskney, includes some tense debate, but it is clear that Ross had his way, as he ultimately exercised a veto to keep *Beautiful Losers* from the initial series run, declaring it "quite infantile in its thematic conception, & other[wise] pretentious and very self-conscious in its structural methods, painstakingly and repetitively dirty in its imagery and detail."[31] Ross's rejection of *Beautiful Losers*, even in its traditional novel form, indicates that much of borderblur—also characterized at times as self-conscious, juvenile, and controversial—was not aligned with the Canadian literary tradition Ross imagined. The NCL's achievement in moulding a specific tradition inspired several publishers to pursue similar paperback series showcasing supposedly representative works of Canadian literature in the 1960s, including University of Toronto Press's Canadian University Paperbacks in 1963; Oxford's Oxford in Canada Paperbacks in 1965; and Macmillan of Canada's Laurentian Library in 1967.[32]

The kinds of exclusions from Canada's literary mainstream outlined above were deeply felt by those interested in borderblur poetics. Editor and artist Eldon Garnet, for example, published *W)here?* in 1974, an anthology of Canadian poetry featuring UU, Nichol, Copithorne, bissett, and others. Its subtitle, "The Other Canadian Poetry," hints at these artists' outsider status. This location on the fringe of Canadian literary culture at times frustrated the borderblur poets. In September 1968, Nichol asked *grOnk*'s Canadian and international newsletter subscribers, "Aren't we all a little sick of seeing our old standards being anthologized right and left?"[33] Nichol quotes a similarly frustrated bissett in *THE BIG MID-JULY grOnk mailout* (July 1969), sardonically highlighting borderblur's lack of mainstream popularity: "writing what s now calld concrete sound borderblur poetry etc is why we enjoyd so much malnutrition etc for so many years so i feel a special fondness for it."[34] bissett identifies borderblur's unprofitability as a poetic enterprise, despite the rising affluence of Canada's literary public during the boom. Nichol also parodies the Canadian literary establishment in his comic "What Is Can Lit?" "But what the hell is CAN LIT?" quips Nichol's character.[35] Here, he parodies scholarly claims by offering brief perspectives on poets Sheila Watson, Gerry Gilbert, James Reaney, Margaret Avison, and Earle Birney. For example, "Sheila Watson," the narrator explains, "was the first to [illegible] the images of [the] outsider from [illegible] in Canadian [prose]."[36] As evidenced by my attempt to quote these lines, Nichol has obscured certain words in each panel to complicate the possibility of close reading, thus thwarting circumscription

Figure 0.3: "What Is Can Lit?" by bpNichol, 1973.

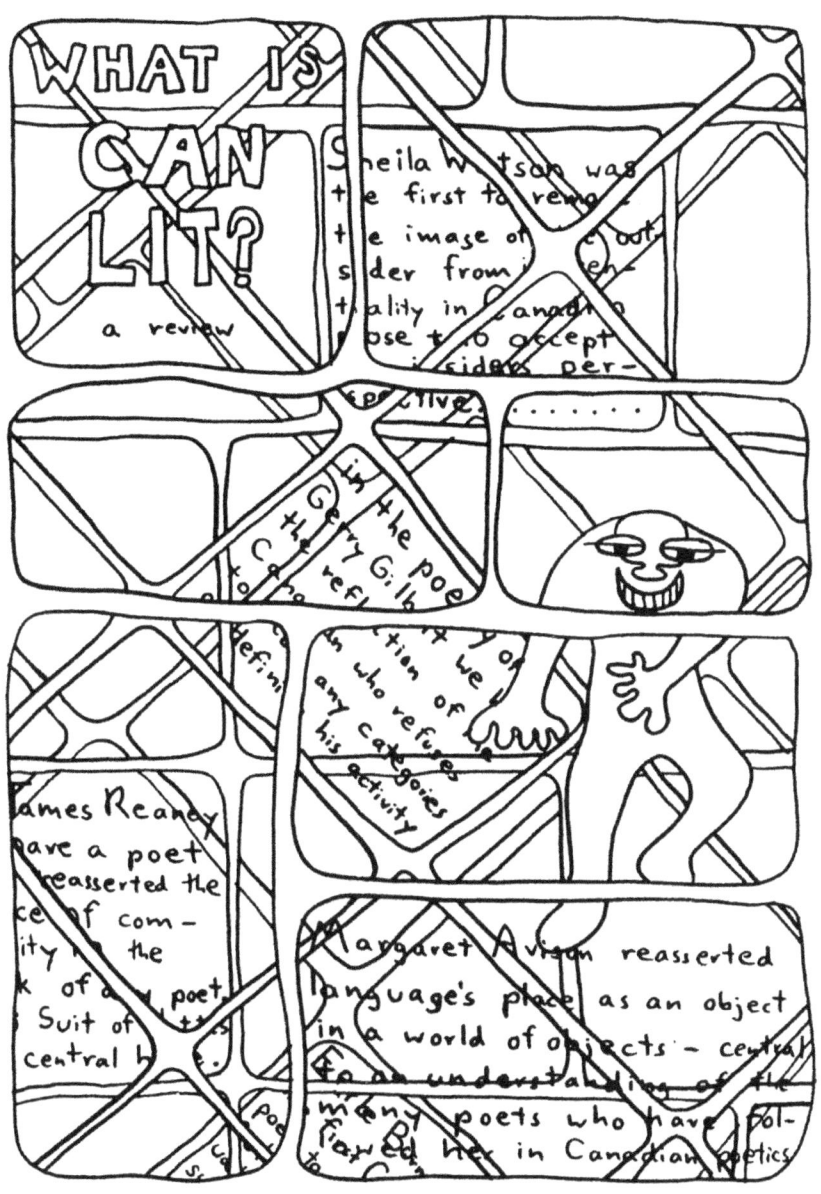

Figure 0.4: "What Is Can Lit?" by bpNichol, 1973.

within a defined national literary framework. By citing five Canadian authors and accounting for their diverse practices while at the same time denying critical closure, Nichol effectively undermines narrow definitions of Canadian literary identity.

The humour of these poets speaks to their belief in borderblur as a viable poetic, which was viewed as a threat by the establishment. In fact, poets like Nichol and bissett were publicly targeted by the government. When Nichol's literary talents were recognized on the national stage, for example, they were deemed outrageous. Nichol received the 1970 Governor General's Award for Literary Merit for four titles that demonstrated his literary prowess via their humour and inclination toward intermedia. These texts include a small collection of lyric poems entitled *Beach Head* (1970), an anthology of concrete poetry entitled *The Cosmic Chef* (1970), a box of minimalist concrete poems entitled *Still Water* (1970), and a fifteen-paragraph prose poem entitled *The True Eventual Story of Billy the Kid* (1970).[37] The latter work tells the story of Billy, whose insecurity with his famously "short dick" explains his self-destructive and violent behaviour.[38] Hardly what scholar Frank Davey refers to as "juvenilia,"[39] Nichol's narrative—with its Gertrude Stein–like repetition and Freudian phallocentrism—effectively deconstructs notions of history, masculinity, truth, and the mythic image of the gun-slinging cowboy in the Wild West. Though Billy the Kid is a significant character within the American national imaginary, Nichol's idiosyncratic prose work parodies romantic notions of colonialism, settlement, and territorial conquest, which also inform Canada's national legacy.

It was not long after the Governor General's Award ceremony that several politicians denounced the judges—including University of British Columbia professor Warren Tallman, former commissioner of the National Film Board George McPherson, and CBC host Robert Weaver—and their decision to award Nichol the honour. On 10 June 1971, Conservative member of Parliament Mac T. McCutcheon rose in the House of Commons to express his "displeasure with the award recommendations in relation to the work *The True Eventual Story of Billy the Kid*."[40] Supporting McCutcheon's disapproval, another MP, W. B. Nesbitt, requested that the government "take immediate steps to make appropriate changes in the personnel of the Canada Council in order to prevent future scandalous, ridiculous, and outright silly awards such as the one referred to" earlier that morning.[41] Later that month, yet another MP, J. P. Nowlan, referred to *Billy the Kid* as "nothing more than rude and pornographic."⁴² These documented expressions of outrage had no formal impact on the procedures and processes of the Canada Council. No motions were officially passed in Parliament, nor did Nichol's detractors have any noticeable impact on his poetry. However, it does indicate that certain members of the government attempted to use their privileged positions to shape Canadian literary culture with their conservative imagination. Offering his stance on the attacks made against Nichol and the jury's decision, McPherson told the *Toronto Star* that he is "annoyed by untutored criticism of artistic and literary awards," adding, "I don't think the Governor General entirely approves of some awards, but he doesn't complain."⁴³

bissett's status as a cultural outsider is documented in the short CBC documentary *Strange Grey Day/This: bill bissett Vancouver Painter & Poet* (1965), wherein a camera crew follows him through Vancouver. He narrates the film, describing his experience as both poet and painter, detailing the times he was harassed for his Beat lifestyle, and telling of his sense of disconnection from Vancouver's major galleries and art scene. Recounting his inclusion in an unnamed gallery show, he confesses that "it was really no fun, the opening of that show. I thought it would be fun because my painting was in it, but there was no glamour, which was the first thing that disappointed me. Really. No one was trying to make a groovy thing out of it, you know?" He continues:

> At this opening, where my painting was, people who for the last maybe three years wouldn't speak to me—They knew who I was. They had heard about me. I knew who they were. I had myself a few times spoken to them, but they would no longer speak to me because I wasn't making it in whatever club they felt I should be making it in—[They] came up to me that night at the opening behind my back and said, "Congratulations, boy. You made the grade." And if that's what becoming a well-known Canadian painter is, or an international painter is, then I really don't want it.⁴⁴

bissett's displacement from the locus of social and cultural life in Canada continued for decades. And just as Nichol had earlier in the 1970s, he suffered damaging assaults from various politicians in the late 1970s.

Starting in 1977, bissett, whose publishing and writing was partially funded by the Canada Council, began to receive similar charges of depravity and pornography from critical members of the House of Commons. According to Tim Carlson, these attacks "seemed to centre on" bissett's concrete poem "a warm place to shit," which repeats this phrase nearly forty times without spacing or punctuation.[45] Scholars Don Precosky and Ryan J. Cox have each produced detailed overviews of the attacks on bissett, some of which bear repeating here.[46] On 2 December 1977, Conservative MP Bob Wenman addressed the House to express his outrage that "the Canada Council is supporting, with public money, individuals to write what anyone in this chamber would term as offensive and demeaning pornography."[47] Wenman's attempt to have the Canada Council's funding procedures reviewed failed, but the Conservatives mounted another attack months later on 3 April 1978, when Hugh A. Anderson identified *blewointment* as "a degradation to the printed word in Canada" and argued that "if publications such as the one I mentioned by the Blue Ointment Press [sic] of Vancouver are published as a result of government funding, I suggest that a thorough examination should be made so that culture rather than Canadian pornography is advanced." Indeed, he went so far as to push for censorship, claiming that "material which should not be published is being published under the auspices of the Canada Council."[48] Responding to these comments in an interview with Alan Twigg, bissett humorously said that "If I was actually writing pornography, I wouldn't need grants."[49]

bissett was attacked not only by Conservative MPs but also by members of the literary community. Canadian writer John Glassco specifically complained of bissett's intermediality in the *Globe and Mail* on 12 November 1977, where he decries the turn "toward the idea of poetry as a mindless emotional release, a kind of pentecostal 'service of witness'—with the poet as priest or shaman—or what is almost as bad, simply as pseudo cultural vaudeville, a form of bad showbiz."[50] Glassco's comments were aimed at bissett, who was referred to by critics as Canada's poetic shaman on account of his high-energy performances, which often incorporate song and chant.[51] Such comments indicate the discomfort established writers felt about the development of an alternative, and in this case explicitly intermedial, poetic. Such attacks on bissett had a significant financial impact on him as well, as evidenced by the fact that he was denied Canada Council funding for *blewointment* and Blew Ointment Press between 1978 and 1979 (having received $9,550 from the same body between 1976 and 1977). In 1983, bissett sold the press to recoup his financial losses. Blew Ointment Press was purchased by David Lee and Maureen Cochrane, who transformed it into Nightwood Editions.

On the one hand, bissett's battle with conservative opinion reminds us of his reliance on national funding bodies such as the Canada Council, perhaps complicating the claims made earlier on *Extension* regarding literature's relationship to national institutions. On the other hand, bissett's years of receiving financial support from the Canada Council—and the many publications he issued in support of writers and artists during those pre-controversy years—also highlights what a nation can do when it supports its writers and artists. Regardless, his work was evidently at odds with what his critics—including the very politicians who supposedly represent the Canadian status quo—believed should comprise Canadian literary culture.

These encounters with Canadian public officials and established writers, and the setbacks they caused, were significant; however, poets like Nichol and bissett persevered. Much like the editors and publishers who sought to establish a recognizable Canadian literary tradition, they, too, saw publishing as a powerful tool for formulating a distinctive literary paratradition. As bissett put it to Twigg, "We started it in the 60's cuz no one else would print us. Visual writing was just too weird for other magazines. I guess that's the way most presses start. You get a bunch of people who are organically together and no one else will print them. It just grows and grows."[52] And it did grow and grow and inspired many similar endeavours—including many of the small presses and little magazines mentioned above—in the process of building a small but receptive audience. These struggles to define Canada's literary culture suggest that the efforts made by borderblur poets to create a literary paratradition were meaningful and significant, making both an impact in the community and national news, and illustrating these artists' political subversiveness.

Readers who are unfamiliar with these poets' exclusion from an emerging Canadian literary hegemony in the latter part of the twentieth century may find the anecdotes recounted above somewhat surprising. From the perspective of the twenty-first century, intermedial literature has been celebrated, albeit as a niche form, to such an extent that disparaging opinions of Nichol's and bissett's poetry have largely vanished from literary discourse. In fact, intermediality, despite Glassco's complaints, has become an increasingly common mode for poets in recent decades. This is a result of these poets' perseverance and their success as grassroots cultural organizers. Today, they are recognized as exemplars of small press publishing, community leadership, and alternative poetic forms in Canadian literature. bissett and Nichol, for example, are often taught in post-secondary literature classes, featured in Canadian literature anthologies, and are the subjects of many articles, chapters, dissertations, and essay collections analyzing their work. This has led several critics and educators to sensibly locate them within the Canadian literary canon, positioning them as emblematic of a particular subset of the 1960s countercultural zeitgeist, as indicated perhaps by Nichol's inclusion in two major Canadian Literature anthologies, volume 2 of Laura Moss and Cynthia Sugars's *Canadian Literature in English: Texts and Context* (2009) and Russell Brown and Deanna Bennett's *Anthology of Canadian Literature* (2019). This is at least partly a reflection of Canadian literature's historical tendency to absorb dissident voices so as to nullify critiques of literary nationalism. But as I argue throughout this book—and despite this introduction's predominant focus on bissett and Nichol—borderblur formed a concerted avant-garde paratradition comprising identities, positions, and texts that do not tidily fit into nationalist literary discourse.

Bordering the Book: Critical Parameters

In *Designed Words for a Designed World: The International Concrete Poetry Movement, 1955–1977* (2016), Jamie Hilder criticizes nationalistic analyses of concrete poetry, suggesting that the "movement had no geographical centre."[53] While *Borderblur Poetics* does not solely engage concrete poetry, and instead looks to other and related borderblur forms, Hilder's point is worth considering here since I have indeed adopted a nationalist framework. Hilder might contend that my approach "prevents readers from discussions of how the very concept of nationhood was being challenged and transformed at mid-century, especially in relation to the re-drawing of borders after World War Two."[54] I agree with Hilder; as this book argues, internationalism and transnationalism inflect the principles of borderblur poetry, whose practitioners in turn see their work as a paratradition that conflicts with the dominant Canadian literary tradition that emerged in the 1960s. In other words, it is in some senses an aspiration toward internationalism that characterizes borderblur in Canada.

This study begins in 1963 and concludes in 1988, a twenty-five-year period during which Canadian literature underwent numerous significant transformations. These temporal parameters may at first seem surprising since critics often contend that enthusiasm for consolidating a national literary identity was maintained from approximately 1967 to 1974. The former was, of course, Canada's centennial year, a significant milestone for Canadian culture, as indicated by Webb's *Extension* program, major events such as Expo 67, and Canadian historian Pierre Berton's subsequent history of the time, *1967: The Last Good Year* (1997). The latter year, 1974, is generally acknowledged as the peak of this activity. For critics like Mount, this serves as the end point of a period that had seen the publication of several field-defining treatises with a thematic focus on archetypes and the nature/culture divide, notably Northrop Frye's *Bush Garden: Essays on the Canadian Imagination* (1971) and Atwood's *Survival: A Thematic Guide to Canadian Literature* (1972). While this seven-year span marks a significant phase in the establishment of a predominantly white, anglophone, and traditional literature, this study investigates borderblur as a distinguished paratradition that emerged concurrently and then continued beyond these developments.

Eschewing these expected parameters, this study begins five years before Canada's centennial, in 1963, a significant year for the development of experimental and avant-garde writing in Canada, especially on the West Coast.[55] It was in 1963 that bissett, along with his then partner Martina Clinton and friend Lance Farrell, began publishing *blewointment*, the same magazine that was denounced by Conservative politicians in the 1970s. As Michael Turner notes, *blewointment* signalled the birth of a new literary spirit that was largely unseen in Canada up until this time.[56] The arrival of *blewointment* proved to be formative for concrete, sound, and kinetic poetry in Canada, beginning as a forum for bissett and likeminded writers who struggled to find their footholds in Canada's established literary forums. It was also a catalyst for poets like Nichol, who felt compelled to promote this kind of work in Toronto, where he channelled it into a publication named *Ganglia. blewointment*, Ganglia Press, and the related *grOnk* were crucial forums on the international level, since, as will be detailed in the next chapter, they provided necessary connections to an international avant-garde network, including communities of writers in the United States, the United Kingdom, Europe, and South America.

Ending in 1988, this study follows and then exceeds *blewointment*'s lifespan as a literary magazine and press, concluding instead at a crucial point for Ganglia Press. During this time, many other significant publications had started and ceased; in addition to those mentioned above, these included projects organized by Copithorne, UU, McCaffery, and others. Most tragically, however, Nichol died on 25 September 1988 as a result of complications during a surgery to remove a tumour from his back. As evidenced by this introduction, Nichol was an early and central actor for borderblur poetics, helping to open writers and readers to its powers and remaining committed to expanding the poetic field throughout his life. In the wake of Nichol's death, friend and composer R. Murray Schafer wrote to UU on 12 September 1992, confessing that "It has been different without Barrie around, I think we all feel it."[57] Nichol's death left a tremendous feeling of loss in the avant-garde literary community that he participated in. During his lifetime, he directly motivated and supported, and shared a creative life with, many if not all the poets mentioned in this book. He also influenced a younger generation of writers such as Stuart Ross, Gary Barwin, Margaret Christakos, and jwcurry, among many others—all of whom would develop complementary poetic trajectories.

The year 1988 signals a variety of interpersonal and communal shifts in Canadian literary culture. However, this year is also notable for its social and political significance. Borderblur emerged from the fervour of the sixties counterculture, a movement predicated on the ideals of individual freedom, nonconformism, free speech, and grassroots organizing in the service of social, political, and cultural change. With the formation of their alternative poetics, small presses, and little magazine networks, the practitioners of borderblur undeniably emerged from a countercultural ideology. However, 1988 marks roughly the midpoint of Progressive Conservative prime minister Brian Mulroney's years in office, during which he adopted a neoliberal agenda in kind with that pursued by Margaret Thatcher in the United Kingdom and Ronald Regan in the United States. Neoliberalism's oppressive marketization and normalization of human experience are among the issues that borderblur poetics worked against. However, the advancement and subsequent adoption of these principles in the 1980s is a consequence of neoliberalism's co-optation of countercultural rhetoric and its promises of freedom. It could be said, then, that the perspective of borderblur poets, whose works were animated by the spirit of the sixties, represented a major turning point in the late 1980s, when the countercultural ideology espoused by many members of their generation had been largely nullified and absorbed into a dominant system they had once opposed.

Between 1963 and 1988, the poets who championed borderblur poetics created a particular dynamic of rapid change that mirrored the many seismic social, political, and technological shifts that occurred throughout these years, both nationally and internationally. This period is comprised of significant and often controversial episodes that repeatedly challenged the nation's faith in the possibility of a unified identity. The 1960s were a turbulent time for Canadian youth, many of whom partook in uprisings and protests prompted in part by the rise of the civil rights movement and the horrific violence of the Vietnam War. In the late 1960s, Liberal prime minister Pierre Elliott Trudeau tried and failed to advance the 1969 White Paper policy, which proposed an end to the legal relationship between the Canadian government and Indigenous peoples in Canada. Trudeau then declared in 1971 that Canada would adopt policies of multiculturalism and bilingualism to preserve individual cultural freedoms. There was also the 1970 October Crisis, which saw tanks roll through the streets of Montreal after Trudeau invoked the *War Measures Act* in response to the kidnapping of provincial cabinet minister Pierre Laporte by the Front de libération du Québec (FLQ) in the name of Quebec sovereignty. That same decade, younger baby boomers faced stagflation as they struggled to find work, and second-wave feminism began to gather force as middle-class women returned to the workforce in large numbers, seeking to define themselves beyond maternal roles. In the 1980s, Canada continued these transformations by acquiring its own constitution in 1982, and, under Mulroney's government, the *Canadian Multiculturalism Act* was passed in 1988 (building on Trudeau's multiculturalist policy, introduced in 1971). As prime minister, Mulroney developed his neoliberal policies and negotiated the Canada–US Free Trade Agreement, which did much to affect the cultural and economic direction of the country and the flow of US culture and commodities into Canada. For Western countries more generally, this was a period when human life was being transformed on an international scale, typified by the proliferation of electronic telecommunication systems that circulate ideas, words, images, and sounds across disparate geographies; a rapid increase in consumerism; burgeoning military operations around the world; and the newfound ease with which products and services could be moved across national borders. McLuhan referred to this period as the "electric age," but theorists such as Michael Hardt and Antonio Negri describe it as the rise of "*postmodernization*, or better, *informatization*," which accounts for the economic and social transition away from "the domination of industry" and toward the informatization of the economy and social life as well as the emergence of affective labour.[58] All of these conditions captured the imaginations of Canadians and, as this book demonstrates, inflected the proliferation of Canadian borderblur poetics as an internationally conscious, intermedial paratradition.

Though this book articulates borderblur as a significant paratradition, thus making it recognizable as a substantial alternative to the established Canadian literary culture that formed in the mid- to late twentieth century, an encyclopedic inclusivity of all borderblur writers and their texts is not my intent here. Avid readers and scholars of Canadian experimental and avant-garde writing will likely find certain poets missing from these pages, or they might appear only a perfunctory fashion. On the other hand, I also anticipate that some readers may find my critical approach risks a degree of romanticism or hagiography, or that it tends to reinforce a canon of Canadian avant-garde writers—especially since, in the following pages, I frequently return to Nichol and bissett. Many other writers discussed in this book, however, have hardly been discussed within the field of Canadian literature. Thus, I dedicate much of the book to exploring these writers' statements and discussions of borderblur to offset this imbalance; I believe that these poets had intelligent and compelling things to say about their own work. Regardless, and despite the risks these strategies may hold, I concur with Betts, who claims "that until very recently Canada has not been a good or encouraging setting for avant-gardism."[59] Thus, in turning to borderblur as a literary subject, and by maintaining a critical focus on these poets, this book enriches the discussion of avant-garde paratraditions by turning to poets who have received scant critical attention in the past. In this way, my work attempts to expand our "history of diverse local narratives of emergence" by recognizing oft-overlooked writers who contributed to the development of borderblur as one node of poetic activity within a vast "alternative poetics network."[60]

By focusing on borderblur and the network that formed around that idea, I hope to make clear that my intent is not to romanticize or canonize a certain group of poets. Rather, it is to contribute to the discourse of alternative literary histories in Canada formed by the scholarship of Caroline Bayard, Derek Beaulieu, Charles Bernstein, Gregory Betts, Christian Bök, Pauline Butling, Stephen Cain, Frank Davey, Jack David, Johanna Drucker, Paul Dutton, Lori Emerson, Barbara Godard, Jamie Hilder, Peter Jaeger, Steve McCaffery, Roy Miki, Marjorie Perloff, Susan Rudy, Stephen Scobie, Dani Spinosa, Stephen Voyce, Darren Wershler, and many others. My work is significantly indebted in direct and indirect ways to their scholarship, without which none of this would be possible. Alongside this established discourse, my contribution could be appropriately considered as one additional node that will continue to require maintenance, correction, expansion, and development.

I feel inclined to issue one final note regarding the exclusion of certain writers from this book. Although any recovery of neglected poets or texts is often subject to the contingencies of individual taste and experience, and, in this case, circumscribed by the ephemeral nature of avant-garde literary production, I am troubled by the way my omissions and exclusions may be read. Indeed, though this study includes women such as Copithorne, Rosenberg, Kemp, and McMaster, whose works have been eclipsed by dominant masculine personalities, it lacks representation of Indigenous poets, whose works have similarly been overshadowed by white anglophone writers in Canada. Illustrated prose works such as *Song of Raven, Son of Deer* (1967) and *Potlach* (1969) by visual artist and writer George Clutesi, as well as *My Heart Soars* (1974) and *My Spirit Soars* (1982) by Chief Dan George (both with illustrations by Helmut Hirnschall), are notable works published during the period studied here. These books feature illustrations that factor into the process of meaning-making. As tempted as I have been to include these books in this study, Clutesi and George were not evidently part of borderblur's avant-garde network. To my knowledge, there is very limited correspondence between the intermedia writers discussed in this book and writers working within Indigenous traditions and networks.

This book also engages with certain writers and performers who are connected to the borderblur network in somewhat perfunctory ways. Caribbean-Canadian dub poet Lillian Allen, for example, is only briefly mentioned in these pages, despite her close affiliation with Nichol and her own intermedial practice, which brings together song, dance, poetry, and spoken word. Though comparisons between Dub poetry and the sound poetries of borderblur are certainly profitable, I ultimately decided not to include Allen in the sound poetry chapter out of respect for the distinctive features that comprise the Canadian-Caribbean Dub tradition that she has pioneered. A related issue emerges with poet Maxine Gadd, whose typographically playful poetry, some of which was published by Blew Ointment Press, is well-suited to my discussions of concrete poetry. However, when poet Daphne Marlatt asked Gadd about concrete poetry, she responded, "It's boring. I see the compellingness of it, especially if you've got to put out a book. . . . But it's boring to read for me."[61] Thus, I have circumscribed my study with a sensitivity, whenever possible, to the specific ways some writers have explicitly located themselves.

My approach is historically contextualized and focused on poets who worked with intermedial forms and shared an avant-garde network.

From Here to There: A Brief Chapter Outline

The turbulent and transformational qualities that characterize the twenty-five years of Canadian avant-garde activity studied in this book inflect many of the texts that were published during this time, as well as the attitudes and view of their authors. We will see, for example, how an increasing sense of the world's interconnectedness encouraged borderblur poets to find an international community of like-minded avant-garde practitioners with whom they would achieve recognition on the world stage. I will also explore how the women's liberation movement of the 1960s underpins the hand-drawn concrete poems of Copithorne, or how feminism motivates Rosenberg's fusion of concrete poetry and prose narrative in *The Bee Book*. What will become apparent over the course of this study is that borderblur, while always maintaining its aesthetic openness, intermediality, and penchant for creative risk taking, is inflected by ongoing events, and that certain decades saw significant developments for each form.

Chapter 1 explores borderblur in terms of avant-gardism, emphasizing the term's implications and limitations, and attending to the ways that this paratradition manifested in Canada within a broader avant-garde network. In addition to working through poetic statements, I further identify some of the specific conditions—local, national, and international—that contributed to borderblur's intermedial formation. In theorizing borderblur as an intermedial and avant-garde form, I also reconsider its particular strain of avant-gardism amid a highly contested field of historical and contemporary avant-garde theories. The next three chapters highlight three specific forms of borderblur: chapters 2–4 examine, respectively, concrete poetry, sound poetry, and kinetic poetry. These chapters present a survey of literary and related activities associated with each form, identifying the implications of each for the formation of this intermedial and cosmopolitan paratradition. Specific exemplary texts are explored in each chapter—sometimes in-depth, sometimes in a perfunctory manner—to tangibly demonstrate the specific contributions these diverse forms have made to the paratradition. Finally, the conclusion will recapitulate my main arguments before turning to consider the ways that borderblur's intermediality lives on today with specific emphasis on recently published works by Nisga'a poet Jordan Abel and feminist-anarchist poet Dani Spinosa. Taken together, these chapters provide a critical history of borderblur that captures the shared elements of this work while gesturing to the ways this poetic enforces, critiques, and questions notions of belonging within Canadian literature.

1

Bordering the Blur

> *blurring frontiers between art & art, mind & mind, world & world, mind art & world*
>
> —Dom Sylvester Houédard (1963)

In their 2019 recollection of borderblur activity in Toronto, poets Brian Dedora and Michael Dean claim that "the explosion of literary and related work of an avant-garde inclination in Toronto from the late 1960s to the late 1980s was without precedent in the production of Canadian letters."[1] They specify that they "aligned [themselves] with an international avant-garde, and were propelled by the force of [their] own creative energies that either did or did not synch with a Canadian zeitgeist."[2] In retrospect, Dedora and Dean describe the marginal status held by the literary avant-garde in Canada—and not just in Toronto, as this book shows—and articulate the sense of affinity that they and many intermedia poets in Canada felt with literary cultures abroad. Nichol's contributions to the concrete poetry anthologies edited by Emmett Williams (1967) and Mary Ellen Solt (1968) were early stages in the alignment between Canadians and other intermedia practitioners, and publications like these did much to foster the sense of connection that Dedora and Dean felt vis-à-vis an international literary network. It should be no surprise, then, that Nichol, bissett, and others latched on to the "borderblur" neologism, which British concrete poet Dom Sylvester Houédard had coined to describe their work. Art critic and scholar Greg Thomas identifies 1963 as the year in which Houédard first conceptualized the term, describing it, in the context of concrete poetry, as a "rejection of divides & borders, delight in accepting ambiguity/ambivalence: alive blurring frontiers between art & art, mind & mind, world & world, mind art & world."³ Thomas confirms that in 1966, Houédard used similar phrasing to introduce a series of exhibitions held at the Arlington Mill in Glostershire when he commented that "Arlington-une begins w/ the idea that poetry frontiers have been shifting & in fact are being shifted. . . . [B]y crossing and demolishing boundaries [poets] have made it clear that only an aesthetics of nationalism & apartheid could ever continue to defend them."⁴ Finally, Thomas suggests that the term "borderblur" was also explicitly used in 1969 to introduce an exhibition of concrete poetry that was hosted by another British poet, Bob Cobbing, this time to refer to Houédard's poetic contributions to the show.⁵ Since Nichol credits Houédard for the term in 1967, it is likely that borderblur was coined *at least* two years earlier than 1969.

Nichol and Houédard were, in fact, in correspondence in 1965. That year, Houédard wrote to Nichol to update him on the status of a concrete poetry exhibit at the Institute of Contemporary Art entitled *Poetry and Painting*. Houédard coordinated Nichol's involvement in the show⁶ and in their correspondence he recommended that Nichol contact other poets, including Cobbing and Scottish poet Ian Hamilton Finlay. In this same letter, Houédard asked about Nichol's possible relationship with Marshall McLuhan:

> in canada dyou know marshall mccluhan? his books have big influence on especially furnival -- cour bougre - just looked up address - he is yr neighbour - 29 wells hill toronto-4 - like photography liberated from art from having to be a reporters lens -- radio-tv-&c liberates poetry from (& prose from) i mean ALL communication artwise from being written descriptive report - so abstract or concrete poetry is cool in mcluhan sense⁷

While the letter does not explicitly use the neologism "borderblur" to discuss the work of these writers, Houédard's update for Nichol provides even earlier evidence of Canada's connection to an international poetic avant-garde whose proponents Houédard would have likely considered to be representative of borderblur poetics. It also provides evidence of the relationship between borderblur, Canada, the international avant-garde, Marshall McLuhan, and the impact of electronic media on poetry. This chapter explores this relationship to identify how borderblur in a Canadian context comprises literary works that transcend artistic boundaries and is inflected by an awareness of an international avant-garde network.

As discussed in the introduction, Houédard's characterization of borderblur was rehearsed and promoted by Nichol and bissett, both of whom used the term to articulate their poetics during their 1967 television appearance. Irene Gammel and Suzanne Zelazo associate Canadian borderblur, and Nichol in particular, with currents of twentieth-century artistic production that include modernist artist Florine Stettheimer and Fluxus artists such as Dick Higgins, Alison Knowles, and Yoko Ono. Gammel and Zelazo recognize that "the generic 'borderblur' of bpNichol's art practice between poetry, prose, sonic performance, and illustration significantly altered Canadian cultural expression in the 1970s and '80s."[8] Their description of borderblur as a "betweenness" aligns Nichol with others located under the banner of intermedia, suggesting that they see clear commonalities between Nichol and intermedia artists like Higgins. However, the "betweenness" of this creative practice—not limited to Nichol's work alone—is historically under-represented in the Canadian literary context. Despite earlier international avant-garde precedents—Dadaism in the early twentieth century, say, or international concrete poetry in the 1950s, or Fluxus in the 1960s and '70s—Canada in the mid- to late twentieth century, and especially during the so-called CanLit Boom, was home to a dominant, page-based literary tradition in which language was more often than not the sole expressive medium. Canadian literature's historical emphasis on language as the central means for expression is represented by books, anthologies, and collections such as those published as part of the New Canadian Library (NCL). These projects, with their emphasis on the written text, were detrimental to the development of other diverse literary practices in Canada. Not only did they segregate literature from other artistic disciplines, but they also suppressed oral traditions; this was the case with Indigenous storytelling, for example, whose practitioners were consequently banished to the margins of the country's literary culture. While borderblur is not necessarily analogous to Indigenous traditions, and, in fact, certain aspects of borderblur were appropriated from Indigenous cultures (a problem I touch on later in this chapter), Canadian literature's hegemony displaced poets who sought to expand literary artistic practices beyond the singular medium of language.

To develop such expansive literary practices, borderblur poets consciously sought to merge literature with other artistic modes in some of the ways that Houédard had earlier identified. Houédard evidently used the term "borderblur" to describe concrete poetry; however, in its Canadian usage (of which more below), it came to signify the folding of poetry into many other arts forms. I recognize borderblur poets' work as contributing to the discourse of intermedia—that is, the creative combination of separate artistic domains into a singular work that eludes typical categories and genres. As a critical discourse (and as noted in this book's introduction), intermediality was theorized by Nichol's contemporary, Higgins, who tried to provide a critical vocabulary for creative works that "fell between media."[9] In the case of borderblur, a shaped concrete poem involves the analysis of the visual layout of the poem and the actual language on the page—and, often, the material elements used to compose the poem (whether it is hand-drawn or typewritten, for example). This methodology implicitly informs the existing criticism of concrete, sound, and kinetic poetries, and will do so in this book. Borderblur poetics comprise an intermedial approach to literary production wherein meaning emerges from the simultaneous interaction of diverse creative media.

As part of a movement that emerged in the 1960s, borderblur poets stood at the vanguard of a dynamically evolving and shifting field of literary production in both the Canadian and the international contexts. The accessibility of printing technologies such as the mimeograph machine; the increasing presence of electronic media such as television, radio, and film; and a shrinking sense of the globe did much to inflect these artists' poetic purview. This chapter explores borderblur in the Canadian context as a loosely defined intermedial poetic. It articulates the features and concerns of borderblur poets' work, beginning with the early formation of bissett's *blewointment* and its subsequent proliferation throughout Canada. It then discusses Canadian borderblur's connectedness to a concurrent international avant-garde that gave Canadians the very word that would come to describe their work, while also providing them with a receptive audience when one was lacking at home. Building on this international component, this chapter continues to highlight the increasingly globalized sense of literary life and culture that was then developing in Canada, with a particular emphasis on McLuhan's influence at the time. The chapter concludes with a discussion of borderblur and its connections to historical and contemporary theories of literary avant-gardism.

In doing so, I establish a preliminary, context-based theorization of borderblur as a recognizable avant-garde paratradition.

Before I begin any such theorization, I must admit that any attempt to critically account for this activity violates the spirit of borderblur, which actively worked against discursive closure. As a scholar, I am complicit in such an imposition, yet I am not dissuaded from this task since it adds more complexity to the standard narrative of Canada's national literary development. If the mid- to late twentieth century announced a new phase in the modernization of Canadian culture, then this chapter outlines in broad strokes poets' responses to a rapidly changing cultural landscape that led them to conceive of their work as a cosmopolitan alternate poetics network. I do this work while trying to be cognizant of the movement's open spirit and of the advantage that a term like "intermedia" can offer by breaking down singular categories and circumventing the problematic language of "discipline" as it is frequently applied to the arts (i.e., interdisciplinarity).[10] Readers should keep in mind, of course, that this chapter presents only one of many ways to account for this activity. Nevertheless, I proceed from the premise advanced by Nichol's friend, the Canadian poet and critic Stephen Scobie, who claimed that Canadians came to borderblur and its various iterations "first of all from their own experience."[11] This is a point that Nichol confirms when he suggests that avant-garde poets of his time "were operating much like amnesiacs" since avant-garde literature "was not accessible" to them in the 1960s.[12]

In Search of Experience: Borderblur Poetics in Canada

Borderblur in Canada is unlike many of its avant-garde predecessors in that its proponents resisted the impulse to issue programmatic manifestos declaring specific principles, beliefs, and intended courses of aesthetic action. Those statements that were written by borderblur poets in Canada, for example, are unlike the manifestos of André Breton, the French Surrealist, who declared that Surrealism is "[p]sychic automatism in its pure state, by which one proposes to express—verbally, by means of the written word, or in any other manner—the actual functioning of thought. Dictated by thought, in the absence of any control exercised by reason, exempt from any aesthetic or moral concern."[13] In contrast, as Dedora and Dean state, poets affiliated with Canadian borderblur typically "did not name [themselves] or prepare a manifesto" to articulate their work.[14] These poets more often issued artistic statements related to specific texts or forms that outlined their individual intent and at times their perceived position within literary history. We shall see this with concrete poetry in the case of David UU (see chapter 2) or with sound poetry in the cases of Steve McCaffery and Susan McMaster (see chapter 3). An emphasis on the flexibility of individual practices and aesthetic exploration are primary characteristics of borderblur poetics. This also helps explain why these poets might have eschewed more oft-used terms such as "interdisciplinary" or "multidisciplinary" when describing their work. To refer to borderblur in terms of discipline runs counter to the individualistic, rebellious, and convention-breaking nature of this work. As Houédard describes it above, borderblur is a means to revel in ambiguity and blur artistic and communal lines, not adhere to them. As manifested in Canada, the form remains true to this spirit, which is emphasized by the fact that it has no intentional point of origin. Though evidently circulating in an international network in the 1950s and early 1960s, borderblur was not at first consciously adopted by Canadians. Rather, it grew impulsively and organically as a poetic in Vancouver and only later became associated with Houédard's term, by which point Canadian practitioners had joined a network of international counterparts.

It was in the summer of 1958 that nineteen-year-old bissett departed from his home and birthplace of Halifax, Nova Scotia. He and his then boyfriend hitchhiked across the country, leaving behind his repressive middle-class upbringing to eventually arrive in Vancouver, British Columbia. It was there in the early 1960s that he gradually developed his place within the city's downtown art and literary scene as well as his recognizable, though ever-shifting, poetic signature characterized by a unique orthography, strong visual components, and charged performances. It was also in the early 1960s that he, friend Lance Farrell, and then partner Martina Clinton began to reject traditional writerly practices—namely, by eschewing narrative conventions and experimenting with alternative presentations of poetry on the page. They felt restricted by the mono-spaced linearity of the typewriter and the page's rectangular shape, and instead sought to explode them.[15] These transgressive impulses manifested in a hybrid poetic—an expansive intermedial practice combining poetry, sculpture, collage, drawing, music, and other artistic forms.

Vancouver in this era was in the midst of an artistic and literary renaissance spurred by the arrival of Beat culture and jazz in the city's cafés and music venues.[16] *TISH* was launched in 1961 by a group of young poets, including George Bowering, Frank Davey, David Dawson, Jamie Reid, and Fred Wah, and others at the University of British Columbia (UBC), who drew influence from American poets such Charles Olson, Robert Duncan, and Allen Ginsberg, as well as professors such as Warren Tallman. In doing so, they announced themselves as the new generation of poets that Canada's established literati would soon have to recognize. Members of the *TISH* group—along with several other poets from across the city—gathered for what is commonly referred to as the 1963 Vancouver Poetry Conference, the soon-to-be-legendary meeting between established American poets Olson, Duncan, Ginsberg, Robert Creeley, Denise Levertov, Philip Whalen, and Canadian poet Margaret Avison, along with an eager cohort of local emerging writers. Arts and culture were thriving in Vancouver at this point, as further evidenced by Léonard Forest's short film *In Search of Innocence* (1964), created for the National Film Board of Canada. Featuring philosophical conversations, roaming shots of Vancouver's cityscape and surrounding landscape, and soundtracked by jazz musician and writer Al Neil, the film presents a documentary montage of Vancouver's jazz, visual art, and poetry scenes, and includes appearances by sculptor Donald Jarvis, painters Jack Shadbolt, Joy Long, and Margaret Peterson, printmaker Sing Lim, and others. bissett and Farrell actually appear in one scene of the film but are not credited.

bissett's *blewointment* magazine and Blew Ointment Press emerged alongside this creative fervour as a little magazine and press for poets and artists who were outside of established cultural vortices.[17] *blewointment* was "a house for the houseless bissett," writes Tallman, and bissett invited many like-minded writers and artists to join him.[18] Thanks to Tallman, they became known as the "downtown poets," a group comprised of bissett, Copithorne, Gadd, Farrell, Clinton, Gerry Gilbert, Roy Kiyooka, John Newlove, and others who "distrusted what seemed like a heavily academic orientation" toward poetry and poetics then being cultivated at UBC.[19] Despite these suspicions, the first issue of *blewointment* was not published as a response to or refusal of UBC's academic poetics; rather, it was a response to Forest's *In Search of Innocence*. The first issue of *blewointment*, published in 1963, includes bissett's reflection on the making of the film:

> In a gestalt of montage wgich [sic] dug in
>
> further and further into us you reveald [sic] the questions

> of all our lives
>
> what can we know
>
> what is eternal, outside us
>
> what can we do
>
> artists poets, outside the abstraction.[20]

blewointment, then, began as a response, not to a specific set of poets, nor to UBC's academic literary circles, but to the local culture of visual art and music in Vancouver. bissett positions *blewointment* as an outsider press and little magazine, describing the artists and poets of this first issue as "outside the abstraction."[21] The abstraction, for bissett, is not the fringe that these bohemian artists occupy; rather, society itself is the abstraction, as it is removed from what he perceives to be the conditions of true living. This was hardly a combative reflection; rather, it complements the film by featuring Vancouver-based artists and poets bissett, Clinton, Copithorne, Farrell, and Maria (Gladys) Hindmarch—none of whom were recognized in the film. Thus, it further expands the sense of community that *In Search of Innocence* began documenting. The first issue of *blewointment* was published prior to the film's 1964 release, thus *blewointment* unwittingly parallels the film's open-ended, narrative-free structure—"a gestalt of montage"—in its aesthetic. In this way, *blewointment*, and its aesthetic, was seemingly more influenced by film than literature, which is hardly surprising given bissett's appreciation for intermedial poesis and cinema.

Recounting his memories of *blewointment* in 1967 and 1968, Patrick Lane describes how it was literally and figuratively a house not just for bissett and his family, but for this wider faction of like-minded bohemian writers and artists in Vancouver. Recalling the time he spent at their home, Lane writes, "We walk around the room and talk about poetry as we collate the pages of *blewointment*. They are stacked on tables and chairs and we go in a long slow circle picking up page after page of poems until we have a single issue of the magazine then we staple it."[22] Lane's comments suggest that *blewointment* was at the centre of bissett and Clinton's life, taking up a large portion of their home space with artists and writers coming in and out to help with the magazine, including Copithorne, Shadboldt, Neil, Gilbert, and Farrell, as well as Milton Acorn, Gregg Simpson, Beth Jankola, Scott Lawrence, Kurt Lang, and many others. Credit is usually given solely to bissett for *blewointment*'s aesthetic. Poet and critic Ken Norris, for example, states that the project "reflected bissett's experimental and organic poetics."[23] However, *blewointment* and its aesthetic were not bissett's alone; rather, they were developed in dialogue with Clinton. Discussing these early days, bissett recollects with poet Barry McKinnon that

> Me and Martina Clinton were working the press together for the central part of the mid-sixties—63–67. Before starting, ie. the press, we would take all night, all day, in going over how we wanted to present the language on the page, paper, to let—have the poem to be a map for a mood/statement, show and tell of feeling message, articulate space between words for pause-emphasis-measure visual presence of that poem.[24]

In the same interview, bissett further explains that he and Clinton "talked a lot about poetics, what later became known as poetics"[25] and that they wanted "each poem to be different than any other poem."[26] Thus, it was through collaboration with Clinton that *blewointment*'s intermedial direction emerged, with its inclination toward aesthetic diversity and attention to the way materials and design shape literary meaning-making. Clinton evidently played a significant role in the development of *blewointment*'s editorial and aesthetic principles, a point often overlooked in critical accounts of the project's history. While it is difficult to determine the precise degree of Clinton's involvement, her poetry regularly appeared in the magazine until 1972, though the first few issues featured more of her work than the latter issues. Clinton eventually disappeared from the *blewointment* nucleus, likely because bissett and Clinton ended their relationship in the late 1960s. However, the magazine and later Blew Ointment Press maintained the direction they had established, becoming increasingly intermedial.

The eclecticism of the magazine is apparent, too, when looking over the diverse selection of authors published by bissett. "He published hippies, feminists, red-power advocates, socialists, communists, environmentalists" at many career stages and representing various aesthetic persuasions—from more established figures like Dorothy Livesay, P. K. Page, and Earle Birney, to the rising stars of mainstream Canadian literature such as Margaret Atwood and Dennis Lee, to Vancouver's downtown artists such as Vincent Trasov (also known as Mr. Peanut) and photographer Ian Wallace, to many of the Canadian and international borderblur poets mentioned above.[27] The magazine's radical openness—both in terms of its aesthetic and its editorial principles—articulates bissett's sense of Canadian literature as an open field, not limited to a single aesthetic or social viewpoint, regardless of the dominant trends of the time.

blewointment began as an essential reference point for borderblur, and it often served as a model for other like-minded writers. Nichol published his first poem, "Translating Translating Apollinaire," in *blewointment* in 1964, which evolved into one of his life-long projects. *blewointment* evidently influenced Nichol's work as a publisher and community organizer; it set him on a course to extend the ideas he found in Vancouver to other communities. Until *blewointment* magazine ended in 1977, Nichol—if we don't count bissett—made the highest number of individual contributions to the magazine (with Copithorne and UU just behind them). Nichol was living in Vancouver during the early days of *blewointment* but eventually moved eastward to Toronto in the spring of 1964. As Nichol had claimed during the 1967 television interview with Webb, Toronto was not yet home to the bohemian literary culture that he found out West. So he had to develop it himself with the 1965 launch of his own mimeo press, Ganglia Press, which produced *Ganglia* magazine and later *grOnk*. Poet David Aylward (whom he met while working at the University of Toronto's Sigmund Samuel Library) was one of his earliest collaborators on these projects.[28] The first issue featured poets such as Aylward, bissett, Copithorne, Nichol, and others, which indicates that—as Nichol has admitted—it first served primarily as a venue for introducing the avant-garde poets he met in Vancouver to a Central Canadian audience.

In January 1967, Nichol, Aywlard, UU, and Rob Hindley-Smith, also known as rah-smith began a Ganglia Press publication called *grOnk*, which was dedicated to "concrete sound kinetic and related borderblur poetry."[29] The title was a neologism expressed by a dinosaur character in the famous American comic strip *B.C.* (created by Johnny Hart), which emphasizes *grOnk*'s focus on sound and visuality—the comic strip is identified by Higgins as an intermedial form.[30] The allusion to the *B.C.* comic strip also subtly connects this work to British Columbia, thereby acknowledging the influence that Vancouver had on this work at the time. Occasional editors later included bissett, McCaffery, Nelson Ball, jwcurry, and R. Murray Schafer. These writers and artists formed a basis for Nichol's Toronto literary community, and their presence and assistance with these ventures helped transform borderblur from a localized aesthetic that Nichol found in Vancouver into a transnational paratradition.

The creative energy generated by these publications inspired similar and no less significant forums for the proliferation of borderblur, such as UU's Fleye Press and *Spanish Fleye* magazine, the latter of which was limited to a single issue. This first issue appeared in 1966 and adopted the editorial principles and mimeo aesthetic UU used with Nichol on *grOnk* and features a mix of lyric and pattern poems, asemic writings, line drawings, and a book review. UU had ambitions to continue publishing the magazine with three further issues, none of which materialized. Though the magazine was short-lived, UU continued to publish through Fleye Press, including a series of pamphlets by himself and Nichol and a book by bissett entitled *Where Is Miss Florence Riddle?* (1967).

With more longevity than Fleye, Underwhich Editions was formed in 1979, a joint effort by Nichol, McCaffery, Riddell, Michael Dean, Brian Dedora, Paul Dutton, Steven Ross Smith, and Richard Truhlar. Dutton, the remaining steward of the publishing imprint, describes their mission thusly: "unorthodox content, unorthodox publication, efforts to economise (the projects being self-financed, with costs barely recovered and any surplus going into subsequent publications), low print-runs and individual initiative."[31] Each member of the collective was responsible for their own projects, giving them the freedom to publish a variety of authors with a wide range of media and formats, including books, broadsides, chapbooks, pamphlets, cassettes, vinyl, microfiche, and more. The collective managed several significant projects that widened the network's reach, such as sound poetry scores by Ottawa-based collective First Draft—*Pass This Way Again* (1983), composed by Susan McMaster, Andrew McClure, and Claude Dupuis, and *North South* (1987), composed by McMaster, McClure, and Colin Morton. Sound poetry was central to the imprint's operations. Indeed, its flagship publication was *Sound Poetry: A Catalogue* (1978), edited by Nichol and McCaffery on the occasion of the eleventh International Sound Poetry Festival, which was hosted in Toronto and organized by McCaffery, Smith, and Sean O'Huigin. Truhlar and McCaffery would later develop the Underwhich Audiographic series, which published tape cassettes of sound poetry by national and international

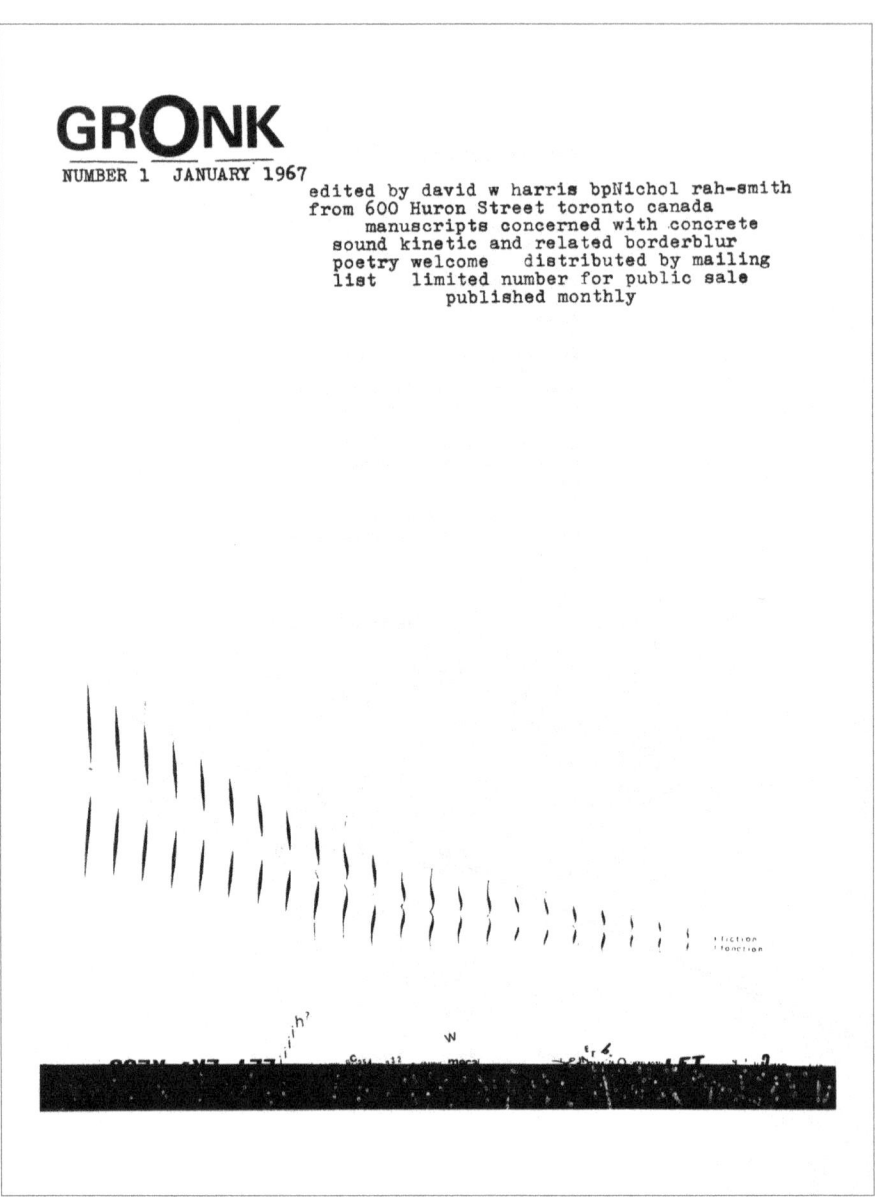

Figure 1.1: Front cover of *grOnk*, no. 1, published January 1967.

practitioners, including Paula Claire (England) and Susan Frykberg (New Zealand/Canada).

As these projects emerged and proliferated, borderblur and its poetic subcategories were debated and discussed by Canadian practitioners. Nichol, for example, outlined his poetics on the back of his intermedia publication *Journeying & the returns* (1967; sometimes also referred to as *bp*). The publication comprises a slipcase of poems and poem-objects, printed and recorded across a variety of media, including a perfect-bound book, postcards, flipbooks, an audio disc, and more. Adhered to the back of the slipcase is Nichol's "Statement." He writes,

> now that we have reached the point where people have finally come to see that language means communication and that communication does not just mean language, we have come up against the problem, the actual fact, of diversification, of finding as many exits as possible from the self (language/communication exits) in order to form as many entrances as possible for the other.[32]

Further down the slipcase, Nichol continues to state that "there are no barriers in art. where there are barriers the art is made small by them," and he further recognizes that "traditional poetry is only one of the means by which to reach out and touch the other."[33] While Scobie refers to this text as a "manifesto," Nichol's language is far less combative and programmatic than the language found in many manifestos of the historical avant-garde.

Nichol here articulates his outlook on language's relationship to communication in the late 1960s, a period during which the technological landscape of media and communication technologies was rapidly transforming. For Nichol, these shifts expand the possibilities for human connection since image and sound, for example, have begun to occupy more prominent positions in everyday life, as described in the writings of McLuhan (which Nichol likely knew well, as we will see later in this chapter). It is worth noting, too, that Nichol does not seek to disparage traditional poetic modes; rather, he stresses that traditional poetries such as free verse are only one of many modes of literary expression. Instead, Nichol muses, "how can the poet reach out and touch you physically as say the sculptor does by caressing you with objects you caress?"[34] With such provocations, Nichol invokes borderblur as it is described by Houédard, to envision a means of broadening aesthetic scopes and transmission in communal exchange.

Nichol's "Statement" establishes a set of common presumptions that other poets could gather around (and they did). However, his anthology *The Cosmic Chef* (1970) functions even more like a manifesto because it directly invokes borderblur while actively forming a loose coterie of poets. It is useful here to consider poet and anthologist Jerome Rothenberg's notion of the anthology as a manifesto and, by example, an articulation of this active poetic.[35] *The Cosmic Chef* features work by Aylward, bissett, Clinton, Copithorne, McCaffery, Riddell, UU, Hart Broudy, Earle Birney, Jim Brown, Barbara Caruso, Victor Coleman, John Robert Colombo, Greg Curnoe, Gerry Gilbert, Lionel Kearns, Seymour Mayne, David McFadden, Sean O'Huigin, Jerry Ofo, Stephen Scobie, Peter Stephens, and Ed Varney, alongside perhaps unexpected—but aptly selected—poets such as Margaret Avison, Phyllis Webb, Michael Ondaatje, and George Bowering. In the afterword, Nichol claims that "this whole book is best described by the term dom sylvester houedard coined BORDERBLUR," and he goes on to explain, alluding to the notion of intermedia, that "everything presented here comes from that point where language &/or the image blur together into the inbetween & become concrete objects to be understood as such."[36] While emphasizing the way these works occupy an in-between space, Nichol specifically treats borderblur as a visual form but does not preclude sound or kinetic poetry. The poems range drastically in style and method. Webb's sparse minimalism is presented alongside McCaffery's multidirectional typestracts, Birney's thinly handwritten text spiral "Like an Eddy" is featured next to Copithorne's thickly lined asemics, which in turn appears beside bissett's chant-poem comprising the lines "yu are imprisond in th city."[37] It is clear from these selections that Nichol's sense of borderblur is broad and inclusive. By using Houédard's coinage to describe their work, Nichol identifies an emergent poetic community within a larger, international avant-garde network and theorizes an expansive poetic during a time when definitions of poetry were narrowing as part of Canada's nationalist surge. This was representative of a larger movement in Canadian poetry that Dean and Dedora described as an effort to get "outside quatrain, couplet, maple leaves, and snowshoes."[38]

As I have demonstrated thus far, Nichol and bissett saw their work as distinctive from the mainstream literary culture that was forming around them. The discussions of their poetics that Canadian audiences saw on television in 1967 continued privately in mail correspondence in 1972. As evidenced by a thirty-page, mostly handwritten letter from bissett to Nichol, they were evidently still working toward a sense of their poetics, determining where it fit within established literary cultures. This letter was written and sent just before the release of his book of poems and collages *pass th food release th spirit book* (1973). It addresses an essay Nichol had recently drafted for inclusion in the collection but ultimately excised from the final version of the book at bissett's request. As evidenced by the letter, bissett was initially excited by the connections Nichol made between bissett's work and other writers in their nexus, including their contemporaries and modernist predecessors. Ultimately, though, more than twenty pages into the letter—and having read the essay many, many times—bissett asks Nichol to remove it, preferring to let the work speak for itself and pointing out that few of Nichol's own books have an explanatory apparatus. Nichol's essay eventually appeared reworked for publication in *BRICK* in the winter of 1985 under the title "PASSWORDS: The Bissett Papers," wherein he attempts to situate bissett within a tradition of poetry that extends from and includes Birney, *TISH*, Gertrude Stein, James Joyce, and Raoul Hausmann. Nichol's essay usefully contextualizes bissett's practice within national and international currents of literary and artistic innovation. In the letter, however, bissett is adamant that his work exists separately from these modernist predecessors and other international writers with whom he may share aesthetic similarities: "i meen a <u>new</u> line has startid like yu say in PASSWORDS. it dont fit in with anything els apriori really," he contends.[39] bissett, eager to differentiate his own work and that of his peers, is reluctant to give too much credit to European or American literatures as an influence on their work. While he is eager to articulate his cosmopolitanism—as he did with Webb on television in 1967—he is also careful not to give himself over entirely to other established traditions. bissett's comments are undoubtedly hyperbolic and perhaps too narrow—consider, for example, the fact that he and Nichol use Houédard's coinage to describe their work. However, it does underline what is at stake for bissett in these discussions: to ensure openness and an open perception of his poetics that is neither part of the dominant Canadian literary mainstream nor merely a transplant of American or European modernism. Borderblur, for bissett, must be, as the name implies, a blurring of borders between aesthetic, historical, and national contexts.

Borderblur, and notably Houédard's definition of the term, was still central to Nichol's conception of writing even in the late 1980s. Echoing his "Statement," Nichol maintained that writing inherently blurs borders between media; he writes, "Writing, precisely because it is *written*, is, at least in part, a visual art. It's also a sound art. . . . It lies, therefore, at the juncture between painting & music, taking something from each but remaining itself. . . . between those juncture points is the area which Dom Sylvester Houedard [*sic*] referred to as 'borderblur,' the area where the distinctions break down and become useless."[40] He lamented, however, that even after decades of sustained publishing of intermedial works like his own and many of his peers, this approach to writing "still seems to be news to some people."[41] For Nichol, literature was often misunderstood as being singularly expressed through language. Despite the substantial cultural capital that Nichol accrued over the course of his life as one of its leading practitioners, borderblur in Canada was always a fringe poetic. Writers tend to focus on language as a container for content, for communicating meaning rather than focusing on it as a medium that is also inherently visual and musical. To a lesser extent, the conservative conception of literature in Canada had returned in the 1980s according to Nichol: "That is to say, attacks on experimental writing, attacks on deconstructionism or anything that has a certain life and vitality to it."[42] Highlighting these other dimensions of writing and their importance to communication is a tenet of borderblur activity. It is the form's persistent outsider status that makes it one of Canada's significant literary paratraditions.

Dropping Off the Borders: An International Network of Alternative Poetics

While Nichol seemingly felt that borderblur poetics was relegated to the margins of Canadian literary culture, the creation of vibrant and active borderblur communities made it relevant to a niche group of writers and readers. In the previous section, I mentioned a limited number of small presses and little magazines that provided essential forums for borderblur poetry in Canada. More could also be said about the importance of Copithorne's *Returning*, Very Stone House press (edited by bissett, Patrick Lane, Seymour Mayne, and Jim Brown), or even the role of Stan Bevington at Coach House (where Nichol worked as an apprentice typesetter) in the creation and sustaining of borderblur as a Canadian avant-garde paratradition.[43] In *Imagined Communities*, cultural theorist Benedict Anderson convincingly suggests that print media is one of the crucial ways in which people—whether in local, national, or international contexts—come to think of themselves as part of an identifiable community.[44] Literary production in the late 1960s and '70s lends support to this thesis, especially the critical projects bolstered by literary Canada's then emerging mainstream "stars" such as Margaret Atwood and Dennis Lee, projects such as McClelland and Stewart's NCL, and studies such as *Survival* (Atwood) and *Savage Fields* (Lee), which did much to promote the writers in Anansi's catalogue at the time. Poets like those mentioned above, however, also saw publication as a powerful tool for formulating an alternative literary community. As quoted in the previous chapter, bissett speaks to this conception of print in a 1978 interview with Alan Twigg: "We started it in the 60's cuz no one else would print us."[45] From the beginning, all of these projects were formed out of a desire to create vibrant literary and artistic communities—whether that meant providing additional venues for Vancouver's overlooked downtown poets or creating a bohemian literary culture that was missing in Central Canada.

The sense of community cultivated by and through these projects extended to an international network of poets and artists who were also exploring borderblur, indicating that not only was this an alternative literary community that opposed mainstream culture in a domestic context, it was also connected to a broader avant-garde tradition. McCaffery has described magazines like bissett's and Nichol's publishing ventures as having a "loose editorial policy of national alongside international content."[46] After the first issue of *Ganglia*, its pool of contributors expanded well beyond Toronto and Vancouver, to include Ian Hamilton Finlay (Scotland) and d. a. levy (United States) in *Ganglia* number 3, and John Furnival (England) in *Ganglia* number 5. Series 1 of *grOnk* continued this tradition in 1967: number 1 features Pierre Garnier (France) and d. r. wagner (United States), number 2 features Furnival and Cavan McCarthy (England), number 3 features Ivo Vroom (Belgium) and Ernest Jandl (Austria), and numbers 6 and 7 feature Hansjorg Mayer (Germany), Jiří Valoch (Czech Republic), and Edwin Morgan (Scotland). *blewointment* magazine had similar but comparatively smaller roster of international contributors, including d. a. levy, Diane di Prima, and Richard Kostelanetz (United States); Vroom and Pierre Albert-Birot (France); bob cobbing (England); and others.

With *grOnk* and Ganglia Press, "Nichol made concerted attempts to expose different literary communities to one another,"[47] as did bissett, evidently by bringing together British, Czech, American, Canadian, German, French, and Austrian poets in the pages of their publications. Nichol also used *grOnk*'s mailouts to make interested readers known to one another so as to effectively trace the connections of this international avant-garde network. He acknowledges, for example, their presence by listing writers involved or connected to *grOnk* in the 1969 *END OF AUGUST GRONK MAILOUT*. The list includes Nichol, UU, bissett, d. r. wagner, John Simon, David Aylward, Rob Smith, Dave Phillips, Andy Phillips, Captain George Henderson, Andrew Suknaski, Eleanor Hiebert, John Riddell, Cavan McCarthy, Nicholas Zurbrugg, Jiri Valoch, David McFadden, Michael Ondaatje, Nelson Ball, Barbara Caruso, Judith Copithorne, Gerry Gilbert, Victor Coleman, Stan Bevington, Hart Broudy, Barry McKinnon, Denise Phillips, Carol Giagrande, Julie Keeler, Colin Jackson, Paul Dutton, Ivan Burgess, Scott Lawrence, Jo O'Sullivan, Pearline Beaton, Rene Young, Wayne Clifford, and Julie Clifford. According to Graham Sharpe's count, *grOnk* had acquired a national and international subscriber base, comprising 273 individuals. Many readers were based in Canada but there were 45 in the United States, 14 in South America, 3 in Japan, and 55 across Europe.[48] Sharpe claims that this subscriber base "provided international exposure" that served "to validate the work that was begun and ongoing here [in Canada]."[49] This was undoubtedly because borderblur was nearly invisible to the literati at home, but this cultivated sense of internationalism is also crucial to understanding the poetic.

The role of internationalism looms large in the imaginations of Canadian borderblur poets as the poetic emerged and proliferated from 1963 onward. This period saw the dawning of a global age and the emergence of new networks that challenged the theoretical foundations of what it meant to be a national community. McCaffery recalls the feeling in Toronto in 1968 as being "backward and repressive" on account of his "feeling this terrible pressure as an artist to contribute to the dissemination of national identity."[50] As an immigrant from England, McCaffery's sense of community exceeded geographic boundaries. "The fact that both sound and concrete poetry emerged as international phenomena, was what I found attractive,"[51] he says. McCaffery did not occupy this position alone. Four Horsemen collaborator Rafael Baretto-Rivera immigrated from Puerto Rico in the 1960s, evidently with similar interests since he approached McCaffery and Nichol in 1970 to "jam." Similarly, but travelling in the opposite direction, Gerry Shikatani lived for many years in France, where he performed and developed close bonds with

```
END OF AUGUST GIANT grOnk MAILOUT

bpNichol - co-ordinating editor
david uu & bill bissett - editors at large (yuk yuk - i just realized
                             someone else who has that title)
D.r.Wagner - RUNCIBLE SPOON/grOnk brotherhood of mimeo madmen chief
John Simon - holy ghost
David Aylward & Rob Smith - founding editors (along with bp & dave)
Dave Phillips - head of old friends department
Andy Phillips - head of agriculture & photography department
Captain George Henderson - guru of comic books
Andrew Suknaski - guiding light of the FREE POEMS department
Eleanor Hiebert - tender love and care division (also circulation)
John Riddell - chief of the "it's great but where do we get the
             bread to publish it" suggestion box
Cavan McCarthy - "hands across the ocean" department
Nicholas Zurbrugg - questions & prodding
Jiri Valoch - soul brothers of brilliant con corporate division
Dave McFadden, Mike Ondaatje, Nelson Ball, Barbara Caruso, Judy
Copithorne, Gerry Gilbert, Victor Coleman, Stan Bevington, Hart
Broudy, Steven McCaffery, Barry McKinnon, Denise Phillips, Carol
Giagrande, Julie Keeler, Colin Jackson, Paul Dutton, Ivan Burgess,
Scott Lawrance, Jo O'Sullivan, Pearline Beaton, Rene Young, & a
cast of thousands participating friends.
                                   Hello Wayne Clifford &
Julie Clifford wherever you are.

ANNOTATED LIST OF GOODIES IN THIS MAILOUT

series 4 #4 - WAR AGAINST THE ASPS (time wise this work pre-dates
              TYPESCAPES (published in 1967 by COACHHOUSE PRESS
              401 (rear) Huron Street, toronto) as does his WOURNEYS
              (also included in this mailout). we should have pub-
              lished these years ago but hit a giant two year period
              of lethargy) - David Aylward
series 5 #1 - done somewhat in the runcible spoon format to turn you
              on to that variouslyrapidly moving magazine edited by
              D.r.Wagner. send him bread & love c/o P.O. BOX 4622
              Sacramento California 95825 USA. also numbered Synapsis
              2 because in terms of what synapsis is attempting to
              do it fits that format.
series 5 #2 - excerpt from CARNIVAL by Steve McCaffery. author's note
              explains everything.
series 5#3 - WOURNEYS David Aylward (see $4#4)
series 5 #4 - SOMETHINGin - poems by Martina Clinton - an excerpt from
              her long awaited eventually to be published MAY..N
              FRACTURES.

we've been getting a lot of action lately about erratic numbering.
therefore (as a service to our readers) here's the lowdown on what
we've published so far.
               series 1 - numbers 1 to 8
               series 2 - numbers 1, 2, 3, & 7/8
               series 3 - numbers 1 to 7
               series 4 - numbers 2 & 4
               series 5 - numbers 1 to 4
                                   there are eight numbers
to a series. the gaps in series two are being filled by John Simon
at some unspecified point. the gaps in series 3 & 4 are cause i'm still
putting those numbers together.
```

Figure 1.2: Excerpt from *END OF AUGUST GIANT grOnk MAILOUT*, published 1969.

French sound poets such as Bernard Heidsieck. Notably, too, Shikatani is a second-generation Japanese Canadian, and his 1981 anthology *Paper Doors* (co-edited with Aylward) confronts, among other things, the legacy of the Canadian government's racist internment of Japanese Canadians during the Second World War. The global flows of travel and immigration, as theorist Arjun Appadurai suggests, were among the factors at this time that created an "instability in the production of the modern subjectivities,"[52] which in turn could destabilize the subject's sense of self within a nation. With increasing access to international travel for the middle class in the mid- to late twentieth century, it's surprising that Canadians had not yet conceived of a broader conception of their literature in their efforts to define their own, unique literary identity.

Alongside the increasingly commonplace activity of international travel, electronic media was becoming a core component of everyday life during the twentieth century, which in turn affected the flow of news, culture, ideas, and visions across national lines. Appadurai recognizes the proliferation of electronic media—notably television, radio, and film—as part of a globalizing modernity that offered new resources and disciplines for the imagination of self and community. This includes the transmission of entertaining television shows and films, horrifyingly violent images broadcast from the war in Vietnam, and the paranoia of the Cold War arms race channelled directly into the living rooms of many Canadians. Within this context, "Neither images nor viewers fit into circuits or audiences that are easily bound within local, national, or regional spaces," which in turn affects the production of the modern nation.[53] This sense of the world provides the larger backdrop against which we must view these poets' work—Nichol, and especially bissett, adopted a global perspective: they wanted to "drop off the borders."[54] With that said, their relationship to global flows is complex and should not be assigned one specific meaning, just as their relationship to national literary identity encompasses many complexities. Rather, their work embodies a collision of the local, national, and global, one that serves to highlight the oversimplification of nationalist essentialism. Electronic media also opened new possibilities for art and culture. As Houédard, recognized for coining the neologism "borderblur," mentions in his above-cited letter to Nichol, television and radio encouraged some poets to escape realist aesthetics and to pursue more abstract forms. They certainly pushed the borderblur poets featured in this book to conceive of their work in dialogue with the multiple modes of communication they encountered in their day-to-day lives. To fully appreciate this foundation, it is crucial to look at one critic in particular whose influential work captures much of the anxiety and optimism that attended a rapidly changing, seemingly borderless world as it formed in real time: Marshall McLuhan.

Intermedial Poesis in the Electric Age

The Toronto-based, internationally renowned media critic Marshall McLuhan shared with Nichol, bissett, McCaffery, and others a notable distrust of nationalism in the mid- to late twentieth century. McLuhan's vision for Canada was pluralist and dynamic, subject to the influence of a rapidly changing mediascape. "The vast new borders of electric energy and information that are created by radio and television," he wrote in 1977, "have set up world frontiers and interfaces among all countries on a new scale that alter all pre-existing forms of culture and nationalism."[55] This thinking, however, was apparent in the much earlier *Counterblast* (1954)—a short, eighteen-page manifesto that McLuhan self-published. An expanded version of *Counterblast* was published in 1969 (somewhat surprisingly, perhaps) by McClelland and Stewart, "making it likely," as Stephen Voyce suggests, that "Steve McCaffery and bpNichol encountered it."[56] In *Counterblast*, McLuhan lambastes Canadian nationalism:

B L A S T (for kindly reasons)
    C A N A D A
   The indefensible canadian border
  The SCOTTISH FUR-TRADERS who haunt
  the trade routes and Folkways of the
  canadian psyche
  B L A S T all FURRY thoughts
    The canadian BEAVER,
  submarine symbol of the
   SLOW
     UNHAPPY
       subintelligentsias.
  ....
    Oh BLAST

> The MASSEY REPORT damp cultural igloo
> for canadian devotees of
> TIME
> &
> LIFE
> ...
> BLESS
> THE MASSEY REPORT
> HUGE RED HERRING for
> derailing Canadian kulcha while it is
> absorbed by American ART & Technology.[57]

McLuhan criticizes the insularity of Canadian nationalism, deploring its symbols such as the beaver. McLuhan takes aim at the findings of the 1951 Massey Report (the product of the so-called Massey Commission, officially known as the Royal Commission on National Development in the Arts, Letters and Sciences), which would eventually lead to the formation of the Canada Council in 1958 and the pressure to create a national literary identity in the 1960s—exactly the sort of pressure that McCaffery and others found oppressive. McLuhan jabs at the commission, suggesting that its findings reduce Canadian life to the sort of discourse found in commercial magazines such as *Time* and *Life*. McLuhan's vision of Canadian culture was far less segregationist than the report's definition of culture, with its emphasis on high art and the separation from American culture. Rather, McLuhan's notion of Canadian culture acknowledges the blending of cultural forms, including sports ("B L E S S / French Canadian HOCKEY PLAYERS / for keeping art on ice") while acknowledging the unavoidable influence of American culture on Canadian life ("B L E S S USA cornucopia of daily / SURREALISM"). This conception of Canadian culture and its interconnectedness to international contexts is directed by his understanding of media in the mid-twentieth century.

In *The Gutenberg Galaxy*, McLuhan advances his theories of media with a special focus on print and literacy. A fundamental thesis of the work is that the adoption of new (especially electronic) technologies is causing major shifts in human speech and writing.[58] McLuhan theorizes differences between auditory cultures and literate cultures as an attempt to understand what he believed to be the drastically different world views conveyed in manuscript culture, on the one hand, and typographic culture, on the other. McLuhan further suggests that the new electronic age—the so-called post-typographic world—renders "individualism obsolete" and "corporate interdependence mandatory."[59] This concept of corporate independence is modelled on what McLuhan refers to as "tribal" or oral and auditory cultures—the new image of the global village. However, it also effectively captures the promise that media could present a way of opening the world. In his biographical note to his poetry collection *Nobody Owns Th Earth* (1971), bissett hopes "that th world be mor open as what is possibul that ther be less imperial isms"[60]—despite, perhaps, not yet seeing the imperialism at the heart of some aspects of rising global modernity and this newly mediated world. Nonetheless, the arrival of electronic media facilitated this shrinking sense of the world and offered new access to other cultures since they so easily transmit images and ideas from elsewhere.

In McLuhan's next book, *Understanding Media: The Extensions of Man* (1964), he situates even more forcefully the role electric and electronic media play in connecting persons and places around the globe: "after more than a century of electric technology, we have extended our central nervous system itself in a global embrace," he writes, before suggesting that media is an "extension, whether of skin, hand, or foot, [that] affects the whole psychic and social complex."[61] His chapters on radio, film, and television, for example, reflect on the ways these media have impacted the development of social and psychic life. These media compelled new collective formations between audience and producer. The radio is a means of broadcasting distant voices into the home while the television, a relatively new medium, delivered the horrors of war, and particularly the Vietnam War, directly into the homes of television audiences.

McLuhan's conception of culture, media, and borders effectively articulated the dynamic social and technological shifts taking place at the time. He declared the arrival of the electronic age, a term that adequately describes the intensifying conditions of globalized modernity with an emphasis on mass media's role in shaping an emergent human imaginary. McLuhan's description of this period matches characterizations of the global age offered by later theorists such as Arjun Appadurai, who in subsequent decades would echo the claim that the imaginations of artists, poets, and citizens are altered by electronic media that, in turn, alter their sense of belonging within the nation.⁶² Nationalism, as a basis for communal belonging, is complicated when daily life is interfaced with ideas, things, persons, and art from elsewhere. In Canada, this has always been the case; yet many of the existing narratives—some old, some surprisingly recent—affirm a desire for a definitive sense of Canadian identity produced by the country's art and culture. Within this paradigm, borderblur poetry offers a compelling case study since it emerged concomitantly with Canada's nationalistic surge, and yet, the work of these artists did not contribute to the same mode of belonging. McLuhan's theories are essential to this context for the way he expressed the perceived impacts of global mediation for a whole generation of people, and especially the borderblur poets.

McLuhan's writing also presented new ways of understanding the relationship between artistic production and the media used in such production—that is, the ways of producing art in a society comprising competition between multiple mediums of communication. In his "Statement," Nichol articulates his sense of the seismic shifts underway among his generation: "there's a new humanism afoot that will one day touch the world to its core."⁶³ Nichol offers no clear description of what this new humanism looks like, but it seems to signal a possible departure from previous systems of thought that centre humans instead of the divine or ecological. For Frank Davey, this claim of a new humanism places Nichol on one side of the debate regarding the relationship between literature and national literary politics. He describes the "aesthetic/humanist" camp as being concerned with humanity, detached from nationalist ideologies, while the literary nationalist argues for the "particularity of human social forms within specific national boundaries."⁶⁴ It seems likely that Nichol, in his conception of a new humanism, may have been revising what he perceived to be a humanist system in order to consider the implications of the new technological moment that he and his peers were living in. Those conditions stretched across national boundaries and affected human life wherever it was present. Nichol opens his "Statement" by generalizing this conception as a universalism: "we have reached a point where people have finally come to see that language means communication and that communication does not necessarily mean language."⁶⁵ For Nichol, this raises problems of human relations and commonality. The fact that Nichol describes language *as* communication in this passage, and specifies that not all communication is language, corresponds to the emergent conditions faced by his generation while also indicating his faith in intermedial works. The dominance of electronic media suggests there needs to be a new way of expressing life—a new humanism—and also speaks to how language now fits within that paradigm.

While it is profitable simply to acknowledge that a shared interest unites McLuhan and the borderblur poets in exploring the emergent conditions of the electric age, there is evidence to suggest that McLuhan was particularly influential on these poets and assisted in articulating the grounds from which much of their work was produced. McLuhan made a significant impact on Vancouver, including in the late 1950s, when he gave a lecture at the Arts Club, and in 1965, when the Festival of Contemporary Arts paid tribute to McLuhan with its nickname "The Medium Is the Message." McLuhan's most striking early appearance in the work of the borderblur poets is in the epigraph to bissett's 1966 book of poetry *We Sleep Inside Each Other All*, published by Nichol through Ganglia Press. bissett writes,

> Marshall McLuhan sz we are poisd between th typographic individualist trip th industrial revolution & the electronic age we have been in for sum time, between a unique dis tance and alienation privacy well now iullbe in th study for th rest of th night with my nose in a boo k & th corporate image tribally we are a part of out extensions do reach now have been reach thruout all time th historical jazz consumd in th greater fire of mo vies t v & lo ve.[66]

As a partial explanation of his book, bissett locates his writing at the intellectual vanguard, articulating, through McLuhan, an awareness of the shifting nature of the mid-twentieth century from the industrial age toward the electronic age. It is not entirely clear if bissett is positioning *We Sleep Inside Each Other All* as a response to McLuhan's theorization of the age, for there is a cheeky quality to his quip "iullbe in th study for th rest of th night with my nose in a boo k."[67] bissett's tone may be unclear, and he does have a complicated relationship with academic modes of thought and writing; however, a survey of his poetry from 1966 onward suggests that he was writing in response to many of the cultural maladies and trends identified in McLuhan's writing.

McLuhan's influence was apparent in many of the borderblur poets' subsequent activities and publications. Though McLuhan's name is not explicitly used in the previously mentioned segment on *Extension*, his thinking permeates Webb's discussion with Nichol and bissett regarding their "nonlinear" poetics, a buzzword likely borrowed from McLuhan since he, too, liked to use that as a description for his aphoristic style of writing. bissett's mention of Canada within an international network of poetry—encompassing Brazil, Belgium, Holland, England, Scotland, and Japan—is indicative of the McLuhanesque conception of the world as a "global village." Webb also mentions Nichol's tape machine experiments and asks, "Is this just extending yourself, or is it more connected with leaving the meaning out of the word?" Nichol suggests that it is more about giving an "electric context to the word," and Webb's use of the word "extending" in reference to the tape machine is equally telling.[68] It is a reference to the notion of extension that McLuhan develops in *Understanding Media*, which Webb uses to understand Nichol's and bissett's poetry.[69] The interview is indicative not only of McLuhan's influence on bissett, Nichol, and Webb, and of their understanding of poetry more generally, but also of just how deeply McLuhanesque thinking had embedded itself in the cultural zeitgeist during this period.

Nichol most directly engaged McLuhan's thinking in 1982 in an essay that remained unpublished until 1989 (when it was featured in a special issue of the *Journal of Canadian Poetry*). The text was initially intended to appear in a book on McLuhan, presumably to be edited by Fred Flahiff and Wilfred Watson, but was never published. Nichol draws a clear connection between his work and McLuhan's writing style by way of the pun, a literary device both authors evidently loved. "No one punned more seriously than McLuhan," writes Nichol, suggesting that McLuhan's punning "is not trying to fix 'a' or 'the' reality—he wants to open realities."[70] This inclination toward "openings" guided Nichol, as seen in many works, including *Still Water* and *The Martyrology* (the latter his life's work). Indeed, McLuhan and Nichol both share a linguistic playfulness and a desire to liberate its meaningfulness from singular and standardized usage. The pun is one of the many ways Nichol's writings engage an aesthetic register of borderblur since the pun is typically used to blur the multiple meanings that might be assigned to a single word.

McLuhan directly influenced Nichol and bissett in ways that apparently affected their writing. They found inspiration in his work and used him as a foil. However, McLuhan is cited by many like-minded poets throughout the second half of the twentieth century. In the catalogue for the exhibiton *Concrete Poetry: An Exhibition in Four Parts*, held at UBC in 1969, Ed Varney declares that concrete poetry is "medium as message."[71] He made this claim on behalf of sixty-three artists and poets from Canada and abroad, including Nichol, bissett, Copithorne, Gerry Gilbert, and Stephen Scobie. In his 1970 revolutionary statement "for a poetry of blood," McCaffery refers to sound as "the extension of human biology,"[72] echoing the subtitle of McLuhan's *Understanding Media: The Extensions of Man*. One year later, John Robert Colombo uses McLuhan as a point of entry for readers of *New Direction in Canadian Poetry* (1971), an anthology of mostly concrete poetry that featured Nichol, bissett, McCaffery, Copithorne, UU, Aylward, Hart Broudy, and Andrew Suknaski. In a note accompanying McCaffery's contribution, an untitled work that would later be featured in *Broken Mandala* (1974), Colombo asks, "Is the ape-man emerging from what Marshall McLuhan called 'the age of literacy' into a post-literate age of electronic communication?"[73] There are more examples to be catalogued, but all of this is to say that McLuhan's writings loomed over this generation of writers, who engaged with his work explicitly so as to theorize their own practices. They took seriously both his prophetic concepts of media and community, as well as his warning about media's impacts on human life. Most importantly, however, their poetry resonates with McLuhan's theorizations of an emergent culture that in turn informed their own avant-garde poetics.

"Fuck the Avant-Garde": Borderblur and Theories of the Avant-Garde

The previous sections of this chapter have portrayed Canadian borderblur as an intermedial approach to literary production that was influenced by the intellectual vanguard of its day and was incongruous with an ascendant mainstream Canadian literary tradition. These writers positioned themselves as anti-establishment individuals who produced work that was aesthetically and often sociologically distinct from Canada's nationalist tradition. These characteristics neatly align borderblur with conventional definitions of the avant-garde, which, according to scholar Pauline Butling, identifies "both a social position—ahead of the mainstream—and to a subject position—that of adventurous, forward looking individuals."[74] Similarly, Gregory Betts and Christian Bök describe avant-gardists as "deviant writers who, against prudence, decide to break from the orthodox pathways to fame in order to become not so much unseemly to their contemporary peers as untimely to their contemporary epoch."[75] To a great extent, these attributes are drawn from foundational avant-garde theorizations by such writers as Peter Bürger, Renato Poggioli, Matei Călinescu, Charles Russell, and others. At the risk of oversimplifying, this body of scholarship has assisted in creating roughly two frameworks for thinking about the avant-garde: a traditional aesthetic model and a sociological model. The former emphasizes challenging and reinventing artistic expression, while the latter, according to Bürger, tends to advance institutional critique and offer alternative forums for aesthetic activities and is often guided by programmatic texts. These two approaches to avant-gardism have dominated the discourse for decades.

In her 2014 essay "Delusions of Whiteness in the Avant-Garde," poet and critic Cathy Park Hong criticizes the historical avant-gardes on account of their exclusionary logic. Writing within the American context, she states that "to encounter the history of avant-garde poetry is to encounter a racist tradition."[76] "American avant-garde poetry," she continues, "has been an overwhelmingly white enterprise, ignoring major swaths of innovators—namely poets from past African American literary movements—whose prodigious writings have vitalized the margins, challenged institutions, and introduced radical languages and forms that avant-gardists have usurped without proper acknowledgment."[77] Hong further explains that poets who write about issues related to identity, especially racial identity—though they may write in ways that are recognizably avant-garde in terms of their aesthetic (take Theresa Hak Kyung Cha's *Dictee* [1982], for example)—are excluded and instead framed as "anti-intellectual, without literary merit, no complexity, sentimental, manufactured, feminine, niche-focused, woefully out-of-date and therefore woefully unhip, politically light, and deadliest of all, used as bait by market forces' calculated branding of boutique liberalism."[78] Hong offers an understandably polemical solution to this problem: "Fuck the avant-garde. We must hew our own path."[79] Importantly, Hong identifies a crucial aporia within the thinking and art making of the historical avant-gardes, highlighting avant-gardism's lack of self-criticism regarding the historical and ongoing exclusion of writers of colour from its canons. While Hong's necessary critical intervention is focused primarily on American avant-garde poetry, her critique can be applied to a variety of national contexts.

In Canada, similar critiques of avant-gardism have been periodically advanced in recent decades. Preceding Hong's call by nearly a decade, Butling suggests that the established discourse of avant-garde theorization requires reinvention because, in Canada as in the United States, it is typically bound to white, masculinist cultural rebellion that excludes women and writers of colour. Like Hong, Butling's solution is to abandon such descriptors as "avant-garde" and to instead theorize unorthodox, disruptive, and deviant writers and texts. Butling therefore calls for new terminology, privileging the word "radical" to describe this work and seeking to characterize it by underscoring the power of the prefix "re" in this context. Butling here draws from Fred Wah's notion of "re poetics," which gestures toward processes of "*re*defining, *re*writing, *re*claiming, *re*articulating, *re*inventing, *re*territorializing, and *re*formulating."[80] For Butling, such gestures constitute a kind of literary radicalism: "*re*writing cultural scripts and *re*configuring literary/social formations. The goal is to *change*, not conserve, past and present constructions."[81] Working within this revisionist framework, the avant-garde's hopefulness and unorthodoxy are preserved, but in a way that is potentially less exclusionary than established models.

Butling's and Hong's concerns regarding the avant-garde's overwhelming exclusionary logic are not to be ignored, and both writers make useful interventions in the field. While I am certainly an advocate for inventing entirely new ways of thinking about literature, and especially unorthodox literature, I worry that doing so in this context might disconnect Canadian borderblur poetics from historical and concurrent avant-garde movements with which they identified. Additionally, along with a new generation of avant-garde scholars such as Sophie Seita, Jean-Thomas Tremblay, and Andrew Strombeck, I believe there is something worth saving, or at least salvaging, from the term "avant-garde." To counter the exclusionary logic that informs the legacy of avant-gardism, these scholars advocate for a redefinition of the term, approaching it with more flexibility and a willingness to tie it to a wider variety of aesthetic, social, and political commitments. They outline new, alternative models to reinvigorate the discourse, and these inform my thinking in the remainder of this chapter. As I outline in this section, Canadian borderblur is representative of both the aesthetic and the sociological arms of avant-gardism, but there are incongruities between existing historical theorizations and the literary practices of borderblur in Canada that prompt me to consider an alternate formation of avant-garde theory, drawing from post-1945 considerations of avant-gardism as advanced by Seita, Charles Bernstein, and David Antin. Doing so allows me to locate Canadian borderblur within avant-garde discourse while acknowledging its distinctive qualities.

As suggested above, the principles of avant-gardism are largely drawn from the foundational writings of such theorists as Bürger, Călinescu, Poggioli, Russell, and others whose work paints a complex portrait of historical avant-garde movements and their identifiable leaders, goals, manifestos, and coherent aesthetics. The canonization of Surrealism and its goals, for example, as outlined in Breton's manifesto (noted earlier in this chapter), is evidence of the mutual interrelationship between established avant-garde theorizations and avant-garde movements. Movements like Surrealism informed the discourse of avant-gardism, and, in turn, theories pertaining to the avant-garde secured Surrealism's lasting presence within the discourse. The work of Bürger and other scholars have formulated what I understand to be conventional theorizations of avant-gardism. Their theories, however, do not fulsomely support discussions of Canadian borderblur, whose adherents gathered around a loose set of social and aesthetic principles. They were not necessarily writing collectively out of an allegiance to a specific social or political cause, but they did seek to expand the field of writing and publishing in Canada by opening more pathways between artistic modes so as to expand the possibilities of expression.

The word "avant-garde," as a descriptor for borderblur, is problematic in itself since it denotes militarism. It was used early on by the French military to describe a small group of shock troops who would scout ahead of the main body of soldiers and clear a path for its safe arrival at the place of battle. According to traditional theories of avant-gardism, avant-gardists are the literary counterparts to the military shock troops forging ahead to intercept an oncoming force. Hence, one of the customary objectives of avant-garde writing and art is to shock its audience, either morally or psychologically. The violent connotations of the word tend, however, to overshadow the history of avant-gardism itself. While avant-garde movements such as Futurism undoubtedly embraced violence within their aesthetic and social purviews, other movements like Dadaism and Surrealism were decidedly anti-war and populated with pacifists who co-opted the language of physical conflict to describe their own war against the violent culture of their time. It seems wholly inappropriate to dismiss the term on the grounds of its violent connotations; rather, Futurism aside, we might say that one of the central aims of the historical avant-garde was to invert violent connotations, or, in the case of Surrealism and Dadaism, to turn the violence back onto the violent culture in which these artists were working.

As with these historical examples, the militaristic connotations of the avant-garde label are incommensurate with borderblur since many of these writers held anti-war sentiments. One of the founding editors of *TISH*, Jamie Reid, a poet and friend to bissett, Nichol, and others, describes the psychological threats posed by the Cold War and the lasting traumas of nuclear destruction during the Second World War: "[We] lived every day and dreamed every night in fear that the city might actually be incinerated, the entire earth of people wasted and destroyed."[82] bissett, as critic Jim Daems argues, "has been critically attuned to the infiltration of militarization in Canadian culture—from his early anti-Vietnam work to the present day conflicts in Iraq and Afghanistan, along with Canadian corporate complicity in these military theatres."[83] Copithorne, too, highlights her involvement in the anti-war movements as fundamental aspects of her experiences in the literary scene in 1960s Vancouver.[84] In noting these two figures, whose writings helped to lay the foundations of this paratradition, it's appropriate to suggest that borderblur also grew out of the counterculture's anti-war values.

For these reasons, traditional conceptions of the avant-garde are somewhat incongruous with Canadian borderblur. The work of these poets, then, also asks us to reconsider and reinvent certain facets of avant-gardism in order to swerve from the word's erroneous associations with violence and monolithic theories to acknowledge new possibilities for appreciating these artists' status as cultural outsiders. Betts, for example, has claimed that poets such as bissett, Copithorne, McCaffery, and Nichol comprise an avant-garde node he identifies as *Canadian postmodern decadence*. As such, their work is characterized by "a liberating turn away from convention, order, and Western traditions." Echoing Perloff, Betts also sees in these writers' work a "poetics of rupture . . . that gleefully cast aside meaning, closure, and denotative signification."[85] As an emergent force during what is now often recognized as the advent of Canadian postmodernism, their work signified a loss of faith in language as a communicative mode, a process that played itself out in acts of "creative destruction" to "explore and expose the limits of an overly conventionalized language."[86] Betts notes, too, that despite this inclination toward disruption, a "sense of possible redemption or even revolution, never quite formulated or realized, lurks behind a great deal of this experimental activity."[87] Instead, the borderblur poets' work—without the autotelic aims of a revolutionary order—"halted their rebellion at the stage of personal liberation."[88] Betts's argument captures borderblur's spirit as a concerted movement characterized by linguistic disruption and eschewal of literary convention, but his account ends in the early 1970s, even though these poets continued to work in the modes described here well into the 1970s and '80s. And some of course continue to do so today. However, regardless of the particular temporal frame, I am concerned that characterizing borderblur poets broadly as negative revolutionaries who stopped at personal liberation will inadvertently obscure the sociological dimension of avant-gardism and its centrality to Canadian borderblur.[89] This social dimension understandably exceeds the scope of Betts's analysis. However, for all the emphasis on the avant-gardists' intention to blur "life and art," as is frequently repeated by scholars like Bürger and Russell, borderblur poets' role as social agents active within various local, national, and international networks must be accounted for. While Betts's theory of Canadian postmodern decadence is quite robust, a wider and more open definition of this particular avant-garde paratradition is needed to account for both the aesthetic and sociological aspects of Canadian borderblur.

Theorist and artist Sophie Seita adds much-needed nuance to the discussion of avant-gardism when she refers to *avant-garde proto-forms*, which she defines according to four specific criteria: "(1) the avant-garde is a print or publishing community consisting of multiple participants and heterogenous materials; (2) it usually engages inventively with its medium of publication; (3) it is provisional in its aims, practices, and participants; and (4) the avant-garde is what is called avant-garde. It is a discursive and malleable construct within a not necessarily cohesive interpretive community."[90] This definition largely informs my own understanding of avant-gardism, and in subsequent chapters I try to show how these characteristics resonate in the context of Canadian borderblur. Seita's theory combines the aesthetic and sociological sides of avant-garde theorization. She "conceives of avant-gardes as provisional networks of affiliation rather than rigidly demarcated groups, where *proto-* suggests provisionality and heterogeneity, while *forms* stress media, genres, and groups."[91] Given that the poets considered here formed a loose constellation based on intermedial approaches to poetic practice, a "network of affiliation" is already a better description for borderblur's Canadian proliferation since it acknowledges the group's interconnectedness even in the absence of programmatic texts around which the poets would rally. This comes from Seita's focus on little literary magazines that challenge common conceptions of how avant-garde networks form. These networks, for example, accommodate avant-gardist movements that do not fit neatly within a single aesthetic or medium and lack manifestos, and that accommodate a broad range of related activities. Much of the work examined in this book was published in either little magazines or through poet-run small presses; likewise, the performance-based works were often staged at alternative venues such as artist-run centres and independent art spaces. These forums emerged in response to the gatekeeping mechanisms of established and authoritative Canadian cultural institutions. Seita's model of avant-gardism accounts for the social structure and heterogenous aesthetics of these networks.

The sociological aspects of Seita's theorization are drawn in part from poet Charles Bernstein's writing on the value of alternative poetics and the social and economic networks that form around them. Put differently, Bernstein concretizes the sociological dimensions of avant-garde practices, with an emphasis on their propensity for community building. He describes alternative poetics as conveying a "refusal to submit to marketplace agendas,"[92] a phrase that describes numerous avant-gardes and resonates with borderblur's relationship to mainstream Canadian literary culture. However, the "power of our alternative institutions of poetry," Bernstein writes,

> is their commitment to scales that allow for the flourishing of the artform, not the maximizing of the audience; to production and presentation not publicity; to exploring the known not manufacturing renown. These institutions continue, against all odds, to find value in the local, the particular, the partisan, the committed, the tiny, the peripheral, the unpopular, the eccentric, the difficult, the complex, the homely; and in the formation and reformation, dissolution and questioning, of imaginary or virtual or partial or unavowable communities and/or uncommunities.[93]

Bernstein's analysis is notable for the way it also presents avant-garde poetic paratraditions as sites of opening rather than opaque, closed communities that abide by predefined sets of principles. Bernstein claims that "when you touch this press, you touch a person."[94] His conception of avant-gardism as social work directly connects with Nichol's conception of borderblur, wherein he emphasizes that intermedial approaches to literary practice open new ways of communicating and connecting with people: "how can the poet reach out and touch you physically as say the sculptor does by caressing you with objects you caress?"[95] Seita and Bernstein, for their part, outline an avant-gardism that connects to some traditional meanings of the word while reinventing certain facets of it. "Avant-garde," then, comes to describe a constellation of like-minded poets and their aesthetic practices without imposing an artificial homogeneity or adopting a nakedly exclusionary lens.

If Seita and Bernstein create an aperture in the discourse through which to better articulate a sociological reading of the non-programmatic avant-garde, there remains the issue of accounting for both the rebellious aesthetic of borderblur and its timeliness in the context of Canada's cultural development. There is substantial evidence to suggest that these writers and their aesthetics were seen as rebellious—recall the descriptions of Nichol's and bissett's work in the House of Commons. However, their work also asks us to reconsider the avant-garde's relationship to time and the common association of avant-gardism with futurity to which Butling, Bök, and Betts earlier gestured. Thus far, I have implied that borderblur is not necessarily a forward-looking movement—though, in hindsight, we can see how these poets' intermedial approach to literary production anticipated the work of certain digital literary forms (as discussed in the conclusion to this book). While McLuhan's writings represented an intellectual vanguard in the 1960s and '70s, they were also the work of an intellectual trying to make sense of the emergence of media in his exact moment. Borderblur was a response to these ideas, and these poets were clearly trying to reconceive art's meaning-making possibilities within these conditions. Likewise, Canadian literary scholar Caroline Bayard, in her book *The New Poetics in Canada and Quebec: From Concretism to Post-modernism* (1989), outlines the ways in which concrete poets like Nichol, bissett, and McCaffery drew from emergent post-structuralist and deconstructionist ideas. Thus, to describe borderblur with reference to the avant-garde's supposedly "forward-looking" ethos risks misrepresenting Canadian borderblur. These poets were, in fact, quite timely.

Poet David Antin offers an interesting reconfiguration of avant-gardism in his talk poem "what it means to be avant-garde." Antin, who as an associate of Fluxus during the 1960s and '70s has been described as an avant-gardist himself, rejects a monolithic view of avant-garde scholarship, knowing that this largely means describing work in reductive terms such as "shocking or making new."[96] For Antin, avant-gardism is characterized by responsiveness to the conditions of the present, to the time and place in which one is working, without necessarily being preoccupied with innovation, newness, or shock. A transcription of this talk poem relays these ideas in the following terms:

> and i did the best I could   under the circumstances   of being there   then   which is my image of what an artist does and is somebody who does the best he can   under the circumstances without worrying about making it new or shocking   because the best you can do depends on what you have to do and where and if you have to invent something new to do the work at hand you will   but not if you have a ready-made that will work and is close at hand and you want to get on with the rest of the business
>
>   then youll pick up the tool thats there   a tool somebody else has made that will work   and youll lean on it and feel grateful.[97]

Antin thus conceives of the avant-garde artist as someone who is responsive to their moment, to the specific conditions in which they are working.

This decentering of newness and invention directly applies to borderblur since these poets began with the pursuit of something they thought was new only to learn that the possibility of intermedial poetics was already being actively explored by other poets around the world. Antin continues: "and as for the future   it will find us all by itself   whether we look backwards or forwards it will be there at the top of the stairs."[98] Antin here encapsulates a flexible avant-gardist ethos, not as a forward-looking and militaristic operation but as an openness to the present and willingness to work within it. The work of Canadian borderblur poets, as will be seen in subsequent chapters, offered responses to the emergent conditions of the electronic age—its technologies, economies, culture, and aesthetics. We shall see how much of this intermedial work emerged in dialogue with the dominant communication technologies of the time—mimeograph machines, typewriters, television, tape recorders, and more—and how these technologies gave shape to borderblur poetry. Combined with Bernstein's and Seita's sociological theories of avant-gardism, Antin's ethos captures the spirit of borderblur with its networked affiliations, its emphasis on finding alternatives to artistic hegemonies, and of its willingness to create a dialogue with the conditions of the present.

Antin's characterization of avant-gardism as a response to the conditions of the present point back to Hong's comments regarding the exclusionary logic that informs conventional avant-gardism, and especially the historical avant-garde's overwhelming whiteness. Theoretically, Antin's positioning of avant-gardism as an art concerned with the present should serve to create space for excluded writers. Placing the present at the centre of avant-gardism should create room for works that are aesthetically recognizable as avant-garde but that have been dislocated on account of the dominant focus on identity. Identity, after all, is always a central concern in any present context, and contemporary avant-garde scholarship should recognize its relevance. With that said, positioning Canadian borderblur within the avant-gardist discourse described above does not entirely shield it from the critiques made by Hong, Butling, or others. In the case of borderblur, the poets comprising this paratradition are, with some exceptions, predominantly white men, with some white women.[99] While issues related to race and cultural appropriation evidently stirred relatively little debate at the time, I believe, at the risk of being accused of presentism, that these issues are worth briefly examining here. What follows is neither defence nor condemnation. Rather, I point to these issues so as to recognize that so-called progressive literary movements intended to create openings can also have their limits.

We might take Nichol's interest in non-European cultures as an instructive example of Canadian borderblur's complex relationship to questions of identity, race, and cultural appropriation. In *Doors: To Oz & Other Landscapes* (1979), Nichol states that he described his earliest concrete poems as "ideopoems," a term that nods to Ernest Fenollosa's *The Chinese Written Character as a Medium for Poetry* (1919). He was, as he admits, "very interested in Chinese, Japanese, Haida, and Kwakiutl poetic modes."[100] Referring to the latter Indigenous poetic mode, Nichol indirectly describes his approach as working in consonance with these poetics while conversing with Butling and Wah in 1977 and 1978. Discussing Wah's *Pictograms from the Interior of B.C.* (1975), Nichol and Wah acknowledge their approach to Indigenous cultural forms as outsiders, remarking upon how they project their own experience onto what they see in pictographic writings. Wah used pictographs as a kind of raw material for his poetry, an approach that Nichol seems sympathetic to during their discussion. Though such practices did not seemingly cause a stir at the time, Hong might identify this as an instance where "avant-gardists have usurped without proper acknowledgment."[101] Such an approach suggests a lack of sensitivity to problems caused by the appropriation of Indigenous cultures by non-Indigenous poets.

In terms of race, ethnicity, and cultural identity, some poets' inclination toward what they considered "openness" enabled them to cherry-pick certain aspects of other cultures with seemingly little consideration for the significance of their actions. I find possible traces of this in bissett's early sound poetry, wherein he integrates tropes of Indigenous chant into his work. Maxine Gadd has described bissett's use of both Indigenous and cowboy imagery as a form of escapism, an "attempt to get the hell out of being a weak, miserable, near-sighted, undernourished, physically rundown, feeble city intellectual."[102] Gadd explains away bissett's actions as mere "fantasy."[103] However, bissett's seeming appropriation of Indigenous chant forms may inadvertently contribute to Canada's long-standing history of colonial violence through the appropriation and misrepresentation of Indigenous traditions.[104] As I will explore in the next chapter, McCaffery's poetry—especially *Carnival*—makes privileged assumptions about the body and disembodiment. Poet and critic Andy Weaver argues that McCaffery occupies a position of white male privilege and that this positionality is at the core of much of his work.[105] Many writers who are marginalized by culture are forced to acknowledge the subject position from which they write, while white, able-bodied male writers can assume that the body is a neutral, non-signifying thing. This underscores a seeming problem with the universalist principles that guide the poetics of some of the artists within Canadian borderblur's network of affiliation, leaving them blind to the nuances of white privilege and cultural appropriation.

On the other side of this, we will also see in the following chapters compelling works by writers who take issues of identity seriously. Copithorne, Rosenberg, Kemp, Shikatani, and others treat their intermedial work as more than just a means of resisting the Canadian literary tradition in order to advance sharp social critiques of racial and gendered oppression. Subsequent chapters will at times address these issues in the context of individual works. For now, the issues that arise when considering identity and borderblur's general desire for an expansion of Canadian literary traditions illustrate two key points. First, I see these poets' efforts to both appeal to other cultural forms and to privilege disembodiment as attempts to divorce themselves from the resoundingly white, anglophone colonial literary and artistic traditions on which Canada was founded—traditions that were being formalized and enshrined during the mid-twentieth century as Canadians were supposedly formulating an image of their own. They engaged with and appropriated other cultural forms in an attempt, perhaps, to escape their own. On the other hand, issues such as cultural appropriation highlight one of the consequences of perceiving a vast, open world amid the thrall of globalizing processes: these poets saw the world as a more open space for increased cross-cultural dialogue, even if they had not yet perceived the ethical quandaries and colonial legacies that such an approach entails. The following chapters will examine how this emergent sense of an electronic, networked, and open world compelled intermedial poetics of Canadian borderblur to create new forms, and, more importantly, how its conditions informed the creation and proliferation of a significant Canadian literary paratradition.

2

Concrete Poetry

> *In no other form of society in history has there been such a concentration of images, such a density of visual message.*
>
> —John Berger (1972)

The year 1955 marks the beginning of an explosive period of aesthetic risk taking by an international network of poets and artists who eschewed conventional verse for the expansive possibilities of visually oriented expression. Their work could undoubtedly be recognized under the umbrella category of borderblur; however, many of the poets who were part of this wave preferred other descriptors. Some poets, like Bolivian-born German poet Eugen Gomringer, called their work "constellations," but it is most commonly known by the term "concrete poetry." The dynamism of this generation's poetics is comprehensively captured by three anthologies published before 1970: Stephen Bann's *Concrete Poetry: An International Anthology* (1967), Emmett Williams's *An Anthology of Concrete Poetry* (1967), and Mary Ellen Solt's *Concrete Poetry: A World View* (1968). Together, they feature poets from Brazil, Britain, Germany, Japan, Sweden, Switzerland, Turkey, the United States, and elsewhere. Nichol was the only Canadian-identified poet acknowledged among these international selections, with poems in two of the three anthologies—Williams's and Solt's.[1] These poems are exemplars of Canadian intermedia poetry and are among the work produced by Canadian poets that closely resemble representative works by first-generation practitioners. Nichol's poem "eyes," for example, bears certain visual resemblances to other pieces in Williams's anthology, such as Aram Saroyan's minimalist poems and Williams's rubber stamp poems. Relatedly, Nichol's celebrated poem "Blues" (in the Solt anthology) is remarkably similar to Gomringer's "constellations," especially his famous poems "Wind" and "Silencio," which create slippages between signifier and signified and feature ordered typographic arrangements of black letters surrounded by white negative space, suggesting the inverse of a star-filled sky. However, Canadian concrete's leading practitioners in the early 1960s, such as Nichol, bissett, and Copithorne, did not begin to publish their work until nearly a decade after the form's banner had first been raised by Gomringer and the Brazilian Noigandres poets Décio Pignatari, Haroldo de Campos, and Augusto de Campos in 1955. The use of the moniker "concrete poetry" in reference to a visual literary form arrived in Canada belatedly, and Canadians seemed to have adopted it after they began their own avant-garde practices.

There are many definitions of concrete poetry that gesture toward its intermedial features—so many, in fact, "that it is difficult to say what the word means," writes Solt.[2] Avant-garde poet and theorist Richard Kostelanetz defines concrete poetry straightforwardly as the reduction of "language to its concrete essentials, free not only of semantic but syntactical necessities. . . . Simply letters or disconnected words scattered abstractly across the page."[3] Kostelanetz's definition is useful but risks oversimplification since it cannot capture concrete poetry's full range of aesthetic nuance, and really it most aptly describes earlier forms of concrete poetry, like those composed by Gomringer and the Noigandres poets. After a scan of the anthologies mentioned above, one can quickly gather that concrete poems can appear disconnected and scattered, but they can also be quite rigid and uniform; they can be tight minimalist works like Nichol's "eyes," but they can also be sprawling and chaotic multi-page works like both panels of McCaffery's *Carnival* (discussed below). Within the larger international borderblur network, the Canadian node of concrete poetry is difficult to precisely distinguish and define. Critics such as Stephen Scobie and Lori Emerson have referred to much of this activity as *dirty concrete*, which describes works that resist the "clean lines and graphically neutral appearance"[4] characteristic of the work of the previous decade—the opposite of Perloff's description of the first wave of international concrete poetry as "ideologically suspect . . . advertising copy."[5] These are subtle yet critical distinctions that overly narrow definitions cannot capture. Yet, again, not all works published during this time by Canadian borderblur poets necessarily correspond to this more specific definition. In fact, when comparing bissett, Copithorne, McCaffery, Nichol, David Aylward, Paul Dutton, Roy Kiyooka, David UU, Ann Rosenberg, Shaunt Basmajian, and Brian Dedora—whose works provide this chapter's case studies—we see a diversity of aesthetic iterations.

Like Scobie and Emerson, UU argues in "Beyond Concrete Poetry," published in the December 1972 issue of the *British Columbia Monthly*, that Canadian concrete poetry is dissimilar to the first wave because it is dirty, disordered, and chaotic. He refers to Canadian concrete poetry as "Canadada," a neologism that fuses "Canada" with the historical European avant-garde movement known as "Dada."[6] For UU, concrete poetry begins with concrete art—as represented by the Bauhaus School and artists such as Laszlo Moholy-Nagy and Joseph Albers—and its principles of intellect, organization, and construction.[7] Canadian concrete poets do not share these values but instead operate intuitively with "physical/destructive" tendencies.[8] "Concrete Poetry embraces the visual (image) while Canadada is emotional and embraces the auditory (lyric)"; it is "an illogical search for no meaning in an ordered universe (a body without mind)."[9] While UU's characterization of Canadian concrete poetry is somewhat limiting—Canadian poets did after all produce carefully constructed and intellectually driven poems—and though concrete poetry could have a sonic element if performed, it is not necessarily lyrical. As a descriptor, "Canadada" did not survive, but UU's argument captures the contemporary perspective on concrete poetry as it emerged under the auspices of Canadian borderblur. Notably, too, UU's neologism also contains "nada," subtly indicating that concrete poetry had no place in Canadian arts and literary culture at the time, so the poets were forced to create a cultural context of their own. UU achieves this, in part, through his astute comparisons to international cultural movements, thus developing the cosmopolitan purview that this book partly traces.[10]

Since there is such a diversity of definitions for concrete poetry in Canadian and international contexts and a vast heterogeneity in its aesthetics—clean, dirty, partly washed, whatever you would like to call it—I appeal to an expanded definition to invite the many formations of concrete poetry that emerged within the publishing activities of the borderblur network. Concrete poetry is a visually oriented form that places language as one medium within a framework shared by visual artistic media and modes, including design, illustration, painting, photography, and more. Concrete poetry may emphasize linguistic content and semantics, but it can also underscore and revel in language's materiality and the expanded creative possibilities generated when language is placed in dialogue with non-linguistic materials. Concrete poetry is intermedial in that it explicitly relies on a creative interaction between language and visual modes, elements that can include shape and pattern as well as imagery, the latter raising certain similarities with collage. Its cultural and historical touchstones are many, as are its aesthetic manifestations. Casting a wide net in this way enables us to perceive a group of practitioners whose work might have otherwise been excluded from overly stringent definitions.

As I now proceed into the first of three poetic forms examined in this book, I want to stress again that Canadian borderblur is an umbrella term that describes a contextually situated intermedial poetic and avant-garde network of affiliation. Concrete poetry—like the sound and kinetic poetry analyzed in later chapters—is one manifestation of borderblur's expressive forms (and this book cannot possibly deal with them all). This chapter focuses on Canadian practitioners of concrete poetry and continues to develop my argument that Canadian borderblur is an avant-garde paratradition inflected by a cosmopolitan awareness that complicates assumptions about Canadian poetry as an expression of Canadian identity. Again, my modest intent is to add nuance to the story of this nation's literature and to emphasize that, while we may call this literature Canadian, it is motivated by considerations that complicate and at times exceed a cultural-nationalist discourse.

In this chapter, I treat concrete poetry as one vector of borderblur activity within two interrelated contexts. First, I demonstrate how this Canadian network of affiliation was in dialogue with international concrete poets in order to emphasize the cosmopolitanism underpinning of this paratradition. Furthermore, along with this chapter's discussion of how concrete poetry is ostensibly shaped by an emergent sense of international connectedness, I also explore the form's investment in the transnational conditions of an emergent visual and technological culture—with a focus on advertising, typewriters, film, and television—that was rapidly transforming life in Canada, the United States, and England at the time. As avant-garde poets "mainly concerned with the present,"[11] the broader implications of a transnational, technologically driven, and media-saturated culture preoccupied Canadian borderblur poets more than the prospect of a national literary culture formulated on the literature of the past.

Beginning Again: A Confluence of Encounters

Identifying a single point of genesis for any national literary tradition or paratradition is a monumental task, and the job is often confounded by the flows of influence that inevitably pervade the written form. Literature should never be envisaged, in Wai Chee Dimock's words, as "the product of one nation and one nation alone."[12] Rather, it is always a confluence of temporal, geographical, and cultural encounters and influences. With its combination of British, French, American, Asian, and Indigenous foundations, critics today recognize Canada's literature as undeniable evidence of this truth, but this was not adequately reflected in the dominant cultural-nationalist discourse of the late 1960s and early 1970s, which largely overlooked the breadth of Canada's diversity. Gregory Betts pursues this line of thinking in *Finding Nothing* (2021), recognizing that concrete poetry's specific aesthetic and cultural foundations are evidenced in many lines of influence, beginning in the early twentieth-century with the materialist experiments with language championed by the European avant-garde: the calligrammes of Guillaume Apollinaire, which are evocative of seventeenth-century pattern poetries such as George Herbert's "Easter Wings," and which prefigure the emergence of the American E. E. Cummings's shaped poems; the esoteric Symbolist poetry of Stéphane Mallarmé, including his spatially cognizant, book-length poem *Un Coup de Dés Jamais N'Abolira le Hasard*; the rebellious Italian Futurists such as F. T. Marinetti, who advocated for a typographic poetry modelled after modern industrialization; the colourful typographical experiments and collagist anti-artworks of Dadaists Hugo Ball, Kurt Schwitters, Hannah Hoch, and Baroness Elsa von Freytag-Loringhoven; and Ezra Pound's call for precise diction, clarity, and scrupulous imagery in the Imagist manifesto, which draws from his fascination with Chinese written characters. These are vital poetic nodes of avant-gardism that comprise the international artistic and literary zeitgeist that culminated in 1955.

The many materialist explorations of language that took place in the first half of the twentieth century laid the groundwork for the emergence of concrete poetry's first wave. "The international movement of Concrete Poetry owes its origin," writes Bann, "to a meeting which took place in Ulm in 1955. It was in this year that Eugen Gomringer, then working as a secretary to Max Bill at the Hochschule fur Gestaltung, made the acquaintance of Décio Pignatari. . . . Both were already active in the field of experimental poetry."[13]

The meeting "opened a channel of communication between Gomringer and the Noigandres poets, but also led to an agreement that their work should henceforth be identified by one common title."[14] This one common title was *poesia concreta*, or concrete poetry. Following the Ulm meeting, these poets gained increasing recognition as they advanced separate but concurrent manifestos regarding the ambition of their work. In 1956, Gomringer typified first wave concrete in phraseology that reflected conventional avant-garde theories and emphasized that it does "not follow the traditional verse and line order."[15] Two years later, the Noigandres poets echoed Gomringer's denunciation of the past: "Assuming that the historical cycle of verse (as formal-rhythmical unit) is closed, concrete poetry begins by being aware of graphic space as structural agent."[16] Embodying traditional characteristics of avant-gardism, first wave concrete poetry is understood as a break with tradition and was said to represent innovative possibilities for creative expression with a focus on language's materiality. Thus began the international movement of concrete poetry, which would be critically lauded and enthusiastically anthologized well into the late 1960s.

In contrast to this oft-accepted narrative describing the origins of the first wave of concrete poetry, its Canadian iteration is unique. Instead of formulating itself as a mutated version of a pre-existing movement, some Canadian concrete poets, like the poets of the first wave, also thought they were starting anew. Canadian concrete poetry—as part of borderblur as an international whole—was established discretely and only then recognized within the broader, rich tradition of visually oriented intermedial poetics. The confluence of writing and thinking that set the stage for Canadian concrete poetry is well-documented. Tracing the vectors of poetic and artistic confluence allows us to elucidate some of the ideas and encounters that animated Canadian concrete poetry and to demonstrate these poets' eschewal of a single line of influence, a denial of a linear narrative that authoritatively connects events. Poets such as Nichol, bissett, Copithorne, and UU outline variegated influences on Canadian concrete poetry's earliest stages, some of which overlap, some of which do not. Many influences shaped Canadian concrete poetry (and there are more to be identified than those highlighted here). This is suggestive of its heterogeneity as well as a distrust of singular narratives that informed the nationalist discourse and were solidified by the subsequent outpouring of publications that advanced a tradition of poetry in verse.

Having started his work in the late 1950s and early 1960s as a visual artist and poet, bissett was living and working within Vancouver's transnational nexus of writers and poets. During his earliest developmental phases, bissett experimented alongside such poets and artists as Lance Farrell and Martina Clinton, "eschewing th narrativ line" to rethink the page as surface and space and the placement of poems upon it to effectively fold together his artistic practices.[17] In a 1972 letter to Nichol, bissett eagerly identifies Clinton and Farrell as part of his lineage, in contrast to other distant poets and traditions. Vancouver at the time was also a destination for American poets thanks to the UBC professor Warren Tallman, who invited several Beat and Black Mountain poets for visits, including Allen Ginsberg, Charles Olson, Denise Levertov, Robert Duncan, and others, who represented a new wave in poetry and poetics at the time (as anthologized in Donald Allen's *The New American Poetry*). The presence of these poets has been well-documented, and the 1963 Vancouver Poetry Conference remains a cornerstone in Canada's avant-garde literary history. bissett did not formally attend that event, nor was he affiliated with the academic poetry that Tallman bolstered, but he did meet poets like Ginsberg, who passed through Vancouver on more than one occasion. Unlike bissett, Copithorne did attend some parts of the Vancouver Poetry Conference, and, like bissett, was also aware of the city's lively downtown literary culture, especially the intermedial activities at Motion Studio, the Sound Gallery, and Intermedia. She was inspired by the work of American poets like Kenneth Patchen (who visited Vancouver in 1959) and enamored by the genre-defying poets and artists whose work she saw in San Francisco at City Lights in 1961: Brion Gysin and Henri Michaux, both of whom share with Copithorne an affinity for asemic writing—that is, writing that has no specific semantic content. bissett and Copithorne, then, like others in Vancouver's poetry scene at the time, were circulating within multiple international networks composed of a fertile mixture of different poets, aesthetic approaches, and ideas.

As we saw in the previous chapter, Nichol drew inspiration from Vancouver's cosmopolitan scene and its vital confluence of artistic forms, which he brought eastward to Toronto through his various publication efforts. It was reportedly in 1965 that Nichol came into direct contact with international practitioners of concrete poetry. In the *Ganglia Press Index* (1972), he credits George Bowering with assisting him in making connections to the concrete poetry scene that thrived in the wake of the initial manifestos published by Gomringer and the Noigandres poets. While Frank Davey contests this point in *aka bpNichol*, offering a slightly different version of this timeline, the critical point is that in 1965, at nearly the beginning of his work as a poet and publisher, Nichol began to correspond with Cavan McCarthy, an English poet and publisher of *Tlaloc*, as well as with the aforementioned Houédard and French poet Pierre Garnier. McCarthy, in 1965, published a special Canadian issue of *Tlaloc* featuring contributions from bissett, Bowering, Nichol, Gerry Gilbert, and Lionel Kearns, with non-Canadians Houédard, McCarthy, and Robin Page. These connections to McCarthy, Houédard, and Garnier granted Nichol and his Canadian affiliates access to this international network, and likely also led to Nichol's inclusion in the major international concrete poetry anthologies.

Like the page space of books, periodicals, and correspondence, the art gallery was a central nexus that evidences a direct and incontrovertible relationship between international and Canadian practitioners. UU organized notable exhibitions that demonstrated the way concrete poetry blurs the borders of media and disciplines—bringing poetry into spaces typically dominated by visual arts—while also demonstrating its international reach. The first of these exhibitions was *Brazilia 73*. It was held at the Mandan Ghetto and featured the work of Canadians bissett, Nichol, UU, and Stephen Scobie, with international contributions from Houédard (England), Henri Chopin (France), Ian Hamilton Finlay (Scotland), Ernst Jandl (Austria), and d. a. levy (United States).

After that, in 1971, UU organized another ambitious show at the Avelles Gallery in Vancouver entitled *Microprosophus: International Exhibition of Visual Poetry*, which ran 9–28 September. The press release for the show notes that it featured 153 works by 30 contributors from 11 countries. The lineup included Canadians such as bissett, Copithorne, Coupey, Wallace, Gary Lee Nova, Mr. Peanut, Gregg Simpson, and Edwin Varney. The names of the international contributors were not included in the press release; however, the title of show is clear evidence that some Canadians explicitly acknowledged their relationship to the broader international avant-garde. Finally, in 1969, UBC was host to the *Concrete Poetry: An Exhibition in Four Parts*, from 28 March to 19 April. Like *Brazilia 73*, the exhibition featured Canadians such as bissett, Nichol, Copithorne, Varney, and Scobie, as well as international practitioners such as Houédard, Finlay, Bob Cobbing, John Furnival (United Kingdom), Hansjorg Mayer (Germany), Carlo Belloli (Italy), Niikuni Seiichi

(Japan), and more. Thus, it is evident that by the late 1960s and early 1970s international practitioners had become frequent contributors to Canada's concrete poetry exhibitions and periodicals, solidifying Canada's place within a broader international avant-gardist network.

It would perhaps be tedious to map these relations any further, even if stopping here admittedly risks omitting essential references that may further illuminate the many artistic and intellectual vectors intersecting this poetic and the poets who practice it. However, before moving on, more might be said about later concrete poetry anthologies such as Canadian poet Peggy Lefler's 1989 *Anthology*, published by a scenario press. The mini-anthology was initially created for a grade-school workshop, which never took place, yet the book itself demonstrates the strong connection between Canadians and the international network of concrete poets even decades after it had been formed in the 1960s. Lefler's selections include Canadians bissett, Nichol, Hart Broudy, jwcurry, David Aylward, Shaunt Basmajian, and Gerry Shikatani (as well as Lefler herself), alongside Crag Hill, Richard Kostelanetz, John M. Bennett (United States), Fernando Aguiar (Portugal), Shoji Yoshizawa, Seiichi Niikuni (Japan), Bob Cobbing (England), and others. As such, even at this later stage in the history of Canadian concrete poetry, *Anthology* is reflective of an ongoing commitment to the earlier principles of concrete poetry in Canada, with its intermedial aesthetics and its connections to a broader international network.

To many critics, and especially critics like Dimock (noted above) or Jahan Ramazani (mentioned in the introduction), this confluence of temporal, geographical, and cultural influence is hardly surprising. It demonstrates how Canadian concrete poetry is composed of many textual strands, and these convergences force us to acknowledge the cultural, temporal, and contextual diversity at the root of Canadian concrete poetry (and borderblur more broadly). Nichol, reflecting on his early days, confessed to poet Stuart Ross that "it was almost a necessity for stimulation to look across the borders, towards Europe, or towards the States."[18] Once the network formed, Nichol found it stimulating, but this activity first needed to be animated by poetics from abroad.

Canadian Concrete Poetry and the Electric Age

Media and technology were central to the encounters that expanded Canadian borderblur's sense of itself beyond the traditional verse redolent of a Canadian literary nationalism. Many technologies facilitated the flow of persons, ideas, texts, and sounds into concrete poets' awareness, thereby shaping their poetics. Cars, planes, and trains moved poets toward city centres like Vancouver; likewise, the typewriter, postal service, and telephone ensured pathways of communication across vast distances. However, the rapidly changing conditions of the mediascape in the mid- to late twentieth century more directly shaped Canadian concrete poetry. The press release for the 1971 exhibition *Microprosophus* succinctly captures the cosmopolitan dimension of concrete poetry while also acknowledging the influence of new theories giving shape to the electronic age. UU conceives of concrete poetry as a meeting point between media and disciplines and describes it as "a desire to experience the elements of literature and communicate this in a world which is besieged by electronic media and no longer understands the importance and progression of tradition."[19] With electronic media, then, came possibilities for poetry that prompted poets to sever their connections to traditional literary lineages in a way that neatly aligns with Antin's conception of avant-gardism as "mainly concerned with the present."[20] It is also important to underscore UU's use of the phrase "in a world," which I interpret literally as a reflection of his sincere belief that Canadian concrete poetry was connected to similar activities in other geographical contexts involving poets who were also interested in the emergence and proliferation of electronic media. The worldliness of UU's thought is made explicit in his curated roster of international artists and poets, and it further confirms Canadian borderblur's status as a paratradition that is both within and without Canadian literature, and by the same gesture, within and without an international network. In a way, it occupies a liminal space wherein these poets are geographically located in Canada—reacting against the formation of a literary tradition contingent on a narrow conception of national identity—while responding, along with poets in other geographical contexts, to the social and cultural transformations happening within the world around them. These poets were concerned with the role of electronic media in their daily lives and adopted intermedial approaches to reckon with these new conditions. UU's identification with electronic media resonates with poet Ed Varney's claim that concrete poetry is "medium as message,"[21] highlighting the media-centredness of concrete poetry with its nod to McLuhan's oft-used phrase "the medium is the message." Both Varney's and UU's claims find common ground not only in gesturing toward McLuhan's influence on borderblur, and especially Canadian concrete poetry, but also in illustrating that concrete poetry cannot be reduced to a simplistic expression of Canadian national identity. Instead, it is concerned with how human life "in a world"[22] is being reshaped within an emergent electronic context. These conditions reconstituted possibilities of poesis and, by extension, formed part of the ground upon which this Canadian avant-garde paratradition flourished.

The emergence of electronic media, which evidently preoccupied the imaginations of Canadian concrete poets, is captured in McLuhan's writing on what he termed the *electric age*, or what might be recognized more commonly today as the early emergence of postmodernity. McLuhan's 1951 book *The Mechanical Bride: Folklore of Industrial Culture*—at the time, a cutting-edge analysis of newspapers, advertisements, radio, and film and their modulation of human thought, behaviour, and desire—effectively articulated these conditions for a whole generation of writers and thinkers. He continued this work with varying degrees of optimism and caution in *The Gutenberg Galaxy* and *Understanding Media*. *The Mechanical Bride* captures both the limits and possibilities that emergent media promised this generation. McLuhan writes,

> Ours is the first age in which many thousands of the best-trained individual minds have made it a full-time business to get inside the collective public mind. To get inside in order to manipulate, exploit, control is the object now. To keep everybody in the helpless state engendered by prolonged mental rutting is the effect of many ads and much entertainment alike.[23]

McLuhan recognizes this impetus toward control as a vital issue as the Western world transitions from an industrial age to the electric age. He writes that, in this age, the "Imagination flickers out," the "Markets contract,"[24] life becomes monotonous and boring, and "conformity"[25] becomes increasingly rampant. The forms of media becoming more commonplace in McLuhan's day, he suggests, seemingly reduce the possibilities for an enriched human experience and point toward the emergence of a society controlled by corporations, advertisers, and entertainers.

Michael Hardt and Antonio Negri confirm, with the advantage of hindsight, the conditions that McLuhan observed in his own time. They refer to these as symptoms of postmodernization—the transition from an industrial to a service-based economy, which includes everything ranging from "health care, education, and finance to transportation, entertainment, and advertising," and which is "characterized in general by the central role played by knowledge, information, communication, and affect."[26] As outlined in chapter 1, and emphasized by UU and Varney above, communicative possibilities were developing as communication became increasingly bound with electronic media. This brought multimedia methods of communication including television, film, and mass advertising, which in turn transformed social, economic, and cultural interactions. This is a moment that, for Hardt and Negri, "marks a new mode of becoming human,"[27] one that reformulated possibilities for expression, communication, and belonging. This concern with the present is a key distinction between borderblur as a literary paratradition and the dominant Canadian literary tradition that emerged in the 1960s. These poets were not concerned with the formation of a Canadian literary identity as much as the broader implications of electronic media and its impacts on human life. It is worth remembering, too, Arjun Appadurai's point that electronic media has the power to transform our understanding of what it means to belong to a nation.[28] The rise of this new visual culture evidently influenced the compositional approaches that Canadian concrete poets adopted during the 1960s and into the 1980s. What I show in the remainder of this chapter, however, is that their responses to the conditions of the electronic age were multifaceted. Historical theorizations of avant-gardism might seek out particularly radical and rebellious responses to these conditions; however, as will be seen in the work of these poets, they responded with a sharp sense of rebellion—at times resisting emergent economic and social configurations—while also embracing the possibilities that electronic media offered them.

Against Manipulation: Advertising and Consumer Culture

John Berger's 1972 book *Ways of Seeing*—based on the BBC television series of the same name—confirms that the late twentieth century was charged with anxiety as the conditions of entertainment and consumer capitalism intensified under postmodernization. The image was gaining inordinate ubiquity. "In no other form of society in history," Berger writes, "has there been such a concentration of images, such a density of visual message."[29] Like McLuhan, he acknowledges the troublesome bind of an optically centred consumerist culture that he calls *publicity*: "Publicity is not merely an assembly of competing messages: it is a language in itself which is always being used to make the same general proposal."³⁰ Advertising presents the illusion of free and sundry consumerist choices but actually offers limited variegation to benefit corporations, a point that echoes McLuhan's concern about manipulation and exploitation. Publicity works, according to Berger, primarily by motivating and manipulating a person's feelings. "Capitalism survives," he writes, "by forcing the majority, whom it exploits, to define their own interests as narrowly as possible."³¹ This is a familiar premise to us today, but it was among the most salient contentions of Canadian borderblur poets as they confronted the conditions of their own present. And concrete poetry was one poetic form for exploring the effects of this emergent visual culture.

While this chapter has so far maintained the distinction between the first and second waves of concrete poetry, both waves actually shared a fascination with postmodernization's emergent phase as typified by McLuhan and Berger. In "From Line to Constellation," Gomringer declares that "the language of today must have certain things in common with poetry. . . . Headlines, slogans, groups of sounds and letters give rise to forms which could be models for a new poetry just waiting to be taken up for meaningful use."³² Gomringer's declaration conveys his ambition to mend the fragmented world that emerged from the destruction and divisiveness of the Second World War. Gomringer attempts to overcome poetry's antiquity by synthesizing it with the popular media of the day, thus making poetry more appealing to a contemporary audience. As Perloff points out, however, Gomringer's "ambivalence" toward "the related visual poetics of advertising and the media" undercuts any kind of radical project intended to improve the conditions of human life.³³ She echoes Berger and McLuhan, noting that humans are "vulnerable" to "prefabricated messages, bogus claims to authority, and endless dubious prescriptions," and that advertising exploits these vulnerabilities.³⁴ She is skeptical, too, of the Noigandres poets, whose work is aligned with a radical anti-advertising agenda and as such is demonstrative of a sort of prototypical culture jamming. Pignatari's "beba coca cola" critiques Coca-Cola through visual wordplay to suggest that consumption of the beverage is a "form of infantile regression and at worst the consumption of excrement."³⁵ Following from Rosemarie Waldrop's careful reading of this poem, Perloff ultimately regards first wave concrete poetry's divergent approaches to advertising thusly: "The Concrete poem as anti-advertisement . . . is perhaps not all that different from the Concrete poem as proto-advertising logo."³⁶ In other words, first wave concrete poetry, to return to Perloff's claim that it is "ideologically suspect," too closely resembles advertising copy.[37] Aesthetically replicating the conditions of the present, as many of the first wave concrete poets did, according to Perloff, is counter to any attempt to transform society.

This relationship to aesthetics and the mechanisms of advertising and visual media is said to mark Canadian concrete poetry's difference from the first wave that began in the 1950s. McCaffery epitomizes the form's anti-capitalist and anti-consumerist ethos when he argues that linguistic expression is intricately bound up with capitalism and its problematic program of homogenizing and standardizing the expression of the lyrical subject. "Capitalism begins," he writes, "when you / open the dictionary."[38] In a separate context, he suggests that "language . . . functions like money and speaks *through* us more than we actively produce *within* it."[39] McCaffery and his contemporaries believed that language was being systematically regularized to the extent that expression of the self had become imitative of the power structures that, as McLuhan also contends, manipulate, control, and exploit human subjects. This is a problem directly related to Perloff's critique of first wave concrete poetry's politics. By contrast, McCaffery would likely describe concrete poetry—especially its most disruptive variations—as writing that "extends far beyond scriptive practice and would include all non-utilitarian activities of excess, unavoidable waste and non-productive consumption."[40] In other words, writing that does not directly or intentionally reproduce language as it has been systematically regularized; instead, it is illegible, disordered, and challenging to absorb.

Building on McCaffery's work, poet Derek Beaulieu applies this theory of a heterogenous poetics directly to concrete poetry. In "an afterword after words: notes toward a concrete poetic," he advances an aesthetic theory for concrete poetry. Situating himself between Sianne Ngai's "poetics of disgust"[41] and Roland Barthes's semiotics, Beaulieu argues that concrete poetry "can also be closely read in conjunction with the idea of concrete poetry as an 'inarticulate mark,'" suggesting that it "interferes with signification and momentarily interrupts the capitalist structure of language."[42] While I am cautious of privileging a single way of thinking about concrete poetry's intervention into social and economic contexts—for these poets had diverse concerns and political leanings—some Canadian concrete poets were apprehensive of capitalism and conscientious of how their poetry figured within the rapidly intensifying dynamic of a capital-driven visual culture.

Figure 2.1: "Blues" by bpNichol, from *As Elected: Selected Writing*, 1981.

With its minimalist exploration of the single four-letter word "love," Nichol's "Blues" is a compelling case study of Canadian concrete's relationship to capitalism and the conditions of a consumerist culture that reached beyond national borders. The poem is similar to Gomringer's "constellations" but surpasses the latter's interest in the technical language of science or the simplicity of advertising and popular culture. If publicity, according to Berger, is the business of manipulating human emotion, "Blues" transforms the idea of love, an emotion that is often referenced in the capitalist marketplace to compel consumers to purchase products to increase their chances of gathering affection.[43] Nichol explores love as a complex idea and affect. In "Blues," love is not merely an emotion that connotes a powerful social bond, nor is it an emotion for the service of a consumerist economy.

Critics like John Robert Colombo and Caroline Bayard have identified a binary in "Blues" that emphasizes a single permutation of the word "love." They highlight "evol" as an alternative spelling of "evil," a seeming opposition to love. Nichol, however, speaking through another poem, refutes dualistic readings of "Blues." In "Captain Poetry in Love," Nichol writes,

> love
> spelled backwards
> is evol
> is
> 'nature's way' (i've
> overworked it
> in a dozen
> poems) has
> nothing to do
> with evil
> but rather evolves
> new themes. how
> impossible
> to overwork them.[44]

For Nichol, the poem contains at least a triad of words and meaning: love, evil, and evolve. Scholar Stephen Voyce, whose paper at the 2014 Avant-Canada Conference helped make these connections, notes that love for Nichol, especially in his early writing, "shares an operative logic" with borderblur.[45] Voyce looks upon a passage from the sequence "JOURNEYING & the Returns," one part of the 1967 slipcase of the same name, in which Nichol writes,

> love is some sort of fire
> come to warm us
> fill our bodies
> all in these motions
> flowing into each other
> in despair - the room -
> one narrow world
> that might be anywhere.[46]

Love, as Voyce suggests, is for Nichol "an integration of subjects, bodies flowing into one another, into the space between."[47] Love, then, embodies the core principles of borderblur: a means of overflowing a space, of transcending borders—genre, meaning, media, and materials. This point is unsurprising since, as Nichol writes on the back of the slipcase of *Journeying*, "The other is the loved one and the other is the key."[48] Nichol demonstrates this clearly in his arrangement of a single word to offer at least three conceptual pathways into and out of the poem, offering an idea of love that embodies the term's significance as an expression of feeling, belonging, and poetic form.

Adding to the poem's complexity, Nichol is not so naive as to suggest that love overcomes evil. Rather, the poem acknowledges love to be intricately bound up with evil—or, at least, love's negative emotions. "Blues" highlights love's misgivings. In the context of romantic love, one must acknowledge the negative feelings that attachment can generate: jealousy, possession, insecurity, anxiety, and so on. Similarly, the poem's invocation of evolution—via "evol"—suggests that love is a feeling that is always in flux; it expands, dissipates, and shifts over time. We come to love others, and our lovers can leave us too. Love is a process, and embedded within it is a series of entrances and exits to the self and the other. For Nichol, love's meaning exceeds its conventional definition and its simplistic use in advertising as a positive feeling to connote affection and a deep social bond that can be mobilized by advertisers for economic gain—as we well know, for decades products have been advertised with the promise of making the consumer more desirable to lovers and friends. With all its additional negative complexities, the concept denotes a feeling that is not easily consumed or consumable. Love is complex and multidirectional; it is comprised of both positive and negative feelings and, as Nichol's poem seems to suggest, any application of the word that reduces its complexity does so in the disservice of human emotion and the service of capitalist gain.

Love was evidently on the minds of other concrete poets within the Canadian borderblur network. Love is at the centre of UU's chapbook *Touch* (1967), published by Ganglia Press. The title itself directly invokes notions related to intimacy—touch, of course, is how one person can reach out to another and impress themselves upon the body and mind, to mark the surface of another's body, to generate bodily sensation in the skin and nerves. Except, in this case, the other body is a textual body: that of *Touch* itself, a staple-bound chapbook, wrapped in a slightly mottled, deckle-edged cover paper. The texture of this paper—unlike cheaper and more commercially available papers—highlights the importance of physicality and intimate interaction. Like Nichol, UU puts his faith in language and the poem to reach out and impress themselves upon the reader in a way that is akin to human touch—to reach out through the poem and touch another.

Touch includes an introductory note written on 20 March 1967 that foregrounds love as the work's central feeling. With a somewhat romanticized tone, UU claims that "all poemz arr lessonz tooe love."[49] UU's conception of love is demonstrated in the series entitled "a story," which closes the collection. This is a four-page suite of plot-driven concrete poems consisting of a single quasi-phonetic spelling of the word "luv," composed using a "mask" method to create perfect circles that are then overlaid on one another. The sequence depicts the movement of two circles, both created from the repetition of "luv" running in straight lines—vertically, inside one circle, and horizontally in the second. The two circles are side by side, almost but not quite touching, and poised with a seemingly intense attraction to one another. The remainder of the poem depicts the movement of these two formations as they succumb to each other's magnetism, at first overlapping only slightly before becoming fully overlaid upon one another. In the final page of the sequence, the two figures are situated side by side again, but this time enveloped by a larger circle also composed of the same word. If we were to project a story onto this sequence, as the title suggests, then this is a story of two figures attracted to one other. It is a story about desire—a "luv" story, if you will.

UU's concrete narrative poem is demonstrative of typical renderings of love, especially love as it is mobilized within consumerism. Advertisers seek

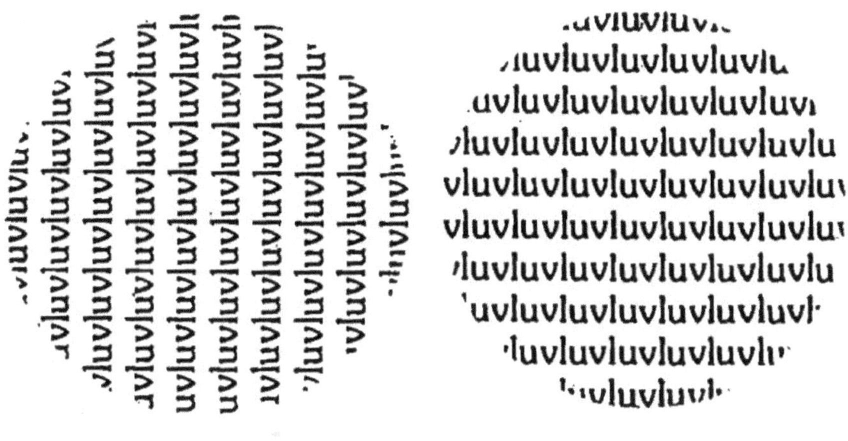

Figure 2.2: Excerpt from *Touch* by David UU, 1967.

to sell goods to consumers that, among other things, will ensure the loving embrace of another through the promise of an attractive image and social status. However, UU displaces this conventional notion of love in his introductory note to the poem, wherein he encourages the reader to "forget our social insurance number maybiy therr iz noe god eor tooemorroe but therr iz love."[50] In the same breath, he suggests that love is a method for bringing people together and a site of communal resistance that exceeds the mechanisms of the state. Love, then, in this poem, is not conceived as a convenient means of bringing together persons in the promise of a happiness easily packaged and sold to consumers; rather, it is a site of intimacy, identity, and sociality that rejects conventional consumerist and state-sanctioned modes of togetherness.

Nichol's "Blues" and UU's *Touch* offer an oblique commentary on emotional complexity and consumerist manipulations of feeling and gesture toward the fundamental humanist and political concerns of their work. These were crucial concerns for their peers too, like bissett, whose poems often address social and political dynamics. bissett directly engages the genre of advertising as part of his poetry and publishing. *blewointment*, for example, would include advertisements for issues of the magazine that would never appear. As Betts points out in *Finding Nothing*, the back cover of volume 4, issue 1 of *blewointment* advertised an upcoming piece by jazz musician Al Neil entitled "Chums," which was ostensibly to be included in issue 2; however, that issue of the magazine was never published. Instead, the next installment of *blewointment* was volume 5, issue 1, which did feature Neil's "Chums." The mysteriously absent second issue of volume 4 may have simply been a result of a mismanaged publication schedule, yet this enticing offer of a new issue in that volume plays with readers' expectations and their relationship to advertisements. bissett offers the promise of a specific cultural product without fulfilling that promise in the manner specified. Notably, too, *Th Combind Blewointment Open Picture Book nd the News* (1972) contains an advertisement for a steak house in Puerto Vallarta offering New York–style steak imported from the United States. The ad's placement inside both the front and back covers of the anthology is out of place, considering that bissett's core readership is likely far removed from the advertised destination (though bissett did spend time in Mexico in the mid-1960s). Instead, the appearance of this ad in 1974 highlights the transnational influence of American imperialism.

The advertisement in *Th Combind Blewointment Open Picture Book nd the News* is also indicative of the way bissett experimented with the materials of consumer culture, and especially its detritus, in his concrete poetry. bissett would occasionally print his publications on the backs of one-sided commercial ads.[51] *Pass th food release th spirit book* (1973), for example, prominently features such mass-produced debris: torn imagery reassembled in collages, crushed papers with barely legible text, gum wrappers, and torn newspapers. One page of the collection consists of what appears to be crumpled and crushed paper, looking as though it had been forced through a duplication machine, with the phrase "whunawhunaw" written over it. Another page in the collection contains a torn page of advertisements from an 1871 newspaper printed in the then colony of British Columbia showing sugar, molasses, champagne, and other miscellaneous groceries; it is overlaid with fanged-shaped cut-outs along the top. The collage is notably anti-colonial in its posturing since these advertisements from earlier colonial days are given a threatening appearance via the fang shapes; it also comments more generally on advertising as a business.

These collagist concrete poems literally engage McCaffery's notion of writing as "excess," since bissett in these poems uses literal waste to mark the page, challenging conventions of poesis while also forcing us to confront the textual and material detritus of consumer culture.

Another striking poem from this collection begs readers to rethink or resist consumer culture. bissett places a Dentyne-brand gum wrapper at the centre of the page and frames it with a black rectangular box to identify the debris, like a picture frame, as an art object. Aside from reproducing and framing the wrapper, bissett's intervention is minimal, confined to his placement of the word "help" in the empty white boxes on the wrapper. "Help" echoes the slogan on the wrapper—"Helps Keep Teeth White"—but the repetition of the word is altered in the poem. There, in the word's second appearance in the poem, the typewriter line visibly slips and only a portion of the *h* is visible. The slippage suggests a struggle, thereby reinforcing the request for assistance. Moreover, in this way, the poem is a cry of desperation reflecting on the production of consumerist waste and its effect on the earth's atmosphere. It commands the reader to help, to become a better steward of the earth, and to think more consciously, as the frame of the poem suggests, about consumerist excess.

Breaking the Typing Machines

Implicated within the mechanisms of control that underpin the culture and values of publicity and advertising are the corporate offices where the "best-trained individual minds have made it a full-time business to get inside the collective public mind."[52] The twentieth century, as Darren Wershler explains, saw "the emergence of large corporations and global markets [that] produced a blizzard of documents—accounting ledgers, purchase orders, memos, correspondence, and so on."[53] The typewriter, though not always electronic, was an essential writing device that aided the work flows of corporations. Thus, the typewriter is emblematic of the capitalist and communicative conditions of the period. Not only is the typewriter emblematic of corporate culture, but, as Wershler explains (drawing on Michel Foucault's *Discipline and Punish*), it is also representative of a form of disciplinary control that "operates by dividing the world into grids: spaces designed to contain and manage different segments of a population."[54] Discipline is the subtle modulation of bodies and behaviours to ultimately optimize the productivity of citizens, labourers, and consumers as contributors to a socio-economic system. Advertising does this by influencing the desires of consumers, prompting them to buy specific consumer goods. But as Wershler writes in regards to the typewriter, "nowhere

Figure 2.3: Untitled collage from *pass th food release th spirit book* by bill bissett, 1973.

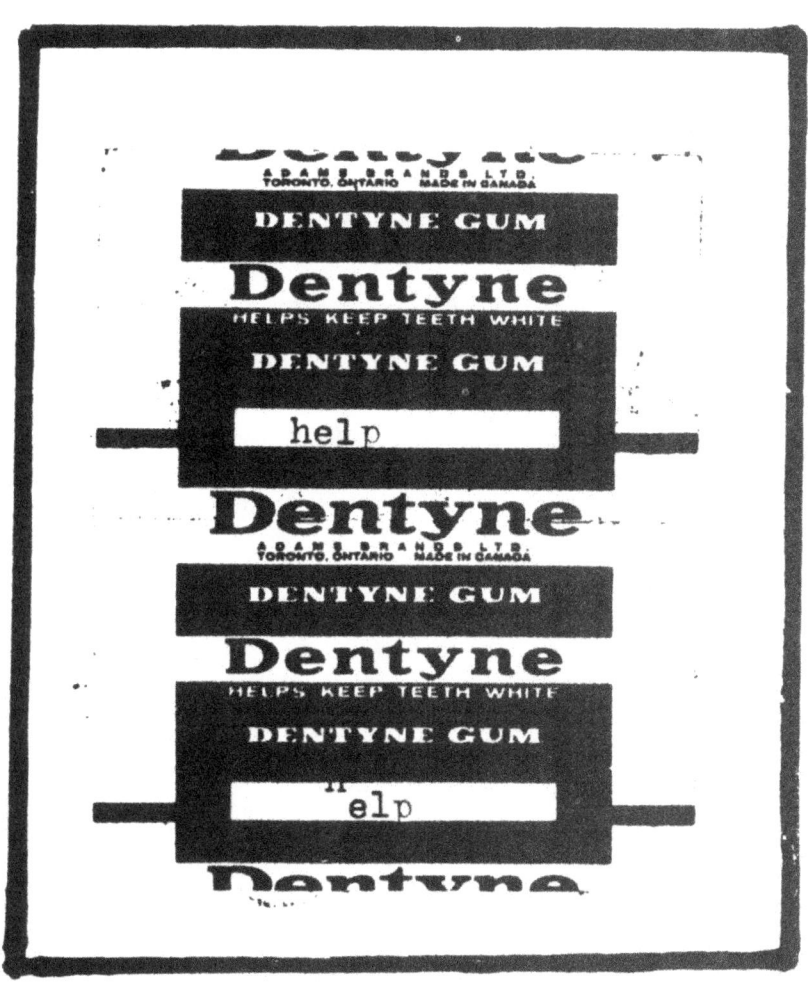

Figure 2.4: Untitled collage from *pass th food release th spirit book* by bill bissett, 1973.

does this system of discipline become more clear than in the standard classroom typing manual,"⁵⁵ which provides detailed instructions on the proper ways for engaging the typewriter's mechanisms, including the placement and movement of fingers across the keyboard for optimal typing efficiency. So, for all the usefulness of the typewriter as a writing tool—one that poets in the mid- to late twentieth century often relied heavily upon to produce their mimeographed publications—it was also a site of control that dictated the movement of language on the page and the bodily movements of the typist within grid systems that were designed to increase the speed and clarity of printed communication. In the typewriter, we find both the literal modulation of communication and the symbolic modulations of corporate culture. Some poets reacted against these controlling mechanisms, creating concrete poetry that misused and abused the typewriter in order to free language from the discipline to which it has traditionally been submitted.

In *Reading Writing Interfaces*, Lori Emerson draws together the typewriter-based concrete poetry of Canadian borderblur poets McCaffery and Nichol and English borderblur poet Houédard, whose work she argues represents a form of media-based activism. During "the era from the early 1960s to the mid-1970s . . . poets, working heavily under the influence of Marshall McLuhan, sought to create (especially, so-called dirty) concrete poetry as a way to experiment with the limits and the possibilities of the typewriter," writes Emerson.⁵⁶ She argues that Canadian concrete is visually unlike its first wave predecessors and is perhaps more aptly described as *dirty concrete*, a term that some Canadians preferred to use when describing the "nonlinearity and illegibility" of their work.⁵⁷ For Emerson, dirty concrete represents an aesthetic that actively contests the limits of communication devices such as the typewriter. If the typewriter is a "particular kind of mechanical writing interface that necessarily inflects both how and what one writes," then dirty concrete is a means of breaking its material specificities.⁵⁸

The desire to respond to technologies that control communication and enable the development of postmodernization is strongly foregrounded by McCaffery, whose intermedial works "resolutely resist categorization and containment," claims Stephen Cain.⁵⁹ McCaffery's oeuvre is exemplary of borderblur, exploring as it does many intermedial possibilities, including concrete poetry, sound poetry, game-like works, and more. I will return to McCaffery's work numerous times in subsequent parts of the book, but for now, I focus on his exemplary work of typewriter-based concrete poetry,

Carnival. *Carnival* is a work consisting of two panels, the first of which was composed from 1967 to 1970 and the second from 1970 to 1975 (both published by Coach House Press). McCaffery describes this work as "essentially cartographic; a repudiation of linearity in writing and the search for an alternative syntax in 'mapping.'"[60]

Carnival is multidirectional, coloured with both black and red typewriter tapes, and employs printing and copying devices that are typically found in corporate offices, such as rubber stamps, xerography, dry transfer lettering, and stencils. Each of these techniques are used in unconventional ways, creating a visual disorder on the page that is augmented by McCaffery's use of textual overlay and abstract shapes. To consume the text as intended, a reader must destroy the book by removing each page and then following the instructions provided with the text and assembling the panels to create a largescale artwork. In effect, *Carnival* "challenges" not only "the sequentiality of the book" but the sequentiality of syntax and conventional reading processes writ large so as "to achieve a calculated annihilation of semantic meaning."[61] That McCaffery created a book that must be destroyed foregrounds his interest in exceeding the conventional limits of the medium, since here the book as a container for language needs to be broken before the work can actually be consumed. In doing so, McCaffery also theoretically frees the body from the disciplined practice of reading. *Carnival* is not a work that is meant to be held in your hands and read following the traditional left-to-right reading pattern. It breaks with this tradition while also breaking the linear, gridlike construction of the typewritten page. When assembled by the reader as instructed, it most loudly pronounces its intermedial aesthetic, blurring the medial borders of the book and framed artwork, of language and visual mark.

When assembled into its intended form, *Carnival* is also indeed "cartographic" and map-like. The typewritten words are freed from conventional linearity and both panels are maps for an imagined space, outside of syntax and semantics. In *Carnival*, there is no recognizable order. The book echoes the tradition of Western Christian and Greek Orthodox festivals, which include public celebrations, parades, and entertainment attended by persons in costumes and masks. It is traditionally a time for participants to free themselves from the strictures of their daily lives within the state. In his introduction to the book, McCaffery suggests that one can enter the text using one of many definitions of the word "carnival," which in this case comes "from Med. L. carnelevale, a putting away of the flesh and hence a prelental language game."[62] *Carnival* is a space in which the rules of linguistic meaning-making are ignored in order to open a space of possibility in which readers can revel—much like the attendees of a carnival—in disruption, image, and play. As a text that seeks to free itself from the state, it also gestures toward the possibility of being outside of Canada, and, as a work of literature, of imagining the possibility of forming a textual community divorced from nationalistic forms of cultural expression.

Among the critiques of McCaffery's *Carnival*, poet and scholar Andy Weaver foregrounds the problem of the socio-political art project in relation to issues of identity politics, which highlights some of the complexities of the book's status as an avant-garde text, especially as they relate to privilege, masculinity, whiteness, and ableism. If this is, by one reading, an intermedial text meant to free language from the control of corporatized writing devices, whose language is allowed this freedom? Who is able to follow McCaffery's prompt, that this text is about the putting "away of the flesh?"[63] For Weaver, this compromises the socio-political project of *Carnival* because, as he notes, McCaffery's text is a call for "moving past the physical body, towards an ideal relationship between mind and language."[64] The validity of McCaffery's political project is problematized by the fact that this negation of the body ignores the conditions that deny other bodies—those of visible minorities, people with disabilities, queer bodies, etc.—the luxury of leaving their corporeality behind. These bodies are effectively locked within the social conditions produced by the stigmas that target them. The second panel of *Carnival* thereby ignores "the socio-political and economic differences that cause real strife in the world, an oversight that leaves the text dealing with ethereal problems at the expense of offering any thoughts on practical matters."[65]

Like Weaver, I seek to locate my analysis in the pitfalls of McCaffery's conceptualization of *Carnival: The Second Panel*. The first pitfall concerns the problem of putting away the "flesh." The whole body is not composed of "flesh"—flesh is but one part of the body, which is also composed of skin, bone, nerves, and blood, in addition to the emotions, sensations, and ideas that inform how the body experiences the world. Furthermore, McCaffery's seeming attempt to negate the body by placing the "reader, as perceptual participant, within the center of his language" seems to be a mere provocation.[66] Body and language are intricately and totally assembled; they are inseparable. McCaffery himself describes the bodily aspects of language in processes of enunciation and vocalization: "Voice is the polis of mouth, lips teeth, tongue, tonsils, palate, breath, rhythm, timbre, and sound."[67] Similarly, the production of concrete poetry depends on an assemblage of bone, cartilage, and muscles: movements of the hand and eye and more. From these two points, I offer a complimentary reading that builds on the observation with which Weaver begins his essay: the text's relationship to notions of disorientation, which seeks to free language from the controlling mechanisms emerging in the twentieth century. This might cut against McCaffery's conceptualization of his own work; however, I think it is only fair to analyze his writing on its own terms. If *Carnival: The Second Panel* is a text within which the reader "confront[s] [language] as material without reference to an author or to any otherness," then McCaffery, too, must be banned as authorial referent.[68]

I propose that *Carnival: The Second Panel*'s call to move away from the body could be also understood not as a movement away from flesh toward the abstract, but as a move deeper into the body—into its feelings, intensities, and affects. In bold, rubber-stamped text an elongated form of the word "plunge" begins in the upper-left corner of the assembled version; it then moves diagonally toward the centre—signifying not a movement away from but a movement deeper *into* the body. In the assembled form of *Carnival: The Second Panel*, the movement of the word "plunge" draws the reader's eye further into the centre of the text, not away from it. A similar sentiment is expressed on page 6, perhaps summarizing the book's overriding project: "the message being that we are all poets one and all as long as we have lungs the moving into the body's ritual of repeated semaphore / a perception of clarity beyond all measure of meanings."[69] Again, there is a distinctive invocation calling the reader to move *into* the body—not away from it. I can only assume that the "message" is the poem itself. This message, as indicated by Weaver's analysis, could rightly be characterized by disorientation, an effect traditionally used in many avant-garde artworks to, as theorist Charles Russell explains, allow readers to "perceive things of previously unimagined beauty, or experience states of abruptly expanded consciousness."[70] *Carnival: The Second Panel* is deranged, mobilizing disorientation with the intention of offering a possible place within which an individual may find liberation, even just for a moment. As a receptive reader of *Carnival: The Second Panel*, one invites the text into one's body and allows one's sense of typewritten language to be disrupted, opening up new possibilities for writing and reading.[71] McCaffery demonstrates these possibilities with his intermedial, multi-panelled book cum visual artwork. Typewritten language was essential for ordering society during the mid-twentieth century. It allowed personal communication, but it also, as both Wershler's and Emerson's writings imply, facilitated the controlling mechanisms of corporate and disciplinary cultures. By reading McCaffery's poem, our "body's ritual of repeated semaphore" is disrupted, and that disruption is essential. It opens language to new possibilities of configuration and movement free from controlling mechanisms at the economic, social, and cultural levels.

Paul Dutton, like McCaffery, destroys his writing device in *The Plastic Typewriter* (composed in 1977), and creates a book using "a disassembled plastic-case typewriter, an intact typewriter, carbon ribbons, carbon paper, metal file, and white bond paper."[72] McCaffery and Dutton share an interest in exploring the communicative functions of the writing machine by using those of its parts not usually designated for the production of typed language. The typewriter is an assemblage; thereby, all its parts in interplay are involved in the process of producing the typewritten word. However, the separate function of certain parts (e.g., the carbon paper, or the letters themselves) are more integral to the production of language than, say, the aligning scale or the spool cover. That being said, in the spirit of borderblur, Dutton's text is thematically linked to song and music. For example, lyrics from "Certainly Lord," a traditional Black spiritual commonly sung in churches and adopted in the 1960s as a civil rights anthem, is imprinted on some of the pages.[73] "Flamenco Sequence/1977," Dutton's contribution to the *Sound Poetry Catalogue* (1978), presents an excerpt from *The Plastic Typewriter*, where he writes, "Poetry consists of language; and language consists of sound and sight, of idea and emotion, of intellect and body, of rationality and irrationality,"[74] and he further explains that one should "Work with it, play with it, act on it. And most of all (ultimately, hopefully) enjoy it."[75] And perhaps, a work like *The Plastic Typewriter* is just that simple: a text wherein readers should find pleasure outside of the conventional communicative modes of his time.

If, for McCaffery and Dutton, breaking open the restrictions of the typewriter is about revelling in the pleasure of textual freedom, Copithorne, in the 1960s and '70s, developed an intermedial concrete poetic in concert with the core principles of borderblur, but deviated from her peers with her emphasis on the hand and body in her work. In an interview with Lorna Brown, Carole Itter describes Copithorne as one of the "astounding young women" of the Vancouver scene, someone "who insisted that their statements be heard

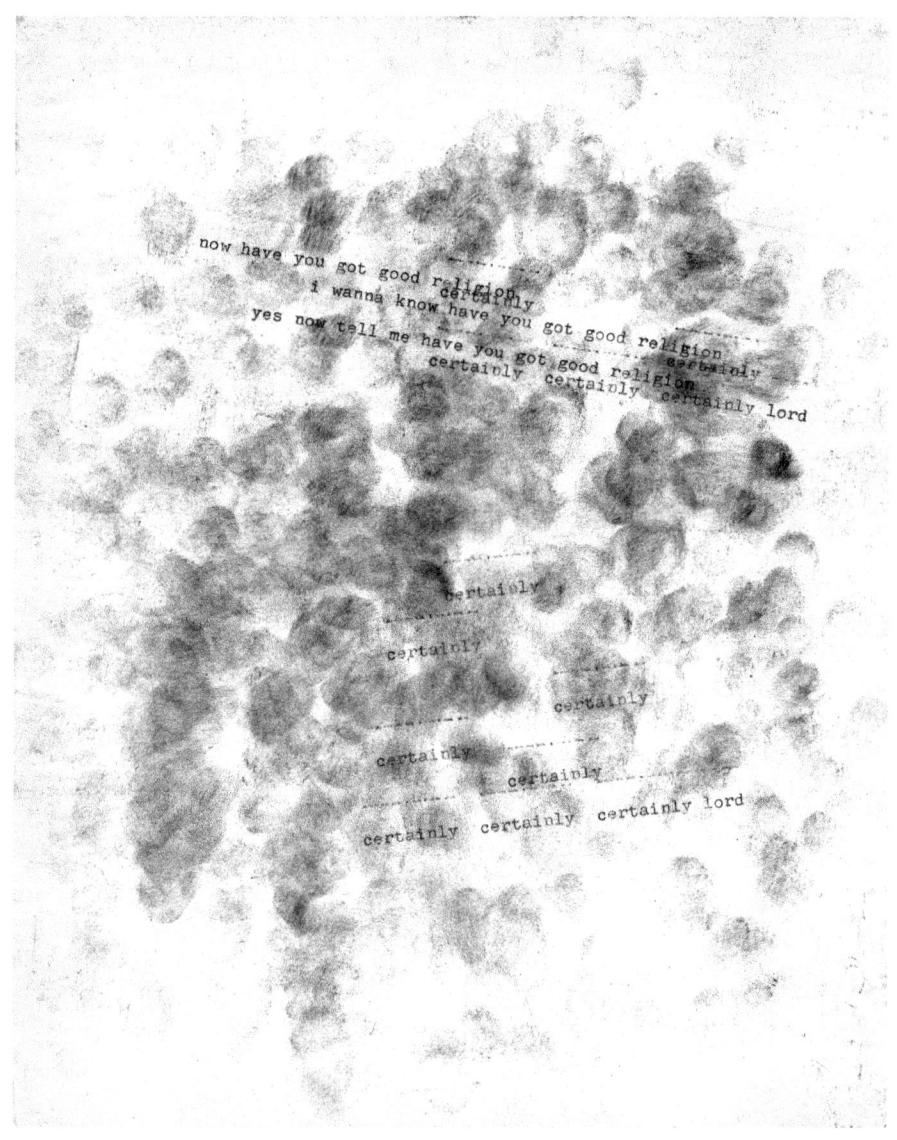

Figure 2.5: "The Plastic Typewriter, 12" by Paul Dutton (text sourced from the traditional Black US gospel song "Certainly, Lord").

and that they could be artists."⁷⁶ Indeed, active in both poetry and dance, Copithorne's work stretched across local, national, and international literary networks.

Copithorne's privileging of less mechanical writing media is significant for a variety of reasons. First, it becomes a way of folding together both of Copithorne's artistic media: poetry and dance. The latter of the two is a fully embodied art, founded on principles of kinesis and proprioception. Second, it offers an expansion of Canadian concrete poetry discourse beyond its largely mechanized mode of poetics. Unlike some of the work by her male counterparts, Copithorne's poetry and her choice of hand-drawn methods are significant because the relationship between typewriters and women's bodies is troubling. Wershler himself questions critics who have hailed the typewriter as the mechanical device that "was the major means of women's emancipation."⁷⁷ Due to the increasing demand for clerical work in the late nineteenth and early twentieth centuries, women were more frequently employed in secretarial positions, including what Wershler, echoing the derisive usage of the time, refers to as the "Type-Writer Girl." However, as Wershler points out, the typewriter led to "losses of power" as well as "gains."⁷⁸ While women gained employment, equity was not the primary goal for the businesses that employed them: women were paid significantly lower wages than their male co-workers, and as "more Type-Writer Girls joined the workplace, corporations restructured themselves to ensure that these women would rarely if ever enter the management stream."⁷⁹ Furthermore, as Wershler points out, many women were attracted to employment because popular culture painted a glamorous image of such work, yet this "imagery exaggerated the independence of the Type-Writer Girl, [and] it did so only to imply that part of her longed to be swept away by the right man."⁸⁰ In effect, "fiction and advertising alike turned the Type-Writer Girl into something of a fetish object."⁸¹ For these reasons, the typewriter's role within the history of women's emancipation has been overstated and should garner greater skepticism.

Wershler's account of women and the typewriter illustrates the complex and alienating relationship between the two at the material level, yet a vast majority of the labour performed by women typists was also exploitive at an immaterial level. Much of what typists transcribed during this period was information received in dictation from men in superior workplace positions. The information that women typists worked with was derived from men's voices and was not an expression of their own ideas. In other words, women's labour—in assemblage with the typewriting machine—was doubly estranged since not only was it the first step in an exploitative labour environment for women workers, but this information was employed in the service of men operating as agents of the capitalist marketplace. In the clerical space, women were relegated to a mechanical status, treated as a conduit for the transference of information within a capitalist economy. In this way, the typewriter anticipates the conditions of the computing age and its problematic conceptions of embodiment. While the typewriter became increasingly ubiquitous, anticipated our own relationship to computers today, men's voices had already become perceived as a "bodiless fluid" that could be transmitted through an assemblage of women's labouring bodies and analog writing machinery.[82] Considering this narrative of media archaeology, it becomes clear that McCaffery's typewriter-based concrete poem *Carnival* is problematic. According to Weaver, it posits male privilege as a universal experience. At the helm of the typewriter, women were unable to type themselves onto the page. But in Copithorne's decisive swerve away from the typewriter, she refused to entangle herself within its alienating mechanisms. Instead, she sought to write her body upon the page, to allow her body and its movements to take up space among a network of discursively dominating male practitioners.

In her early concrete poetry, Copithorne makes the body apparent by using graphic design tools such as sketching pencils and calligraphy pens, which require precise movements of the body that are distinct from the movements applied to typing machines. Betts notes that Copithorne's poems "bring the body back into the text by breaking the monotony and standardization of type."[83] Similarly, Bayard finds that Copithorne's concrete poetry traces "a narrative in space, and more than a transmitter of lexical meaning, each letter is carried across the page as a trace, the aesthetic and graphic energy of a specific mood, of a specific feeling."[84] Similar threads connect Bayard's and Betts's analyses of Copithorne's work: both draw attention to the importance of the body—its movements, feelings, and capacities to take up space on the page. However, I suggest that Copithorne's work is not just "breaking" the standardization of type, nor is it merely a "trace" or representation; instead, it is an embodied concrete poetic that responds to the gendered politics of writing media and literary culture in the 1960s and '70s. The typewriter requires the movement of hands and fingers to register a mark upon the page—the result of a type hammer striking typewriter tape and then page—thus, through this small form of violent impact the mechanical apparatus effaces the movements of the finger. Conventionally used, the typewriter can render only the force of the typist. A forceful application of the finger upon a key might register a bold mark on the page, or even puncture the paper. With that said, this is not possible on all typewriters. Hand-held writings tools, like those used by Copithorne, much more effectively render bodily movement, speed, and pressure upon the page, affecting the overall texture, size, and style of the piece. In this way, the body is an undeniably integral part of the hand-drawn text's composition.

Copithorne ostensibly announces her difference and the capacities of her hand-based concrete poetic in her 1969 book *Release*: "There is another Order / to things," she writes, articulating the stakes of her poetic for us.[85] The necessarily broad invocation of "things" speaks to all aspects of material life: systems, bodies, language, affects, and so on, which become reconfigured in her poetry. Though not explicitly stated, this gesture toward the possibility of a new order suggests a dissatisfaction with the current order, which I recognize as the patriarchal conditions that arranged her communities as well as the increasing effacement of bodily materiality. Furthermore, she writes that this alternative order can be figured through "the games / that children play," "a doodle," and "delight."[86] Each of these elements corresponds to Copithorne's practice: there is indeed something playful about her work; the abstract graphics of her poetry might otherwise be referred to as doodles; and "delight" invokes pleasure, which is integrally bound with bodily processes. It is precisely from the body and its processes that Copithorne's poetry emerges, seeking a new order. It is, she writes,

> produced from
> my body of bliss
>   growing
>   beyond
>   my mind[87]

Beyond the mind, in Copithorne's conception, is the body; this is where she locates her poetry and from where a new order may be attained. It is an order wherein intelligence, bodies, materials, and affects are intricately bound. Atop these words is a drawing of a winged creature, sitting on the opening words as if about to take flight, suggesting that this mode of bodily poetry offers agency and a pathway out of the "order of things" as they are.

Figure 2.6: Excerpt from *Release* by Judith Copithorne, 1969.

The first poem in this same collection, begins with the word "No," and announces Copithorne's resistance to the conditions and mainstream poetics of her time. The decipherable language of the poem, embedded within the curlicues of an abstract, hand-drawn graphic, elaborates on the opening sentiment:

> No
> I say
> I don't have to play
> games your way
> I can play any game
> I please
> and still say
> No[88]

Copithorne's "No" is a matter-of-fact assertion of independence, announcing a poetry that is premised entirely on the pursuit of her own impulses.

"Play" is a foundational concept to many of the works published under the guise of concrete poetry in Canada. Nichol and McCaffery, in "The Open Ladder Essay," articulate the stakes of "play" for poetry. While this piece was only published in 1992 (and had only been performed in full once before, in 1982), play with text and image was a driving force for many concrete poets long before they articulated the stakes. Despite the seeming innocence that accompanies the idea of play, its use in poetry is often encoded. Much of what is considered play in concrete poetry corresponds to a playfulness vis-à-vis writing machinery, as in McCaffery's two panels of *Carnival*—a title that even foregrounds playfulness by gesturing toward the carnivalesque. Less recognized is the type of play that Copithorne's concrete poetry explores. She plays with her hands—following not the program of a typing machine, but her desire for movement as her hands, clasping a pen or marker, pull across the page to create what might otherwise be read as doodles. Instead, these marks are the body's imprints on the page as it interacts with writing materials. In doing so, Copithorne refuses to "play by the rules," resisting what was becoming, at the time, an aesthetic norm of machine-driven concrete poetics.

(Moving) Images: Film, Television, Photography

While Copithorne's concrete poetry explores the sensuality of the body, the lesser-known Armenian-Canadian poet Shaunt Basmajian (born in Lebanon) explores feeling and desire in conventional, heteronormative relationships.[89] These instances of desire in Basmajian's poetry are noteworthy for the way they take their cues from popular culture, with Nichol identifying rock 'n' roll as a major influence on Basmajian, whose work he says conveys an "infatuation which is so often taken as love, emoted as such in the rock & roll radio wave world we live in."[90] Nichol's point reminds us that he was thinking carefully about the meaning of love and the way the word circulates within popular culture, and Basmajian's exploration of the word here extends some of Berger's concerns around consumerism, advertising, and entertainment, as outlined in a previous section of this chapter. The influence of rock 'n' roll is apparent in Basmajian's concrete sequence "Personal Traumas," from his 1980 chapbook of *Boundaries Limits and Space*, which includes many poems that recall the playful minimalist poetic of Aram Saroyan. The words of "Personal Traumas" move across the five horizontal lines of a musical staff. The words themselves pay homage to rock 'n' roll and the well-worn lyrics about unrequited love typical of the genre.

"Personal Traumas" consists of only six pronouns—"me," "him," "her," "she," "they," "them"—and the adjective "alone," variously arranged across the staff, blurring the boundaries between musical and poetic media. In their own way, each word is a note in the poem, generating visual rhythms. The poem captures the speaker's romantic fixation with a woman who is in a relationship with another man, and the speaker's repeated disappointment with his inability to get close to her (hence the melodramatic reference to "trauma" in the title). The poem, which is composed across six pages, places these words in such a way as to describe the speaker's varying successes (or failures) in approaching the woman, who is sometimes quite close and other times blocked by another suitor. The poem ends with a penultimate "Breakdown" that uses overlaid text that communicates the speaker's anguish—as though the word "me" were falling or collapsing into itself—and then ends with the single word "alone." While Basmajian's poem is distinct from other concrete poems mentioned in this chapter, such as Nichol's "Blues," UU's "Touch," or poems from Copithorne's *Release*, since it lacks the kind of radical social and political thought that informs these works, "Personal Traumas" highlights

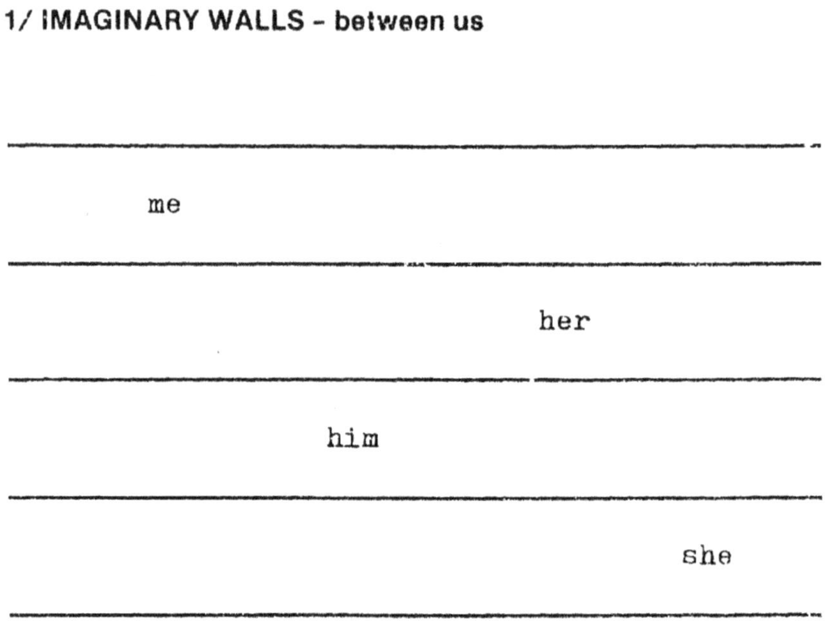

1/ IMAGINARY WALLS – between us

──────────────────────────────────────
      me
──────────────────────────────────────
                                     her
──────────────────────────────────────
                him
──────────────────────────────────────
                                       she
──────────────────────────────────────

Figure 2.7: Excerpt from Shaunt Basmajian's "Personal Traumas," 1980.

the way modes of expression move across disciplines, informing each other in terms of both meaning and form. In this way, Basmajian enthusiastically transposes the schmaltzy musical expressions and lyrical archetypes that define the mid- to late twentieth century into a series of minimalist concrete poems that tell the same classic tale conveyed in many rock songs.

Basmajian's minimalist engagements with music and popular culture are in stark contrast to bissett's *Stardust* (1975), a maximalist book of concrete poetry that takes up the complexity and problems of complicity experienced by a person living in a media-saturated environment. *Stardust* indulges bissett's deep affinity for Hollywood, which he describes as a "dreem/nightmare uv a poor man in a / countree that has not its own / freedom independence intact / nd is mostly a capitalist countree." bissett states at length that

> yu maybe cudint get a buk like ths
> stardust writtn at all but   in ths
> kind uv oligarghy ths ar th gods
> nd goddesses nd also th vessuls uv our
> own ideaz nd in any kind uv society
> tho prhaps diffrently paid nd glamorizd yu
> have to have th prforming arts from street
> theatre to opera whatevr so ths buk it
> self is not a capitalist xpressyun
> so forget that if yu ar thinking it
> coz thats not wher its at ok[91]

bissett's poetic preface to *Stardust* makes clear his awareness of film's relationship to capitalism, inequity, and consumerism, especially in the way it represents false configurations of reality. bissett, too, is likely critical of Hollywood cinema as a container for the export of US ideology, promoting capitalism and consumerism as desirable ways of living. In this way, Friedrich Kittler's writings on film in *Gramphone, Film, Typewriter* (1999) offer a useful reference point for understanding bissett's complicated relationship to film. As Kittler points out, "films are more real than reality and . . . their so-called reproductions are, in reality, productions."[92] As such, they effectively undermine assumptions that film is a documentation of life. Films are, he writes, "scans, excerpts, selections."[93] In other words, films are momentary interventions into, and selections of, the stuff of real life, reconfigured mainly for popular consumption. As such, the power of film as a medium is in the hands and minds of those who cut and splice the stuff of life. This point may underscore why bissett, in the very first issue of *blewointment*, felt compelled to advance an open letter responding to Forest's *In Search of Innocence*, with its partial representation of Vancouver's arts scene. While bissett does not accuse them of misrepresenting their subject, he does suggest that their film does not wholly represent the community he saw coming into existence at the time. The consequences of this deficit, bissett seems to recognize, will be a misperception of the reality of the 1960s Vancouver arts scene among future generations.

Poems from *Stardust* directly intervene in the entanglement of film, capital, and consumerism, with their collagist elements (mainly pictures of bissett and celebrities), shaped lyric poems, hand-drawn images, and dirty typewriter concrete poems. The book is both a celebration of Hollywood, celebrity, and film, and an investigation of film's impact on the shape and perception of everyday human life, hence bissett's framing of the book as both a dream *and* a nightmare. Following the title page, *Stardust* opens with a collage combining a photograph of twentieth-century media darlings Fred Astaire and Jane Powell in *Royal Wedding* (1951) placed overtop a repeated pattern of the letter *x*. Gaps in the pattern leave room for white spaces, like stars against a night sky, falling upon the kinetic grace of Astaire and Powell as a celebration of their musical prowess and celebrity status. On the following page, there is a similarly designed collage depicting a scene from another film: *Kim* (1950), based on Rudyard Kipling's novel of the same name and starring Errol Flynn and Dean Stockwell. In the image, Stockwell (playing Kim) is taken into custody by the police to escape a group of persons following him. Unlike the collage with Astaire and Powell, however, the pattern above the photograph is more solid, with the addition of a somewhat ominous, tentacular-looking type drawing over top. While both images share a context—the so-called golden era of Hollywood cinema, when audiences were promised spectacular visuals and storytelling—and both represent Metro-Goldwyn-Mayer productions—they are nonetheless in stark contrast with one another. One depicts the agency and grace of Astaire and Powell as onlookers watch with pleasure; the other presents a boy in captivity, glared at by a group of stern-looking men. In comparison, these images capture both the dream-like and the nightmarish sides of Hollywood film, seen here as a source of entertainment but also of containment.

Figure 2.8: Untitled (Astaire/Powell) from bill bissett's *Stardust*, 1975.

bissett moves beyond this initial binary in the shaped poem "THE TUBE IS GASEOUS," which considers film, much like Kittler, as a medium for displaying and obfuscating the conditions of human life. In this poem, the speaker reflects upon *Royal Wedding* and asks, "will we all ever compleetly know / what m g m was   and has done / to ourselves or the royal family," a question that reveals a desire to know how media and corporations, like Metro-Goldwyn-Mayer, impact the conditions of human life. bissett suggests that the impact is the warping of reality:

> jane powell did not shite or   piss
>   i remember that clearly   how cud shee
>   nor did the
>   royal family[94]

Anticipating Kittler's theory of film as a medium that fractures and splices the actual events of real life, bissett identifies how film veils basic human functions and instead treats actors as "heaven / incarnate."[95] For bissett, there is a classist dimension to such portrayals:

> m g m may not
>   have been in the nashun
>   sintrest th board
> a governors so plottud n conivd against us poor
>   white
>
>   quakers[96]

In this way, bissett draws attention to how Hollywood films cultivate a cult of celebrity, a tiered vision of human life that places some people in more privileged places than others.

First published by bissett's Blew Ointment Press, McCaffery's *Panopticon* (1984) is also thematically concerned with film while, perhaps, expanding the definition of the concrete poem to engage the problems of film as a visual medium that includes visual, sonic, and gestural domains. *Panopticon* is not a concrete poem like those examined above. It is, rather, a book-length work that at first glance looks more like prose than poetry. However, *Panopticon* engages optically centred media and displays the same material consciousness that other concrete poets have advanced in their work. McCaffery engages the

Figure 2.9: Untitled (*Kim*) from bill bissett's *Stardust*, 1975.

realm of narrative but with poetic intent. *Panopticon*'s narrative, if one can call it that, is ruptured in terms of both content and form by the integration of many concretist elements. As such, the book closely corresponds to concrete poetry as a materially conscious form: unconventional typography and layout; collagist techniques with images, grids, and false errata; and, perhaps most strikingly, a section containing the image of a static band that differentiates the white page space from a strip of pixelated grey, which reviewer Sam Rowe suggests is "meant to represent a filmic image."[97]

Hailed by poet Charles Bernstein as the "exemplary antiabsorptive work," *Panopticon* engages film as a visual, narrative-driven medium by returning to and remediating the same scene: a woman emerging from a bathtub, reaching for a novel, as she prepares to see a film.[98] This scene is reconfigured in *Panopticon* across three sections, beginning with part 3, "The Mind of Pauline Brain," followed by part 2, "Summer Alibi," and ending with part 1, "The Mark"—a sequence that resists linear convention. As Rowe explains, "the woman both appears in and watches a film variously titled *Summer Alibi, Panopticon, The Mark, Toallitas* and *The Mind of Pauline Brain*, a film which at certain points inexplicably changes into a novel, in fact, the very novel that the woman reaches for in her bookshelf after stepping out of the bath."[99] *Panopticon* shifts between media quickly by invoking the typewriter, photograph, novel, play, film, and more. As an extremely fragmented work, it engages the optic realms of media with an eye to how they present disparate sequences of events with coherence, a point that Kittler, as noted above, describes as fantasy. In its fractured form, *Panopticon* reminds us that media presentation is part fantasy as it problematizes conventions of narrative and visual media as representations of life.

With its repeated ruptures, returns, and remediations, McCaffery's book also engages problems of control. The title invokes Jeremy Bentham's notion of the "panopticon," a prison model predicated on omnipotent surveillance as a means of control. *Panopticon* engages this intensity of seeing by way of exhaustive, meta-conscious descriptions wherein the reader is at times placed in a position closer to that of author or filmmaker:

> Let the image of the bath persist and split a second time. Place the woman in the room and in the theatre. This time allow the man to walk away. Follow him until you reach the study door. Don't bother to describe the room, just put him in it. Let him

meet another man. Don't mention names. Allow them to leave the room and walk down into the street where a planned complication will occur. Finish the chapter. Switch off the machine.[100]

As Bernstein claims, the "mark" is "the visible sign of writing," and he further claims that "to make a movie of the 'mark,'" as *Panopticon* does, "is to theatricalize it."[101] McCaffery foregrounds the fact that reading often makes the material signifier of the mark invisible: "A TEXTUAL SYSTEM UNDERLIES EVERY TEXTUAL EVENT THAT CONSTITUTES 'THIS STORY.' HOWEVER THE TEXTUAL HERMENEUSIS OF 'THIS STORY' DOES NOT NECESSARILY COMPRISE A TOTAL TEXTUAL READING."[102] The "total textual reading" is further obscured by film as a medium (with the exception of early silent films, which employed text to convey dialogue and even sound). Without subtitles, later twentieth-century films make language transparent as a medium—it initiates and drives the actions of any film, which often begins as a written text; however, in the end, the written word is erased, replaced by moving image and audio. While engaged by film, we can hear the word, but we cannot see it. *Panopticon* reverses the filmic privileging of images and sound over letterform, forcing us to turn our gaze away from the spectacle of media and back toward language and its necessary interaction in McCaffery's media-saturated world.

In *The Bee Book* (1981), Ann Rosenberg fuses the montage techniques of moving images—as used in film and television—to create a nearly two-hundred-page intermedial novel that fully embraces the materially conscious spirit of borderblur. Like McCaffery's *Panopticon*, Rosenberg's *The Bee Book*, which Nichol shepherded through production while at Coach House, extends the definition of the concrete poem. Is it a novel? A poem? A collage? A play? *The Bee Book* blends all of these genres to create a meditation on a woman's desire and sexuality that relies on the interaction of visual and linguistic media. The novel's nine sections each take the form of narrative prose fragmented by elements of concrete poetry (which are integral to the story), including hand-drawn images, photographs, diagrams, musical scores, asemic writings, and typographic arrangements of text that resemble waves, lips, and genitalia. Over a series of connected vignettes, *The Bee Book* follows Habella, a bee enthusiast and natural science teacher, as she navigates the complexities of sexuality as a young woman nurtured by Catholic principles and traditions. Rosenberg uses the lives and language of bees, with a particular emphasis on their mating patterns and internal hierarchies, as a counterpoint to Habella's understanding of human relationships. In part, the book follows Habella through relationships with two men as she tries to understand what she needs and wants—emotionally, physically, and intellectually—in partnership. *The Bee Book* traces Habella's shift from her belief in patriarchy and her desire for marriage toward self-reliance and an embrace of matriarchy. In this way, the book is located at a critical juncture of interest for the concrete poets: that of visuality and the limits of individual expression through multiple media (which might also explain why Nichol appears to have been a steward of the book).

The text employs image in a variety of ways; however, text and image are used most strikingly in places where conventional language does not fully capture feelings and ideas. Like other concretists of her time, Rosenberg uses visuality where consciously apprehended language fails. For example, in chapter 3, "The Drone," Habella courts a man who claims he is an Egyptologist named Solomon. She is quickly infatuated with him and loses her virginity, a decision she later regrets. Their brief courtship is described in prose fragmented by the interjection of images. As they flirt, they draw hieroglyphics and diagrams of bee dances to impress one another with their knowledge, and these are presented as physical imagery in the book.[103] They also dance together to suggestive music, which is described in the typographic arrangement of the morphemes "UUHHHHH," "MMMAHHHH," and "oooooooo."[104] When they finally have sex, Rosenberg conveys this encounter with a typewritten concrete piece consisting of the letters *n*, *m*, and *o* in repetition, and a letter-based depiction of a penis and vagina.[105] This final depiction is augmented by the language used to create these images: "I want to," say both Solomon and Habella, which leads Solomon to reply insensitively, "why why do you cry habella oh what damn it is the matter with you."[106] Later in the book, when in conversation with her close friend Matthias, she expresses of regret: "Damn it, damn it. I I'm so ashamed. I I gave up my virginity to someone I I'll p probably never see again. I I j just lost my head."[107] On the one hand, this expression is enough to convey Habella's feelings in the moment of her encounter with Solomon—she is overwhelmed, impassioned, infatuated. However, the fragmentation of the narrative through the incorporation of concretist image effectively depicts Habella's feelings. These feelings are heightened and passed on to the reader, who, in a similar way, might feel disoriented by the mixture of text and image, which simultaneously breaks the logical flow of conventional narrative.

Eventually, Habella marries a man named Fred, with whom she raises several children. Over time, though, Habella grows unhappy in her marriage. She is bored of Fred and seemingly unhappy with her children. She begins to seek a way out of the reality she has found herself in, which is largely the result of her fulfilled desire to be married: "why can't I *create* my own dream and *choose* the people who live it with me? Why can't I become *in charge* of my reality?"[108] From this utterance, the story dramatically shifts toward the surreal. Habella proceeds upstairs and begins rearranging the furniture so as to build a "hexagon in her room with one side open," where she feeds "herself on Royal Jelly."[109] In so doing, Habella has transformed herself into a queen bee, thereby fully emulating the species she has admired so deeply all her life. Near the end of the novel, Habella's son Harry seems to voice Habella's esteem for bees when he "announced for some reason with ten-year-old earnestness that he would build a colony where workers shared equally in labour and where there would be no sexual rivalry."[110] *The Bee Book* ends with Habella leaving her hexagon, transformed into a queen bee. Once the narrative confirms Habella's flight, the text ends not with language but with photographs of an open sky, indicative of Habella's newfound freedom.

By framing it as being in dialogue with the visual culture of mass media—especially film and television—we might locate *The Bee Book* in the context of important discussions regarding the representations of women in media. While Copithorne's hand-drawn poems can be understood as a response to the various patriarchal structures embedded in arts and literary communities, and reinforced by the typewriter's gendered history, Rosenberg's text does similar work in relation to narrative and television. While the novel is not preoccupied with television as a medium, its narrative structure is disrupted (or expanded) by its montage-like qualities. In *Panopticon*, McCaffery, too, finds stimulus in the ruptures of narrative brought about by electronic media, which is routinely signalled by *Panopticon*'s return to a voyeur-like moment that focuses on a woman emerging from the bath. *The Bee Book* makes for an interesting companion to McCaffery's book, presenting a more robust characterization of women and desire. Furthermore, not only is *The Bee Book* driven by a conventional narrative about self-discovery, but nearly every page integrates a new visual element—drawings, diagrams, charts, photographs, musical score, and other images. It reconfigures media, like television, so as to disrupt and expand upon the production of meaning. In *The Bee Book*, Rosenberg shifts her focus away from the woman as a subject of the male gaze; instead, she follows Habella's development in dialogue with a culture that objectifies women's bodies and desires, a problem that continues to haunt advertising in the twenty-first century. Rosenberg claims the strategy of the fractured narrative to better represent the experience of Habella's coming of age, reclaiming media's collagist strategies to better represent the complexities of a Habella's life.

While Rosenberg, McCaffery, and bissett produced works connected to moving images, Roy Kiyooka's *Stoned Gloves* (1970) focuses on the still image—the photograph. As George Bowering recounts, "Kiyooka had gone to Osaka to install his brightly coloured sails at the Canadian pavilion at Expo '70. While there, he photographed gloves discarded by workers at the site. The photographs and some of his words, rendered large, made a travelling exhibition in Canadian galleries, and were translated into a book by Coach House Press."[111] In a work that is equal parts poetry and art book, Kiyooka fuses black-and-white photographs with text (overlaid or accompanying) and "traces the history of race labour in the foundations of the Canadian nation-state, and attempts to redress state policies of racial exclusion and discrimination in Canada's national narrative."[112] Kiyooka's photographed found gloves synecdochically represent the erasure of immigrant labour in crucial nation-unifying projects such as the building of the transcontinental railway, just as the gloves discarded around the site of the 1970 Expo represented the local workers who assisted in building the Canadian pavilion.

Blurring the borders of art and life, Kiyooka utilizes the photograph as a mechanism for witnessing these unacknowledged bodies of workers: "the way they fell / the way they lay there / the dust sifting down / hiding all the clues."[113] The photographs are the only evidence of these labouring bodies before the dust of history settles upon them, perfectly occluding their narrative lines. Instead, in this sequence of photos, Kiyooka announces their presence and, in a simple equation, speaks to the interconnectedness of body, earth, and nation:

> glove
> equals
> leaf
> equals

    stone
    equals
    wood
    equals
    bone[114]

This equation is particularly striking since it was during this period that poets and critics like Atwood were investigating such natural images as foundational aspects of settler life in Canada, where an earlier generation of newcomers had struggled against the natural environment. The photographs in *Stoned Gloves* effectively gesture toward the various internationalizing movements of ideas and, especially in this case, bodies across borders that are foundational to the formation of Canada as a nation thus undermining claims to a national identity by critiquing how this singular mindset risks effacing racialized bodies and labour.

    Kiyooka draws attention to the frame of an artwork in *Stoned Gloves*'s exploration of absence, presence, race, and identity. The text could be profitably compared to the work of poet and craftsman Brian Dedora, who has at times similarly explored the way aperture obscures and reveals a subject. The most obvious comparison here would be Dedora's 1988 chapbook *The Compact Edition of HUGE* (published by UU's Silver Birch Press), which brings together poetic text and photographs of the "HUGE" brand of notebooks. Dedora's privately published 1978 poem *CRACK*, however, captures my attention for the way its form is more sharply distinguished from *The Compact Edition of HUGE*. In *CRACK*, Dedora's skills as a photographer and framer are apparent. The poem is comprised of a single piece of black, 8.5-by-11-inch cardstock containing a small aperture that reveals a thin white line and a few letters, like an opening on or within the page. The effect of such a presentation emphasizes the role of the reader as viewer. When looking at this poem one may feel as though one is peering through a door left ajar or a crack in a wall. Composed of only a few letters, the poem is void of semantic content; it is impossible to know what words are seemingly concealed by the matte black of the page. In its own way, like many poems addressed in this chapter, *CRACK* unsettles the conventions of the traditional page-based poem. Typically, readers expect the high contrast of a white page covered in black text to ensure legibility. Yet here, Dedora has overwhelmed the page with a stark blackness to obscure legibility.

Beyond these reversals, it is difficult not to read Dedora's *CRACK* within the historical context in which it was written, specifically the oppression of Toronto's gay community in the 1970s and '80s. In "I Have a Remember When," Dedora remembers his experiences during this tumultuous period, which are "entirely unknown with the corollary apprehension of what else is unknown, forgotten, or lost."[115] He highlights, for example, the various forms of violence and surveillance that Toronto's gay community faced at the hands of the Metropolitan Toronto Police. "Vice arrests" at bars such as Toronto's Parkside Tavern "were made easier through collusion with the owners of the Parkside, who allowed police surveillance in the downstairs washrooms."[116] Officers would entrap gay patrons by constructing a surveillance hole in the bathroom that allowed them to peer from the other side and look, say, for any signs of cruising, and anyone found participating in such activity would surely face "grievous consequences."[117]

Dedora's *CRACK* recalls the same kind of optics employed by police. The reader is a viewer peering through a crack in the wall, surveilling the language on the other side, hoping to seize upon its meaning. Likewise, surveilling officers peer through the wall, intending to seize gay patrons. There is distinct violence that unites each instance; both language and subject are meant to be forced into systems that make them known and knowable. Yet *CRACK* resists legibility and closure; it thwarts our attempt to reduce it to a singular meaning. The language remains open to possibilities more significant than semantics. In this way, and through this analogy, Dedora's *CRACK* reminds us, too, that the queer subjects behind those tavern walls—whose identities may not be legible to an ignorant public and police force—are people who can be recognized in ways that are far less reductive and complex than sexual identity. Taking a step back and recalling Dedora's interest in photography as a visual mode, *CRACK* reminds us that in the era of the ubiquitous image, the visibility images may offer can also be willfully misread and used to manipulate people toward unjust ends.

Though lacking the resonant images of surveillance and police oppression evoked in Dedora's *CRACK*, this chapter offers a minuscule aperture through which to view the vast matrix of Canadian concrete poetry produced under the aegis of borderblur. Another way of reading Dedora's *CRACK* is to read it as a metaphor for the creative openings that intermedia offered this generation of poets, including a wider array of strategies for expression. All these poets, in one way or another, demonstrate how their expansive, intermedial

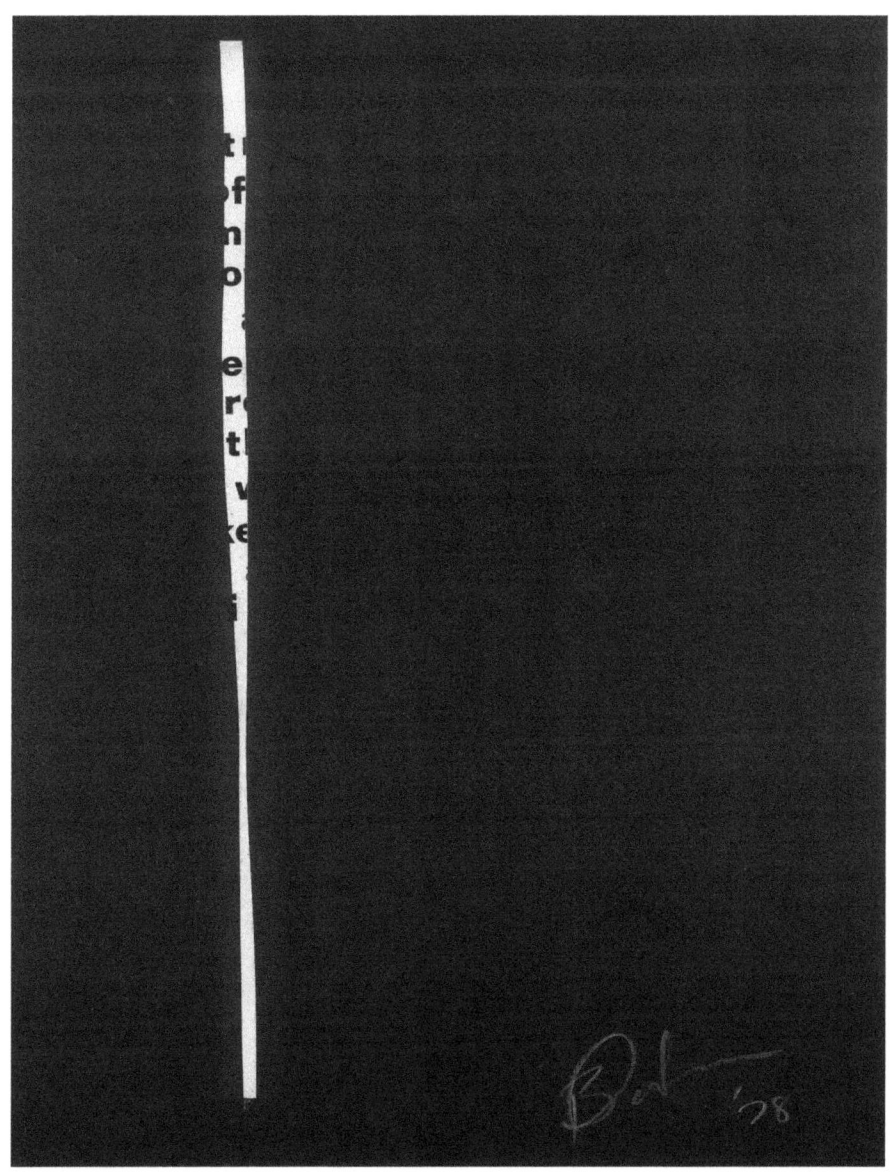

Figure 2.10: *CRACK* by Brian Dedora, 1978.

poetics challenge literary tradition through their inimitable fusion of poetic language with optically centred modes. As detailed above, their concerns far exceed the project of cultivating a national literary identity; rather, they were often wrestling with the implications of what it meant to create in a world in which, for better or worse, images were making their presence ever more forcefully felt.

3

Sound Poetry

AAAAAAAHHHH

—The Four Horsemen (1982)

ahh, ahhh ahhhh

—Penn Kemp (1987)

On the occasion of the 1970 spring equinox, people assembled at Nathan Phillips Square in downtown Toronto at exactly noon for a one-minute event called the Scream-In. Anticipating a turnout of a thousand attendees, poet, Ryerson Institute of Technology psychology teacher, and event organizer George Swede obtained a permit for the gathering, but, according to the *Globe and Mail*, only a relatively small group of seventy-five people turned up. Photographs published by the *Globe* and the Toronto Italian-language newspaper *Corriere Canadese* suggest that there was perhaps closer to the one hundred and fifty attendees. But regardless of the numbers, for that whole single minute—from exactly 12:00 to 12:01 p.m.—participants loosed a roaring cacophony to achieve what they hoped would be the "World's Loudest Sound Poem." As the minute concluded, their collective scream "withered to a sigh."[1]

While overlooked as a noteworthy moment in Canada's literary history, the Scream-In neatly exemplifies Canadian sound poetry's estrangement from the dominant literary culture of the day. Swede planned first to herald the arrival of spring, and second, to encourage participants to gather "to seek the elusive identity" of Canada.[2] "If a person can't get to the square to scream for the Canadian identity," continues Swede, "he should stop where he is at that time and scream for it on his own."[3] Swede's latter stated intention flirts with the rhetoric of cultural nationalism, but he explained that "screaming establishes contact with the subconscious mind, that well-spring of all activity,"[4] thus situating the Scream-In as a moment connecting participants with the immediacy of their place and company through expressivist action. The actual minute-long scream suggests that a nation's identity is not produced through literary themes or images; rather, it stems from an ongoing commitment to voice, action, connection, and process. Swede, then, seemed to be parodying Canada's urgency to define itself, and by extension its literature, since this act of collective screaming—void of semantic content—emphasizes the futility of those efforts. If taken with the dose of irony that would seem to be implied by Swede's statements on the event, the Scream-In refuses the Canadian literary discourse of the CanLit Boom and its overstated authority over the formation of national literary identity.

Swede is among the lesser-known figures of Canadian avant-garde literary history, though his Scream-In certainly enriches the story of Canada's literature. I start this chapter with the 1970 Scream-In since it underscores many of the topics of interest here—namely, sound, poetry, networks of affiliation, and literary paratraditions—and because 1970, and the collective screaming of at least seventy-five people, inadvertently marks the momentous arrival of a sonic wave in Canadian poetry. This year is also remarkable as it saw the formation of an undeniably influential Canadian sound poetry collective: the Four Horsemen (comprised of bpNichol, Steve McCaffery, Paul Dutton, and Rafael Barreto-Rivera), who, Joe Rosenblatt has written, dug their "electromagnetic spurs into the flesh of our complacency, inspiring the tribe."[5] Indeed, they joined the forces of their vocal talents to forge connections to an international network of poets while stoking the imaginations of like-minded poets and performers in Canada and abroad. Their work inspired companion ensembles who explored similar poetic terrain, including Owen Sound (Michael Dean, David Penhale, Steven Ross Smith, and Richard Truhlar), Re: Sounding (Stephen Scobie and Douglas Barbour), and First

Draft (Susan McMaster, Colin Morton, Andrew McClure, and others), while working alongside kindred solo performers such as bill bissett (who also performed with bands such as the Mandan Massacre), Penn Kemp, and others. With sound poetry, the network of affiliated Canadian poets expanded just as the intermedial dimension of borderblur extended into sonic realms.

Sound poetry in Canada grew out of and in tandem with the development of concrete poetry, both as a widening of the form (concrete poems were often performed as sound poems) and as a separate mode in itself. Marshall McLuhan's comparison of the written and spoken word elucidate this turn toward the utterance in dynamic performance and helps explain sound poetry's prominence as one face of borderblur poetics: "The written word spells out in sequence what is quick and implicit in the spoken word."[6] If Canadian concrete poetry is an intermedial form in dialogue with visual media, then oral transmission, according to McLuhan's claim, can be understood as a more immediate and flexible means of pursuing similar goals. Sound poetry is inherently intermedial, prompting us to reconsider the borders between poetry, music, sound art, and performance. For some sound poets examined in this chapter, the body is the locus of poesis. Sound poetry typically explores a range of linguistic (words, phrases, etc.) and extralinguistic soundings (breathing, laughter, howling, grunting, body slaps, etc.) that are projected from the inner and outer surfaces of the poet's body. In this way, acoustic sound poetry (in comparison to electroacoustic sound poetry) is often a practice of immediacy and intimacy, happening in real time and in performative contexts, like the choreographed howling of the Scream-In. For other sound poets, however, electroacoustic devices—microphones, recording equipment, etc.—posed opportunities to de-familiarize and expand the possibilities of vocalization in poetry. Both acoustic and electroacoustic sound poetry are representative of intermediality for the way they often bring together aural, visual, linguistic, and gestural modes of artistic expression, including singing, acapella, chant, prayer, drama, vaudeville, and other kinds of performances. When compared to the concrete poetry of the previous chapter, which was shaped by the increasing interaction between linguistic and visual modes, borderblur's specific Canadian formation of sound poetry is informed by the mutating conditions for sound and sound technologies during the same moment.

On this last point, I look again to the diagnoses offered by Michael Hardt and Antonio Negri, who recognize the international arrival of *postmodernization* and *informatization*[7] in capitalist modes of production in the mid- to late twentieth century. As described by Hardt and Negri, this shift signals a transition away from industrial modes of labour toward "service jobs (the tertiary), a shift that has taken place in the United States, since the early 1970s," including in the sectors of health care, education, finance, advertising, and entertainment,[8] occurring in "the United Kingdom, and Canada" around the same time.[9] These very topics thematically occupied much of the poetry examined in the previous chapter. Among the many implications of this shift, the role of affect in social and material contexts takes on a new life in these later-stage capitalist countries. The arrival of *affective labour* announces a mode of work "characterized in general by the central role played by knowledge, information, affect, and communication,"[10] and "marks a new mode of becoming human."[11] Here, we might catch an echo of Nichol's claim that in the 1960s a "new humanism" was afoot.[12] Nichol, living amid these conditions, could sense these changes. While Nichol limits his assessment to a vague but compelling wording, Hardt and Negri explicitly recognize that affect comes to bear on the postmodernizing economy in unprecedented ways, especially a postmodernizing economy that is reliant upon the homogenization and standardization of feeling and expression. Consider, for example, the last chapter's discussion of advertising and how it relies on the manipulation of desire. In a context in which affective labour is becoming a dominant mode of production, the body's processes, expressions, and feelings are rapidly standardized to serve commercial and capitalist interests as they gain increasing control over the affective aspects of life, especially in Western countries.

The transnational conditions of affective labour, as Hardt and Negri describe them, are the conditions and premises that, directly and indirectly, shaped the work of sound poetry practitioners in Canada at this time. Swede's 1970 Scream-In exemplifies this: it was motivated by an attachment between participants secured through expression while parodying Canadian literary discourse. If affect is "an impingement or extrusion of a momentary or sometimes more sustained state of relation," and "is found in those intensities that pass body to body (human, nonhuman, part-body, and otherwise),"[13] then Swede's Scream-In is undeniably an affective poem that articulates body-to-body relations through sonic expression. As such, Swede's gathering reclaims affect from nationalist and commercial contexts by binding people together outside of those frameworks. It eschews the efforts of Canadian writers and publishers to bolster a literary economy of printed books that contributed to Canada's rapidly developing national literary identity. I understand these underlying aspects of the Scream-In to be indicative of a major factor that shapes and motivates Canadian borderblur sound poetry during this period. This chapter examines how the conditions of postmodernization—and specifically the emergent role of affect within it—informed sound poetry as it circulated within Canadian borderblur's network of affiliation.

Questioning the Cadence: Sound, Nation, Affect

Sound is deeply entangled with the dominant Canadian literary discourse, and specifically the idea of what it means to create Canadian literature. It informed the work of Dennis Lee, Canadian lyric poet and co-founder of House of Anansi in 1967—the year of Canada's centennial. Lee struggled to triangulate a relationship between sound, poetry, and national identity. In "Cadence, Country, Silence: Writing in Colonial Space" (delivered first as a talk in Montreal in 1972), he explains that the immediacy of aurality is essential for developing a national literary identity. Lee describes a period of writer's block, or what he calls "silence," that he began to endure in 1967. He struggled with the absence of a distinctly Canadian language under the pressures of American and English colonial influences. Lee's language, he felt, was not his own. This resulted in a period of authorial silence during which he was unable to authentically write with an earnest sense of himself. Lee found a solution in listening to what he describes as *cadence*: "the medium, the raw stone. Content is already there in the cadence. And writing a poem means cutting away everything in the cadence that isn't that poem," until the "poem is what remains; it is local cadence minus whatever is extraneous to its shapely articulation."[14] Lee's solution, to listen to the cadence of the local—or "what is already there"—was his way of overcoming the debilitating problem of external, imperialistic pressures to build an authentic national literary identity.

While Lee's privileging of the nation was a position that many Canadian writers shared, an interest in the relationship between listening, nationalism, and international influence is far more complex than Lee suggests. On the one hand, if we take his notion of listening literally, we must remember that the geographies and cultures that comprise Canada have many of what R. Murray Schafer refers to as *soundscapes*. The sounds of the harbours on the East Coast are perhaps out of tune with the sounds of the fields of the Prairies since the sounds in each of these locales appreciably differ. And of course, one can sense significant differences without travelling great distances: the urban soundscape of Kensington Market, in downtown Toronto, conspicuously contrasts with the soundscape of the farm fields of the Niagara region. I confess that I may be taking Lee's notion of listening too literally; however, certain questions arise: What sounds actually comprise the cadence that Lee is listening to? What and who does he not hear or ignore? Does Lee listen for the Indigenous peoples who sounded on this land long before him? Since so much of Canada's population is made of first- and second-generation immigrant families, what exactly is distinctly "Canadian" in these soundings anyway? As Benedict Anderson, Arjun Appadurai, and others remind us, nationalism is an imagined project, not something innate to the land. Some would make a case that the sound of Canada is a multicultural soundscape, but that is not what Lee here conceives. Instead, he makes a case for a mythological cadence that emanates from Canada without considering that what makes up his idea of Canada is necessarily cultivated and contrived. Despite Lee's romantic portrayal of the cadences of Canadian life, Canada at that time, like other Western countries, was undergoing significant shifts in its sonic composition, and these changes complicate any suggestion that a geographical space has a particular cadence. Rapid changes in social and material conditions, and the emergence of a world wherein borders are believed to be, as bissett says, "dropping off,"[15] brought with them the sounds of other spaces and times, and these were conveyed by new technological means.

By declaring the arrival of a new phase of capitalism in Western countries based on the manipulation of affect in the mid- to late twentieth century, Hardt and Negri draw attention to the changing role of feeling and expression for persons living in post-industrial countries such as the United States, the United Kingdom, and Canada. The conditions of this economic model are felt in all aspects of life, according to these authors, and affect plays a more significant role in that it modulates human behaviour on a molecular scale. They do not define affect in terms of emotion,[16] nor the swerve of sensation;[17] however, their argument suggests that communication—and I would suggest the communication of emotion—is changing within this paradigm. Within an economy characterized by affective labour, the body's processes, expressions, and feelings are forcibly standardized and calibrated to serve this postmodernizing economy. Myrna Kostash confirms that the shift toward a new capitalist modality, characterized by affective labour, was felt by Canadians before the 1970s:

As the percentage of the Gross National Product (GNP) represented by government revenue grew greater and greater, so did the percentage of the labour force employed by the state: 12.6 percent in 1956, 16.3 percent in 1962 and 19.1 percent in 1966. Besides the professionals, these workers were the clerical staff and the service and support staffs. By 1964 the Canadian Union of Public Employees would be the second largest union in Canada after the United Steelworkers of America.[18]

With clear statistics and data, Kostash corroborates and expands Hardt and Negri's claim, highlighting the shift toward an affective economy in Canada as early as the 1960s.

Hardt and Negri's conception of affective labour emphasizes the standardization of communication for the efficient purpose of mobilizing thought and feeling in the service of commercial capitalism—sales, entertainment, moving information, communication, etc. The conditions of affective labour play a significant role, then, not just in an individual's life but also on the scale of "social networks, forms of community,"[19] since communities are formed through processes of affective bonding. Swede's 1970 Scream-In at Nathan Phillips Square suggests that Canadian borderblur's strain of sound poetry emerged in dialogue with the rise of affective labour. In Swede's conception of the event, the collective scream was motivated by a desire to develop an attachment to nearby participants through sound, voice, and action. Though the sound poetry event writ large is a niche cultural form, one that may seem somewhat sheltered from the social and material shifts outlined above, I contend that these conditions acted upon it, at times directly forming the field within which sound poets worked, while at other times forming the background against which we can understand their work. If affect is a state of relation, then the efforts that I explore in this chapter—including the work of sound poets; the network formulated by their local, national, and international performances; and their independently produced and circulated recordings—all suggest that these social and material shifts permeated their work. I suggest, then, that Canadian sound poetry, under the auspices of borderblur, is an affective poetic form that exceeds print via the intermedial interaction of sound, language, and gesture, which is in turn shaped by the conditions of an emergent affective economy.

A Network of Sonic Affiliations

Highlighting a core tenet that shapes avant-garde literary paratraditions, Charles Bernstein refers to the work of provisional institutions such as small presses, little magazines, and artist-run reading series as a form of "social work."[20] In that work, there is an inherent affective dimension in that it facilitates tight networks of affiliation between poet and publisher, poet and audience, and poet and poet—one that is arguably tighter than those created through larger and more diffuse mainstream publishers. For the concrete poetry of the previous chapter, the poets' abilities to print their work in their own magazines, books, and pamphlets enabled them to contribute to the creation of a transnational network while facilitating connections to avant-garde communities in other parts of the world. They mailed their work to and corresponded with other artists, traded it during face-to-face encounters, exhibited together, and wrote to one another about each other's work. In this way, provisional print operations were also necessary for creating the paratradition of intermedial works that were largely excluded from Canada's literary mainstream. The sound poetry analyzed in this chapter offers a compelling case study for considering affective labour and the formation of literary traditions since it is such an ephemeral form. Even when circulated in recorded formats through provisional publishing operations, it resists the established model of Canadian literary culture that emerged during the CanLit Boom. By attending to the social and material conditions of sound poetry, we see how the paratradition is formed but also how these poets championed an alternative vision of what literary production, circulation, and reception might look like.

According to Steve McCaffery, writing in the late 1970s, sound poetry, as an international form of literary expression, advanced in three distinctive phases. The first stretches back to a period of what he refers to as "archaic and primitive poetries," including chant, song, and incantations "still alive among North American, African, Asian and Oceanic peoples."[21] In other words, this is poetry that supposedly precedes modernized and industrial formations of society, but I note that many oral traditions exist today. The second phase began in 1875 and ended in 1928, and includes Lewis Carroll and avant-gardists such as the Dadaists, Italian Futurists, Russian Futurists, *De Stijl*, and *Lettrisme*. The final period in McCaffery's timeline is his own, beginning in the 1950s, which builds on these legacies and includes international poets and artists interested in acoustic and electroacoustic compositions, such as Henri Chopin, Bernard Heidsieck, Bob Cobbing, Paula Claire, Ernst Jandl, Jackson Mac Low, Jerome Rothenberg, Michael McClure, and many Canadian practitioners. Had it been published decades later, McCaffery's survey might be extended to delineate another phase comprised of poets who have both extended and deviated from this line, including Caroline Bergvall, Maja Jantar, Tomomi Adachi, Jorg Piringer, a. rawlings, Kaie Kellough, and many others.

Canadian sound poetry, McCaffery argues, began "not with Bill Bissett or bpNichol, but with Montreal Automatiste Claude Gauvreau,"[22] who in the 1950s, along with peers like Thérèse Renaud and Françoise Sullivan, explored an extension of European Surrealism known as *Automatisme* (or "automatic writing"), a term that describes writing done with a liberated consciousness (or at least without any intentional meaning to the language being put on the page). Instead, words rise from the subconscious or a spiritual or supernatural source. Gauvreau's "Trustful Fatigue and Reality," for example, is a short, characterless, and set-less play consisting almost entirely of extralinguistic sounds that vaguely gesture toward semantics, comparable to the Dadaist sound poetry. In identifying Canadian sound poetry's genesis with *Les Automatistes*, McCaffery makes an important point since he acknowledges the significance of the Québécois literary avant-garde. However, his claim also elides Indigenous oral traditions in Canada, which are conspicuously absent from McCaffery's historical overview given that he gestures toward chant and prayer in his account of sound poetry's three waves. Notably, too, by referring to oral traditions as "archaic and primitive," McCaffery has dislocated these traditions from the discourse, reinforcing the colonial view of Indigenous traditions as backwards and out of step with the present.

The absence of careful consideration of specific Indigenous traditions from McCaffery's account is noteworthy given the currency that Indigenous poetries and orature from North American, African, Asian, and Oceanic cultures enjoyed during the 1960s, specifically through poet and editor Jerome Rothenberg's 1968 anthology *Technicians of the Sacred*. As Rothenberg put it in 1984, the anthology served as a response to the "inherited view" that the "idea of poetry, as developed in the West, was sufficient for the total telling."[23] On the one hand, I find it necessary to resist the urge to subsume Indigenous oral traditions under the term "sound poetry" so as to avoid the problem of categorically determining and defining poetry from cultures that are culturally dislocated from that context. On the other hand, Rothenberg's anthology was highly influential for sound poetry in the 1960s and '70s. It resonated, says Rothenberg, with "the sixties maelstrom" and "confronted an audience that was already waiting for it, often with more preconceptions about the 'tribal' or the 'oral.'"[24] For Rothenberg, the anthology was evidence that poetry "appeared not as a luxury but as a true necessity: not a small corner of the world for those who lived it but equal to the world itself."[25]

Some critics see Rothenberg's anthology as controversial, but it at least reminds us to treat possible connections between Indigenous cultural traditions and sound poetry with greater care. As mentioned earlier, bissett's identity as a poet, for example, is frequently linked to concepts of Indigeneity. Summarizing these connections, Scobie points out that "the oral is important, as his [bissett's] readings demonstrate—especially the chants, based on Native chanting as much as on the tradition of sound poetry, and conveying a mesmeric, meditative effect that provides one of the foundations of his vision."[26] I will note, too, that when I hear bissett's sound poetry, I also notice similarities with Buddhist chants, and indeed Buddhist practice was growing in popularity in North America in the 1960s alongside the counterculture movement. While any direct connections between bissett and Indigeneity remain unclear, the feeling of openness in the world at the time, facilitated in part by the increasing sense of international connectedness ushered in by the electronic age, led to problematic appropriations and imitations of non-Western cultural practices (as briefly discussed in chapter 1). Sound poetry undoubtedly provides further evidence of this problem. This complicates the claim that borders were "dropping off" and the assumptions of universality embedded within some aspects of the counterculture in the 1960s and '70s, of which sound poetry—and borderblur—were direct outgrowths. The turn toward Indigenous and non-Western forms of chant and prayer, which many artists in the 1960s pursued with enthusiasm, indicates that poets turned to these cultural forms to access rhythms, sounds, and modes of vocal expression that felt distinct from the sounds they experienced in their own cultural contexts. In other words, they were in search of sound, feeling, and expression to help them conceptualize the possibility of getting outside of their immediate cultures and, in Canada, colonial contexts.

An understanding of these contexts is necessary if we are to locate and assess sound poetry as a broader poetic form. Sound poetry, as it relates to Canadian borderblur, could be traced back to the early efforts and experiments of individual poets, which anticipate the maelstrom of activities, collaborations, communities, and national and international tours of the 1970s. In tracing this trajectory, I return to some familiar figures: namely, bissett and Nichol. The Underwhich collection *Past Eroticism: Canadian Sound Poetry in the 1960's: Vol. 1* (1986) contains recordings from as early as 1964, including Nichol's "Beach at Port Dover," which is also likely his first recorded sound poem. Nichol recounted the poem's composition to an audience at a 1968 reading at Sir George Williams University (now Concordia University): "I wrote it at Port Dover, in, on Lake Erie. It's one of those days when I was flaked out on the beach."[27] As Stephen Cain explained in his paper at the 2021 Modern Language Association convention, Nichol "wrote this poem lying on the beach at Port Dover while nearby loudspeakers played both Vera Lynn's WWII standard 'The White Cliffs of Dover' and Tom Jones's cheesy pop song 'What's New Pussycat?'"[28] Nichol wrote the poem in response to the absurd combination of these site-specific conditions, and it reveals his characteristic fascination with sound and play since most of the content of the poem pivots around a *puh* sound in a sequence of paratactic soundings and varying rhythms: "um pa pa . . . perch peach park . . . paper cup paper cup . . . pitter patter pitter patter pit pat pit pat . . . um pa . . . po dunk . . . part diver . . . port dover."[29] In this way Nichol lets sound form the pathway of his vocabulary with an emphasis on *p* sounds. In the recording, Nichol's voice is nearly overwhelmed by the throbbing bass of Jones's and Lynn's songs in the background of his recording. This version of the poem, as an early recorded example of Canadian sound poetry, suitably captures Nichol's interests in improvisation, spontaneity, and especially borderblur. From the vantage of the beach at Port Dover, Nichol overlooks the Lake Erie borderline that separates Canada and the United States, and, further, Nichol's poem fuses a variety of sources and experiences into a single poetic expression. This seemingly chance assemblage between poet, environment, and sonic nexus foregrounds one trajectory for sound poetry with its emphasis on process, action, feeling, and non-semantic language.

Two years later, in 1966, bissett "moves into word-mergings, soundings, [and] chantings." This was the same year that American poet Michael McClure visited Vancouver to read at the psychedelic Trips Festival, hosted at the Garden Auditorium of the Pacific National Exhibition and organized by Sam Perry, Ken Ryan, Al Hewitt, Mike Coutts, and Dallas Selman.[30] It was around this time that McClure had transitioned into his "beast language" poems, as featured in *Ghost Tantras* (1964), where he writes, "Grahhr!

Grahhhr! Grahhhrrr! Ghrahhr. Grahhrrr."[31] McClure and bissett performed on the same night, Sunday, July 31, in the company of the Grateful Dead and the Al Neil Jazz Trio and alongside showings of films by Charlie Chaplin, Andy Warhol, Sam Perry, and Gary Lee Nova. This meeting of media and personalities was typical of bissett's sound poetry. bissett was an avid solo performer who, like Nichol, played with language and sound, with the integration of rhythms and intonations with chant- and prayer-like inflections. bissett also brought these expressive forms into direct dialogue with music, notably with the Mandan Massacre (Roger Tentrey, Terry Beauchamp, Wayne Carr, Gregg Simpson, Ross Barrett, Harley McConnell, Ken Paterson, and Martina Clinton), who performed with bissett and are featured as part of his 1968 record/book *Awake in the Red Desert*. bissett's primal, aggressive raging with the Mandan Massacre can be recognized, somewhat reductively, as an extension of McClure's animalistic sound poetry. McClure's writing also proved to have a formative impact on Nichol, who recalls that "his work opened up new possibilities for me," though it is unclear if Nichol also attended the Trips Festival or had come to McClure by other means.[32] According to Frank Davey, Nichol left Vancouver for Toronto in 1964 so the latter option seems more likely. If he did see McClure on the West Coast, then his influence indicates that sound poetry, as part of the borderblur ethos, followed a pattern of proliferation similar to that of concrete poetry: it began in Vancouver and travelled eastward to Toronto with Nichol. If Nichol came to McClure by other means (and this theory is perhaps bolstered by the fact that Nichol's first published sound poem was recorded in 1964), this suggests that Ontario is a central locale for sound poetry's emergence in Canada during this time. In either scenario, Nichol played a significant role in introducing intermedial forms to poets in Central Canada.

As early as 1966, David UU was also evidently experimenting with chant forms in poetry, as indicated by his 1984 Underwhich Audiographics album *Very Sound* (discussed below), featuring fourteen sound poems written before 1970 and recorded in the 1970s and '80s. The cassette's A-side features UU's collaboration with the Avalettes (the Avalettes comprised Gregg Simpson, Phil Morgan, Ingrid Harris, Patricia Garrett, and Bob Coleman) while the B-side contains mostly solo works by UU. UU's work with the Avalettes is closely aligned with the sounds of Canadian free improv noise group Nihilist Spasm Band (founding members included Hugh McIntyre, John Clement, John Boyle, Bill Exley, Murray Favro, Archie Leitch, Art Pratten, and Greg

Curnoe), whose 1967 noise track "No Canada" satirizes the Canadian national anthem across six minutes and twenty-eight seconds of erratic kazoos, drums, strings, screams, hollers, horns, farts, moans, and invented instruments. The Avalettes are similar, too, to bissett's Mandan Massacre. In comparison, the pieces that UU composed in the 1960s and presented on *Very Sound*'s B-side offer us his single voice using chant-like rhythms, often delving into the sounds of words and short phrases. The thirty-one-second track "how can i touch you now," exemplifies this approach. Here, UU gently sings the title words, omitting a word with each repetition until arriving at "now now." He then builds the phrase back out, imitating through sound the act of moving toward and then away from a lover. These earlier sound poems, though less "noisy" than his work with the Avalettes, are undeniably like the equally playful, repetitive, and chant-like sound poetry of Nichol and bissett.

During this early period of borderblur sound poetry, Nichol, too, experimented with noise, which can be heard thanks to Jim Brown, who in 1968 undertook the curation and production of the short-lived "record magazine" *See/Hear*, an ambitious project that resulted in two recordings. Brown intended to produce a quarterly series

> of recordings of contemporary sound arts. Contemporary sound arts are usually discussed in terms of certain categories such as electronic music, experimental acoustic music, sound poetry, projective verse, chance music, improvised forms and so on, however what should probably be recognized is that sound arts are continually evolving and to create categories only restricts the way in which we think about sound. Mixed media, combinations of sound and visual arts, or combinations of different modes of sound art, are easily seen as results of our electric environment, and are as valid as the already accepted sound forms.[33]

Brown's description of *See/Hear* reflects an intermedia ethos given his emphasis on diverse "media" and "combinations" while also acknowledging, echoing McLuhan, his "electric environment." Though not exclusively dedicated to sound poetry, the first issue of this record magazine contains electroacoustic spoken word poetry. Lionel Kearns's permutational poem "The Woman Who" is perhaps typical in this regard, as it uses stereo panning to produce the effect of multiple voices in conversation. Nichol's electroacoustic contribution is seemingly void of language and consists of squealing frequencies. The second issue of *See/Hear* consists entirely of contributions from Brown, Wayne Carr, and Ross Barrett (all of whom appeared on the first record installment). Despite its two-issue run, the record magazine anticipated some of the spoken and electroacoustic poetic experiments that would be more deeply explored in the following decades.

These formative but fringe moments of the 1960s led to the flourishing and vibrant network that emerged in the 1970s. Caroline Bayard hails 1970 as the official starting point for sound poetry in Canada since it also saw the aforementioned arrival of the Four Horsemen (active from 1970 to 1988). There are competing accounts of the group's formation; however, Butling and Rudy confirm that shortly after they met in 1969, Nichol and McCaffery performed as a duo, and during the following year were joined by Baretto-Rivera and Dutton, both of whom were involved with the Therafields psychotherapy community (where Nichol worked). They began workshopping and performing and released their first studio recording, *Canadada* (1972). They performed at Vancouver's the Western Front and Toronto's A Space and Music Gallery, in university auditoriums like York University's Curtis Lecture Hall, and at festivals like the 1982 Summer Solstice Festival in Damrosch Park, Lincoln Centre, New York, the Sound Poetry Festival at La Mamelle, San Francisco, in 1977, and at a festival in Amsterdam in 1981.

The Four Horsemen's work inspired other Canadian poets to take up sound poetry and thereby consolidate it as a significant part of borderblur, and as such a Canadian paratradition. Owen Sound—comprised of Michael Dean, David Penhale, Steven Ross Smith, and Richard Truhlar—began workshopping sound poetry in 1975 in a Toronto framing studio on Dupont Street operated by Brian Dedora.[34] The group drew influence from the Dadaists, composers such as Steve Reich and Philip Glass, and poets such as Nichol. They performed privately until 1976, when they held their first performance at Fat Albert's Coffee House on Bloor Street in Toronto. Owen Sound, like the Four Horsemen, became well-known as a sound poetry collective and performed in Montreal, Ottawa, Owen Sound, Toronto, Vancouver, and abroad in Amsterdam at the Stedelijk Museum and in London, England, at the Canada House and National Poetry Centre. The group stayed together until 1984.

Like Owen Sound, another group of poets were inspired by the Four Horsemen: a duo comprising Stephen Scobie and Douglas Barbour, who began collaborating in Edmonton, where they taught at the University of Alberta. "In the best Canadian tradition of The Four Horsemen (not to mention The Rolling Stones)," Barbour says, "we gave ourselves a group name—Re: Sounding."[35] Referred to in *Music Works* as "Canada's undocumented sound poetry group,"[36] they travelled the same pathways as Owen Sound and the Four Horsemen, performing "in Canada, the U.S., Austria, Denmark, Sweden, West Germany, Germany, and Australia & New Zealand, and at the 12th International Sound Poetry Festival in New York, 1980,"[37] and later, in 1999, Barbour and Scobie compiled *Carnivocal: A Celebration of Sound Poetry*, which also featured a newer generation of sound poets including Christian Bök, W. Mark Sutherland, Stephen Cain, and others. There are no available recordings of Re: Sounding.

The Four Horsemen, Owen Sound, and Re: Sounding are often given pride of place in narratives describing Canadian sound poetry; there are, however, numerous, less frequently acknowledged figures whose work is nonetheless worth considering. Toronto-based Sean O'Huigin,[38] for example, a Scottish-Canadian poet who co-organized the eleventh International Festival of Sound Poetry in Toronto, was a vital member of the community. Before the formation of Owen Sound, and just as the Four Horsemen were gaining critical notice, O'Huigin was experimenting with sound poetry, working with musicians like Ann Southam and artist Aiko Suzuki. With Southam, he released *Sky Sails* (1973), a record for which Nichol wrote a note for the back cover:

> there is no sense here of a poet reading with musical accompaniment there is only the piece itself that this is possible is only because of the years these two people have spent working with one another & their sensing of where the other is   that this search this struggle towards community in a context of isolation should be (& i hesitate here to use this term) the theme of their album seems right.[39]

They documented their collaboration once more in 1978 with *Poe [Tree]*, a book which also included their work on the B-side of a split seven-inch, *Appendix*. Like O'Huigin, Gerry Shikatani was also an active member of the Toronto sound poetry community, but his work has received scant critical attention. The reason for this oversight, at least in the context of Shikatani's sound poetry, can partially be explained by the fact that many of his sound

EAR RINGS
Penn(y) Kemp

EAR RINGS   Penn(y) Kemp

EAR RINGS is No. 33 of
the Underwhich Audiographic Series.
First Edition of 100 copies. August 1987.

Cover drawing by Vachel Lindsay

Side 1

* with David Prentice (music)
** with Charlie Morrow (mix)
*** with Anne Anglin (voice/music)

Re Solution*	4 min. 15 sec.
All the Men Tall**	2 min. 15 sec.
The Trick Is*	3 min. 23 sec.
Trance Form**	2 min. 17 sec.
Her Mind Set*	8 min. 32 sec.
Matter Matters***	12 min. 37 sec.
Divining***	2 min. 33 sec.
Tiger Skin***	3 min. 5 sec.
Displacement***	2 min. 53 sec.
Wishes***	4 min. 45 sec.
On and On*	2 min. 28 sec.
What the Ear Hears***	2 min. 56 sec.
When the Heart Parts*	3 min.
Don't***	1 min. 45 sec.
Please*	3 min. 45 sec.
Ka***	54 seconds
Attention Shifts***	1 min. 52 sec.

Side 2

* with David Prentice (music)
** with Charlie Morrow (mix/voice)
*** with Anne Anglin (voice)
**** with Coby Stoller (mix)

List Ten*	2 min.
Ven Ear*	1 min.
P'Leisure*	2 min.
Wait Late*	3 min. 55 sec.
Won (ce)*	45 sec.
Once****	3 min. 35 sec.
Won (ce)*	2 min. 38 sec.
Ms*	1 min. 45 sec.
Is s/he*	2 min. 31 sec.
Fall*	1 min. 18 sec.
Something About a Bear**	5 min. 5 sec.
Won (ce)**	5 min. 37 sec.
Pan Ta Re**	2 min. 33 sec.
Map Oracle***	2 min. 50 sec.
Bone Poem***	7 min. 53 sec.
Pan Ta Re*	4 min. 15 sec.
Lord He Rose*	3 min. 15 sec.

Published by Underwhich Editions, P.O. Box 262,
Adelaide St. Stn., Toronto, Canada M5C 2J4.

Figure 3.1: Liner notes to Penn Kemp's *Ear Rings*, 1987.

works were not documented—a problem that Re: Sounding shares—even though he "ha[d] been performing sound poetry since the 1970s."[40] Shikatani's performance work is engaged more fulsomely in the next chapter.

Penn Kemp, Nichol's friend, is also deserving of a more forceful acknowledgement as a central protagonist within the development of sound poetry in Canada. She began publishing in 1972 with her book *Bearing Down*, which launched a generative life of work in poetry, including lyric, sound, and concrete poetry, performance, and prose. This first book, published by Coach House Press, places her work directly within the mesh of borderblur as Coach House was an avid publisher of intermedial and exploratory literary works. Kemp has rigorously pushed the boundaries of not only poetry but sound poetry itself, collaborating with musicians and theatre performers—evidence of her aesthetic and medial diversity. One of her earliest recordings is *In Spirit Trees* (1977), which contains "Feminist sound poems and chants."[41] Since then, she has published well over a dozen recordings, including 1987's *Ear Rings* (published by Underwhich), for which she collaborated with American violinist David Prentice and Canadian actor Anne Anglin, and which was mixed by American sound poet, artist, and musician Charlie Morrow.

There is at least one more overlooked sound poetry collective that must be noted here to clarify our sense of the network at the time: First Draft, which formed in 1980 and comprised core members Susan McMaster (who studied with Barbour in 1972), musician Andrew McClure, and poet Colin Morton. First Draft welcomed a revolving cast of collaborators, yet it seems that McMaster and Morton were anchors for the group. Their names are included on each of the group's published volumes of scores and poems (some of which were published by Underwhich). First Draft was a performance group that explored the sounds of poetry, and on various occasions it collaborated with visual artists, performers, and musicians. It was not until 1982, two years after they formed, that First Draft officially entered the Canadian borderblur network. That year, the seventh annual Great Canadian Writers' Weekend was held at the Cranberry Inn in Collingwood, Ontario. Many poets attended, including members of the Four Horsemen and First Draft.[42] In her autobiography, McMaster recalls meeting Nichol at the event: "I've just seen the Horsemen perform, and am still quivering from the excitement and energy of their presentation. . . . bpNichol is *it* in sound poetry in Canada."[43] Recognizing their shared interest in intermedial poetics, she feels compelled to introduce herself: "I can't stay away: the power of the performance, the clearly visible warmth and kindness of the man, the fact above all that he is doing a version of what Andrew and I are working on in First Draft in our wordmusic—working with many voices together as sound as well as meaning—draw me towards him."[44] She soon initiated a friendship with Nichol, thereby bringing First Draft within the orbit of this network of affiliation. Nichol seemed to develop a close relationship with members of First Draft, whom he supported in a variety of ways; he helped them workshop their pieces, edited their two books of scores, and helped them build an audience. As McMaster says, Nichol went to Ottawa on his own expense "to be the 'big name' at the launch of First Draft's first wordmusic book."[45] First Draft was distinct from their predecessors and eschewed the masculine homo sociality of the other collectives who began performing in the 1970's. First Draft, in other words, was not a group of men exploring the limits of their sounding bodies; rather, their sound poems carefully developed a working relationship between the voices of all members regardless of gender. First Draft, as McMaster claims, is "a feminist, a humanist, adventure. . . . We are all collaborators on equal terms."[46] Kemp's and McMaster's works represent essential contributions to a poetic field that is otherwise dominated by masculine personalities (a point I come back to later in this chapter).

It is doubtful that the work of the sound poets described above would have flourished had it not been for the infrastructure developed in such forums as artist-run centres, poet-driven reading series, and small press publishing efforts. The artist-run centre, in principle, is an alternative space that provides artists a refuge from big galleries and corporately managed spaces. In a sense, these spaces might also be recognized in Bernstein's terms as "provisional institutions,"[47] since they share a commitment to local, peripheral, and exploratory art forms over the desire to maximize profits and audience numbers. In other words, they are meant for artists and writers who typically work outside of the mainstream. These kinds of spaces in Canada include the Western Front and the now defunct Intermedia, both in Vancouver, A Space and the Music Gallery in Toronto, and Véhicule Gallery (also defunct) in Montreal, as well as lesser-known spaces such as Vancouver's Mandan Ghetto (created by bissett, Joy Long, and Gregg Simpson) and the Sound Gallery (also founded by Simpson). There are few publicly available recordings of performances in these spaces, of which notable examples include the Four Horsemen's performances at the Western Front in 1974 and 1977 as well as bissett's 1978 reading in the same space. These were remarkable spaces that did more than offer "a public venue and supportive environment for play and experimentation;"[48] they were also instrumental in the growth of borderblur as an avant-garde paratradition. Not only did they provide an environment for the development of artistic and literary paratraditions, but the artist-run centre brought together poetry and many other artistic modes and media.

It is important to recognize, however, that Canadian sound poetry was not performed solely in provisional spaces. In fact, Canadian sound poets embraced the possibilities of performance in a range of larger institutionalized spaces, from university classrooms and radio stations to larger art centres like the Harbourfront Centre in Toronto. Such a gesture may signal sound poetry's institutionalization or transition toward a more mainstream audience. Indeed, it may seem as though sound poetry did enjoy some degree of popularity (yet, if true, this enjoyment was fleeting). But despite this flirtation with established institutions, Canadian sound poetry remains outside of Canada's dominant literary tradition and is often perceived more as a novelty than a serious mode of poetic expression. On this note, I wonder why and how some Canadian sound poets were invited into these spaces. It seems likely that sound poetry, far from being wildly popular, was appreciated by a small few who also had access to institutional spaces and invited sound poets to perform there. Truhlar, for example, worked at the CJRT radio station, where he produced two programs: *The Art of Sound Poetry* and *Canadian Poetry in the 1980s*. In September 1979, CJRT's *Music and Literature* program featured the Four Horsemen. With that said, CJRT was by no means a conventional station, having been established in 1949 at Ryerson Polytechnic. As for university performances, some of these poets were university instructors. As noted above, Barbour taught at the University of Alberta. Both Nichol and McCaffery were connected to York University, where the Four Horsemen on occasion performed. McCaffery received his master's degree from York in 1970, and Nichol began teaching at the school in 1980.

Rather than see these forays into institutional settings as borderblur's invitation into Canada's dominant literary culture, we can see them as opportunities for poets to disrupt the conventions of these spaces where thought and feeling are often expressed in standardized language and where modes of communication are typically recognized as distinct. Take, for example, York University's Curtis Lecture Hall, where the Four Horsemen performed in January 1973. This is typically a place where speech is used as a passive container for thought, logic, and meaning.[49] A lecturer communicates thoughts to the students in attendance; the students are in turn often expected to record those thoughts and sometimes respond in a meaningful way. A Four Horsemen performance was radically unlike the lecturer's delivery of content. The Four Horsemen revelled in nonsensical and non-semantic meaning—very much unlike most university lecturers. Instead, they, and other Canadian sound poets who were occasionally welcomed into institutionalized settings, took over these spaces, disrupting the flow of speech and logic to redefine and subvert their intended purposes.

Though the materialistic dimension of Canadian sound poetry has been diminished as an impure representation of the art, audio recordings are one of the few ways sound poetry continues to enjoy circulation within borderblur's affiliated network. As part of Underwhich's publishing program, several editors developed the Underwhich Audiographic Series, which focused on the production and dissemination of cassette tapes (and later compact discs). McCaffery initiated this series and was joined by Truhlar, Smith, and Nichol. Truhlar eventually maintained the series "thru his publication of numerous new music cassettes and his efforts to get the entire series better known in the alternative press."[50] Underwhich primarily relied on the audiocassette. Rising to prominence in its standard form in the mid-twentieth century, the audiocassette opened new possibilities for sound poetry because of its affordability and user-friendliness. Underwhich took advantage of this accessibility; their published cassettes were very much provisional affairs, sometimes dubbed using home stereos and store-bought tapes.

All the activities accounted for above provide a clear sense of the social and material processes that set the emergence and proliferation of Canadian sound poetry under borderblur into motion, and, in so doing, made Canadian sound poetry audible to an international network, which Nichol and McCaffery helped to foster. Most notably, *Sound Poetry: A Catalogue*, edited by Nichol and McCaffery, was published by Underwhich on the occasion of the eleventh International Sound Poetry Festival, hosted in Toronto and organized by McCaffery, O'Huigin, and Smith.[51] As Rudy and Butling have noted, "this is an annual event that began in Sweden in 1968 and was the first time the festival was held in North America." It was recognized for the prominent billing it gave to group and collective performances.[52] Poets from Canada, the United States, the United Kingdom, France, Italy, and Holland attended and participated, including the likes of Dick Higgins, Bob Cobbing, Paula Claire, Henri Chopin, Jackson MacLow, Jerome Rothenberg, and others.

The event was a high watermark for sound poetry in Canada. It was not only a crucial nexus at which an international array of practices and practitioners gathered, but it also foregrounded (like other festivals), the importance of community as a major component of sound poetry practice—both in the coming together to collaboratively compose and perform sound poetry, and in the persistence of collectivity among festival attendees (at this point, eleven iterations of the festival had already occurred). The eleventh International Sound Poetry Festival highlights the aesthetic diversity of sound poetry, including both acoustic (by the Four Horsemen and Owen Sound, for example) and electroacoustic performances (Jackson Mac Low and Henri Chopin), as well as collaborative and solo performances. More than anything else, the festival is clear evidence of Canadian borderblur's unique approach to sound poetry while also validating practitioners' connections to an international community.

The events, personalities, and materials that I highlight in this section in no way amount to a holistic portrait of sound poetry during the 1960s through to the late 1980s. Significant figures are missing due to a lack of accessible documentation—Basmajian, for example, is listed as a participant in the eleventh International Sound Poetry Festival, yet it seems that no recordings exist of his sound work. Similarly, few recordings by Shikatani—who places silence at the core of his performance—exist, and those that do have been minimally documented (I return to Shikatani's performances in the next chapter). With that said, an exhaustive depiction is not my purpose here; the goal, rather, is to highlight the many ephemeral cultural processes around which affiliated practitioners gathered to make sound poetry one face of Canadian borderblur. All of this work is what Bernstein would call "social work," in the sense that it sought to forge a paratradition outside of Canada's dominant literary community. With its emphasis on community and face-to-face encounters, we see how by sheer necessity affect was already at the centre of Canadian sound poetry.

Language and Sound in the Electronic Age

While Canadian sound poets in the 1960s through to the 1980s at times engaged the idea of Canadian identity or nationality—though they more often than not maintained a critical or ambivalent position vis-à-vis nationalist concerns—their work can be generatively situated as responses to two conditions related to the electronic age and the transnational rise of affective labour: sonic media, on the one hand, and the increasing standardization of speech, on the other.

New technologies had an effect on sound production and sonic mediation in that they disrupted traditional processes of imagining community since new technologies allowed the voice to travel great distances and thereby exceed national borders. As with concrete poetry, McLuhan's writing articulates how electronic media ushered in new possibilities for understanding the relationship between community and oral/aural communications at the time. Critic Richard Cavell explains that McLuhan "was writing in a transitional moment, when a primarily literate culture was experiencing aspects of oral culture as they were being retrieved by electronic media."[53] Jamie Hilder echoes this point when he writes that "The drastically altered mediascape that arose at mid-century alongside electronic media is what led Marshall McLuhan to theorize the experience of space as acoustic rather than visual."[54] Like Dennis Lee, McLuhan was acutely aware of the power of sound and how it shapes one's sense of place. In *Understanding Media*, he recognizes that "in speech we tend to react to each situation that occurs, reacting in tone and gesture even to our own act of speaking,"[55] and further that "the power of the voice to shape air and space into verbal patterns may well have been preceded by a less specialized expression of cries, grunts, gestures, and commands, of song and dance."[56] For McLuhan, sound, and particularly the voice, rely on the intimacy of the spoken word—that is, the unaided voice's capacity to fill a space, to vibrate within it without travelling far beyond it. Unamplified speech typically requires an immediate audience, and thus has communal implications. Nevertheless, as McLuhan knew well, electronic audio technologies were transforming sound and lending it an itinerant quality, permitting the voice to move beyond its immediate environs. The voice could travel—across the airwaves or inscribed onto tapes and records—far from its source of origin, which also meant that sound had new capacities for shaping the communal imagination through the distant voice.

Working in consonance with McLuhan's writing, R. Murray Schafer, the Canadian composer and sound theorist, and a friend to many borderblur poets, lamented these mutations in the soundscape that were catalyzed by the rise of electronic audio technologies: "Modern man is beginning to inhabit a world with an acoustic environment radically different from any he has hitherto known," which has alerted researchers "to the dangers of an indiscriminate and imperialistic spread of more and larger sounds into every corner of man's life."[57] For Schafer, these shifts delivered two interrelated problems. First, was the impact of sonic technologies—like the telephone, radio, and phonograph—on human life. In particular, he focuses on the concept of "schizophonia," the separation of sound from its original context because of these technologies' capacities to record, store, and transport sounds around the world. In Schafer's words, schizophonia refers "to the split between an original sound and its electroacoustic reproduction" so that it "may be restated at other times and places."[58] He deems schizophonia unnatural and suggests that it leads to "the territorial expansion of post-industrial sounds [which] complemented the imperialistic ambitions of Western nations."[59] The possibilities offered by sonic technologies of the mid- to late twentieth century were implicated within the problematic conditions of this electronic age. Schafer's position is reactionary and now out of fashion, but he believed that new technologies dismantled the immediacy of the face-to-face meeting of vocalizing subject and listening audience.

The second problem with electroacoustic technologies, as far as Schafer was concerned, has to do with the blending lo-fi and hi-fi soundscapes. The lo-fi soundscape is overcrowded with signals that are obscured and lack sonic perspective (the acoustic foreground and background). In contrast, the hi-fi soundscape is less crowded, sonically sparse with a clearly defined acoustic perspective. These two problems, resulting from the proliferation of electroacoustic technologies, create another crucial problem for Schafer: "a synthetic soundscape in which natural sounds are becoming increasingly unnatural while machine-made substitutes are providing the operative signals directing modern life."[60] For Schafer, the changes imposed on the sonic environment have tremendous impacts on human life, altering our interaction with it. This "synthetic soundscape" casts some doubt on Lee's claims, detailed earlier, of having found an authentic cadence by listening to the soundscape immediately available to him. Implicit in Schafer's study is a fear that the new electronic soundscape will detrimentally alter the social work of listening since sonic technologies could now modify depth and distance. These concerns directly informed the work of the poets themselves.

For sound poets like McCaffery, schizophonia had significant implications for the body's expressionistic capacities. In 1978, he claimed that "the body is no longer the ultimate parameter, and voice becomes a point of departure rather than the point of arrival."[61] He further suggested that "technological time can be superadded to authentic body time to achieve either an accelerated or decelerated experience of voice time. Both time and space are harnessed to become less the controlling and more the manipulable factors of audiophony."[62] McCaffery used Schafer's concept of schizophonia as a marker for categorizing sound poetry practices. As a collective, the Four Horsemen largely swerved from schizophonic sound poetry, preferring sound poetry unaided by acoustic technologies, presumably in an attempt to return to "authentic body time" and as a gesture of resistance against the problems posed by electronic media (according to Schafer).[63] Echoing McCaffery, Nichol characterized the Four Horsemen's work as a body-centred practice: "phonograph recordings and tapes . . . remove the living performers from the audience's presence, and freeze what should be an ongoing process."[64] Schafer's concept of schizophonia, then, captures the anxiety some poets felt about the separation of sound from its bodily source. This resistance to the recorded sound poem also gestures toward the Four Horsemen's resistance to the materialistic dimension of literature's conventional literary economy. While they circulated their concrete poems outside of the mainstream Canadian publishing industry, they rarely circulated recordings of their sound poetry performances, thus emphasizing the creation of a community through tangibility, presence, attachment—in the spirit of Swede's Scream-In.

While groups like Owen Sound and Re: Sounding largely shared some of the convictions of the Horsemen, it would be an over-generalization to frame the sound poetry of borderblur as a practice that was interested solely in this turn away from the schizophonic. It would be too exclusionary to definitively argue, as McCaffery did in 1978, that Canadian sound poetry is typified by a swerve away from electroacoustic technologies, as doing so excludes collaborative works by Nichol, bissett, Jim Brown, Lionel Kearns, Sean O'Huigin and Ann Southam, Richard Truhlar, Penn Kemp, and the musical groups that formed in the 1980s such as Tekst, Phenomenθnsemble, and CCMC—all of whom worked with technology, musical instruments, and tape to some degree. These poets and performers actively embraced these technologies as a way of augmenting, amplifying, distorting, and extending the human voice within a synthetic soundscape that resists homogenization. McCaffery himself would eventually experiment with tape, as heard in his 1981 collaboration with Truhlar, *Manicured Noise*. Schizophonia, however, as McCaffery and Schafer describe it, offers a concept around which we can understand the polarizing effects of sound technologies and their relationship to an emergent affective economy. By responding to schizophonia—either in the form of a rejection of it, or by excitedly exploring its possibilities—sound poetry emerged as part of a dialogue with the pressures of the affective economy and the electronic age.

This brings me to the second aspect of the electronic age and the affective economy against which borderblur sound poets reacted: the standardization of speech. According to Hardt and Negri, "Language, as it communicates, produces commodities but moreover creates subjectivities, puts them in relation, and orders them."[65] Thus, language, as a basis for communication, in terms of both its methods and its purposes, takes on a particular dimension within the new, international, affective capitalist paradigm. McCaffery's writings on sound, capitalism, and language effectively triangulate these as points of crisis for some sound poets. In his manifesto "for a poetry of blood," he declares his utter faith in sound's liberating and transformative capacities: "EITHER YOU TRANSFORM OR YOU / DESTROY," he writes.[66] McCaffery's statement positions emotion and sound and its value over language and semantics. For McCaffery, poetry and sound share the same essential qualities, "rhythm & pulse," and it is through sound and its affect that one achieves "the successful assimilation of your own [biology] into another biology."[67] This creative undertaking was also reflected in Nichol's description of his poetic projects as seeking expression beyond standard semantic speech (or writing, for that matter): "language means communication and that communication does not just mean language."[68] Nichol's intermedial literary experiments seek to transcend the limitations of singular corporeality and linguistic homogenization, or as he puts it, to find "as many exits as possible from the self (language/communication exits) in order to form as many entrances as possible for the other."[69] Thus, I see these poets reaching toward the expansive possibilities of an intermedia poetic—for sound poetry brings together expressive modes such as language, sound, and gesture—that recognizes the complexities of communication in a postmodernizing era.

We should also recognize that these poets saw sound poetry as a tool for creatively unsettling linguistic convention. For McCaffery, linguistic expression is intricately bound up with capitalism and its problematic program of homogenizing and standardizing the subject's language since, as mentioned before, "capitalism begins when you / open the dictionary,"[70] and, in a separate context McCaffery, while referring to work by Ferrucio Rossi-Landi, suggests that "language . . . functions like money and speaks *through* us more than we actively produce *within* it."[71] McCaffery and some of his contemporaries believed that language had been systematically regularized to the extent that any expression of the self was imitative of the power structures that alienate, suppress, or deny individual expression. This is the same crisis of control that McLuhan identified in his discussions of the electronic age, which are echoed in Hardt and Negri. The standardizing project, in this context, is a subtle means of modulating what language means and does. McCaffery illustrates these connections most clearly when he situates sound poetry in dialogue with theorist Georges Bataille's concept of the "general economy," wherein he figures sound poetry as a matter of total excess: "sound poetry is a poetry of complete expenditure in which nothing is recoverable as 'meaning,'" one that exceeds "semantic order" and "shatters meaning at a point where language commits its move to idealization," which consequently "puts the subject into process."[72] This process contests capitalistic formulations of the self as a total, effectuated being that is thereby serviceable to capitalist society—a crisis that borderblur sound poets sought to work through. Practitioners like Nichol, McCaffery, bissett, and others, then, confronted this crisis and formulated a mode of sonic poetic expression that reflected their awareness of language as a means of exchange, and they sought ways of expressing themselves outside of that system. In other words, taking McCaffery's point as a central tenet, sound poets sought to disrupt capitalism's linguistic standardization by re-imagining language and communication through sound.

Many of the sound poets operating at the locus of borderblur advanced their poetry under somewhat analogous conceptions of sound and social politics. In particular, they saw sound poetry as an affective practice with radical potentialities through which they might engage themselves and others in a process that exceeds conventional linguistic, intellectual, and affective experiences. In addition to McCaffery's "a poetry of blood" and Nichol's concept of "exits and entrances," there are numerous other statements of sound poetics that complement this conceptual constellation. For example, McCaffery's and Nichol's theorizations of sound poetry align with that of another member of the Four Horsemen, Dutton, who in his preface to *Right Hemisphere, Left Ear* (1979), included in *Sound Poetry: A Catalogue*, argues for more fluid forms of expression: "Poetry consists of language; and language consists of sound and sight, of idea and emotion, of intellect and body, of rationality and irrationality. It is my delight to explore all these elements of language and to incorporate them in my compositions. I am not in a camp." He adds, "if some ineffable emotion demands recourse to human sounds beyond the realm of conventional verbalization or if the communication of a particularly pleasing rhythm is hindered by the imposition of intellectual or verbal constructs, then let the everyday words depart to make way for that which is most immediate."[73] Dutton's comments here connect with McCaffery's rejection of standardized modes of expression as denying and obfuscating expression, and especially, for Dutton, the expression of feeling.

Influenced by the Four Horsemen, members of Owen Sound described their practice in similar terms. Dean suggests that "in sound-poetry we give form to the unspoken communication between things."[74] Penhale, likewise, argues that "sound-poetry as we know it is based in **our** language experience, in our emotional experience," and later that "sound without ideation is emotion. The first registration our work has on an audience, beyond the initial shock, is emotional. We are speaking to them in a non-image work manner yet with a good deal of communication."[75] Most pointedly, Truhlar directly links sound, affect, and self-expression: "Sound must be encompassed into an organic process which is greater than the sound itself. . . . Emotion is the expression of a life deeply felt and experienced. One emotes thru sound. We then must make a conscious link for ourselves between our sounds & our lives."[76] Poets such as Kemp and McMaster took these premises a step further since their sound poetry is a mode for the formulation and expression of their subjectivity outside of capitalism and a male-dominated tradition. Patricia Keeney Smith highlights this affective dimension of Kemp's work: "Kemp is an accomplished sound poet, expressing emotion that goes beyond logic or syntax. Sound was first and sound is last, From breath and cry to keening, From gasp to gasp."[77] In the same article, Kemp tells Keeney that "All my books are about the many aspects of being a woman," a statement that can be extended to her sound work as well.[78] Similarly, McMaster identifies that from an early point in her career she conceived of poetry as being intimately linked with emotion, a consideration that she inherited from Barbour, one half of sound poetry duo Re: Sounding:

> At the time when I started coming out of the closet as a poet—which was [the] late sixties, early seventies—poetry as I understood it was very intense, lyrical, the *moment* captured. I had some excellent teachers at that time—W. O. Mitchell, for example, and Doug Barbour—who told me "Don't tell the story, don't

tell the story, make it the pure emotion." And my poems got shorter, and shorter, and very formal, and non-narrative.[79]

It was through her study with the more senior poet Barbour that McMaster began to distinguish lyrical and intermedial literary traditions, in pursuit of an emotive practice. As part of her work with First Draft, this drive toward emotion also became a mode of feminist practice. Situating herself within the sound poetry scene, she writes,

> bp, like Colin and Alrick and Peter and Claude, is a friend simply, so that at one point I think, my life is full of men and I'm not sleeping with any of them. A change from the wild girl who was. In that way, First Draft is also a feminist, a humanist, adventure, in which I and other women involved are there not as ornaments or organizers and the men are there not as Cool Lukes or *artistes*. We are all collaborators on equal terms—people, in fact.[80]

These statements, from both Kemp and McMaster, highlight the affective as well as the avant-gardist dimensions of sound poetry as a means of accessing alternative modes of expression and subjectivation—the process of independently formulating identity, and, I note, an identity that is contingent not on external nationalist factors, but on the interiority of the voicing subject.

In the context of an emergent affective economy and a male-dominated network, the work of Kemp and McMaster is important since, as Hardt and Negri have noted, affective labour is typically *gendered labour*. As Dorothy Smith recognized in 1987, affective labour can also be effectively characterized as "woman's work," which is especially true for caregiving and secretarial work (typically done by women in the twentieth century).[81] So, not only do Kemp's and McMaster's sound poetries intervene into the male-dominated space of the community, but their work also reverberates strongly within the broader context of the emergent economy. Their work stages a resistance to the determined role of a woman's body within it. This is doubly significant considering that the 1980s was a crucial period in the development of feminist poetics, as evidenced by the theoretical and creative writings of Barbara Godard, Daphne Marlatt, Nicole Brossard, and others. Kemp's and McMaster's works aligned with this feminist literary zeitgeist not only for how they write the body but also for how they express the body in sound.

Affect and Extension: Listening to Canadian Sound Poetry

Listening to recordings produced and disseminated by and through the Canadian borderblur network reveals the way sound poetry ripples with affect, extends with audio technologies, and transcends the limits of linguistic expression. Before going further, though, I must acknowledge that sound poetry, under the umbrella of Canadian borderblur, poses numerous challenges for critics assessing such work. First, there is the problem of ephemerality since, in typical avant-garde fashion, many sound poetry recordings were produced and disseminated through the same provisional institutions that support this paratradition as a whole. At the time of writing, much of the sound poetry described in this section remains accessible thanks to databases and websites (such as the University of Pennsylvania's PennSound online archive and the website UbuWeb), rare book and record sellers, and archivists. This is also a testament to the ways that Canadian sound poetry has necessarily circulated outside of the mainstream Canadian literary tradition (though scholarly networks such as the SpokenWeb are working to change these conditions). Adding to these problems of access, some sound poets denigrated the authority of the audio recording and instead privileged the live performance as the most effective way of experiencing sound poetry. Speaking on behalf of the Four Horsemen, Nichol writes, "even phonograph recordings and tapes run this risk [of falsifying their group identity], as they remove the living performers from the audience's presence, and freeze what should be an ongoing process."[82] In this way, we can see that Nichol privileges a "sustained state of relation" between performer and audience and a specific means by which the "intensities" of the sound poem "pass body to body."[83] Thus, I acknowledge, and despite my having experienced many other live sound poetry performances, that listening to some records and cassettes, like the Four Horsemen's, is necessarily a limited engagement with their work since the actual, real-time performance is inaccessible to me. But while I appreciate Nichol's concerns, I must also acknowledge that his position is not true for all Canadian sound poets in the borderblur network. As evidenced by Underwhich's catalogue of sound poetry cassette tapes, recorded audio was an acceptable medium for many poets; thus, the available recordings can, in some cases, be considered satisfactory representations of the work. In this section, I am conscious of these complexities and know that my listening experience is also mediated by my own material and technological context. Thus, in dealing with this poetry I am engaging, at times, with a quasi form of such work. Nevertheless, I proceed.

As the group that is said to have unleashed sound poetry in Canada and situated it as a recognizable aspect of borderblur poetics, I turn first to the collaborative, acoustic, and sometimes improvised work of the Four Horsemen, whose sound poetry resists and responds to the conditions of electronic mediation (as noted above) and the standardization of expression during the rise of postmodernization. Their resistance to so-called schizophonia and standardized communication is audible, for example, in their sound poem "Assassin" from 1977's *Live in the West*, an album that documents three live performances from February 1974, one at the University of Manitoba in Winnipeg, one at the Western Front in Vancouver, and one at the University of Alberta in Edmonton. "Assassin" opens with hissing sounds made by several members, accentuating the double *s* sound in the word "assassin." One member's voice emerges from these hisses with a buoyant, song-like voice, repeating "sin sin sin-a-sin sin sin," playing with the phonemes of the word until the group begins to ecstatically chant "AH-SA-SIN." The chant's tempo accelerates with each repetition until the synchronicity of voices dissolves, followed by sharp breathing sounds that are quickly silenced by another group member's cry. This sequence is then repeated. In this way, the Four Horsemen become assassins themselves, destroyers of standardized language. They deconstruct the title word "assassin," spilling its morphemes and phonemes—words such as "sin" and "ass" as well as related extralinguistic sounds (hisses, screams, shouts, panting, breathing). They charge through these sonic elements, stripping the word of its singular meaning while finding openings to explore. This is the kind of linguistic analysis critics often employ when discussing the Four Horsemen's sound poetry. They focus on the deconstruction of language and logic that results in a discourse of negation, aligning their work with early twentieth-century avant-gardes such as the Dadaists. This kind of analysis is apt, and "Assassin" is indeed a metaphorical killing of speech through the destabilization of the word. However, as theorist Adrianna Cavarero reminds us, "voice is sound, not speech," and, given the Four Horsemen's emphasis on sound and non-semantic language, we know that this is central to their work.[84] Their poems often present the creative process of revealing innate sonic elements that exist just outside of language—living in sound and gesture—but still have a communicative effect.

Thus, the sound poetry of the Four Horsemen signals more than a distrust of standardized language. It emphasizes the materiality and presence of the voice while offering an experiment in formulating connections and belonging through sound. Most strikingly, the Four Horsemen offered opportunities to rethink the conditions that forge a connection to their audience—not through the printed word but through a "sustained state of relation"[85] during a performance. We might listen to another recording from *Live in the West*, "Mischievous Eve," wherein relation and affect are strongly foregrounded. "Mischievous Eve" begins with seemingly maniacal laughter by one member, who is soon joined by the others. As the laughter reaches its peak, it sounds as though the audience has also joined in the revelry. Laughter, as it is used by the Four Horsemen within the first minute of this sound poem, highlights the passage of intensities between bodies. At times, one person may begin to laugh while another joins in, unable to control themselves. As I listen to this first minute, I find it hard not to laugh myself, and I expect the live audience might have felt similarly compelled. From this joviality, one group member's voice emerges singing, "Remember, remember the fifth of November," and the group soon enters into intense, chant-like rhythms anchored by the sustained repetition of "remember." Squeals, hums, trills, grunts, and other guttural sounds come from the rest of the group. This continues until McCaffery announces himself with the mock authority of a lecturer speaking on the "history of North American respiration." The clarity of McCaffery's speech in the recording wanes as two members repeat in airy voices, "one voice alone still cannot say what two voices together saying one thing can." They repeat this line, gradually increasing in speed and volume until they overwhelm McCaffery's voice, demonstrating the power of collective action as their two voices overpower the one voice that had previously assumed authority in the performance. McCaffery's voice becomes mostly inaudible; by the time it re-emerges, he has dropped the didactic tone and is instead chanting, "get them speaking your way," along with the other voices, until their collective chant dissolves into a variety of post-linguistic sounds, including hisses, squeaks, and grunts. McCaffery's vocal transformation and realignment with the group signifies the power of the collective voice and the transference of intensity between bodies.

Considering the references to Guy Fawkes Day (5 November), a British holiday commemorating the radical plot to explode Parliament, and the biblical story of Eve—who transgresses the command of God—Stephen Voyce argues that these allusions "collude in significant ways: both involve a transgression against property by figures whose traditional status as villains is challenged."[86] "Mischievous Eve," then, engages notions of transgression in unusual ways. In performance, it is the voice and its affect that transgresses the borders of the body (both the performers' and the audience members'). The group employs laughter at the beginning of the work as a cathectic mechanism, a means of unifying or tuning the audience into the piece, the performers, and each other. It is a transferable sonic thing that spreads throughout the audience, inciting pleasure and briefly drawing the audience into relation. We can also understand the sound of laughter in "Mischievous Eve" as a sonic extension of the self into a larger body of organisms (recall here McLuhan's notion of extension and McCaffery's remarks on biology and sound's transformative qualities). The power of sound is thematized by the exchange between McCaffery's didactic voice and the other members' chant. They do not chant persuasively at McCaffery's didactic voice to convince him to speak their way, but in so doing they nonetheless exemplify the power of their unified voice.

As implied by my brief discussion of laughter above, it was not uncommon for the Four Horsemen to encourage audience participation during their performances. As performers seizing upon the expansive capabilities of intermediality—using song, language, and performance—their work is immersive and relies on a feedback loop of energy transferred between themselves and the audience. The Four Horsemen, however, facilitated direct interactions with their audience, inviting them to be performers too.[87] Journalist Marq de Villiers described such a performance in the *Globe in Mail* in 1973:

> Waiting for a moment to begin. Then, quietly, a humming began in the front row of the audience, a nasal droning. It grew louder. The audience craned its neck to see; it was coming from a tall blonde man in a blue suede jacket. The humming broke into separate sounds, resolved itself: it was nichol [sic], and he had seemingly plucked the words from the minds of the crowd: he was chanting very softly ... "We are waiting for the moment to begin to begin we are waiting for the moment to BEGIN TO BEGIN ... " and by the end, when the beginning was done, The Four Horsemen had the audience uproariously chanting their own phone numbers while they themselves gibbered and danced up

and down and neighed shrilly into the wind and gave off harsh baboon barkings.... Images glowed and faded and slid into each other, none staying long enough to be called, really, a poem.[88]

De Villiers captures the excitement and the infectiousness of a performance by the Four Horsemen: the audience, overcome by the performance, becomes part of it, thus highlighting the "intensities that pass body to body."[89] At the opening, it seems that the Four Horsemen utilize anticipation—the feeling that combines excitement, impatience, and suspense—as the audience might eagerly wait for the event to begin. In this case, the Four Horsemen push this feeling to the fore by chanting, "We are waiting for the moment to begin to begin we are waiting for the moment to BEGIN TO BEGIN."[90] De Villiers's comments also highlight the sound poem's status as a nexus of feeling: not only do the poets express themselves, but the audience finds themselves swept up—voluntarily or not—by their energy and express themselves in unconventional ways, in this case "by uproariously chanting their own phone numbers." While the presence of sound always establishes what Steve Goodman calls a "vibratory nexus"—where sound transcends the distinction between performer and audience to create a "mesh of relation in which discreet [sic] entities prehend each other's vibrations"[91]—these cases of audience participation most directly reveal the meshing of bodies through sound and immediacy. Within the space of the Four Horsemen's events, sound, gesture, and language (as abstract as it might be in some cases) provide a means of connection; it is here that the community vibrates outside of standard modes of expression.

Owen Sound followed in the wake of the Four Horsemen, exploring similar possibilities for sound poetry, employing chants, song, polyvocal arrangements, heteroglossia, and a range of guttural and bodily soundings. They thrived, too, as a performance group, touring similar circuits as the Four Horsemen in Canada and internationally. And like their predecessors, Owen Sound composed and performed sound poetry, believing that "performance . . . was the life of sound poetry, its only real existence."[92] A sound poem like "Kinderspielgesange," performed and recorded at the eleventh International Sound Poetry Festival, reveals some of the similarities between the groups and their shared interest in facilitating energetic exchanges between themselves and their audience. "Kinderspielgesange," from their cassette *Beyond the Range: Owen Sound 1976–1979* (1980), is a ten-minute sound poem consisting of high-pitched squealing, gurgling, whistling, and animalistic sounds accompanied by harmonica, percussion, and deflating balloons. It is reminiscent of work by the Nihilist Spasm Band. The poem's title, "Kinderspielgesange," roughly translates from German to "children's game song," highlighting the work's focus on pre- and post-linguistic soundings, but also, since it uses a German title, perhaps acknowledging the beginnings of twentieth-century sound poetry with the German Dadaist Hugo Ball. The poem itself, with its strange, seemingly improvised soundscape, pushes the limits of what we consider voice, language, and sound. One such effect of this type of work, however, is not necessarily alienation or confusion but, much like the Four Horsemen's use of laughter in "Mischievous Eve," the production of pleasure and joy. Throughout the performance of "Kinderspielgesange," I hear audience members giggling and laughing intermittently, perhaps in the same way one may delight in the non-linguistic utterances of a young child.

Owen Sound's first released recording, *Meaford Tank Range* from 1977—named after a military training base and actual tank range near the city of Owen Sound, Ontario (thus invoking traditional militaristic notions of the avant-garde)—features, on its B-side, an acoustic sound poem entitled "Kesawagas." The title may reveal the group's familiarity with Rothenberg's *Technicians of the Sacred* (Rothenberg also participated in the eleventh International Sound Poetry Festival in Toronto). The piece was composed and arranged by Truhlar and, according to the album's liner notes, is based on works by Hugo Ball and American composer John Cage. Those influences can be heard in the recording, both in the phonemic play (Ball) and in the references to silence and indeterminacy (Cage). In the multi-page score to the piece, which resembles a hand-drawn concrete poem, performers are instructed to improvise their way through certain parts by reading in unison, out of sync, choosing words at random, or from different texts altogether. In part, the piece embodies, as one performer says, its status as a "lecture on composition which is indeterminate."[93] While these features are notable, Owen Sound's appropriation of the *kesawaga* is also worthy of investigation. According to Rothenberg, a *kesawaga* is "a [dance] ceremony performed by four drums, the smallest of which 'plays the complex rhythms that serve as instructions to the dancers and that can be identified and repeated in speech patterns'" native to the Trobriand Islands of Papua New Guinea.[94] Owen Sound's connection to this cultural ceremony is unclear, if indeed one exists at all. Rather, I understand this title to be a way of engaging the idea of ceremony itself, as well as the relationship between percussion and voice. This heteroglossic poem employs four voices and uses complex rhythms and repeated speech patterns. The track begins with two voices in a canon-like sequence repeating the seemingly invented words "mâ mâ piaûpa mjâma," which then fades into a vocal hum that gradually crescendos before breaking into frenetic, jazz-like vocal percussion. The loose invocation of the *kesawaga* connects the sound poem with notions of ritual, and a space for community that is guided by a specific ordering of actions and sounds in pursuit of a specific effect. "This is a lecture on composition," multiple voices state, "it cannot be repeated,"[95] which speaks to the performance's spontaneous and improvisatory elements and highlights the unique state of connection vis-à-vis the vibratory nexus that this poem seeks to offer. If Owen Sound's "Kesawagas" is to be considered a ceremony at all, it might fittingly be described as a cleansing ceremony, a poem that cleanses the listener's palette, effacing preconceived notions of what a poem can be and the ways that one can gather around the idea of poetry. It privileges spontaneity and the sense of immanence experienced by both performers and audience. With that said, this poem is another example of how an interest in global currents, and especially, non-Western cultures, led some white, anglophone poets of this generation to appropriate Indigenous traditions, a problem that requires more rigorous analysis and discussion.

While "Kesawagas" demonstrates the group's interest in heteroglossia, ceremony, non-semantic vocalization, and blurring the borders between writing and music, the influences of minimalist composers are noticeable on later releases, such as their 1987 Underwhich cassette *Sleepwalkers* and such tracks as "In the Cells," with its rhythmic pattern reminiscent of Steve Reich and Philip Glass. These musical influences partly distinguish Owen Sound from the Four Horsemen, but the group further distanced themselves by incorporating electroacoustic instruments and effects. "A Spiral of Forgotten Intimacies," composed by Steven Ross Smith and Richard Truhlar (performed and recorded at the Kontakte Writers in Performance series in Toronto on 23 February 1985), is an example of this kind of work. It consists of a single speaking voice accompanied by a low, constant, pulsing rhythm and an electroacoustic voice modulator producing a slight echo. "A Spiral of Forgotten Intimacies" is a nexus point that investigates the human acoustic voice within the context of the electronic age. The speaker meditates on feelings of alienation and confusion, and the limits of language: "What boat has brought me here / living within the walls of language / within a perplexity of cells / in an atmosphere of contained apartments / the everyday cuts in, lurking / within false language."⁹⁶ The speaker laments the disintegrating world: "we are deaf among worn stones, some former image / muscle, bone, dissolving / as the senses fade" and the natural world becomes nothing more than "green memories."⁹⁷ Given the interaction between voice and electroacoustic effects, the poem engages schizophonia and the loss of the world's natural sounds and rhythms. The electroacoustic effect has a spectral presence, distorting the natural qualities of the voice by lurking behind it as though threatening to overtake it, much in the same way the conditions of the electric age threaten the autonomy of the individual subject. The speaker describes the natural world as "a location left behind" and "a spiral of forgotten intimacies."⁹⁸ The invocation of "intimacy" characterizes the human connection with the natural world not as a chance encounter, but one of deep feeling, sensation, and intensity. "A Spiral of Forgotten Intimacies" approximates a neo-Romantic outlook in its longing for the natural world, with its rhythms, vibrations, and acoustic order.

The members of First Draft, by contrast, swerved from the path laid down by their masculinist predecessors. Recall McMaster's claim in *The Gargoyle's Left Ear*: "First Draft is also a feminist, a humanist, adventure, in which I and other women involved are there not as ornaments or organizers and the men are there not as Cool Lukes or *artistes*."⁹⁹ Though their exploration of themes and ideas related to women's subjectivity was less explicit than Kemp's in her own sound poetry (discussed below), First Draft's feminist politics were to be found in the act of collaboration itself.¹⁰⁰ The writing and performance credits for cassettes such as *Wordmusic* indicate that each member shared in these tasks, and it appears as though McMaster in many cases would write a poem and then Andrew McClure would compose the "wordmusic"—the neologism they used to describe their intermedial blend of poetry, music, and performance. In turn, that work was performed by central members McMaster, McClure, and Colin Morton (often accompanied by others). Though one group member may write a piece, there did not appear to be an onus on a single member to produce compositions, and the men in the group did not appear to eclipse McMaster or the other women.

First Draft's ambition for open and equal collaboration among members is strongly foregrounded in their sound poems. Works like "Dream Song" and "Death of a Youngish Man" use multiple voices, often simultaneously. In both pieces, however, no voice dominates another. Instead, all remain at the same volume, intonating with subtle inflections and stresses. The performers strive not for dissonance but for consonance: for example, two or more performers will speak the same lines in unison with a song-like harmony as though they are in thoughtful dialogue rather than striving for the contrived chaos we often hear in the work of the Four Horsemen or Owen Sound. First Draft strongly embodies the principles of intermedia, with multi-vocal sound poems, music, and hybrids of the two. In other cases, their recorded compositions sound more like spoken word or dramatic monologues, while others resemble the chant-based sound poetry of bissett or Nichol. Demonstrative of a borderblur poetic, First Draft's work corresponds to no single medium or genre.

Nichol edited their first book, *Pass This Way Again*, for Underwhich Editions, and they performed across Canada in libraries and universities. Surely, he would have been attracted to a poem like "ABCD" from their cassette *Wordmusic*, one of their most striking pieces, with its exploration of letters, words, and linguistic fragmentation and its dynamic shouting, whispering, and hissing. McMaster begins the poem speaking plainly: "And such divine nonsense."[101] Her words are immediately followed by the three performers, in turn, repeating, "A B C D A B C D A B C D" with varying vocal inflections. Following this sequence, they begin to repeat letter sounds as occasional words emerge from the sequence, like "abracadabra," followed by the varying repetition of "dada" until McMaster, McClure, and Morton collectively shout. As the poem nears its end, they chant "DNA" before closing with a play on the opening phrase, "such nonsense, divine." Like other sound poems produced by First Draft's contemporaries, this work, too, explores the sonic capacities of individual words and letters while carefully and precisely exploring how the sounds relate to one another. The section of the piece during which each member exaggeratedly enunciates multi-syllabic words that start with the letters *a*, *b*, *c*, and *d*, such as "ambergris," "antinomy," "arsenic," "Beelzebub," "Circes," "cinnamon," and "demon," effectively foregrounds the texture embedded in the sound of each word. The poem is informed by the idea of "divine nonsense," with the group's seemingly disconnected but calculated babbling effectively demonstrating, and perhaps reflecting upon, the arbitrary relationship between word and object.

The principles that guided many collective performances of sound poems—presence, spontaneity, a resistance to standardized language, and an emphasis on affect and emotion—also guided the work of solo performers.

A B C D

Susan McMaster

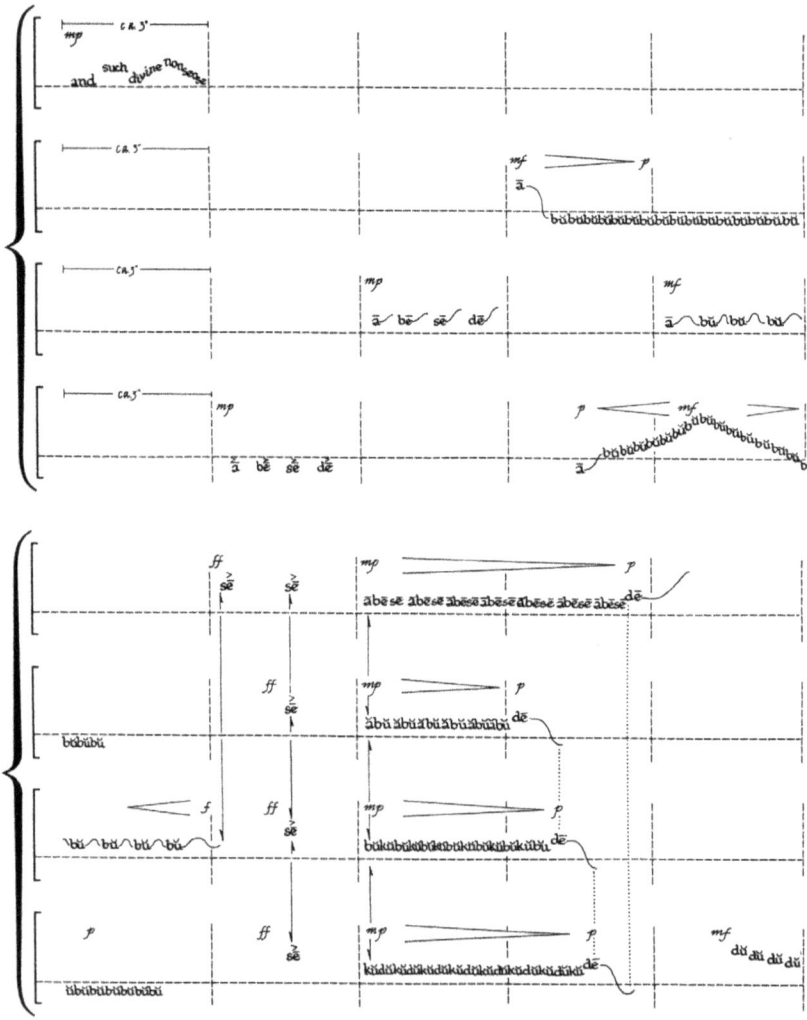

Figure 3.2: Excerpts from score for "ABCD" by Susan McMaster for First Draft, 1987.

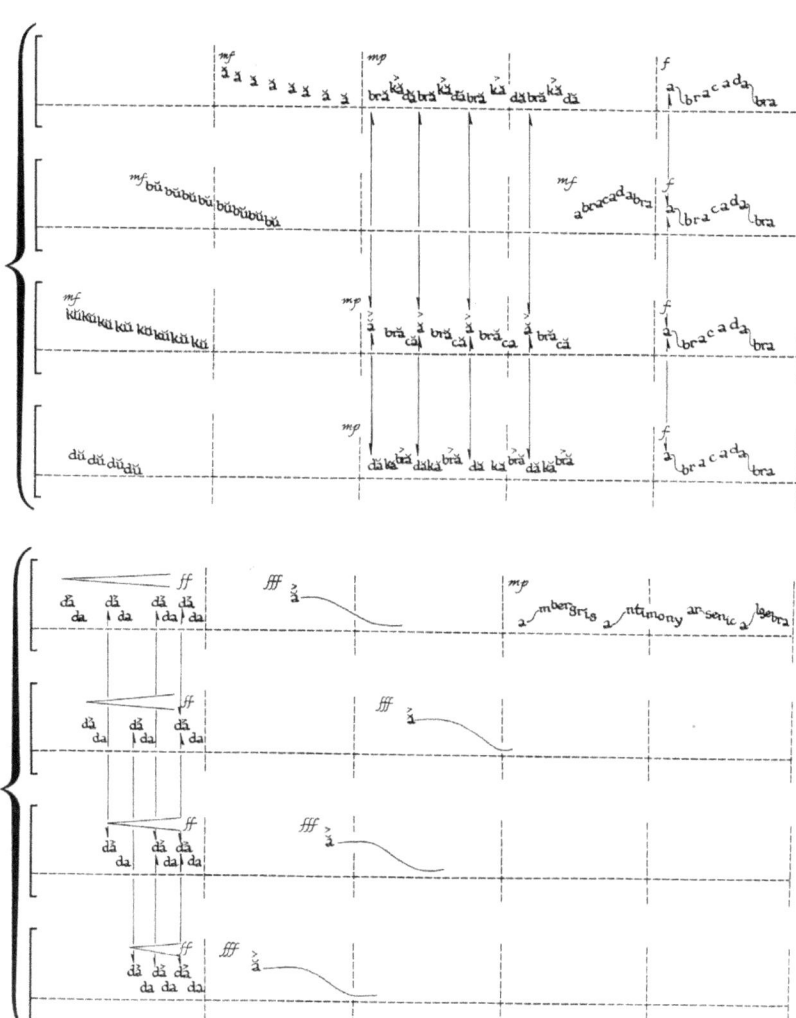

For Nichol, the sound poem was one of the fastest and most effective ways for him to access emotion. At the beginning of his poem "A Love Poem for Gertrude Stein," from the 1971 cassette *bp Nichol*, he states, "My name is bpNichol, and I'm going to approach this tape the way I would any poetry reading, and for me the best way, the thing that gets me the fastest into the poems, into the feeling, into my own breathing body, is to begin with some of my sound poems."[102] The breath, body, and feeling are what guide Nichol through his sound poems, not an imposed, formal logic or intellectual approach. Nichol's "The Incest Song," from his 1968 album *Motherlove*, illuminates his concern for sound, language, communication, and systems in the electric age. The stereo panning effect shifts Nichol's vocalizations from left to right and foregrounds Nichol's interest in the type of movement that rejects the stagnancy of systematization. "The Incest Song" is composed using parts of the word "system." He breaks the word into its phonemes, resulting in a hissing sound from "sys," which is repeated and prolonged variously throughout the poem, as well as "stem" and then the full word, "system." The poem opens with a prolonged "sysssssssss," followed by the same sound in repetition, imitating white noise as though the poem begins *in medias res* as part of a communication breakdown.[103] If the communication devices of the electric age have broken down, we are left with nothing more than sounds that exceed conventional linguistic communication: static and word fragments as the voice struggles through the electronic apparatus. Nichol's poem on communication technologies is trapped within the system he seeks to criticize: it relies on the panning mechanisms of the machine to mount the critique itself, thus expressing an implicit reliance on the system. Considering this reading of the poem, it should come as no surprise that Nichol's interest in electroacoustic sound poetics were mostly abandoned after this and other early experiments.

The systematization of language continues to trouble Nichol in a poem like "Son of Sonnet," from *bp Nichol* (1971).[104] Instead of engaging the conditions of the electric age, Nichol expands poetic convention as a way of expressing feeling, especially "love." The invocation of "son" in the title conjures a kind of Oedipal drama, a conflict between past and present and a struggle for power: the son (Nichol's poem) seeks to escape/overthrow the authority of the father (the tradition of the sonnet). The sonnet, of course, is a rule-governed form, traditionally associated with expressions of love, as typified in the works of Edmund Spenser and William Shakespeare. Nichol's poem intersects with the tradition of the sonnet, as indicated by the title, yet it discards the sonnet's conventions entirely. Instead, it consists of largely extralinguistic sounds—shouts, chants, and trills—thereby rejecting conventional literary expressions of love and affection. Indeed, if this in fact a love poem, it offers a totally alternative way of voicing that feeling. In its rhythm, the sonnet is dominated by iambic pentameter—based on the false notion that this rhythm is most like the rhythm of the human heart. Nichol's poem rejects this notion of a natural bodily rhythm from the outset, and instead continually alters the rhythm of his vocalizations which are variously rapid and frantic, slow and elongated. Nichol's poem recognizes that the body has no "natural" rhythm, just as love exceeds conventional poetic expression.

bissett's sound poetry uniquely intersects with considerations of bodies, sound, and what constitutes the idea of the "natural." Though his sound poetry continues to evolve, even to this day, I will here look at two distinctive phases of his sound poetry. The first can be situated among McLuhanesque considerations of technology as an extension of humankind, while the second represents a return to nature through vocalization (akin to Owen Sound's previously mentioned lament for a lost world). Both phases, which overlap with each other, stage radically different responses to the conditions brought about by electronic communication. In the 1960s, bissett explored the intersection of technology and language. This was perhaps most evident in his concrete poetry and his explorations of the typewriter and mimeograph machines, but it can be heard in his sound poetry too. bissett's sound poetry exceeded the vocal chanting and word merging that Tallman noted. In his performances at places like the Sound Gallery in Vancouver, bissett was experimenting with sound and lights, and, in collaboration with Lance Farrell and Martina Clinton, with tape machines.[105] These experiments indicate that bissett did not reject sound technologies in the same way as Nichol had.[106]

bissett's book-record *Awake in the Red Desert* (1968) effectively represents the range of his sound poetry and the various ways it intersected with the conditions of the electric age. The audio portion of *Awake in the Red Desert*, a twelve-inch vinyl record, consists of fourteen recordings covering a range of sound-poetic practices: solo acoustic sound poems ("o a b a"), collaborative acoustic sound poems with accompaniment from string instruments and percussion ("2 awake in th red desert!!" and "my mouths on fire"), and electroacoustic sound poems ("heard ya tellin" and "she still and curling"). A poem like "she still and curling," for example, is driven by the repeated phrase "supremely massage," which perhaps alludes to McLuhan's *The Medium Is the Massage*, published only a year earlier in collaboration with the graphic designer Quentin Fiore. The poem itself operates by simultaneously exploring several planes of sonic intensity. There is the lethargically repeated phrase "supremely massage," which is then looped backwards. This repetition is accompanied by a continually shifting synthesizer (I think) and the reading of an erotic text. These various sonic layers shift acoustic perspective as the volume of each layer is increased and decreased to accentuate the different elements of the sound poem. Kostelanetz regards most poems on this record as "widely uneven," and suggests that the instrumentation is "unnecessary, if not detrimental."[107] Presumably, Kostelanetz would find "she still and curling" to be guilty of such an offence. The poem, however, perfectly exemplifies the affective complexities of bissett's time. The poem consists of low- and high-pitched sounds, muffled and clear voices, a mixture of linguistic, post-linguistic, and pre-linguistic sound, natural and synthetic sounds, along with quickly and slowly enunciated phrases. These elements are accompanied by the literal subtext of eroticism, a key component of the poem. Indeed, considering these characteristics, the poem might indeed seem uneven, but so is the soundscape of the electric age, according to Schafer. bissett's "she still and curling" captures the confusion of sonic perspectives that prohibits the listener from situating oneself on one plane of intensity, thereby creating a sense of disorientation. As listeners, I suggest, we expect to be able to locate ourselves within a particular sonic intensity, which is why so much lyric poetry tends to follow sonic trajectories that do not thwart a listener's expectations. In other words, the affective potential of the lyric poem is at times limited by its sonic registers insofar as it fails to explore registers outside of the typical spoken voice.[108] bissett, by contrast, uses the sonic characteristics of the electric age to create a poem that embraces the possibilities of relocating and reconfiguring the self by using sound technologies to create a complex sonic environment that thwarts listeners' expectations of sonic coherence. In this way, bissett's poetry does not necessarily embrace the conditions of the electric age so much as employ the characteristics of that age to mobilize its heterogeneity of affects and create a zone within which listeners can explore and understand their own response to a complex arrangement of intensities, offering them a chance to determine their place within it and against it if they so choose.

bissett, though, is likely best known for his sound poems that explore chant and song structures using one acoustic voice. Indeed, Kostelanetz prefers these solo acoustic pieces, such as "is yr car too soft for th roads," from *Awake in the Red Desert*. Poems like this one, or "o a b a" (from the same album), employ repetitive chant structures to explore the sonic dimensions of certain words, phrases, and letters. bissett's poetry, then, sees letters as more than mere things that orient an audience toward an object. bissett's chants largely focus on letters, single words, or sentence fragments, with the goal of pushing their communicative function away from representational imagery and semantics and into an affective field. bissett's chants are permutational, exploring the potential of letters, words, phrases, and their sounds beyond their expected function in order to mobilize an expanded experience of language's materials. Instead of looking through the letters and words toward a signified object, bissett rightly locates the possibility of affect in the materials of language itself. Letters, words, and fragments, for bissett, are abundant with affective potential or intensity; hence, even when bissett is reciting from a written work, he often improvises his way across the page, leaping from section to section, repeating parts either more or less often than the page dictates. In a poem like "o a b a," bissett's chanting draws attention to the aural similarity between words like "heart" and "artery," which are also, of course, physiologically connected by the body's circulatory system. But more significantly, bissett's chanting opens a sonic field wherein the sounds of the ghostly, the animalistic, the alien, the machinic, and the human commingle in song, whispers, stutters, shouts, and speech, all of which pivots around the sounds of the three letters in the title. Using the *ahh* sound of the *a* as a refrain, bissett chants his way through letters, words, syllables, and word fragments, continually returning to the repeated sound of *ahh*. In a way that's similar to his "she still and curling" and its opening of a sonic zone, bissett's "o a b a" opens up the potential for experiences—perhaps *deeper* experiences—of feeling in linguistic art.

Liberation and transformation were also important elements of sound poetry for Kemp, who pursued a more focused project: sounding a woman's body. Kemp's cassette *Ear Rings* (1987), released as part of the Underwhich Audiographic Series, is demonstrative of these ambitions.[109] With its very title, the cassette establishes a relationship between the body (ears), listening (or hearing), and gender (with the allusion to earrings, read here as a symbol of femininity). Kemp delights in this kind of language play, using repetition, puns, fragments, and a whole range of linguistic, pre-linguistic, and extralinguistic sounds in the service of her feminist project. The opening track, "Re

Solution," which consists of an acoustic voice and accompanying violin, suggests this outright. Kemp incrementally repeats and builds morphemes into a complete sentence: "we're going to begin writing some time when electric light descends from fingertip onto computer keyboard and sets us freeeeeeee . . . may-- be--."[110] The sound poem acknowledges its socio-historical location amid a period characterized by the proliferation of electric technologies, and also indicates a belief (though hesitant) that writing can be a liberating exercise. So while *Ear Rings* meditates on several subjects, it seems, importantly, to be one of the few sound poetry albums emerging from this network to focus expressly on issues of women's sexuality, motherhood, family, and birth.

Kemp's concern for liberation is seemingly much more focused than many of her contemporaries. While others produced work that unleash free-flowing acoustic sounds, Kemp's sound poetry seeks to release her womanly body and affects. The second sound poem from *Ear Rings*, "All the Men Tall," demonstrates this, as Kemp works through a series of puns on the title phrase, moving from "All the Men Tall" and "Ele Men Tal" to "In Cre Men Tall" until finally landing on "All Men" and "A men, Amen," "ahh, ahhh ahhhh."[111] As Kemp approaches the final enunciation of "ahh ahhh ahhhh," her voice takes on a tone that seems to convey a greater sense of pleasure, perhaps an expression of orgasmic gratification through sexual intimacy with a man. In this way, Kemp rejects prudish taboos preventing women from expressing bodily pleasure in public. This type of work continues in other poems on the album. In a work like "Her Mind Set," she refers at the beginning of the sound poem to a "feminist creation myth,"[112] and a poem like "Matter Matters" continues to delight in puns to foreground issues of motherhood as the poem's title phrase is gradually transformed into "Mater Matters" and "Mother Matters."[113] These are public expressions of a woman's agency, sexuality, and desire—and an act of resistance to the patriarchal oppression felt by women displaced and alienated in a literary community dominated by masculine personalities. Kemp uses her sound poetry to oppose these conditions and instead expresses her emotions, affects, and desires in her recorded sound poetry.

The sound poetry I hear on Kemp's *Ear Rings* points me back to the conditions of the electric age, its post-modernizing economy, the emergence of affective labour, and especially the gendered characterization of such labour as "woman's work."[114] Kemp's poetry, deserving of further critical exploration, reminds me of the imagined emancipatory prospects that imbue avant-gardist practice as it has been explored in this book so far. Sound poetry, with its intermedial combination of music, poetry, and performance, is a potent means for exploring gendered and bodily autonomy, especially given the male-dominated field of sound poetry in Canada during the period under study. Like many of her peers, Kemp sought not only to find ways to bring together what are often considered disparate disciplines and thereby expand literary traditions in Canada, but she did so in the service of a greater, liberatory feminist project. Kemp was exploring these issues in the mid- to late twentieth century, and more specifically in this case the late 1980s, a time when an increasing number of voices were calling for a substantial reckoning with the problems of gender inequality. These calls, while they came from within the feminist literary movement in Canada, nonetheless transcended national borders and geographical contexts. Kemp was approaching her work with an explicit focus on gender, but to some extent, all of the sound poets explored in this chapter tried to find other, alternative means, outside of the conditions of an oppressive capitalist regime, for expressing the self, for communicating, and for developing community.

In addition to accounting for the persons and means that comprise sound poetry in Canada, the project of this chapter (and, really, of this book more generally) is to build on the existing scholarship and more forcefully place these practitioners alongside each other in order to recognize that they have all in their inimitable ways contributed to the formation of borderblur as a networked, literary paratradition in Canada. One of my hopes is that by finding common ground between better-known (among avant-garde networks at least) sound poetry groups like the Four Horsemen and Owen Sound and lesser-discussed practitioners such as Kemp or First Draft, we can begin to expand the narratives around avant-garde and intermedial literary practices in Canada. In doing so, I hope to find common ground between poets and artists across a series of projects that exceed the nationalist context and engage with the greater implications of a rapidly changing world.

4

Kinetic Poetry

> *syntax equals the body structure.*
>
> —bpNichol (1982)

In 1982, Daphne Marlatt and George Bowering asked bpNichol to elaborate on a statement he had previously made in a 1978 interview in *Outposts* to the effect that "syntax equals the body structure."[1] Admitting that his earlier statement was "over-condensed," Nichol offered the following clarification:

> I discovered—and this is what the statement comes out of—that emotionally and psychologically speaking we learn that we often armour the body, the easiest illustration of which is: if I live in a house with a low doorway, I'm probably going to end up walking like this a lot. (Hunching) I've seen tall people do this when they've lived in situations where the ceiling is low. You get an armouring of the body. I discovered that the order in which I wrote my poems allow certain contents in and keeps other contents out, i.e. the syntax that I choose, the way I tend to structure a piece, form per se, permits some contents and excludes others. So what I was trying to find, because that is part of a larger thing I've been working towards, is a way to increase my own formal range (something I'm still trying to do), and therefore not merely be stuck, shall we say, by the physical limitation of my body at that point, i.e. just because I'm walking around with my

> shoulders up like this, if I can learn to relax I can see the world in a slightly different way and so on. If I can keep moving the structure of the poem around, hopefully I can encompass different realities and different ways of looking at things.[2]

Nichol's explanation articulates a relationship between the body, movement, spatial limits, and creative processes, or, as Bowering puts it, Nichol "replaced the syntax of the image," the foundation of modernism's imagist tradition, "with the syntax of the body."[3] Nichol suggests that the body is shaped—*armoured*, to use his word—by a range of physical movements and extensions, and he uses this as an analogy for how the form of a poem shapes linguistic expression, limiting the extension of words in comparable ways. A traditional poetic form—say, a sonnet—is a type of poetic armour or container that manipulates linguistic content to make it fit within the poem, determining the language's movement, pattern, and flow. Nichol's poetic practice explores a wide range of poetic forms to extend the limits of his poetry. In other words, by employing and exploring manifold poetic structures, Nichol's poetry can be more expressive and expansive, and in the case of his kinetic poems, can invite the reader to engage with elements beyond language such as materials, bodies, movements, and sensations as though they are integral parts of the poem.

Nichol's comments to Marlatt and Bowering reveal a belief in the fundamental linkage between language, movement, and bodies. For Nichol, language instructs and influences the engagement of bodies in and with the world, shaping a person's understanding of and interactions with reality. We can interpret Nichol's suggestion that "syntax equals the body structure"[4] as a rationalization for his indulgence in unconventional poetic forms; however, such an interpretation would regretfully elide the processual relationship between body and poetry that his statement effectively highlights. While concrete poetry and sound poetry situate combinations of visual, sonic, and linguistic media and forms, these poetries partially subordinate a more holistic engagement that includes the body's capacity for movement and physical sensation (though it should be noted that some sound poetry involves theatrical performances). As a result, the previous chapters have elided a plethora of unique and under-examined activities that emerged as part of borderblur in Canada and that often exceed representation on the page, the cassette, or the vinyl record. Along with Nichol, poets such as Steve McCaffery, Gerry

Shikatani, John Riddell, First Draft, and others pursued similar ideas, creating kinetic works that combine performance, installation, game making, and more to facilitate an inward turn toward the body's complexities. Thus, much like sound poets, they also challenge us to reconsider the production of literary culture since their work did not convey the conventional materiality that characterized Canada's burgeoning national literary economy at the time. Like the works discussed in previous chapters, kinetic poetry circulated outside of the mainstream via borderblur's network of provisional institutions, effectively turning away from the national scale.

Nichol and his peers published to bring a nascent Canadian avant-garde paratradition into existence, and they did so with the intention of creating a community for concrete and sound poetries as well as kinetic poetry—indeed, they explicitly called for the latter form on the front cover of *grOnk* in January 1967. I see kinetic poetics occurring at two main interfaces: first, the intimate and unconventional encounters with the codex, and second the semi-public encounter of the performance and installation, especially those that are immersive and interactive and supported mainly by a do-it-yourself (DIY), artist-driven culture. Focusing on these two types of encounters, this chapter examines how these poets continued to explore the possibilities of intermedial expression by attending to how bodies (the poet's body and the bodies of the audience members) figure in the poetry itself as a moving, feeling thing through performances and "happenings," installations, site-specific and time-based works, interactive and game-like works, and interdisciplinary collaborations. The kinetic poem, perhaps more than any other form, most directly answers the question Nichol first posed in 1967: "how can the poet reach out and touch you physically as say the sculptor does by caressing you with objects you caress?"[5] Nichol's sound poem "Pome Poem" (1982) conveys his commitment to linking the poem to the body, as when he chants, "What is a poem is inside of your body body body body," and then proceeds to locate the poem in the eyes, toes, head, etc.[6] Here, the invocation of "your" acknowledges that the poem structures both the poet and the audience.

With these characteristics (elaborated at greater length below), kinetic poetry formed one more aspect of the multi-faceted Canadian paratradition that this book outlines. If concrete poetry can be understood as a way of grappling with the conditions of visual media amid a rapidly technologizing consumerist society, then kinetic poetry also represents a turn away from those conditions in favour of the site-specific, localized workings of body and poem in time and space. The body—the primary site of kinetic engagement—is also a site of subject formation, the underlying foundational point of Nichol's concept of "armouring" (i.e., the subject and their relation to space literally, though not entirely, determines the shape and movement of the body and its relation to the world). Thus, in its effective blurring of life and art, the kinetic work of the borderblur poets can be critically figured as a response to the conditions of the electronic age—especially electronic mediation—while troubling the idea of literature as an expression of national identity. The audience's physical experience of the work unfolds through their interactions with the poem, and the poem can only unfold (sometimes quite literally at times) in tandem with the audience's physical movements. If, in the late 1960s and early 1970s, Canada's literary community was modernizing by finding words to express its own identity on the page and to distinguish itself from other developed literary traditions, the kinetic poet turned away from that project. Instead, it came to be grounded in the fleeting immediacy of the intimate encounter with the poem itself.

I come to this work with my own body, characterized by my own abilities, thus representing my own reading/interacting experience as an able-bodied person. My readings are not meant to be authoritative in the sense of setting forth a definitive experience of each poem; rather, in the spirit of the work, they seek to embody and reflect my own physical experiences, and for this reason they may very well differ from the readings of others. At times, especially for site-specific works such as installations and performances, I come to these works more speculatively, re-imagining and reconstructing those works through careful research and dialogue with the practitioners when possible. From here, I consider the relationship between the corporeally and materially focused work of borderblur and the movements, sensations, and physical feelings that a reader may experience during the process of reading/engaging. Since kinetic poetry, in a pre-digital context, is the least theorized of the intermedial poetries examined in this book, in this chapter I first establish a theoretical framework by outlining both the critical problems related to kinetics in poetic discourse and the theorists who are crucial to my understanding of this poetic. While I have thus far often relied on statements from the poets and artists themselves to provide a contextually based sense of how borderblur proliferated in Canada, I diverge slightly from that approach here since kinetic poets have produced fewer written statements on their work. With the theoretical framework established, I then offer a historical survey highlighting the key nodes of international activity that have—inadvertently or not—affected and influenced the emergence of a kinetically focused poetic in Canada. The goal is to develop a sense of the international paratradition to which the Canadian context relates. I then map a network of activity in Canada, attending to relevant publishers, events, and organizations in an attempt to effectively capture the spirit of kinetic poetry in the English-Canadian context and to develop an acute sense of its proliferation. I conclude the chapter by looking at some illustrative works by such poets as Nichol, McCaffery, Michael Dean, First Draft, John Riddell, and Gerry Shikatani.

Toward a Theory of Kinetic Poetics

When compared to the other poetries explored in this book, kinetic poetry engages the body holistically. Sound and concrete poetry engage the body, but their domain is primarily the ocular and cochlear realms of human experience. Kinetic poetry necessarily foregrounds a different aspect of sensorial engagement: the somatic encounter with language and language's materials via the poem. Etymologically, in the Western tradition, the word "kinetic" comes from the Greek word κῑνητικός, meaning "moving," and is defined more precisely as that which pertains or relates to motion.[7] I welcome connotations of the word from sciences like kinesiology—that is, the study of bodily movements. Suzanne Zelazo's article on Nichol's bodily poetics and the female triathlete is a necessary precursor to this chapter, as she follows a similar discursive strain, examining Nichol's work from a bio-poetic critical perspective. Nichol, she writes, "emphasizes the body itself as a site of meaning and language as a site of sensation, thus generating an embodied poetics."[8] And while I do not draw from Zelazo's discourse of mind and bodily experience to examine the bodied poetics in this chapter—preferring instead Brian Massumi's and Sara Ahmed's writings on movement, bodies, and culture—her work animates my considerations of kinetic poetics as a bodily and mobile poetic form.

Kinetics, as it relates to literary studies, is usually associated with "kinetic poetry," poetry wherein the words themselves are literally in motion. Kinetic poetry is a term almost exclusively ascribed to the poetic sub-genres of video poetry and digital poetry, which are enabled by the technological advances of transnational corporations like Apple and IBM. In both digital and video poetries, movement is abetted by the fact these types of poetry use film, programming, or animation to capture and depict motion. Notable examples of this kind of work include Ana Maria Uribe's *Anipoems* (1997–2003), minimalist poems that extend the principles of 1950s modernist concrete poetry into cleanly constructed digital animations that blink, move, dissolve, transform, and shift in repeating structures; Jim Andrews's interactive poem "Seattle Drift" (1997), which investigates connections between the digital hyperlink, sado-masochism, and issues of pathway control in the digital environment; and, most relevant of course, is Nichol's *First Screening* (1984), which consists of a suite of twelve poems programmed in the Applesoft BASIC programming language on an Apple IIe computer.

My use of the term "kinetic," however, as one face of borderblur poetics, precedes digital contexts to examine poems that utilize movement as an essential part of the poetic encounter and thereby anticipate the prominence of digital tools. Returning to the basic definition of kinetics—as a pure movement—discursively re-engages the field of kinetic poetry to include works that require no electrical or digital interface (initiating a swerve from the electronic context to which so many of the poets discussed in this book responded). Doing so facilitates the inclusion of a plethora of texts, such as Nichol's flipbook poem *Wild Thing* (1967), wherein pages must be flipped in quick succession to see the movement of letter shapes, as well as several game-based works by John Riddell, like the Xeroxed book *A Game of Cards* (1985), which consists of image overlays to be cut out and applied to an existing deck of cards to include textual elements during play. The poets of the borderblur network, however, extended their concern for movement beyond the page and codex by composing performative works that similarly highlight movement and interactivity. McCaffery's 1985 piece *Renting an Apple*, for example, required participants to rent an apple for five dollars; it is a work that folds together textual references to both the Biblical mythology of Genesis and Swiss folk hero William Tell. The apple is accompanied by a choose-your-own-adventure-type pamphlet containing a series of possible performance scenarios that could be carried out with the newly leased piece of fruit. Each of these works—both codex-based and performative texts—exceed the typical scope of traditional literary production and analysis, yet each foregrounds a linkage between language, language's materials, movement, and participatory interaction as integral parts of their composition.

However, while kinetic poetry is a poetry of movement, the very concept of movement invites us to consider a range of somatic registers. Kinetic poems are time-based, interactive, immersive, and haptic. To unpack this expanded definition, I rely upon critical theorists such as Sara Ahmed, Brian Massumi, and Marshall McLuhan, whose writings help situate kinetics in the context of pre-digital poetics. Their understanding of these terms, as will be explained below, inform my thinking about kinetics and give rise to two fundamental questions: How do these poets prompt us to reconsider the limits of bodily sensation in literary texts? Moreover, what meaning is generated when the literary text—the physical materiality of the literary object or performance—emerges as part of a direct, bodily encounter with an audience? But before I seek answers to these questions, I will clarify two key terms—*touch* and *proprioception*. These have been usefully applied to discrete critical contexts, but less so in Canadian poetic discourse. And since they are at the core of my notion of a kinetic poetic, they bear some defining.

Touch is often conflated with tactility, the perception of an object (person or thing) through direct physical contact between the perceiving subject and the perceived object. This type of sensorial engagement can unfurl across at least two different planes of bodily experience. The first is that implied by the common usage of the term "touch," which describes the physiological sensation (also known as tactility) that flashes through the body and nervous system when the skin comes into contact with textures, vibrations, and temperatures, also known as tactility. The second has to do with a more rarified use of the term, which I take up via McLuhan's consideration of touch in *Understanding Media*, where he rhetorically inquires if touch is "not just skin in contact with *things*, but the very life of things in the *mind*?"[9] McLuhan's rhetorical question offers a metaphorical extension of the word "touch," which invokes affect—to touch someone not just physically but also emotionally and psychically. My sense of touch, as part of pre-digital kinetic poetry, then, implies tactility but is not reduced to it; it involves the body without necessarily making a physical impression upon it (though physical impressions do at times occur).

Sara Ahmed articulates the political dimensions of touch in her book *Strange Encounters: Embodied Others in Post-coloniality* (2000). With concern for personal and political borders, Ahmed writes, "The skin allows us to consider how boundary-formation, the marking out of the lines of a body, involves an affectivity which already crosses the line. For if the skin is a border, then it is *a border that feels*."[10] She continues to point out that "while the skin appears to be the matter which separates the body, it rather allows us to think of how the materialisation of bodies involves, not containment, but an affective opening out of bodies to other bodies."[11] Though her writing focuses primarily upon the other produced by colonial logic, Ahmed recognizes that the skin itself, as malleable as it is, demarcates the body's material and corporeal conditions—shape, size, position, and so on. The skin, for Ahmed, is a point of interface—an opening—between bodies, and between body and world: a "border that feels," she says. In part, Ahmed's discussion of the body's border resonates with similar points made by Nichol in his description of body "armouring." It is precisely the interface between the body and the poetic work that Nichol sought to blur with his slipcase *Journeying & the returns*. Nichol sought to directly engage the sensorial realm of touch to produce an opportunity for openness of the type Ahmed describes above. The poem offers a chance for commonality between the reader and poet through the physicality of engaging the work with movement and touch. The kinetic poem, then, when touched, is a zone of contact—a blurring of borders between bodies—from which a relationship and even sense of community can emerge.

Ahmed addresses touch and community in a subsequent book, *The Cultural Politics of Emotion* (2015), wherein she maintains that even in touch's metaphorical sense—i.e., to stimulate someone not physically but emotionally and psychically—it creates social bonds. Ahmed traces the etymological root of the word "contingency," which she recognizes has the "same root in Latin as the word 'contact' (Latin: *contingere: com*, with; *tangere*, to touch)."[12] She writes that

> Contingency is linked in this way to the sociality of being "with" others, of getting close enough to touch.... So what attaches us, what *connects* us to this place or that place, to this other or that other is also what we find most touching; it is that which makes us feel. The differentiation between attachments allows us to align ourselves with some others and against other others in the very processes of turning and being turned, or moving towards and away from those we feel have caused our pleasure and pain.[13]

For Ahmed, whose thinking resonates with McLuhan's point about touch in *Understanding Media*, contingency—as a form of physical contact or emotional touching—is what binds persons to places, things, and other persons. Touch allows a person to form an attraction (personal or political) to another, or, conversely, they can be repelled by it. Hence, a poet like Nichol, and many borderblur poets who reject singular ideas of a poem's form, seek to offer as many pathways into and out of the poetic work as possible. In doing so, they open as many channels for communication, and offer the audience as many zones of contingency and attachment, as possible.

With touch comes another important conceptual consideration for this chapter, which is the individual's perception and awareness of their own body in both position and movement. This sense of awareness is commonly referred to as *proprioception*. Proprioception is similar to touch in the way that both terms describe the registration of sensation, a feeling or awareness that is external to language. Like touch, proprioception requires an engagement with the perceiving subject's body, but it is distinguished from touch by the fact that the actual interface of the perceiving subject and the perceived object need not make surface-to-surface contact. Referring to it as the unrecognized sixth sense, Massumi provides a succinct definition of proprioception; he suggests that proprioception is "defined as the sensibility proper to the muscles and ligaments as opposed to tactile sensibility (which is 'exteroceptive') and visceral sensibility (which is 'interoceptive')," and further that it "folds tactility into the body, enveloping the skin's contact with the external world in a dimension of medium depth: between epidermis and viscera."[14] Lastly, for Massumi, "Proprioception is a self-referential sense, in that what it most directly registers are displacements of the parts of the body relative to each other."[15] In other words, proprioception is a subject's inner sensibility of one's body in relation to its surroundings and movements—the subject's ability to sense the place or movement of a limb or digit, as well as the subject's ability to sense the body as it moves through space. For example, Nichol imagined a tall person who registers the height of a low-hanging ceiling by hunching as they move below it. This chapter's interest in proprioception, as a means of accessing and understanding the literary engagements of borderblur, is grounded in the way kinetic poetry makes us aware of the position and movement of the body—especially the "reader's" body—in the same way that touch makes us aware of the sensations at the literal zone of contact.

Proprioception, as it applies to borderblur, is fundamentally closer to the physiological usage of the term than previous literary uses (more on Charles Olson, poets affiliated with *TISH*, and their "proprioceptive writings" later in this chapter). The proprioceptive poetry of borderblur is less about the introspection of the writer and more about the poet's and audience's awareness of their bodies in relation to the literary work, in essence how a literary work shapes, positions, and moves the body. Proprioception is essential to consider in any analysis of the performative works of the borderblur poets, especially those that are meant to provide an immersive experience for the audience, like Michael Dean's *The Imagination of Aldo Breun* or Gerry Shikatani's *Sans Titre*, both of which invite the audience into locations designed with specific attention to language, interaction, and space. In addition to the distinction between touch and proprioception, two other distinctions must be made. Kinetic poetry, understood here as a pre-digital creative mode, while it shares characteristics with breath poetics and embodied poetics, which emphasize the somatic registers as represented in writing, is nonetheless distinct from both modes.

Olson is an influential figure for proprioceptive writing and the concept he refers to as "composition by field," a poetry that relies on the typewriter and its capacities to express the poet's breath on the page. As Olson envisioned it, the idea of composition by field sought an expansion of poetic form that deviates from the traditional verse structures of previous centuries. Rather than sonnets and sestinas, Olson argued that "Verse now, 1950, if it is to go ahead, if it is to be of *essential* use, must, I take it, catch up and put into itself certain laws and possibilities of the breath, of the breathing of the man who writes as well as of his listenings."[16] The breath, then, rather than the structures of formally fixed poetry, becomes the guide to the visual movement of language on the page. The poet's breath is said to allow "*all* the speech-force of language back"[17] into the poem. To do so, the breath of the poet is registered on the page by the typewriter. The typewriter, as a primary tool of the poet in the mid-twentieth century, often imprints the page using a monospace font, thus, if the "poet leaves a space as long as the phrase before it," writes Olson, "he means that space to be held, by the breath, an equal length of time."[18] The typewriter, then, allows the poet to guide the reader's breathing through the lines of the poem. For Olson, breathing should only occur at the line break; thus, if lines and line breaks are shorter, then the reader breathes more rapidly. Likewise, if the space after the line break is long, the reader's breathing should be slowed down. The poem, guided by a poetics of breath, seeks the direct transference of the poet's living, breathing self onto the page. In this way, somatics are emphasized in the poetry, thus drawing it into proximity with what I am building as a definition for kinetic poetics. "Composition by field" might best be described as a proto-kinetic mode. In "composition by field," the poem is a metonymic representation of the poet's body on the page as it engages the mechanical operations of analog writing technology. In that case, however, the reader of the poem, if they read the poem aloud and precisely, are partially recreating the author's bodily processes, not their own. So, while this may appear kinetic in that it emphasizes physicality and visual movement, it is an author-driven experience, which differs from the openness of kinetic poetics as borderblur poets have realized it.

Likewise, embodied poetics denote poetries grounded in the somatic, but deviate from kinetic poetry in ways similar to "composition by field." Embodied poetics, in this instance, refers to specific feminist poetic practices that emerged in the 1970s and '80s in the writings of Nicole Brossard and Daphne Marlatt. Embodied poetics refers to the writing of a particular kind of body—women's bodies. This movement in poetics, in part, developed from the 1976 essay "The Laugh of the Medusa" by French critical theorist Hélène Cixous, wherein she proclaims, "Woman must write her self: must write about women and bring women to writing."[19] Cixous's call resonated with poets and critics in Canada, who took up this premise. Canadian critic Barbara Godard, for example, wrote her touchstone essay "Excentriques, Ex-centric, Avant-Garde: Women and Modernism in the Literatures of Canada" (1984), which describes what she calls *texte de femme* and employs specific adjectives to describe women's writing. She calls it "diffuse, disorder[ed], circular, multiple, unpredictable, unstructured and uncensored."[20] The question of how to write women's bodies was by the late 1980s a contentious issue for many writers, including Daphne Marlatt, Lillian Allen, and Jeanette Armstrong, who debated how and why this writing must be done at the 1983 Women and Words/Les Femmes et les Mots conference. Embodied poetics, as a movement in Canada, developed concurrently with the activities of borderblur, and indeed in some cases crossed over into distinctively related poetic territories. However, embodied poetics is distinguished from kinetic poetry because, like "composition by field," it is a *representation* of the body on the page in language. It captures the poet's sense of the body in language, but it does not literally engage touch and the materiality of language. Embodied poetry may register the body in language, but it does not necessarily formulate a literal zone of contact by invoking touch, kinetics, or proprioception.

Each of these experiential constituents, and all of the nuance that must necessarily accompany these terms, inform kinetic poetry that emerged as part of the borderblur network. Kinetic poetry gestures toward language as it encourages the reader's body to move, shape, and engender a physical awareness. This is a type of poetry that centres on a different type of output: that of the feeling that sends sensations to the surface of the skin, to the muscles, and relies upon specific positioning and movements as the core of interaction within the literary work. The process by which such engagement occurs—like concrete poetry and sound poetry—is a creative mode of literary output that purposefully subverts standard literary conventions such as grammar, syntax, spelling, narrative, and, at times, language itself by directly engaging the somatic realm of bodily movement. Just as concrete poetry is composed of the visual materials of language, and sound poetry is composed of the sonic materials of language, kinetic poetry is embedded within and around the poem, in its immediate materials, space, and time. Further, kinetic poetry is embedded within the poem's materials to produce tactile and embodied sensation: it is located within the movements and velocity that a poem requires of a body; in the awareness of a body and its muscles, tissues, and ligaments as it engages the literary object, performance, or space. Kinetic poetry is a poetry that directly impacts the body's relationship with language, materiality, and space, recognizing that a poem can be an open interface. In these ways, kinetic poetry is borderblur par excellence.

Before concluding this section, some initial concerns regarding kinetic poetry must be addressed. Critical discussions of poetry that can be located within a kinetic discourse—notably, the kinetic poetry of borderblur—risk falling into a variety of traps. The first is similar to the problem that I confronted with sound poetry: the problem of materiality. For example, the Four Horsemen's game "Andoas" (1979) was only released as a set of instructions in *Only Paper Today*. The game requires players to make their pieces and board themselves. Furthermore, a game like "Andoas" is entirely dependent upon the production of variable outcomes of the game itself, or in other words, how the players choose to pursue an end point (if they decide to pursue one at all). With four people simultaneously playing this literary game, the outcome can differ in dramatic ways, depending on whether or not the game is played co-operatively or competitively. A number of these works, too, are site-specific, such as the sporadic happenings put on by Ed Varney, Maxine Gadd, and Judith Copithorne in the early 1970s, Gerry Shikatani's performances in the 1980s, and Michael Dean's November 1981 installation *The Imagination of Aldo Breun*, which was part of *The Symposium of Linguistic Onto-Genetics*. These works can never be fully recreated outside of the small geographical and temporal windows within which they were realized, and they exist now only on the periphery of Canadian literary culture; they are documented in books, periodicals, and online, recalled in essays or photo essays, and live on in the memories of performers and audience members. They are not materially, corporeally, or experientially accessible in the present moment.

While recognizing that these works cannot be returned to, and that there is no substitute for primary experience, this chapter relies on secondary materials. In some cases, carefully considered speculation is necessary for understanding these works. Furthermore, as with sound poetry, some literary objects, like Nichol's *Wild Thing*, are less accessible—available only from rare booksellers or institutional archives. Going forward, I am conscious of the complexity posed by these problems as I piece together the narrative and my accompanying criticism. More significantly, the limited availability of these works indicates a resistance to the commodification of the literary object, a necessary component of the CanLit Boom as a print-driven nationalist project. In this way, by keeping the poem enclosed, temporary, and immaterial, kinetic poetics necessarily elides any kind of national literary project and instead privileges the local, immediate, and minute.

Kinetic Art and Literature: Borderblur's Kinetic Context

From the early to mid-twentieth century, before borderblur was established as a paratradition in Canada, kinetics manifested as part of a diverse body of investigations into the promises of intermedial expression. As in the cases of concrete poetry and sound poetry, kinetic poetry emerged in Canada in dialogue—at times inadvertently so—with international nodes of poetic activity, many of which drew from avant-garde and intermedial paratraditions. In the found and ready-made sculptures of Marcel Duchamp, such as his *With Hidden Noise* (1916), a collaboration with Walter Arensberg made with twine, brass plates, long screws, engraved text, and a mysterious unknown object apprehended only by shaking the structure (locked inside of it by Arensberg); in the ever-shifting sculptures and "avant-gardening" of Ian Hamilton Finlay and his immersive poetic environment he called Stony Path/Little Sparta (1966/1983); in Brazilian avant-garde movements like the non-verbal extension of concrete poetics known as *poema processo*, grounded in the use of abstract signs, symbols, and geometric figures, and an emphasis on reader participation and collaboration; in the intermedial and participatory works of Fluxus artist Ben Vautier, especially his destructive artwork *Total Art*

Matchbox (1965); and in the participatory, instruction-based, and de-materialized works of conceptual art by Yoko Ono in her *Grapefruit* (1964), the tactile, kinetic, and proprioceptive aspects of language are vital factors of artistic and poetic experiment.

These nodes of poetic and artistic production—from Dada to conceptual art—provide convincing proof that kinetics, as McLuhan points out, has remained an abiding concern for writers and artists for well over a hundred years.[21] I consider these works kinetic because these artists and poets made conscious efforts to explore the intersection where ergodic interaction and language meet. In one way or another, each of these movements or artists intersect with the discourse of the kinetic, and the ideas embedded within their works found their way into Canada by way of exhibitions, performances, and publications. However, the work championed by Black Mountain–affiliated poets such as Charles Olson and Robert Duncan, known as proprioceptive writing, explicitly affected the development of poetry on the Canadian West Coast. Recounting the work of Duncan, whose writing proved to be influential for the Vancouver editors of *TISH* magazine, Warren Tallman describes the proprioceptive writer as one who "sees the surrounding world in the midst of himself as subject."[22] Tallman further explains that "in the proprioceptive sentence SELF becomes the subject, the WRITING becomes all verb, and the OBJECT is life, to live."[23] Proprioceptive writing, then, according to Tallman, is an arguably ego- and subject-centred adaptation of proprioception that circumvents the actual physiological dimension of the term. Proprioceptive writing, according to Tallman's description, approximates confessional modes of writing wherein the I-voice of the poem represents the divulgence of a personal, subjective account of that subject's experience in the world. It misconstrues the actual proprioceptive elements—namely, that proprioceptive writing is based on the subject-object relationship characterized by constant formation and re-formation. The writing is, in a way, documentation of this processual relationship.

Proprioception is actually more bodily than Tallman seems to recognize, though certainly no less egocentric, since the proprioceptive poem is often, though not always, subject-centred. These ideas are most clearly stated in Olson's writing, both his essay "Projective Verse" (1950) and his manifesto "Proprioception" (1965). Olson introduced the idea of proprioception to North American literary communities, describing it as

> the data of depth sensibility/the "body" of us as
> object which spontaneously or of its own order
> produces experiences of, "depth" Viz
> SENSIBILITY WITHIN THE ORGANISM
> BY MOVEMENT OF ITS OWN TISSUES.[24]

This thinking about the body with its stimulations and tensions runs parallel to Olson's poetics essay "Projective Verse," published half a decade earlier, wherein he developed the idea of the "open poem."

The "open poem" consists of "the syllable, the line, as well as the image, the sound, the sense," and these elements "must be taken up as participants in the kinetic of the poem just as solidly as we are accustomed to take what we call the objects of reality; and that these elements are to be seen as creating the tensions of a poem just as totally as do those other objects create what we know as the world."[25] Olson's description of the poem here is bodily. It is a way of foregrounding the body—as a receptor and holder of these tensions—as the principal element of a poem's composition, rather than rhyme or metre, common to lyric poetry, and the dominant poetic mode of the time, especially in Canada. What holds this together as a coherent work is the tension between the elements of the poem and the poem's relation to the poet's body: "the HEAD, by way of the EAR, to the SYLLABLE / the HEART, by way of the BREATH, to the LINE."[26] Breathing is how the poem is truly projected into voice and onto the page: "It is the advantage of the typewriter that, due to its rigidity and its space precisions, it can, for a poet, indicate exactly the breath, the pauses, the suspensions even of syllables, the juxtapositions even of parts of phrases, which he intends."[27] Therefore, the poet is a receptor of sensations from the world who then engages and projects those sensations in language and breath back out into the world in a poem, organized by the proprioceptive processes of the body: "SENSIBILITY WITHIN THE ORGANISM / BY MOVEMENT OF ITS OWN TISSUES."[28]

Duncan's and Olson's writings—especially their proprioceptive works—were, as noted earlier in this book, influential for the Vancouver poets who gathered around *TISH*. It was Duncan who prompted the young undergraduates to adopt the name *TISH*, an anagram of "shit," as the title of their publication. Duncan suggested the name because archaeologists "had no idea what the people were eating except in those few fossilized remains [i.e., of feces]."[29] The fossil conjures images of excess (bodily waste) but also fertility and growth; it is a deposit from a previous existence. The poem, for *TISH* poets, is a product of particular genealogies and results from consumption. The bodily connotations of the name also correspond to Olson's notion of "projective verse." The newsletter served as a means of projecting the ideas, feelings, and experiences of these young UBC undergraduates out into the world, again corresponding to bodily processes of consumption and excretion. George Bowering's poem "Poet as Projector" provides the best evidence of Olson's influence on the *TISH* poets: "I do not interpret, / I switch on & I switch out, / I enlarge the film, / my latent image of all phenomena."[30] These lines are representative of *TISH*'s adoption of Black Mountain poetics, which emphasizes non-lyrical modes of writing, the page as an open field.

The activities of the *TISH* poets draw us back into proximity with borderblur. For Nichol, these poets served as a foundational foil for his own work, which he developed more intensively in relation to *blewointment*. In 1974, he told Nicette Jukelevics that when he was living in Vancouver he was

> sitting in on a bunch of the workshops that some people from *Tish* were conducting, heavy discussions about the relationship of form and content. At that time this was very new to me, I used to sit there and shudder at the implications of what was discussed. Anyway, this opened up another dimension for me. And when bissett once again came out with the *Blew Ointment* issues, I got a sense of inspiration, the kind of inspiration that comes from a person who is also interested in the same thing, the inspiration of somebody communicating exactly what you are interested in and are doing.[31]

Nichol's comments remind us of the beginnings of borderblur, of bissett and *blewointment*, and the poetics that emerged as they developed a genuinely kinetic poetic that was influenced by both Canadian and non-Canadian texts but was never derivative of those preceding and concurrent influential forms.

International movements like concrete poetry, intermedia, conceptual art, and performance art impacted Canadian arts and culture in various ways. Robust studies and histories offered in books such as *Traffic: Conceptual Art in Canada, 1965–1980*, edited by Arnold Grant and Karen Henry (2012); *Caught in the Act: An Anthology of Performance Art*, edited by Tanya Mars and Johanna Householder (2004); *Performance au/in Canada,*

1970–1990, edited by Alain-Martin Richard and Clive Robertson (1991); and online projects like *Ruins in Process: Vancouver Art in the Sixties*, document some of the ways these international movements influenced certain artistic and poetic communities in Canada. Kinetic poetry in Canada emerged both as a successor to and in concert with these poetic and artistic investigations. However, kinetic poetry has not been treated to the sort of critical, historical, and theoretical writings that stimulated the proliferation of other movements in Canada. In some cases, Canada is among the many locations where these movements flourished (intermedia, performance art, conceptual art), while in other cases, earlier movements prefigured Canadian arts and literary culture, as was the case with Dada in its historical incarnation. The emergence of kinetic poetry as a strain of borderblur had no single catalyst—no event, author, or manifesto. It did not result from the arrival of another art or literary movement. Rather, kinetic poetry—much like concrete and sound poetry—emerged independently in Canada, growing rhizomatically before it was enmeshed within a national and international nexus of art and literary cultures.

It could be said that all of the previously mentioned movements, in some way or another, influenced the development of kinetic poetry in Canada. These other poetic and artistic practices, however, tend to privilege one type of engagement over another: kinetic works of art or performance tend to privilege the somatic over the semantic; likewise, the poetries that approximate kinetic modes are more interested in linguistic expression than somatic expression (as in the case of proprioceptive writing). In each case, language and kinetics are not wholly fused to create what I refer to as a kinetic poetry wherein language, language materials, and the body are intricately bound up in the work. The kinetic poetry of borderblur marks a departure from its historical predecessors in the way that the poets in question brought together these elements to create poetry that breaks down the wall between poet and audience, language, and body.

For the kinetic poetry of borderblur, the wall separating bodies and language was dissolved thanks to a particular and unique relationship that these poets had with media and technology—as was true of concrete poetry and sound poetry. McCaffery argues that sound poetry emerged again in the 1950s in response to electroacoustic voice technologies and the tape machine.[32] Likewise, some kinetic poetry emerged in Canada because of the increased access to print materials and technologies. Canadian poets seized upon newly accessible "portable, inexpensive electric or electronic equipment," which not only permitted a "multiplicity of aesthetic systems, or even value systems," but also gave poets and artists opportunities to more deeply engage with the materials of their work, which allowed them to imagine new possibilities for the way a text can move and feel.[33] In their published works, they therefore paid close attention to layout, design, typography, paper type, binding, and so on. All of these factors became a meaningful part of the process of poetic production since much of the work emanating from the Canadian borderblur network was produced and circulated by provisional institutions. As such, the poet's body (labour) and mind (intellect) were perhaps more deeply embedded or entangled within their work. The bodies of poet and audience also became more closely approximated to the language and the materiality of this work, thus closing the distance between poet, poem, and audience. It was this access to and control over these new media technologies, fused with a DIY sensibility, that prompted the proliferation of kinetic poetry. To gain a deeper understanding of the relationship between media and the emergence of kinetic poetry—and to begin accounting for the development of kinetic poetics in a Canadian context—I turn again to McLuhan, whose writings profoundly influenced the generation of poets covered in this book, and these writings include meditations on touch and extension.

McLuhan's theories of media extension gesture toward kinetic discourse, which—inadvertently or not—underpins his critical considerations of the interface between humans and technologies that are external to the human body. McLuhan's claim that "all media are extensions of our own bodies and senses"[34] is based on a deceivingly simple premise. He asserts that media is a means by which humans extend their abilities. The telephone augments human communication by allowing it to take place at a faster speed and across longer distances. By using the telephone, humans can receive linguistic (and extralinguistic) data that stimulates the mind and body in various ways, depending upon how the individual's feelings unfold from the interaction. In this way, the functional capacities of media literally extend the range of human input and output.

But McLuhan's writings on media as an extension of humans' communicative abilities can also sustain a more complex reading, at which point they appear almost like science fiction. For McLuhan, the significance of media during the electric age exceeds its utilitarian function to become a corporeal prosthetic with a direct impact on the kinetic realms, including touch and proprioception. The media technologies that humans employ in their day-to-day lives directly correspond not just to the outward extension of the human body, nor to the inward reception of stimulation: rather, media directly influences and shapes the physical and psychic life of humans. This is an idea that underpins much of McLuhan's writing, spelled out as early as 1951 in his book *The Mechanical Bride*, wherein, anticipating technological singularity, he anxiously claims that "technology is an abstract tyrant that carries its ravages into deeper recesses of the psyche,"[35] and further that "as terrified men once got ritually and psychologically into animals, so we already have gone far to assume and to propagate the behaviour mechanisms of the machines that frighten us and overpower us."[36] In this case, McLuhan's consideration of technology describes the modulating capacities of media—how a medium attaches itself, parasite-like, to the body of the user and influences that user's experience of tactility, movement, and proprioception. In this way, McLuhan conceives of media and the body much in the same way that Nichol conceives of a poem's form as "armour."

    McLuhan maintains his position on media as a literal extension of the human body in later works like *The Medium Is the Massage* (1967). In this text, McLuhan swerves from the sort of idiosyncratic academic writing found in *The Mechanical Bride* and instead issues a series of provocative statements—"The wheel . . . is an extension of the foot,"[37] "clothing, an extension of the skin,"[38] and "electric circuitry, an extension of the central nervous system"[39]—that, in a collagist fashion, are placed against images. The title, *The Medium Is the Massage*, foregrounds the inherent kinetic quality of media by invoking massage—an engagement with the muscles and tissues of the body via flesh-to-flesh contact that, if successful, has tremendous (if only temporary) effects on the body's feeling and composure. Indeed, the use of media is a similarly intimate affair. For example, a telephone requires a short range of finger motions across a number pad (or along a rotary dial, or today a touch screen) in quick succession to achieve aural contact with another person on the other end of the line. Thus, to use that media, the body must always satisfy a predetermined program of kinetic engagements—primarily movements and tactile sensations—that are encoded within the medium. As the body repeats these movements, they become embedded within the body in what is commonly referred to as muscle memory. Likewise, before the rise of mobile devices, a film required viewers to position their bodies toward a screen and in a position comfortable enough, typically, to remain stationary for longer than an hour. Within the folds of this medium, one should not move, otherwise the film will be missed. Each of these examples demands the body to touch, move, and perceive actions in particular ways and at particular speeds in order for the medium to be engaged. These engagements occurring on the level of kinetics (with touch and proprioception) shape the individual and a community's sense of their world.

With the advent of telecommunication technologies came what McLuhan famously referred to as the global village, a shrinking sense of the distance between persons as well as an increased sense of alienation, since these communications mediate interpersonal experiences, establishing a veil or barrier between one person and another. In this way, McLuhan presciently teased out a core condition of the postmodern age—an increase in the means of communication coupled with an increasing sense of alienation. McLuhan takes note of this problem in *Understanding Media*: "Our mechanical technologies for extending and separating the functions of our physical beings have brought us near to a state of disintegration by putting us out of touch with ourselves" (and, I would add, with one another).[40] For McLuhan, the telephone and tape machine, for example, offer a means of communication, but in a disembodied form. Thus, the possibility of a kinetic encounter with another person as part of a face-to-face meeting diminishes. Instead, this communicative process becomes a kinetic encounter with a non-human mechanism—a telephone, a radio, a book, a poem—thus denying possibilities for an imminent human community. In other words, communication is less intimate.

The problem McLuhan poses here is out of phase with other comments he makes regarding the emotional and psychic resonance of kinesis, or what he refers to as "the life of things in the *mind*."[41] This dissonance in McLuhan's thinking is not easily reconcilable, but it is crucial to keep both points in mind. McLuhan's point regarding the problems of disembodiment and technology highlights an anxiety or discomfort some people may have around the use of new communication technologies and the way these can change the relationship between materials and bodies as well as bodies and other bodies. This is an issue that the poets of the borderblur network addressed in their work in various ways. They sought to renegotiate the conditions governing kinetic encounters with the poem. By taking an interest in touch, this problem is partially solved. An investment in touch during the emergence of an internationalizing world is a means of healing the disintegrating self and subject; it is a means of reinstating a conscious, tactile connection between people's inner and outer lives, a point of interface that McLuhan believes is significantly altered by the conditions of the electronic age.

In *Understanding Media*, McLuhan confirms that the artistic zeitgeist that informed borderblur was concerned with touch as a crucial part of day-to-day and artistic experience: "For more than a century now artists have tried to meet the challenge of the electric age by investing the tactile sense with the role of a nervous system for unifying all the others."[42] For McLuhan, acknowledging touch is crucial during postmodernity's emergence. It is a period characterized by seemingly shrinking distances (thanks to the possibility of telecommunications technologies), but also by increasing mediation between bodies (as a result of those same telecommunications technologies). Understanding the impact of media and technology on the body in this way partly explains the impetus behind the concrete poetry and sound poetry of Canadian borderblur. They purposefully misuse their technologies—writing machines, books, tape machines, and language—to resist standardization, to resist the physical and psychic conditions imposed upon the body of the poet and the user. However, it also begins to explain the impetus for a whole range of related activities wherein the interface of work, with its materials and audience, is engaged on the kinetic level. In Canada, these ideas were the impetus for new and daring artistic endeavours, new communal formations, new publishing ventures, and new ways of blurring the borders between art and life.

Kinetics and Poetics in Canada

To move this discussion from the theoretical and conceptual planes to the level of practice, I return to bill bissett, whose early work, as I have mentioned elsewhere in this book, was influenced by McLuhan. bissett's *blewointment* magazine, for example, proved to be a significant forum for the development and popularization of kinetic poetry in Canada, notably for its collagist aesthetic. Michael Turner gestures toward *blewointment*'s tactile qualities as he recounts differences between *TISH* and *blewointment* in the early 1960s:

> While the TISH newsletter was a clean and neatly-typed affair, filled with poems of a 1950s modernist bent, blewointment's first issue emphasized the concrete nature of the written language, not just in its phonetically shortened form ("reveald") but through misspellings ("wgich," "abstracion"). Although the poems in blewointment also had a localized modernist sensibility, woven

between them were drawings and collage elements made up of newspaper clippings and handbills, many of which ("wgich"?) were supplied by bissett.[43]

bissett's collages are grounded in kinetic experience. For example, in some issues, extraneous materials are pasted into *blewointment* that are more diversely textured than the mimeographed pages; these include hand-painted scraps or pieces of paper that unfold and are handled differently. In some cases, a single issue of *blewointment* would be created using different types and sizes of paper, thus drawing the reader's attention to the way the periodical is touched, held, and moved as they navigate the different paper sizes, flipping the issue around to see upside-down images or running their fingers along a differently textured page. Issues of *blewointment* sometimes varied in physical form quite dramatically. The "Fascist Court" special issue, for example, contains several different types of paper––including smaller papers that fold out, a thin red strip with a quote from John Lennon, and textured paper with a picture of bissett.

Due to the "makeshift conditions of production many of bissett's original collages from these publications [*blewointment*] have been lost."[44] However, bissett began experimenting with collagist techniques well before he launched *blewointment*. Keith Wallace, who organized an exhibition of West Coast assemblages entitled *Rezoning*, suggests that "for bissett, collage and assemblage is a visceral activity, an endeavor to become 'one' with the materials of his world."[45] Like Duchamp before him, bissett employs a variety of at-hand materials to construct his work: one of his sculptural assemblages, for example, sees a wooden frame enclose a visual poem, and a torn scrap of printed media hanging in the top left corner while an *a, s,* and *c* rest in the bottom right corner. The wooden frame is backed by additional triangular materials, and overlaying the piece are the words "ice & cold storage." *Vancouver Mainland Ice and Cold Storage* is also the name bissett gave to a book published in 1974 by Bob Cobbing's Writer's Forum, and a photograph of the assemblage was used for the cover.

bissett was also, for a time, affiliated with a loose organization of artists and poets in Vancouver, known as the Intermedia Society, whose work explored, researched, and promoted the immersive, interactive, proprioceptive possibilities of art and literature (as well as communal working). The group's name was likely derived from Dick Higgins's characterization of the international Fluxus movement and other art forms that fall between media. In 1967, Intermedia leased a building that became a multi-purpose hub for like-minded Vancouver artists. It contained studios for film editing, sound recording, installations, dance, performance, and many other arts. bissett produced work there and performed with the Mandan Massacre. That this collective named themselves Intermedia once again gestures toward the cosmopolitan imagination of these artists and poets, who saw their work as located within cross-cultural currents of activity rather than solely growing out of or in response to the conditions of their immediate culture.

In addition to bissett, members of the Intermedia Society included some other and by now familiar names, including Judith Copithorne, Maxine Gadd, Ed Varney, Gregg Simpson, and Gerry Gilbert. Intermedia first formed to "discuss Marshall McLuhan's theories on how electronic media, particularly television, was transforming our world into a 'global village.'"[46] Stimulated by these ideas and committed to social action and change, the group formed in 1967 with the help of a $40,000 Canada Council grant. The society centred around the creation of environments and participatory installations. Members made objects that were often used in interventions or as props for photographs. There was a great deal of interest in time-based projects, including film and video. Much of the activity was conceptual and process-oriented. The artworks were ephemeral and interpersonal in nature, involving performance, poetry, and dance.[47]

While Intermedia initially formed around media and technology, kinetics—and general somatic stimuli—figured strongly in the work of these artists. Copithorne confirms this element: "I saw Intermedia as to do with process and variety. I saw Intermedia to be the human media, not the mechanical media."[48] A great deal of the work that Intermedia produced incorporated the body in a variety of ways. In 1970, for their last show at the Vancouver Art Gallery, the group organized an installation entitled the *Dome Show*, which took place from 19 to 30 May. The show was organized around a series of geodesic domes, which Intermedia members were invited to build individually or communally. Various performances and events took place within the domes, including poetry readings, listening sessions, and musical performances. The *Dome Show* hinged on process-oriented and temporally based experiences: "if you were present at a happening and were documenting, it meant you weren't in the moment, and that wasn't cool."[49] Within a dome, then, the body—with its interactions and reactions to the event and to the other bodies within that space—served as an integral part of the performance and reading.

Intermedia and *blewointment* were representative of the emergent countercultural movements that were sweeping across Canada during this period—which included DIY sensibilities, artistic autonomy, utopian political visions, collectivity, and drug use. Another common type of event that emerged as part of the counterculture is referred to as a "happening," which is primarily associated with performance, improvisation, and participation. "Happenings" rely upon the energy between artist and audience and demand the audience to be fully present in the moment of the event. The *Dome Show* presented by Intermedia facilitated these types of events; however, they also occurred in less contrived settings. For example, poets Gadd, Varney, Gilbert, and Henry Rappaport staged happenings in front of unsuspecting students at UBC sometime in February 1970. Varney recalls what happened: "Gerry Gilbert, Henry Rappaport, Maxine Gadd and I did a free-wheeling poetry event which mostly consisted of us shouting our poems across the campus and making a lot of noise."[50] After reading this, I recall my own experiences of disruption on university campuses—protests, performances, conflicts, parties—and how those moments quickly redefine my sense of the space and my awareness of my body within it. I can imagine a similar reaction if I were confronted by Gadd, Varney, and company roving across campus, shouting countercultural verse. As Varney tells it, the poetry reading was likely a spontaneous event, and hardly as contrived as some of the more elaborate poetic works examined in this chapter. However, this sort of happening emphasized a desire to create events that would fuse art and life and viscerally immerse people (whether they like it or not) into the flow of the performance.

Of course, kinetics was also explicitly foregrounded by the materiality of printed poetry during this time. Like *blewointment*, other periodicals like *grOnk* sought to publish work that fit into the category of kinetic poetry. In addition to foregrounding the physicality of the publications themselves, by creating unique literary objects of varying size, colour, and construction, *grOnk* was interested in poetry that engaged physicality. As stated on the cover of the very first issue of *grOnk*, published in 1967, the magazine was primarily interested in "concrete sound kinetic and related borderblur poetry," and it remained a forum for this type of work until it ceased publication. These forums were crucial not only for the proliferation of kinetic poetry but also for its related somatic domains in Canada in general. As noted earlier in this book, *grOnk* and Ganglia Press were poet-driven endeavours; the poets maintained an almost total control over their work. Of the many notable works of kinetic poetry published under the Ganglia Press moniker, Earle Birney's *pnomes jukollages and other stunzas* (1969) stands out. Similar to Nichol's *Journeying & the returns*, Birney's text was packaged in a white, 9-by-12-inch envelope. The individual pieces are placed loosely within the envelope and consist of various fold-outs, booklets, and sheets. Each work is unique, altering typical experiences of the literary object, as demonstrated by the multiple versions of "Like an Eddy," each of which requires different types of physical interaction to activate the text (more on this later).

Coach House Press began, like *blewointment*, Blew Ointment Press, Ganglia Press, and *grOnk*, with a commitment to experimentation in design. Founded in 1965 by printer Stan Bevington and designer Dennis Reid, Coach House Press has been described as "arguably the single most important publisher of experimental poetics during the 1970s and '80s."[51] Coach House was driven by poets, including Wayne Clifford and Victor Coleman, and later, an editorial board including Nichol, Frank Davey, David Young, David McFadden, Michael Ondaatje, Linda Davey, Christopher Dewdney, and Sarah Sheard. Committed to small press literary culture, Coach House became a hub for innovative texts. In 1967, it published Nichol's *Journeying & the returns*, which is a "characteristic . . . [Coach House] combination of imaginative book design and innovative content."[52] Like Birney's *pnomes jukollages and other stunzas*, Nichol's *Journeying* resisted the traditional codex form. Instead, it was published in a folder and consisted of a variety of materials including sheets, booklets, a perfect-bound book, and pieces of cardstock, each of which requires the reader to hold and move the unique materials differently. These works can be read like conventional books while others, like "Cold Mountain," must be folded and then burned, reminiscent of Vautier's *Total Art Matchbox*.

Underwhich Editions built on the Coach House spirit with its commitment to uniquely designed publications. For this reason, Underwhich uses the term "editions" rather than "press" because its editors were not solely interested in publishing print-based works like books, chapbooks, and pamphlets, but also published objects, audiotapes, and microfiche. Founded in 1979 by Dean, Dedora, Dutton, McCaffery, Nichol, Riddell, Steven Ross Smith, and Truhlar, Underwhich Editions was perhaps the foremost publisher of kinetic poetic works. Each editor was "given editorial independence

Figure 4.1: "Like an Eddy" by Earle Birney, 1969.

in a spirit of mutual trust & understanding of the underlying mandate," and this resulted in an explosion of "action with an initial series of smaller works from almost all editors, each given the physical attention they deserved to become fully-realized works of book art, in addition to their values as literary artefacts."[53] Numerous significant kinetic works emerged from Underwhich, including several literary-based games by Riddell, such as *A Game of Cards* (1985) and *d'Art Board* (1986). Each of these texts not only resists the standard codex format for literature but also encourages readers to engage the poem through unconventional means and media. To engage Riddell's game-based works, one must follow his instructions. Likewise, to read Truhlar's *Five on Fiche* (1980) today, one must travel to the library to use the microfiche machine, which requires a whole different series of movements when compared to the standard movements of flipping the pages of a book.

Combined, these nodes variously emphasize the different kinetic dimensions of literature that assists in the proliferation of art and poetry by closing the gap between poetry, poet, and audience. These poets, artists, thinkers, and organizers developed publications, events, performances, and happenings to emphasize process, participation, response, movement, materiality, awareness, and the body. These works were part of an expanded program of artistic and poetic approaches that sought to reinvent the state of art and poetry so as to shift it from a static image on the page or invisible sound toward physical action, wherein the particular work in question is engaged by the body. This is a significant gesture in itself since these literary works reconfigure the typical interaction between reader and poem with a less common emphasis on the physicality of hands, fingers, muscle movements, etc. Furthermore, these works demand that the audience consider their role in the meaning-making process and determine how the suspense of the work unfolds from their interaction with it and how it will further unfold into their bodily and material lives. Placing this role upon the audience is crucial since many of the conditions of the electronic age, especially the emergence of new mediating technologies, increase the distance between subjects and the surrounding world, thus disconnecting them from the material conditions of their lives.

Extending the Codex

Consisting of a perfect-bound book of poems, a 7-1/4-inch disc entitled *Borders*, and a variety of poems on sheets and in pamphlets, chapbooks, and flipbooks, Nichol's *Journeying & the returns* (1967) contains several formidable examples of kinetic poetry. All of these materials are encased within a pale mauve folder with a blue cover image on one side and Nichol's "Statement" on the other. The "Statement," a central document in the development of borderblur, situates *Journeying* as a kinetic work: "how can the poet reach out and touch you physically as say the sculptor does by caressing you with objects you caress?" he asks, to which he answers, "only if he drops the barriers."[54] To do so, Nichol explicitly created a work wherein the barriers between reader and poem are made apparent. Each of the works in *Journeying* requests a specific engagement from the reader, breaking down the barrier between poem and reader and treating the actual material container of the poem as part of the work. *Journeying* is a collection that anticipates Ahmed's notion of a "border that feels." These works engage the epidermal boundary with varying textures and movements, and even convey smell.

The slipcase foregrounds Nichol's search for a way to dissolve barriers between the poet, the poem, and the reader. The mauve paper that is used to create the folder is subtly dimpled, drawing attention to its texture. The collection within comprises several paper-based materials containing a variety of textures—smooth, glossy cardstock; laid linen paper with horizontal lines; pages with smooth cut edges; pages with deckled edges; and reflective cardstock. Each of the pieces varies in colour too—olive, orange, cream, metallic, etc. In each case, the poem-object offers a different texture that uniquely stimulates the reader's hands, and this contrast is what highlights the unique feeling of each piece. In the version of *Journeying* I consulted at the University of Toronto's Thomas Fisher Rare Book Library, an envelope contains all of the poem-objects; the words "Letters Home" are printed across it in a handwritten script, signifying an attempt to reach out and communicate with a distant but familiar place.

While longing and desire are emotions that inform the work as a whole—especially Nichol's desire to engage the reader on a somatic level—this is explicitly foregrounded in Nichol's miniature chapbook "Cold Mountain," wherein the poem depicts the speaker's journey away from and return to their lover. Described as "a kinetic poem/sculpt for eventual distruction [sic]," the booklet consists of pages of various sizes and heights, thereby forming a staircase-like structure.[55] As the reader flips these pages, a new sequence of words appears describing the journey of the speaker. The first sequence is "GO / TO / COLD / MOUNTAIN," which, after the first page is flipped, changes to "GO

/ TO / COLD / & high," which then changes to "GO / TO / reach you / i must," and then finally, "GO / from / her side."[56] At this last sequence, the reader reaches the top of the Cold Mountain and then eventually returns "home / in pain," "COLD / to her arms," which signifies the end of the speaker's "RETURN / FROM / COLD / MOUNTAIN."[57] With its unique design, the booklet's materials assist in representing the ascent and descent of the speaker on their journey, as they long for a loved one.

By the end of "Cold Mountain," the speaker has returned cold, resting in his/her lover's arms. This can only be resolved one way: to be warmed by a fire. The back of the booklet contains "assembly instructions" to prepare the reader for warmth:

1) Curl the covers in behind the text

2) Curl the text in individually

3) Uncurl the covers

4) Drop a lit match down the centre cone (optional step)[58]

Recalling Fluxus pieces like Ben Vautier's *Total Art Matchbox*, Nichol's "optional step" is to burn the booklet in an act of creative destruction to warm the reader. jwcurry notes on his Flickr page that few people have probably burned their copies of "Cold Mountain." He is among the few who have. While testing exactly how the piece would burn, curry remarks that it "turns out to be a very controlled burn, the central tube channelling the flame into a volcanic gout, the others following along as it spread from the bottom out until it was all consumed."[59] Nichol, then, according to curry's comments, consciously created "Cold Mountain" to present a distinctive aesthetic experience that hinges on the materials of the work: flame, paper, and ink.[60] The flame moves and appears to follow a specific trajectory through the paper and ink as it produces heat and brings warmth to the skin, a remedy to the cold, mountainous journey depicted by language via the movement of the booklet. The burning would also produce smoke and accompanying smells, likely engaging the reader's olfactory senses (another step in breaking down the barrier between poet, poem, and the reader). In this way, "Cold Mountain" is a poem that touches both the inside and outside of the reader, using movement, combustion, and entropy to articulate longing and regained comfort.

Another significant piece from Nichol's *Journeying*, entitled "bp," engages similar ideas as a poem-object that seeks to break down the barrier between reader, poet, and poem. "bp" is a minimalist poem-object consisting of Nichol's two initials, *b* and *p*, joined together to form a single cut-out. The cut-out is made using paper with a reflective finish and a matte black backing—as though it were a mirror. On the one hand, the piece looks like a celebration of the author, with its a bold and flashy signature that accompanies the other texts and announces the author's presence. In this way, perhaps the piece is a reminder to the reader that there is a body and person intimately related to the texts that they hold. More significantly, however, this deceivingly simple piece effectively blurs the borders between poet, poem, and reader. When looking directly at the piece of paper, the reader's face is reflected hazily back at them. When I look at it, for example, I see my nose, mouth, eyes, and glasses: in effect, I see what I recognize as myself in "bp," but I also see myself as the cut-out of the letters *b* and *p*, which serve to shape the image of my reflection. Within the piece, I am intricately bound with Nichol. In so doing, the work is reflective of an interlinked relationship between the poem, poet, and reader, and, further, of how a reader's consciousness, at the moment of consuming this work, is formed within the intersection of these three elements. As such, the work gestures toward a community comprised of reader, poet, world, and poem—all are simultaneously present within one another.

In addition to a shared focus on their materiality, both poems are also representative of Nichol's interest in the Japanese haiku form, which features most prominently in his translations of Basho's "Frog Poem" (ca. 1680). Like haiku, Nichol's "bp" and "Cold Mountain" embrace minimalist diction to offer a careful meditation on language in order to generate feeling from the poems' specific imagery, rather than offer any explicit statements of feeling. To this end, Nichol primarily focuses on the material aspects of the texts. Nichol's *Journeying* radically brings the material world and its conditions back into the reader's grasp. Both "bp" and "Cold Mountain" draw attention to the poem as *techné*, highlighting the relationship between material and reader, and seeking to close the distance between them. "Cold Mountain," a booklet about the labour of travelling vast distances, reminds its readers that they must knowingly traverse the material realm to reduce feelings of alienation in order to find comfort again. Likewise, the smooth surface of "bp" offers an analogy between the ways that materials are inserted into human life without friction and are thereby normalized, sometimes to our detriment (as in the case with some communications technologies). "bp" is a poem that emphasizes our place within material systems, reminding us of our power despite the seeming inextricability of new technologies.

Techné and kinesis are also critical elements in Earle Birney's interactive work *pnomes jukollages and other stunzas* (1969), issued by Ganglia Press. While Birney may have been part of an established generation of poets, and was not at first interested in the experimental tactics of the borderblur group, *pnomes jukollages and other stunzas* offers an exemplary representation of the visual, sonic, and kinetic concerns of the borderblur poets. This is due, in part, to Nichol's influence. Nichol designed the work, and, like some of his own publications, he encased Birney's *pnomes* in an envelope containing a variety of materials. The envelope is about 9-by-12-inches in size, with the title and Birney's name boldly printed on its face. The printed side of the edition at the Thomas Fisher Rare Book Library, however, is upside down. If you flip the envelope over from right to left (like the page of a book), you have to rotate the envelope 180 degrees to access the flap and remove the envelope's contents. Having been printed this way, *pnomes* resists a reader's intuition to flip print media from right to left, as readers normally do with books. Thus, Birney's collection invites the reader to become immediately conscious of the object they are engaging: to be aware of the way the envelope must be moved, foregrounding the materiality and kinetic aspects of the work.

Birney's *pnomes* begins with the materials: there are various paper types and sizes that vary in texture and colour: creamy cardstock for one version of "Like an Eddy," with thinner white paper used for the second version; long, bright yellow sheets for a horizontally printed and staple-bound "Alaska Passage"; a purple folder containing sound and visual poems; and continuous-feed computer paper with perforated edges for "Space Conquest: Computer Poem." Each piece requires a different type of engagement: the centre-folded computer poem, for example, must be opened to reveal a short, three-stanza poem on the large sheet of lined paper; "Alaska Passage" is staple-bound to be read like a typical chapbook, flipping pages left to right; and "Architecture," while it is folded and stapled, must be unfolded to read the poems tucked inside of it. Each of these unique pieces signals a move away from the conventions of the codex, using paper and binding to become not just a by-product of the poem, but part of the poem itself. Each poem, with their emphases on diverse materials and engagements, brings the reader closer as they more consciously consider the movements and gestures required to read the work.

Of the many pieces included in *pnomes*, most striking are the two versions of the kinetic poem "Like an Eddy" (see figure 4.1). Each version requires a specific type of movement in order for the work to be engaged: one must be rotated, while the other must be cut out and assembled to move by itself. The first is printed on a flat sheet of paper with hand-written text in a spiral. Birney writes, "Like an eddy my words turn about your bright rock," invoking the relationship between reader and author.[61] The piece must be rotated to be read so that the reader's hands enact the "eddying" motion of the poem. The "bright rock" belonging to the reader (implied by the "you"), is, in fact, the body. The reader must therefore move their hands in half-rotations, as the edges of the paper are passed between each hand. A similar idea is manifested in the second version of the poem (a collaboration with Andrew Suknaski), which is printed on a flat sheet, and though it does not have instructions to cut the mobile out, it gestures toward that action. Once excised, the work would be hung like a mobile. In this version, however, the language is altered slightly. Instead of "turn about," Birney writes that it will "move about," suggesting that the mobile may not rotate, but it will move. The mobile hangs in suspension, moving as air passes through it, or someone pushes it with their hand. The "bright rock," in this version, would describe any person below the mobile, looking into it. As a pair, each version of the work offers a meditation on human agency and kinetics. The first version looks to the reader as the point of contact who initiates the poem, while the second is more esoteric, indicating that the poem has a life of its own—its own form of agency and activity in the world.

Like Nichol and Birney, Ottawa-based collective First Draft sought to produce poetic works that exceeded conventional definitions of the poem while also responding to the conditions of the electric age. At times, they would use the phrase "wordmusic" to describe their work, and other times they would call it "sound poetry." They also used the term "intermedia," perhaps in reference to Higgins's characterization of art that falls between media—the same term that informs this book. Indeed, their performances occupy the in-between space of poetry reading, theatre, and musical performance. While the group's shows engaged a multiplicity of sensorial receptors at once (especially sound and vision), these were not necessarily kinetic works.

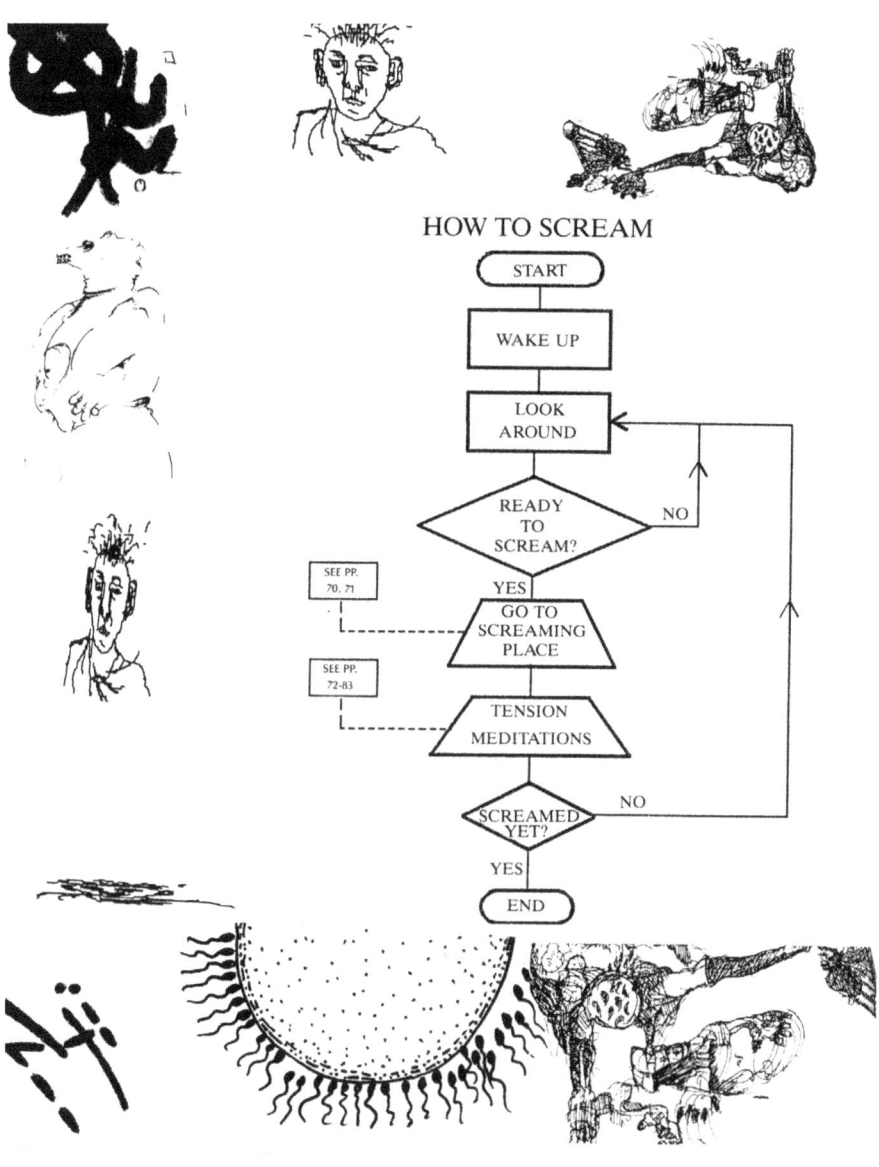

Figure 4.2: Excerpt from "SCREAM (How To)" from *The Scream: First Draft, The Third Annual Group Show* by First Draft, 1984.

Their performances did not require, as far as I know, audience participation. However, outside of performance, they did produce text-based works that incorporate process, proprioception, and movement. Their self-published commemorative book *The Scream: First Draft, the Third Annual Group Show* (1984) is an elaborately designed collagist book composed of photographs, sketches, scores, and abstract imagery and containing several text-based works, including notes, essays, and a brief biographical description of the group. At this stage in First Draft's history, *The Scream* identifies as members of First Draft Susan McMaster, Colin Morton, Andrew McClure, Claude Dupuis, Nan Cormier, David Parsons, and Carol English, all of whom contributed to the book.

Sherrill Grace suggests that "The book deconstructs the usual notion of text to create a new type of multimedia textuality."[62] Their piece entitled "SCREAM (How To)," which they refer to as "a new collaborativeperformance art work,"[63] is most exemplary of an intermedial kinetic work. It presents a "step-by-step guide to refining your own capacity to scream."[64] Accordingly, the piece intersects with Fluxus-affiliated intermedial artworks like Ono's *Grapefruit*. Written by all contributors to the book, "SCREAM (How To)" touches numerous haptic areas: it demands readers consider the locations and positions of their bodies (in preparation for the scream). It instructs them to endure a series of physical activities to affect their psychological and emotional states, building toward emotional release through screaming. They begin by suggesting possible locations for screaming (a phone booth, a street, the National Gallery, a wedding, etc.), which is followed by a series of what they refer to as "tense meditations." These meditations are intended to help one reach "optimal tension" so that one's scream can "express the absolute horror of your existence."[65] These methods of meditation include "not breathing," which may cause one to feel panic or exasperation; "the hang up," which requires one to hang by one's hands from a bar, which may cause exhaustion; and "the loggerhead," which requires one to fist fight, thus, likely, building up stress and anger. Once readers have grown sufficiently tense, the poets provide a flow chart that directs readers through each remaining step. While the flow chart begins with "WAKE UP," it is significant that the step immediately preceding the instruction to scream is actually "LOOK AROUND."[66] It is from looking around that readers are prompted to begin screaming, and, as indicated in the flow chart, if they are not ready to scream, they should continue to look around some more. First Draft, then, ascribes the need to express "the absolute" horror of existence not to existence itself, but to the conditions of existence—that is, the societal conditions in which they live. They clarify this point on the back of the book: "in the midst of your scream you no longer feel like a powerless cog; for an instant you may even experience the illusion that you can control your own destiny."[67] "SCREAM (How To)" provides momentary catharsis from the conditions of the present—specifically, the lack of agency one feels in the face of a quickly evolving social and political landscape that reduces people to mere "cogs" in a system. It seems that even in 1984, when *The Scream* was published, the sense of alienation many began to feel in the 1960s continued to be deeply ingrained within Western society.

Games and Puzzles

Instruction-based poems encourage readers to explore the possibilities of literature off the page, employing a playfulness that assists them in focusing on the material elements of the work in their hands. This playfulness is pushed even further by some borderblur poets who developed a series of literary-based games. John Riddell produced several literary games in the 1980s using the flexibility of Underwhich's production mandate as an opportunity to publish interactive game-based works, including *Game of Cards* (1985), *WAR* (1981), and *d'Art Board* (1987). These works, like many discussed in this book, blur medial and generic borders. Since "Riddell insists that his readers reject passive reception of writing in favour of a more active role," each of his texts requires a unique and mostly unconventional type of engagement.[68] For example, *WAR [Words at Roar], Vol. 1: s/word/s Games* requires the reader to cut up an original text and reassemble the pieces following Riddell's instructions. Riddell encourages the reader to directly contact him to discuss the work: "let me know how you feel about the puzzle!"[69] he writes.

Riddell first conceived of *WAR* as a four-volume work, but not all volumes saw publication. Volume 1 emphasizes kinetics as a fundamental aspect of the work. The book was xerographically produced and created following a collagist aesthetic. The verso of each page contains fragments of a prose text that the reader is encouraged to cut out; on the recto are various bits of text, including quotes, comments, and questions, to which the reader may respond. Riddell is careful with his instructions. He encourages readers to follow his prompts, but he confirms that it is also their decision to engage the text however they want: "you need not cut out designed areas . . . to do so, however, forfeits not only puzzle construct, but your <u>active involvement</u>

Figure 4.3: Front cover of *WAR*, vol. 1, by John Riddell, 1981.

in the /con//destruction of this & (as a further reading will reveal) possibly your <u>own</u> text!"[70] "Your choice," he writes. Instead of cutting and assembling the puzzle, one can still be actively involved with the text, though that choice does diminish the degree of bodily engagement that Riddell promises in volume 1. One could answer Riddell's questions about layout and design or follow his alternative set of instructions to "write poems . . . using extracts &/or 'WAR' proper on each page (or collectively) as your <u>total supply text</u>," thus suggesting that this is not only a text that you cut up but also a text that you write alongside.[71] Regardless of one's pathway through the text, Riddell has established *WAR* as a designated pathway of clear communication and dialogue between author and reader. He includes his address on the fifth page of the text, and in the separate pamphlet, hopes that readers will "accordingly respond."[72]

By these instructions, it is clear that Riddell seeks to destabilize conventional notions of authorship and invite the reader to become an author of the text as well. Though calling *WAR* a poem may seem like a stretch, it indulges in a variety of literary devices, including extensive punning on "peace" and "author." Like a puzzle, "peace" puns on "piece," two terms that propel the text as a textual puzzle and its thematic concern of peace. Not only does Riddell seek to undo conventional notions of authorship by actively involving the reader in the production of textual meaning, but he extends the meaning of the word "author" to include broader notions of power and authority. For Riddell, it seems that the erosion of authorship correlates to the erosion of larger structures of authority. In a pamphlet accompanying *WAR* volume 1, Riddell describes the post–Second World War arms race, highlighting the spirit of industrial competition that animated the United States during the Cold War, but also the competition between the United States and the Soviet Union. Riddell's writing highlights the promise of catastrophe that the arms race represented, recognizing it as the dominant form of "peaceful discourse," or, in other words, the promise of peace as a result of mutually assured destruction. By establishing the text as a clear passage between author and reader, the work becomes a point of contact, a point of discussion wherein both author and reader are equally capable of hopefully undoing textual hierarchies and situating the poem as a collaborative effort.

For the sake of research, I indulged Riddell's request to /con//destruct the puzzle. My primary goal was to answer Riddell's fundamental question: How does the process make me feel? Careful not to destroy my copy, I photocopied

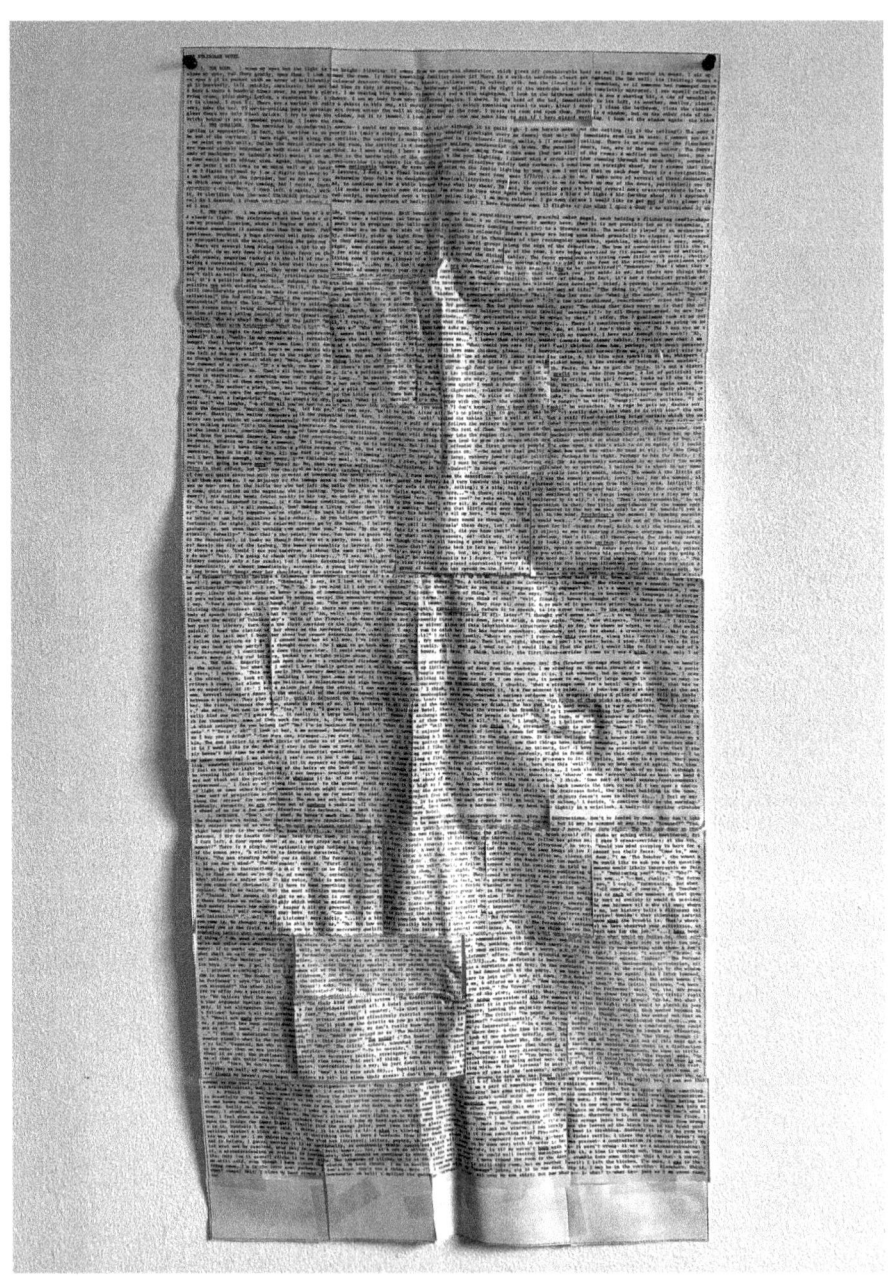

Figure 4.4: The assembled text from John Riddell's *WAR*, vol. 1, assembled by the author in his home.

WAR and carefully cut out each fragment from each page. This took several hours, a period during which I admittedly felt tremendous boredom. At various points, I also felt annoyed, disappointed, and determined. I could see that some of my cutting was less than precise, which meant to me that I might not be able to solve the puzzle successfully. As I cut, I had to control my body and its movements precisely. I could not shake or swerve from the outline of each piece; I had to move slowly and cut as close to the edges of the lettering and lines as I could. As I cut out more pieces, however, I also became more engaged by the text. I was developing a familiarity with the fragments; I was reading across awkwardly broken lines, pieces of words and letters, and soon began to find corresponding fragments. I taped them together as I found them, which I also found encouraging. It generated a desire in me to complete the text. In total, it took six hours to cut up the text and assemble most of it. The process was exhausting, and as I finished taping together what I thought were the final pieces, I realized I was missing a piece, which, of course, left me incredibly frustrated. I woke the next morning to find the missing piece. I am not sure if I threw it out with the scraps or if I had just never printed it. Nonetheless, it illustrated the risk one takes in trying to adhere to Riddell's instructions: carelessness and a lack of attention are an obstacle to completing the work. I reprinted the final piece and put it in place. Having completed the puzzle, I felt satisfied. More importantly, though, what I realized by enduring this process was that the interactive elements drew me into the text. As I worked through the puzzle, I developed an intimate relationship with the work and fashioned a narrative that is singular to me and my specific textual encounter.

Once assembled, the fragments form a large poster containing a prose narrative. The narrative on the poster is conventional. It is a short story in six parts, told by a first-person speaker. We enter the narrative *in medias res*, with the speaker at "The Staircase Hotel." The tone of the narration recalls the grittiness and matter-of-factness of film noir—the hotel itself is shadowy and full of mystery, a mystery that unfolds throughout the text. Moving around the hotel, the speaker, in the third section, happens upon "The Party," where several gentlemen are speaking about business, public relations, and how corporate PR obfuscates public knowledge. Specifically, these men discuss how corporate discourse (and political discourse) sidestep discussions of key issues like air, earth, water, and health, which have been "dismissed."[73] The speaker moves from this conversation and finds himself alone in a library with a young woman, who begins to quiz the speaker on his thoughts about language. The speaker replies, "it's a means of communication, I would say—likely, the best means we have—a way of communicating thoughts, facts, feelings."[74] The woman sighs disappointedly and reflects upon the ways language is misused: "They step all over it. & so much of it goes into print—Books have a way of domesticizing things—ideas—don't you think. If only there was some way to <u>free</u> language again, <u>repoliticize</u> it, return it to speech, to its proper realm. . . . To the speech of the <u>body</u> where the body of speech truly dwells."[75] Shortly after, in the fifth and sixth sections, the narrator finds himself working as a counter-spy for two opposing groups; the woman from the library is on one side of this divide. He agrees to work for both groups, feeling a sense of belonging. In the sixth section, the story shifts again, with the speaker, alone, reflecting on his position as a spy: "An incident (arising on either side) could occur any day now, could conceivably lead to a full-scale confrontation. No one knows what to do about it. We seem to move around in the dark. Words don't seem to have any meaning, any power to initiate action anymore."[76] The speaker continues to reflect upon language in this final scene, mainly its inadequacies, until, after spilling orange juice on his shirt, he begins to stutter, "But now where—I—What—what is—just as I am about ready to—," and there the story ends.[77]

Driven by a tale of shadowy interactions, Riddell's narrative on the poster that comprises volume 1 is a reflection upon the inadequacies of language—with particular attention to how the corporate and bureaucratic uses of language obfuscate essential ideas. Similarly, as in the case of the spy/counter-spy scenario, the speaker joins both sides, with no real attachment to either, for a sense of belonging. Both cases reflect upon the powerlessness of language in these depoliticized and detached scenarios. Without making a clear case for how this might be done, the narrative calls for the return of language to the body, for this is how language will be freed and politicized once more. While the story does not offer a method for reconnecting language and the body, volume 1 of *WAR*, as an interactive and kinetic work, does offer an answer. By providing a text that must be disassembled and reassembled by the reader, Riddell has invited the reader to become invested in the text in a tangible way. In some ways, this is a test that challenges a reader's investment in the task of fully accessing the language of the work and thus the meaning behind it. In this way, Riddell offers a means of returning language to the body by encouraging the reader to invest their body, time, and energy into the text.

Another work, *d'Art Board*, published by Underwhich, consists of a single, semi-glossy sheet of paper that measures approximately two feet square. On the semi-glossy side is the main body of text, which is designed to look like a dartboard. This same text was republished (with rules) in Riddell's *How to Grow Your Own Light Bulbs* (1997) with an alternate title, "Object D'art." In this version, the dartboard is reproduced in pieces that readers cut out of the book to assemble themselves. Riddell provides instructions on how to set up and play the game. The dartboard must be hung so that the "bull's eye is 68" from the floor" and the throwing line is 9 feet from the wall.[78] The outside edge of the board is surrounded by the letters *a* through *z*; each of these letters corresponds to a number: "A = 20, B = 1, C/D = 18 . . . Z = 5."[79] Dense collages of text have replaced the typical colours of the board: we see an evenly spaced series of prosaic textual fragments that are barely legible, followed by collages of bolder, denser, non-semantically arranged letters. The game oscillates between sense and nonsense while blurring the borders between fiction, visual poem, and game.

Riddell's *d'Art Board* employs the same movements as a typical game of darts. Darts is a game of proprioception—one must position one's body per the rules (behind the 9-foot line) and should throw a dart, aiming 68 inches above the floor, at the bull's eye. It demands an awareness of the body as the dart is set in motion—a flick of the wrist with an appropriate amount of force to ensure the dart accurately follows the desired trajectory. Strangely, Riddell's version of darts does not use text to replace the role of numbers in calculating the game's score, leaving me with no clear understanding of the role the text actually plays in the scoring of the game. The title of the second edition of the game ("Object D'Art") suggests that the work is meant to be purely ornamental. An *objet d'art* (or art object) is an ornately created object that has no other function aside from producing pleasure in the beholder or user. Riddell's "Object D'Art," then, offers participants an opportunity of orienting the body directly toward a physical, proprioceptive relationship with language, to reconceive of this relationship purely as a joyous encounter.

Riddell is not the only borderblur poet to develop a literary-based game to create new and unique encounters with language. Like Riddell and his *d'Art Board*, the Four Horsemen jointly developed a game that blurs the line between narrative, poem, and play: it is entitled "Andoas." The instructions for the game—or more accurately, *most* of the instructions needed to play—were published in a 1979 issue of the Toronto arts newspaper *Only*

Paper Today. The players are required to create their own board, pieces, and statistics sheets. The game is designed to resemble other popular games of the 1970s, especially role-playing games like Dungeons & Dragons and board-based games like Monopoly. Like Dungeons & Dragons, "Andoas" is narrative-driven, complete with multiple universes that players can move in and out of as they play in competition or collaboration. Movement around the board follows precisely detailed rules, and the players interact with one another through what in the game are called "encounters" and "situations." The narrative—or "scenario," as it's called—that drives the game is devised entirely by the players and, as an example, can include the following:

> Player A has amnesia & has escaped from hospital. Because his memory is faulty he wanders from place to place not recognizing anyone. Player B has been hired to find him. Since A does not know who he is & does not remember anyone else the key element in the SCENARIO was B's ability to win A's confidence so that he would trust him enough to return with him to the hospital. Thus it was not enough for B to simply find A. The only possible way to show this in the game is to incorporate an element of repeated ENCOUNTERS. "Winning" in this amnesiac SCENARIO depended on B's being the winner in 5 different ENCOUNTERS.[80]

The winners of these encounters are determined by the rolling of dice against a series of odds laid out in a statistics chart; winners of these encounters receive experience points that contribute to their chance of winning while also shaping the narrative arc of the game.

Without an official and complete game, "Andoas" can make for a challenging process; however, my attempts to play have offered me enough insight to situate the game critically. "Andoas" is based in tactility and movement—the players touch the pieces in a virtual space, moving them on and around the board. The game establishes scenarios that are not immersive in a physical sense; instead, they are virtually immersive, intersecting with McLuhan's expanded conceptualization of tactility as "the life of things in the *mind*."[81] The scenarios are played out only through the movement of the pieces and through the players as they imagine the scenario. Part of what propels the game—in addition to strategic thinking—is the excitement provided by the players' encounters with one another, either in competition or co-operation.

Though framed as a game, "Andoas" challenges participants to carefully consider what it means to play, not just as players in a game, but as persons in the real world. In their introductory blurb to the game, the Four Horsemen suggest that the game encourages players to "determine what a 'win' or a 'loss' means to them."[82] In that same blurb, they suggest that this is a didactic game: "It is an educative experience the whole family can benefit from."[83] This didacticism is essential to understanding the significance of the game, especially its treatment of the concepts of winning and losing. Notions like these—synonymous with success and failure, sinking and swimming—comprise some of the dominant forces that drive subjects living under the conditions of capitalism. A subject's place within capitalist society is primarily determined by their ability to play by society's rules, and they are promised pleasure if they can succeed in doing so. On the one hand, "Andoas" offers an escape from that challenge, inviting players into a universe in which they can escape and develop an alternative narrative of their choosing, which speaks to one of the powers of games and play—namely, relief. On the other, it makes a soft but radical gesture insofar as it encourages players to reconsider notions of competition, while not challenging the foundational impetus of competition, and to perhaps more actively determine what outcomes satisfy definitions of winning and losing, in both material and virtual realms.

Immersive and Environmental Works

Each of the works mentioned so far requires a certain level of performativity; players have to follow a set of instructions and/or move or engage an object in a certain way. There are, however, works that foreground performance explicitly so as to create interactive and immersive language-based experiences. In 1981, Michael Dean, a core member of the sound poetry group Owen Sound, developed a similarly immersive installation entitled *The Imagination of Aldo Breun*, which was installed at Studio Gallery Nine in Toronto as part of *The Symposium of Linguistic Onto-Genetics*. The symposium, co-organized by Dean, investigated problems of communication and language's relationship to expression. In a special issue of *Open Letter* focusing on pataphysics, Dean articulates his concerns in the development of a theory of linguistic onto-genetics: "Language is suffering from a deep disturbance. It is not working the way it should. It isn't serving the human function it was meant to serve; that is, it no longer contains the poignancy and energy of Human Communication."[84] The work of the Institute of Linguistic Onto-Genetics, then, is grounded in some of the ideas that intersect those of borderblur—mainly a shared concern for issues of expression during a period of changing communicative capacities. As suggested by Dean's printed introduction to the *Papers Delivered at the Symposium of the Institute of Linguistic Onto-Genetics*—found in the 1985 collected proceedings for the symposium—the institute was part of an effort to repair the "schism between Man and his language," which will "continue as long as we refuse to attend to speech directly." Thus "Man must rebel" against this separation and try to re-fuse language and ontology.[85]

The papers delivered at the symposium variously intersect with the radical premise Dean outlines in his introduction. McCaffery imagines what he refers to as "paleosexuality and fossil speech," a concept that, in his paper, was discovered by the imaginary pseudo-scientist Samuel Gatty.[86] Janine Mather, on the other hand, theorizes the application of "psychometry to language" to examine the "emotional bondage in which speech is now trapped."[87] The symposium itself was a space for creative engagements with materiality, corporeality, and poetic language beyond the book. The participants imagined themselves as part of an alternative universe composed of imaginary scientific investigations that rely upon (for the most part) material realities with the intent of not only highlighting the perceived schism between language and human communication, but also the relationship between body, feeling, and language. Pataphysical experiments like these effectively blurred the boundaries between life and art, fusing scientific discourse (which is perceived to be integral to material and social processes) and the poetic. Some participants also explored the possibilities of blurring these boundaries. This allowed some participants to experiment with notions of corporeality and identity, distributing imagined personas of themselves into material performance and print spaces. Brian Dedora, for example, created his alter ego, Adrian Fortesque, while Riddell composed a correspondence series with his own alter ego, Lleddir Nhan Nhoj. Though seemingly playful, these personalities foreground language's intrinsic relationship to identity and how a body is read and interpolated by others in the world.

The most striking kinetic aspect of the symposium was Michael Dean's centrepiece, *The Imagination of Aldo Breun*, which was also the setting for panel discussions. As part of the symposium, Dean delivered a lecture on the installation, which describes the latter's core pataphysical elements. As participants walked through the gallery, they were walking through (according to Dean) the imaginary landscape of the fictional pseudo-scientist Aldo Breun. Breun is said to have witnessed the schism between language and humankind, indicated by the development of a "mutant letter," the letter *y*.[88] The letter is significant here for the ambiguity it holds in the alphabet. Is it a vowel or a consonant? At the moment of its invention, a moment that Dean says occurred on 14 July 1832, "mute syntax" was born, which describes "the inability of language to find one expression for a fact of state-of-affairs that is dual in nature," or, in other words, "the struggle to find the word."[89] According to Dean, this suggests that "a rupture has grown between our genetic imagination development and our being."[90] Language is no longer material; it no longer functions literally or forcefully in the world, but rather is up for interpretation and analysis. For Dean, "language is a shadow left by light after it has met an object."[91] Human communication with language has become less precise and convoluted. The installation portion of the symposium, the inhabitable companion to Dean's talk, visually and spatially registers this conception of language.

The Imagination of Aldo Breun has been referred to as "probably the largest & most thoroughly contemplative piece to have been built in toronto."[92] Breun, a mysterious character, "developed an interest in 'those conditions which the mind could grasp, but which language could not express.'"[93] That problem sets the stage for *The Imagination of Aldo Breun*, a large-scale and immersive poetic environment. curry described the installation as follows:

> One walked *into* the poem, huge distorted letter-shapes reaching out across the floor & up the walls from a central point in the room. It was also perhaps the most nonsyntactical piece made public: not only were there no words (save those in the title of the piece), the letters themselves defied fixation as specific letters. What appears to be an H at first glance could just as easily be a mutant A. Context is derived entirely from the title, content entirely from the viewers' own interpretations.[94]

In this same article, curry describes *The Imagination of Aldo Breun* as a "logical extension of earlier concepts of concrete & visual poetry," and acknowledges that here "space [is] functioning as field & image."[95] These latter

Figure 4.5: Installation photograph of *The Imagination of Aldo Breun* by Michael Dean, November 1981.

Figure 4.6: Installation photograph of *The Imagination of Aldo Breun* by Michael Dean, November 1981.

terms gesture toward the same elements that comprise kinetic poetics, with their emphasis on space and immersion and the body situated within a field.

Dean's installation gestures toward the relationship between light and shadow, opacity and transparency, object and perspective. Vision is essential to the work—the beholder is supposed to see the shadows—but so is the body, as it orients the degree and angles from which the installed mutant letters may be viewed. As curry notes, "What appears to be an H at first glance could just as easily be a mutant A," which suggests that what each piece might be perceived to be is also determined by how the body is positioned: distance, angle, movement, height, and even the number of people in the room would affect viewers' interpretations."[96] *The Imagination of Aldo Breun* foregrounds how language, even when reduced to its most basic elements, relies on the body's movement and position. In its own way, *The Imagination of Aldo Breun* exemplifies the statement from Nichol that opens this chapter—"syntax equals the body structure"[97]—except Dean's installation offers a twist on that claim, implying as it does that body equals the letter structure. *The Imagination of Aldo Breun* suggests that the processual relationship that Nichol highlights operates in both ways. Nichol argues that "If I can keep moving the structure of the poem around, hopefully I can encompass different realities and different ways of looking at things."[98] Likewise, in the case of Dean's installation, if one keeps moving the body around the space by changing locations, positions, directions, etc., then one can also encompass different realities and different ways of looking at things. The poem, then, is only enacted by a viewer's active movement within the space. Even the letter shapes themselves are left by shadow; they are open to interpretation from the reader and are therefore entirely dependent upon the reader's body.

Like Dean, Gerry Shikatani composed works that are also interactive and immersive, offering the audience a chance to become part of the literary work. An installation like his *Sans Titre* (24 October 1981), also held at Toronto's Studio Gallery Nine but as part of the Kontakte Writers in Performance series, places the audience directly within the work: "Installation of desk, typewriter and visual text in elevator used by audience to reach performance space. Used to activate aural and visual space of language/action of reading."[99] This is likely one of Shikatani's first conceptually influenced poetic installations grounded in his "interest in and relationship to *process* and thus, the moment ephemeral."[100] Recalling the performance in an email, Shikatani writes,

> I do not think there were any instruction for the audience—it was a prop of silence, of potential—and it could be that some did type on it. The reading/performance was no different from a usual one I think—as the main issue was to condition, contextualize the reading as something that pushed the event outside the clear and usual spatial/temporal borders of a literary reading.[101]

Using the small space of an elevator, *Sans Titre* augments audience members' sense of the environment and the installation. Elevators are typically small spaces wherein riders try to maintain a buffer between themselves and other riders. In these situations, one becomes more aware of one's body in relation to others. *Sans Titre* seizes upon the intimacy of the space and the ways by which it informs the body's structure—reminding us, again, of Nichol's argument for the way environments shape the body.

This piece reminds me, too, of the importance of absence in Shikatani's work, especially absent bodies. In the same year that Shikatani installed *Sans Titre*, he published with David Aylward an anthology of Japanese-Canadian poetry entitled *Paper Doors*, a collection of poems in translation that was first privately published and circulated among a small readership in Canada. In his introduction, Shikatani directly connects the dearth of published Japanese-Canadian poetry with what he calls "The Evacuation."[102] He is, of course, referring to the period during the Second World War when many Japanese Canadians were forcibly sent to prison camps or otherwise detained in remote settlements in British Columbia. Even after the war ended, the injustice continued, Shikatani notes in *Paper Doors*. Some young Japanese Canadians, who now held the responsibility for rebuilding their families' lives, felt that pursuing careers in the arts was not viable. Instead, they felt pressure to assimilate by adopting "Canadian middle class ideals, and following careers in business or the trades," says Shikatani.[103]

Returning to *Sans Titre*, the audience would arrive to the venue expecting a night of audible readings, but they first faced Shikatani's Olympia typewriter without a human body. Considering its temporal proximity to the publication of *Paper Doors*, I cannot help but connect the installation to the conditions of the Evacuation and its long-term repercussions that discouraged Japanese Canadians from pursuing the arts. I therefore frame the piece as a lament. The unused typewriter is confined to the liminality of the elevator, a holding space that is always between points of origin and arrival. And this is reflective of the ways that aspiring poets—perhaps the children of the detained families—maybe felt forced to abandon the arts so that they could serve their families and reconstruct their lives. The title, French for "untitled," gestures toward this sense of absence.

Four years after this piece, Shikatani's Olympia typewriter appeared again as a prop of silence in a seemingly related performance entitled "Certain un Certain." This is a hybrid lecture-performance that he did at the Centre for Canadian Culture in Paris, France, on 23 January 1985. Shikatani confirmed that this piece directly references his introduction to *Paper Doors* as well as *Koku*, a one-hour literary documentary that he made for CBC's *Anthology* program, hosted by Robert Weaver, to commemorate the 1977 centenary of the first Japanese immigrant to Canada. From these two direct references, I speculate that the history of the Evacuation and Shikatani's concern for absence and transience survive in this performance. He described "Certain un Certain" to me as a way "to introduce silence" as a "potential of reflection by a public encountering disjunction."[104] For "Certain un Certain," he placed his typewriter in the middle of the room, within the audience, to the left of where he would perform. The typewriter faces a member of the audience. As it did in the elevator in 1981, the typewriter foregrounds the process of writing and, in this case, the typed lecture as a kind of score for performance. Shikatani also placed a kettle in the room, which gradually heated water for tea, which he explained is connected to a tea ceremony (*cha-no-yu*). As I understand it, there is a text for this performance that has never been published; unfortunately, it was either lost or exists only in fragments in Shikatani's private archive. In recounting this event to me, he emphasized that silence more than vocal sound is the core component of this performance. He describes this work as a "minimalist signature" guided by the aesthetics of silence, and by extension, absence. I wonder if the "text" is merely a set of instructions for Shikatani to follow in performance rather than a text for recitation. If there was any vocalization in this performance at all, it seems likely that it was not the main feature. The audience was meant to contemplate the environment of the room, to contemplate the typewriter, to listen to the boiling water. Shikatani emphasized the presence of his body in the room, and by invoking traditional tea ceremonies, he asked his audience to consider his connection to culture and tradition.

Shikatani returned to similar themes for another performance in Paris that same year, held at the ninth installment of the Polyphonix Festival for

International Poetry. He recalled for me that he may have read from his 1984 book of poetry *A Sparrow's Food* during the performance, or from an earlier, unpublished text entitled "Waves," commissioned by Boston-based sculptor and performance artist Bart Uchida. The actual text used during this performance could dramatically alter its meaning. *A Sparrow's Food* consists of a mix of lyrical poems alongside drawings and other visuals that range widely in theme. The latter text, "Waves," Shikatani explained to me, employs English and Japanese words with modulations that fuse the two languages. The main thrust of this performance was its "false ending," a tactic he says he employed in numerous other performances. For this 1985 "false ending," however, Shikatani abruptly stopped his reading and walked off stage as the room faded to black; it was several minutes before he and the lights returned. If we assume that Shikatani read "Waves," then this piece's combination of English and Japanese and Shikatani's sudden departure from the stage could be said to resonate with his other performances. The false ending hypothetically unsettles the audience's expectations of the reading as an event with a clear beginning and end. The result is an even more dramatic creation of absence, an absence of voice and body. Each of these performance pieces were designed to create a unique and intimate experience between the poet, audience, and the performance space, and they did so by drawing attention to bodily absences in spaces where an audience might expect a greater presence on the part of the performing body. In subverting these expectations, Shikatani's performances turned the experience back on the audience members, prompting them to contemplate their relationship to the room and its objects, to Shikatani, and ultimately to each other.

However, Shikatani's immersive performances also prompt us to reconsider the notion of Canadian identity, since each piece, in its own oblique way, points to cultural relations. It is notable that several of the performances detailed above occurred not in Canada, but in France, where Shikatani resided for some time, indicative not only of his own international comportment, but of the ways that Canadian borderblur—in this case through the work of Shikatani—is connected to global networks. His work also has significant implications for cultural relations at home in Canada. Poet and critic Rachel Zolf has described Shikatani as a "Japanese-Canadian man working primarily in English but with an oral/aural knowledge of Japanese from his childhood." She explains that "Shikatani's knowledge base includes the silencing of his Japanese language and identity that the imperialism of the English Language and its inherent racism enacts."[105] Building on Zolf's description, I extend this characterization of Shikatani's practice to his poetic performances and installations. His pursuit of absence—of voice and body—may be understood as a reference to the Canadian government's silencing and displacement of Japanese Canadians during the Second World War. My readings of his performances here, which take place partially through the lens of the traumas and injustices of the Evacuation, would likely displease Shikatani. In the introduction to *Paper Doors*, he reflects upon the historical and social framework he advances to introduce his audience to Japanese-Canadian poetry. "Doubtless, the notion of an absolute and exclusive genre of poetry which addresses 'Japaneseness' and historical data such as 'The Evacuation' may seem attractive to some,"[106] he writes. But he also cautions that "this could narrow Japanese-Canadian sensibility within the ethnoculture and set up a schema for the interpretation of Japanese Canadians in which sociological and historical conditioning are advanced archetypal motives in a linear rationale of the most obvious kind. Ultimately, any approach insisting on the linearity of narrative history to define art is, to me, not totally satisfying."[107] Indeed. Going forward, I hope my analysis here marks a starting point for further investigations into Shikatani's poetry that not only emphasize historical and social events, but that also, as Shikatani suggests in *Paper Doors*, "expand our visions of the nature of the potential of Canadian literature, and that, in effect, will teach us much more about language itself."[108]

These words from Shikatani's *Paper Doors* points me back to the collective work that all poets discussed in this chapter sought to advance—namely, the aesthetically and politically diverse exploration of language as it relates to the body. Poets like Nichol, Shikatani, Riddell, First Draft, and the others mentioned above created poems that directly engage the interface of poem, material, and audience by requiring an encounter on the kinetic level. In doing so, they transformed the poem into a space wherein the audience (and at times the poets themselves) could reconsider and renegotiate the conditions of the electric age, and its impact on the tactile and proprioceptive dimensions of human life. In many of the poems published under the auspices of borderblur, the literary work expands beyond the linguistic content of the poem (with its semantic meaning) to include its materiality as a necessary aspect of the text's meaning. This is not a modernist consideration of form as a mere extension of content. Rather, it is through the careful consideration of these materials that the poet, as Nichol would say, reaches out to touch their audience. The poem and its materiality, then, become a mode of experience that is felt primarily through somatic registers that productively reintroduce the audience to the material conditions of their world.

The electric age was characterized by rampant technological development, which in turn significantly impacted the psychological and physiological conditions of human life during the mid- to late twentieth century. While new communication technologies mediated interaction, a kinetic poetic provided a means by which some might overcome the alienation felt as the world became less human and more technological—especially as human communication and expression came increasingly to rely upon media and its infrastructure. In effect, human subjectivity—and expressions of that subjectivity—became reliant upon these structures threatening to standardize human life, reducing any person to the role of consumer and producer within a capitalist marketplace. In light of this threat, poetry that turns toward the kinetic—with its emphasis on touch, tactility, and proprioception—was a necessary response, offering a means by which the audience and participant could regain an awareness of their bodies within contrived systems (artistic, economic, social, etc.) and consciously attend to how to their bodies enter, exceed, and engage those structures.

CODA

Intermedial Poetry in Canada Today

As it manifested in Canada, borderblur became enmeshed with an emergent sense of the world as the conditions of that world infiltrated the cultural, social, economic, technological, and political aspects of daily life. Poets and writers such as bpNichol, bill bissett, Steve McCaffery, Roy Kiyooka, Gerry Shikatani, Judith Copithorne, Ann Rosenberg, Penn Kemp, and many others created within this world as its lines were being redrawn by the rise of electronic media, mass advertising and publicity, increased travel, and the consequent ease with which ideas and persons moved across time and space. These conditions affected how these poets created their work, and, more significantly, their sense of themselves as cultural creators within Canada's borders and among the artistic currents connecting them to avant-garde communities abroad. In sync with an international network of like-minded avant-garde practitioners, these Canadians created intermedial texts against the backdrop of rapid change to interact with cultural and sensorial domains of visuality (concrete poetry), sound (sound poetry), and movement (kinetic poetry). Their work does not actively consolidate the formation of a Canadian literary identity, even though many of them came to their positions as cultural workers during the peak and in the wake of mid-century cultural nationalism. Instead, taken collectively, it forms a paratradition that challenges the conventional narrative of Canada's literary history while contributing to literary discourse beyond the confines of cultural nationalism.

In "Canada: The Borderline Case" (1977), Marshall McLuhan captures this conception of borders when he declares that "the vast new borders of electric energy and information that are created by radio and television have set up world frontiers and interfaces among all countries on a new scale that alter all pre-existing forms of culture and nationalism."[1] McLuhan suggests an alternative framework for thinking about borders: "A border is not a connection

217

but an interval of resonance."² Inspired by the interface of electronic media, which ushered ideas, persons, images, and sounds across national boundaries and into the homes of Canadians, McLuhan attempted to reimagine borders as liminal spaces wherein oscillating forces produce overlapping frequencies to generate new social, political, and cultural harmonies and disharmonies. Thus, just as Arjun Appadurai, Jahan Ramazani, and others would argue decades later, the imaginations of artists, poets, and citizens are always altered by incoming flows of cultural production that shape their sense of belonging within the nation. Nationalism as a basis for communal belonging is even more complex when we are confronted in our daily lives with ideas, things, persons, and art from elsewhere. This has always been the case for settler literatures in Canada; yet many of the existing narratives affirm a desire for a definitive sense of Canadian identity produced by its art and culture.

Borderblur is compelling since it emerged concomitantly with Canada's nationalist cultural surge, but the poets belonging to this network were seldom interested in contributing to that sense of belonging. Instead, their intermedial, cosmopolitan avant-gardism complicates the belief that Canadian poetry is necessarily an expression of Canadian national identity. The literature created by this loose coterie of artists was generated by the harmonies and disharmonies produced by new forms of communication that afforded them new possibilities for poetic expression. For poets like bissett, as he explained to Phyllis Webb and Nichol during their 1967 interview on CBC Television, a nationally defined vision for literature in Canada was ultimately unsatisfying. To install a literary tradition centred on national placeness, as defined by Margaret Atwood, Dennis Lee, Northrop Frye, and others, recapitulates a colonial model that is similarly restrictive. bissett was attuned to writing that was emerging elsewhere and to the changing shape of cultural production and dissemination in the mid- to late twentieth century. He was compelled by the possibilities of writing when the poetic line is extended beyond the conventions of artistic modes and tradition. Thus, another way of positioning the argument of *Borderblur Poetics* is to consider borderblur as a mode of delineation—that is, as an intermedial poetics that simultaneously effaces the borders separating communicative and artistic modes while at the same time creating a new cluster of poetic activity that thrived outside of the dominant national literary poetics, which is to say the established mainstream in Canada. Borderblur facilitates the simultaneous effacement of artistic and national boundaries, and in so doing also generated new poetic lineages. The lines that define borderblur are many and multidirectional. They overlap; they generate new frequencies as they meet each other. Borderblur poets simultaneously made and unmade the idea of a Canadian poetics while forming their own intermedial, cosmopolitan avant-garde. The paratradition simultaneously enriched and challenged the notion of Canadian poetic expression.

While this book formally ends in 1988, the energy and ideas of borderblur continued to propel poets well after the 1980s. Indeed, some of the poets examined in this book still write and publish today. The earliest-born practitioner of borderblur identified in this book was West Coast poet and painter Roy Kiyooka (born 1926); the latest are the poets Susan McMaster, Gerry Shikatani, and Richard Truhlar, all born in 1950. Many were born during or just after the Second World War. The work of these poets laid the ground upon which new intermedial approaches could expand and evolve, and in the decades since new generations of poets and publishers have been attracted to the possibilities of the approaches described in this book, though they have of course found their own ways of contributing to this paratradition. More work could be done to forcefully situate the poets born in later decades and who established themselves in the wake of borderblur's beginnings in the 1960s. Poets like Margaret Christakos, Gary Barwin, jwcurry, and Stuart Ross—all of whom knew Nichol directly as a friend and mentor—were born around the same time in the late 1950s and early 1960s, just as borderblur was being born in Canada.

In her "poem for bp" from *Psychic Unrest* (2000), Lillian Allen laments Nichol's death and recognizes his lasting impression on writing in Canada: "u never really left," she writes,

> and u became a womb
> birth a child of Canadian culture
> promise destruction of borders
> in the turbulence of language[3]

Allen has made significant contributions to Canadian writing herself—especially through her involvement with dub poetry—yet it is notable that she cites Nichol as a significant figure in the development of Canadian literary culture and recognizes how his work promises the effacement of borders. Allen would identify Nichol as representative of Canadian literary culture, I believe, because he was central in creating a kind of literary zeitgeist in which

Allen's own intermedial work as a dub poet fits nicely. Ojibway poet Wayne Keon similarly praises bissett in "an opun ltur tu bill bissett" (1972), wherein he notes bissett's influence on his writing. In an orthography reminiscent of bissett's own, he writes,

> deer bill
> i don't think
> i evr met yu
> but sum peopul i no did
> the rezun i am riting
> this letr is tu tel yu
> that i used sum of
> yr lines[4]

Keon goes on to thank bissett at the end of the poem. While he gives bissett the same degree of recognition as Allen gave Nichol, Keon's similar orthography suggests that bissett's influence far exceeded the immediate coterie of poets that this book examined.

Like Allen and Keon, many writers in Canada found meaning in the activities and ideas of borderblur. In 1986, Paul Dutton and Steven Ross Smith edited a substantial *festschrift* for *Open Letter* dedicated to Nichol and his work. This issue included contributions from Canadian and international writers, including George Bowering, Bob Cobbing, Robert Kroetsch, Barbara Caruso, Dick Higgins, Margaret Avison, Lola Lemire Tostevin, Stephen Scobie, Daphne Marlatt, Fred Wah, Gerry Shikatani, Earle Birney, Jíri Valoch, and many others. As evidenced by this list, Nichol had a unique ability to formulate relationships across generations, styles of writing, and geographical contexts. Evidence of Nichol's persisting influence appears again in later issues of *Open Letter* showcasing various intellectual and creative engagements with his work. In 1998 a special issue was published, entitled "bpNichol + 10," edited by Frank Davey and with contributions from Nichol's friends and a younger assemblage of writers and scholars, including Lori Emerson, Darren Wershler, Peter Jaeger, Stephen Cain, and Christian Bök. Ten years later, Lori Emerson published two additional issues of *Open Letter* dedicated to Nichol (in 2008 and 2009), featuring Clint Burnham, Stephen Voyce, Steve Zultanski, Marie Buck, and Jim Andrews, a list that speaks to Nichol's continued influence on writers across borders. Nichol's work continues to be revisited by poets and scholars, including Derek Beaulieu and Cain, who have both recently edited volumes of Nichol's lesser-studied writings.

Writings that praise, celebrate, and study the legacy and personalities associated with borderblur have not been limited to Nichol. bissett was the subject of a 1997 issue of the *Capilano Review* containing several anecdotal, creative, and scholarly engagements with his work. Contributors to this issue include Susan Musgrave, Jamie Reid, Adeena Karasick, Judith Copithorne, Maxine Gadd, Darren Wershler, and Renee Rodin. This was later republished by Guernica as *bill bissett: Essays on his Works* (2002), edited by Linda Rogers. McCaffery, too, has had two issues of *Open Letter* dedicated to his work, the first in 1987 (edited by bpNichol) and the second in 2011 (edited by Cain). These issues, like those dedicated to Nichol and bissett, speak to McCaffery's lasting influence in creative and scholarly contexts. In "Becoming Clinamen: McCaffery and the (new) York School of Writing," Gregory Betts describes a "less articulated group [of poets] made up of those who capitalized on the opportunity afforded by McCaffery's employment as a professor in the English Department at York University from 1998 until 2003."[5] These writers include Bök, Cain, Wershler, Angela Rawlings, Bill Kennedy, Suzanne Zelazo, Jason Christie, Jay Millar, and Geoffrey Hlibchuk. This was a group of poets, Betts writes, that

> emerged in the late nineties and "Oughts" during McCaffery's tenure at the Toronto university, and that remains active today albeit in a variety of loci, [and they] might have encountered McCaffery through the auspices of a formal education (if they weren't already actively engaged with his work) but used his influence to provoke multifarious and radical literary practices both inside and outside the institution.[6]

While McCaffery, Nichol, and bissett have received these most apparent forms of praise and recognition from poets, critics, and fans, other writers have undoubtedly had their share of influence, undocumented or less documented.

Poet damian lopes, who ran the Nichol-inspired micro-press Fingerprinting Inkoperated—which released work by Nichol, Nelson Ball, jwcurry, David UU, and others—comes to borderblur with both admiration and critique. His prose poem "requiem for the avant-garde" offers an oblique characterization of borderblur: "twelve whitemen in ordered succession stand in an idle pub to regurgitate carefully rehearsed dada protest commodity. primal screams of ignoble savages in neutral zurich defying the brutality of a world gone mad with African rhythms over pints of beer, around the body counts of colonial armies."[7] The "regurgitation" described here is perhaps a reference to the neo-Dadaism that marked theorizations of borderblur's intermediality by poets such as David UU and others. lopes's critique identifies a critical misstep of borderblur poetics despite its international scope and gestures toward inclusion: the failure of some poets to adequately consider race, ethnicity, and Indigeneity in the formation of their communities and as a factor within their work. This book has provided evidence that numerous, previously overlooked women were integral to the formation and proliferation of borderblur poetics. However, the overwhelming whiteness and various cultural appropriations that informed borderblur's initial vanguard is notable (as discussed at various points in this book). lopes's critique identifies a blind spot in borderblur's program of "openness" and highlights a fundamental problem that emerges when the world is believed to be radically open.

Canada is undergoing a renaissance of poetic activity that began in the 2010s and continues into the 2020s. This later generation of poets has once again extended the intermedial paratradition, working in ways that often consciously address and intervene in social and political contexts, ranging from identity, ethnicity, race, gender, sexuality, class, labour, and religion. Poets like Jordan Abel, Sacha Archer, Kyle Flemmer, Helen Hajnoczky, Kate Siklosi, Dani Spinosa, Matthew James Weigel, and others are empowered by the intermedial environment of the computer, and some embrace a DIY aesthetic when creating and publishing their work. In many cases, these poets engage with the visuality of concrete poetry through various inimitable means, often blending digital and analogue methods of composition. These more recent additions, interventions, and continuations extend, expand, and enrich the legacies of Canadian intermedial poetics, but this work—much like the initial wave of borderblur poetry—has been welcomed into new micro-communities abroad, such as the magazine *To Call* (Germany) and the publishing outfits Timglaset (Sweden), Paperview Books (Portugal), Penteract Press (England), and Happy Monks (United States).

Nisga'a poet Jordan Abel is perhaps the most well-known of these poets since his work has received several well-deserved literary accolades, including the Dorothy Livesay Poetry Prize and the Griffin Poetry Prize. As the recipient of these prizes, Abel has received far less public criticism from members of Parliament than Nichol did in the 1970s. This may be an indicator of a broader acceptance of intermedial approaches today, but it also points to the urgency and necessity of Abel's poetry. Across his books *The Place of Scraps* (2013), *Un/inhabited* (2014), *Injun* (2016), and *Nishga* (2020), he has updated the predominantly analogue methods of concrete poetry by creating with digital tools while advancing decolonial politics. For *Un/inhabited*, Abel datamined the many settler colonial romance novels stored in the online textual repository Project Gutenberg. Abel used the language from these novels as his source text, which he then manipulated to create poems in a variety of forms, including lists, prose poems, erasures, and visual poems in the shapes of maps, landforms, waterways, and abstract palimpsests. As I have argued elsewhere,[8] the section of his book entitled "Cartography" gestures toward a word-world relationship that accounts for how language impacts the shape of the world, and vice versa. Abel's intermedial, map-like poems recognize the impact these novels have had in shaping settler-Indigenous relations by presenting, for example, Indigenous people and nations as "savage others" while presenting white European settlers as romantic heroes. The visual poems of "Cartography," for example, depict the shorelines to which colonial forces arrived before stealing the land from Indigenous inhabitants. The settler colonial novel was one of the ways that colonizers articulated and shaped their relationship to the land and their memories of it, denigrating the presence of the Indigenous people that preceded them. These visual poems are not reclamations of land; rather, they remind readers that language and stories shape the world and the cultural and social values and political systems of any given society. Abel's poetry represents a digital, intermedial poetic that intervenes into literary history and textual representations of settler colonialism.

Like Abel, anarchist-feminist poet Dani Spinosa has also breathed new life into borderblur, most obviously in her book of *glosas*, *OO: Typewriter Poems* (2020), wherein she creates analogue concrete typewriter poems and then digitally manipulates them. These poems imitate the style of many twentieth- and twenty-first-century concrete poets. Spinosa's work, like lopes's, is both inspired by and critical of previous generations of intermedial poets: "I love these poets and these poems, and I mean to show that love," she writes.[9] However, she continues, her "relationship with visual poetics is fraught."[10] While lopes is critical of previous generations on account of their lack of racial sensitivity, Spinosa's book addresses the historical marginalization of women within concrete poetics in Canada and beyond. In her dialogic "Afterword" with Siklosi, Spinosa explains that, before she completed the research for her book, she "had no idea about the long history of women who were doing this work,"[11] which is a direct result of the way previous generations of poets and critics have historicized borderblur, nationally and internationally. Her poem, riffing on the style of Dom Sylvester Houédard, is written in a vertical column of *o*'s that descend while bouncing across horizontal ledges of typewritten dashes. As the *o*'s reach the bottom of the page, the typewritten letters *g* and *d* appear. The poem, then, is an elongated expression of "O God," a reference to Houédard's religious devotion. On the other hand, the poem's elongation of "O God" could also be read as an expression of exasperation, as in the common expression "Oh God," often accompanied by an eye roll. If read this way, and given that Houédard coined the term "borderblur," it could be said that the speaker of this poem is rolling her eyes at the predominantly masculinist tradition that Houédard's notion arguably set in motion in the 1960s. In this way, Spinosa's *OO: Typewriter Poems* is a significant contribution to the legacy of borderblur poetics since it offers an expanded methodological approach while contributing to critical conversations regarding this work and the historical displacement of women from the established narrative.

Though borderblur poets in the mid- to late twentieth century received scant recognition from the literary mainstream, intermedia has evidently become increasingly commonplace. There is much work to be done on Canadian intermedial literature in the 1990s and 2000s, and the more recent examples from Abel and Spinosa confirm that borderblur poetics continues to thrive even though it might not be labelled as such. Borderblur and the intermedial literature of today may be distinguished from the past by their social and political foci, but they share an interest with previous generations in expanding poetic form and the poem's cultural context. In this way, they both share—inadvertently or not—an inclination toward Nichol's expanded sense of the poem in his search for unlimited "entrances and exits" into and out of poetic production. Nichol conceived of his practice, and by extension the work of borderblur more broadly, as a means of expanding linguistic expression, of expressing oneself and one's connection with other individuals and communities. In his time, Nichol saw this as a way of responding to the consolidation of a conventional, nationalistic literary tradition that did not adequately reflect the conditions of expression or connection in the mid- to late twentieth century. Subsequent generations of poets have seized on the possibilities of an expanded field of poetic production, and the combination of image, sound, and movement continues to dominate broader cultural productions today. In these ways, intermedia and the legacy of borderblur poetics expands the possibilities for expressing the complexity of self and community.

Notes

NOTES TO INTRODUCTION

1 The segment can be viewed online in two parts. See "Bill Bissett and BP Nichol - 1 - Interviewed by Phyllis Webb" [*Extension: Here, Now, and Then*; first aired 2 July 1967], YouTube, uploaded by bill bissett, 11 April 2009, 8:38, https://youtu.be/eBmxvfktZaM, and "Bill Bissett and BP Nichol - 2 - Interviewed by Phyllis Webb" [*Extension: Here, Now, and Then*; first aired 2 July 1967], YouTube, uploaded by bill bissett, 11 April 2009, 9:59, https://youtu.be/Vv8BN2NA6nk.

2 bpNichol, "this is the death of the poem," *grOnk*, no. 1 (January 1967): n.p.

3 Katherine McLeod, "Poetry on TV: Unarchiving Phyllis Webb's *Extension*," in *CanLit across Media: Unarchiving the Literary Event*, ed. Jason Camlot and Katherine McLeod (Montreal: McGill-Queen's University Press, 2019), 83.

4 The thirteen-episode show was dedicated to Canadian poetry and aired from 30 April to 23 July 1967. Guests included Earle Birney, Dorothy Livesay, A. M. Klein, and F. R. Scott, George Bowering, Victor Coleman, Gwendolyn MacEwen, and others.

5 McLeod, "Poetry on TV," 74.

6 Marshall McLuhan, *The Gutenberg Galaxy* (New York: Signet, 1962), 14.

7 First mentioned in *The Gutenberg Galaxy*, McLuhan suggests that the rise of electronic media will significantly reshape cultural relations around the world, recreating "the world in the image of a global village" (43). He offers a more specific definition of the "global village" in *Understanding Media*, where he writes, "Our specialist and fragmented civilization of center-margin structure is suddenly experiencing an instantaneous reassembling of all its mechanized bits into an organic whole. This is the new world of the global village. The village, as Mumford explains in *The City in History*, had achieved a social and institutional extension of all human faculties. Speed-up and city aggregates only served to separate these from one another in more specialist forms. The electronic age cannot sustain the very low gear of a center-margin structure such as we associate with the past two thousand years of the Western world" (93).

8 "Bill Bissett and BP Nichol - 1 - Interviewed by Phyllis Webb."

9 Pauline Butling, "Phyllis Webb as Public Intellectual," in *Wider Boundaries of Daring: The Modernist Impulse in Canadian Women's Poetry*, ed. Di Brandt and Barbara Godard (Waterloo, ON: Wilfrid Laurier University Press, 2009), 237.

10 "Bill Bissett and BP Nichol - 2 - Interviewed by Phyllis Webb."

11 "Bill Bissett and BP Nichol - 1 - Interviewed by Phyllis Webb."

12   Nichol, "eyes," *An Anthology of Concrete Poetry*, ed. Emmett Williams (New York: Something Else Press, 1967), n.p.
13   "Bill Bissett and BP Nichol - 1 - Interviewed by Phyllis Webb."
14   Smaro Kamboureli, "Preface," in *Trans.Can.Lit: Resituating the Study of Canadian Literature*, ed. Smaro Kamboureli and Roy Miki (Waterloo, ON: Wilfrid Laurier University Press, 2007), viii.
15   Jahan Ramazani, *A Transnational Poetics* (Chicago: University of Chicago Press, 2009), 14.
16   It is also preferable to other terms such as "sub-tradition" or "subgenre," since they connote hierarchical literary models that the poets in this book actively sought to resist.
17   Dick Higgins (with Hannah Higgins), "Intermedia," *Leonardo* 34, no. 1 (2001): 49.
18   Higgins, 49.
19   Higgins, 52
20   Higgins is careful to distinguish intermedia from mixed media, for example. In "Intermedia," he writes, "Many fine works are being done in mixed media: paintings which incorporate poems within their visual fields, for instance. But one knows which is which" (52).
21   Gunther Kress and Carey Jewitt, "Introduction," in *Multimodal Literacy*, ed. Gunther Kress and Carey Jewitt (New York: Peter Lang, 2003), 3. Emphasis in original.
22   bpNichol, "Statement," *Journeying & the returns* (Toronto: Coach House Press, 1967), n.p. The quote here comes from the back cover of the slipcase itself.
23   Paul Barrett, "The Wild Rise of CanLit," *The Walrus*, 12 October 2017, https://thewalrus.ca/the-wild-rise-of-canlit/.
24   W. H. New, "Canada," *Journal of Commonwealth Literature* 24, no. 2 (January 1989): 40.
25   As per the front cover of *grOnk*, no. 1 (January 1967): n.p.
26   The dates provided here are based on the findings of my research. Given the ephemeral nature of much of this work, some dates were difficult to corroborate.
27   See "About Penn Kemp," Penn Kemp (blog), accessed, 15 December 2022, http://pennkemp.weebly.com/about.html.
28   For more on the history of Coach House and its contributions to experimental and avant-garde writing within the discourse of Canadian nationalism, see Stephen Cain, "Imprinting Identities: An Examination of the Emergence and Developing Identities of Coach House Press and Anansi Press (1967–1982)" (PhD diss., York University, 2002).
29   Janet B. Friskney, *New Canadian Library: The Ross-McClelland Years, 1952–1978* (Toronto: University of Toronto Press, 2007), 154.
30   Similarly, in Joe Rosenblatt's "The Butterfly Bat," the letters W, O, and M are laid out to form a W in one part of the poem, forming probably the closest thing to an example of concrete poetry in this collection.
31   Quoted in Friskney, *New Canadian Library*, 112.
32   Friskney, 63.
33   Nichol, *THE RETURN OF GRONK* (Toronto: Ganglia Press, 1968): n.p.
34   Nichol, *THE BIG MID-JULY grOnk mailout* (Toronto: Ganglia Press, 1969), n.p.

35 bpNichol, "What Is Can Lit?," in *Meanwhile: The Critical Writings of bpNichol*, ed. Roy Miki (Vancouver: Talonbooks, 2002), 118.

36 Nichol, 119.

37 Nichol shared the award with his friend Michael Ondaatje for his own book of prose poems entitled *The Collected Works of Billy the Kid: Left-Handed Poems* (Toronto: Anansi, 1970).

38 bpNichol, *The True Eventual Story of Billy the Kid* (Toronto: Weed/Flower Press, 1970), n.p.

39 Frank Davey, *aka bpNichol: A Preliminary Biography* (Toronto: ECW Press, 2012), 144.

40 Canada, *House of Commons Debates*, 10 June 1971 (Mac T. McCutcheon), https://parl.canadiana.ca/view/oop.debates_HOC2803_06/1008?r=0&s=1.

41 Canada, *House of Commons Debates*, 10 June 1971, (W. B. Nesbitt), https://parl.canadiana.ca/view/oop.debates_HOC2803_06/1011?r=0&s=1.

42 Canada, *House of Commons Debates*, 10 June 1971 (J. P. Nowlan), https://parl.canadiana.ca/view/oop.debates_HOC2803_07/812?r=0&s=1.

43 "Literary Award Juror Annoyed at Criticism of Choice," *Toronto Star*, 10 June 1971.

44 bill bissett, "Part 3 bill bissett documentary" [*Strange Grey Day This*; first aired 1965], YouTube, uploaded by bill bissett, 25 January 2009, 10:26, https://youtu.be/cEbTzMgeD4k.

45 Tim Carlson, "bill bissett," in *bill bissett: Essays on His Works*, ed. Linda Rogers (Toronto: Guernica, 2002), 46.

46 See Ryan J. Cox, "HP Sauce and the Hate Literature of Pop Art: bill bissett in the House of Commons," *English Studies in Canada* 37, nos. 3–4 (2011): 147–62, and Don Precosky, "bill bissett: Controversies and Definitions," *Canadian Poetry*, no. 27 (Fall/Winter 1990), https://canadianpoetry.org/volumes/vol27/precosky.html.

47 Canada, *House of Commons Debates*, 2 December 1977 (Bob Wenman), https://parl.canadiana.ca/view/oop.debates_HOC3003_02/383?r=0&s=3.

48 Canada, *House of Commons Debates*, 3 April 1978 (Hugh A. Anderson), https://parl.canadiana.ca/view/oop.debates_HOC3003_04/710?r=0&s=3.

49 Alan Twigg, "B.C. Poets Faces Critics," *Quill and Quire* 44, no. 9 (1978): 27.

50 John Glassco, "At the Mermaid Inn—Poet as Performer," *Globe and Mail*, 12 November 1977.

51 bissett's appropriation of Indigenous chanting is discussed briefly in chapter 1.

52 Alan Twigg, "#105 bill bissett," *B.C. BookLook*, 2 February 2016, https://bcbooklook.com/105-bill-bissett/.

53 Jamie Hilder, "Introduction," *Designed Words for a Designed World: The International Concrete Poetry Movement, 1955–1971* (Montreal: McGill-Queen's University Press, 2016), 20.

54 Hilder, 20.

55 Nineteen sixty-three saw the pivotal Vancouver Poetry Conference, organized by American expatriate professor Warren Tallman and poet Robert Creeley at UBC, a landmark gathering of mostly established American poets, including Allen Ginsberg, Charles Olson, Denise Levertov, and Robert Duncan, and Canadian Margaret Avison,

for an intensive three-week program of discussions, lectures, and readings on and of contemporary poetry and poetics. This gathering is recognized as a crucial moment for the establishment of an American-influenced Canadian paratradition known as *TISH*, which involved poets such as Frank Davey, Fred Wah, Daphne Marlatt, Jamie Reid, and others.

56 Michael Turner, "Expanded Literary Practices," *Ruins in Process: Vancouver Art in the Sixties*, ed. Lorna Brown, Morris and Helen Belkin Art Gallery and Grunt Gallery, 1 March 2011, http://expandedliterarypractices.vancouverartinthesixties.com/.

57 R. Murray Schafer, "Letter to David UU, dated 16 September 1992," LMS-0217, Box 15 1996-01, David Harris Fonds, Library and Archives Canada.

58 Michael Hardt and Antonio Negri, *Empire* (Cambridge, MA: Harvard University Press, 2000), 280. Emphasis in original.

59 Gregory Betts, *Avant-Garde Canadian Literature: The Early Manifestations* (Toronto: University of Toronto Press, 2013), 7.

60 Pauline Butling, "(Re)Defining Radical Poetics," chap. 1 in *Writing in Our Time: Canada's Radical Poetries in English* (Waterloo, ON: Wilfrid Laurier Press, 2005), 19.

61 Maxine Gadd, *Lost Language: Selected Poems by Maxine Gadd*, ed. Daphne Marlatt and Ingrid Klassen (Toronto: Coach House Press, 1982), 177.

NOTES TO CHAPTER 1

1 Brian Dedora and Michael Dean, "The Symposium of Linguistic Onto-Genetics: An Introduction," *Canadian Poetry*, nos. 84–5 (2019): 56.

2 Dedora and Dean, 57.

3 Dom Sylvester Houédard, "Concrete Poetry and Ian Hamilton Finlay," *Typographica*, no. 8 [1963?]: 48, quoted in Greg Thomas, *Borderblurs: Concrete Poetry in England and Scotland* (Liverpool: Liverpool University Press, 2019), 17.

4 Dom Sylvester Houédard, "Arlington Une/Poetischesuntersuchungen in Glostershire," in *Arlington Une: Summer '66*, [5–11], quoted in Thomas, *Borderblurblurs*, 17.

5 While Houédard is specifically writing about concrete poetry—primarily understood as a visually oriented form in this context—he does acknowledge the importance of sound and sonic extensions in this kind of work. With that said, my understanding of borderblur is specific to the Canadian context, which I contend includes concrete, sound, and kinetic poetries.

6 Dom Sylvester Houédard, "'Between Poetry/Painting' Letter from Dom Sylvester Houédard 07/10/1965," bpNichol.ca, accessed 20 December 2021, http://bpnichol.ca/archive/documents/between-poetrypainting-letter-dom-sylvester-hou%C3%A9dard-07101965.

7 Houédard, "Between Poetry/Painting." Note that the punctuation used here reflects the original style choices made by the author, as is true of many other quotations reproduced throughout this book.

8 Irene Gammel and Suzanne Zelazo, "Introduction," in *Florine Stettheimer: New Directions in Multimodal Modernism* (Toronto: Book*hug, 2019), 4.

9 Dick Higgins (with Hannah Higgins), "Intermedia," *Leonardo* 34, no. 1 (2001): 49.

10   For this reason, I have chosen the notion of intermediality to conceive of borderblur. This strikes me as more appropriate than, say, the concepts of interdisciplinary or multidisciplinary, since it is the very idea of *discipline*, which connotes control, rules, and codes, that these poets sought to resist.

11   Stephen Scobie, *bpNichol: What History Teaches* (Vancouver: Talonbooks, 1984), 32.

12   bpNichol, "Interview: Pierre Coupey, Dwight Gardiner, Gladys Hindmarch, and Daphne Marlatt," in *Meanwhile: The Critical Writings of bpNichol*, ed. Roy Miki (Vancouver: Talonbooks, 2002), 153.

13   André Breton, "Manifesto of Surrealism" [1924], UbuWeb, accessed 15 December 2020, https://www.ubu.com/papers/breton_surrealism_manifesto.html.

14   Dedora and Dean, "Symposium of Linguistic Onto-Genetics," 57.

15   bill bissett, "Bill bissett's Acceptance Speech for Woodcock Award," *BC Booklook*, last modified 2 April 2008, https://bcbooklook.com/105-bill-bissett/.

16   See Jamie Reid, *A Temporary Stranger* (Vancouver: Anvil Press, 2017).

17   I have chosen to use the italicized *blewointment* to refer to the magazine and "Blew Ointment Press" (no italics) to refer to bissett's book-publishing venture. I must confess that my choice still violates the radical and playful spirit of the venture, but, following the lead of other scholars, I opted for this version of the latter title over various alternative renderings, such as Blewointmentpress, or blewointmentpress, which were used interchangeably across different publications.

18   Warren Tallman, "Wonder Merchants: Modernist Poetry in Vancouver during the 1960's," *boundary 2* 3, no. 1 (Autumn 1974): 78.

19   Tallman, 78.

20   bill bissett, "About In Search of Innocence: film by Len Forest, director; Jack Long, camera; addressed to them both," *blewointment*, no. 1 (1963): n.p.

21   bissett, n.p.

22   Patrick Lane, "bill bissett circa 1967–1968," *Capilano Review* 2, no. 23 (1997): 85.

23   Ken Norris, *The Little Magazine in Canada, 1925–80* (Toronto: ECW Press, 1984), 144.

24   Barry McKinnon, "Blewointment," *Open Letter* 7, no. 23 (1988): 74.

25   McKinnon, 74.

26   McKinnon, 76.

27   Gregory Betts, *In Search of Blew: An Eventual Index of* Blewointment *Magazine, 1963–1977* (Buffalo, NY: Among the Neighbours, 2016), 7–8.

28   On the formative role the "Sig Sam" library played in the formation of Nichol's poetics and his Toronto network, see Stephen Cain, "'A Vision in the UofT Stacks': bpNichol in the Library," in *Avant-Canada: Poets, Prophets, Revolutionaries*, ed. Gregory Betts and Christian Bök (Waterloo, ON: Wilfrid Laurier University Press, 2019), 59–75.

29   bpNichol et al., *grOnk*, no. 1 (1967): n.p.

30   Higgins, "Intermedia," 50.

31   Paul Dutton, "Underwhich Editions and the Radical Tradition," Underwhich Editions, accessed 1 May 2018, http://freemarketrecords.com/underwhich/about.shtml.

32 bpNichol, "Statement," *Journeying & the returns* (Toronto: Coach House Press, 1967), n.p.
33 Nichol, n.p.
34 Nichol, n.p.
35 Jerome Rothenberg, "The Anthology as Manifesto & as an Epic Including Poetry," in *Poetics & Polemics, 1980–2005* (Tuscaloosa: University of Alabama Press, 2008), 15.
36 bpNichol, "some afterwords," in *The Cosmic Chef*, ed. bpNichol (Ottawa: Oberon, 1970), 78.
37 bill bissett, "cordially death," in Nichol, ed., *Cosmic Chef*, 67.
38 Dedora and Dean, "Symposium of Linguistic Onto-Genetics," 57.
39 bill bissett, "bissett to bp 1972," MSC 12b.1.11.1, Ganglia Press Archive, Simon Fraser Library Special Collections and Rare Books, 3.
40 bpNichol, "Primary Days: Housed with the Coach at the Press, 1965–1987," in Miki, ed., *Meanwhile*, 422.
41 Nichol, 424.
42 bpNichol, "Interview: Fred Gaysek, Editor, *Artviews*," in Miki, ed., *Meanwhile*, 459.
43 See Stephen Cain, ed., *bp: Beginnings* (Toronto: BookThug, 2014). Also see Cain, "Imprinting identities."
44 See Benedict Anderson, *Imagined Communities: Reflections on the Origin and Spread of Nationalism* (New York: Verso, 2006).
45 Alan Twigg, "#105 bill bissett," *B.C. BookLook*, 2 February 2016, https://bcbooklook.com/105-bill-bissett/.
46 Steve McCaffery, "Trans-Avant-Garde: An Interview with Steve McCaffery," interviewed by Ryan Cox, *Rain Taxi*, Winter 2007–8, https://www.raintaxi.com/trans-avant-garde-an-interview-with-steve-mccaffery/.
47 Stephen Voyce, *Poetic Community: Avant-Garde Activism and Cold War Culture* (Toronto: University of Toronto Press, 2013), 204.
48 Graham Sharpe, "Pushing International Concrete Canada: 'The Communication Link' of Ganglia Press," *Open Letter* 10, no. 6 (Summer 1999): 119.
49 Sharpe, 121.
50 McCaffery, "Trans-Avant-Garde," n.p.
51 McCaffery, n.p.
52 Arjun Appadurai, *Modernity at Large: Cultural Dimensions of Globalization* (Minneapolis: University of Minnesota Press, 1996), 4.
53 Appadurai, 4.
54 "Bill Bissett and BP Nichol - 1 - Interviewed by Phyllis Webb" [*Extension: Here, Now, and Then*; first aired 2 July 1967], YouTube, uploaded by bill bissett, 11 April 2009, 8:38, https://youtu.be/eBmxvfktZaM.
55 Marshall McLuhan, "Canada: The Borderline Case," in *The Canadian Imagination*, ed. Dave Staines (Cambridge, MA: Harvard University Press, 1977), 241.
56 Voyce, *Poetic Community*, 208.
57 Marshall McLuhan, *COUNTERBLAST* (Toronto: n.p., 1954).

58 Marshal McLuhan. *The Gutenberg Galaxy: The Making of Typographic Man* (1962; New York: Signet, 1969), 7.
59 McLuhan, 9.
60 bill bissett, *Nobody Owns th Earth* (Toronto: Anansi, 1971), n.p.
61 Marshall McLuhan, *Understanding Media: The Extensions of Man* (New York: Signet, 1964), 19.
62 Appadurai, *Modernity at Large*, 4.
63 bpNichol, "Statement," n.p.
64 Frank Davey, *Post-National Arguments: The Politics of the Anglophone-Canadian Novel since 1967* (Toronto: University of Toronto Press, 1993), 15.
65 Nichol, "Statement," n.p.
66 bill bissett, *We Sleep Inside Each Other All* (Toronto: Ganglia Press, 1966), n.p.
67 bissett, n.p.
68 "Bill Bissett and BP Nichol - 2 - Interviewed by Phyllis Webb" [*Extension: Here, Now, and Then*; first aired 2 July 1967], YouTube, uploaded by bill bissett, 11 April 2009, 9:59, https://youtu.be/Vv8BN2NA6nk.
69 It is worth noting, too, that Webb also interviewed McLuhan on her CBC Radio show *Ideas* sometime between 1964 and 1969.
70 See Nichol, "The Medium Was the Message," in Miki, ed., *Meanwhile*, 298.
71 Ed Varney, *Concrete Poetry: An Exhibition in Four Parts* (Vancouver: University of British Columbia, 1969), n.p.
72 Steve McCaffery, "a poetry of blood," in *Text-Sound Texts*, ed. Richard Kostelanetz (New York: William Morrow and Company, 1980), 275.
73 John Robert Colombo, *New Direction in Canadian Writing* (Toronto: Holt, Rinehart and Winston of Canada, 1971), 39.
74 Butling, "(Re)Defining Radical Poetics," 17.
75 Gregory Betts and Christian Bök, "Time for the Avant-Garde in Canada," in *Avant-Canada: Poets, Prophets, Revolutionaries*, ed. Gregory Betts and Christian Bök (Waterloo, ON: Wilfrid Laurier University Press, 2019), 3.
76 Cathy Park Hong, "Delusions of Whiteness in the Avant-Garde," *Lana Turner Journal*, no. 7 (Winter 2014): 248.
77 Hong, 248.
78 Hong, 249–50.
79 Hong, 253.
80 Butling, 21.
81 Butling, 21.
82 Jamie Reid, "th pome wuz a store nd is th storee: th erlee daze uv blewointment," in *A Temporary Stranger*, (Vancouver: Anvil Press, 2017), 77.
83 Jim Daems, "'i wish war would fuck off': bill bissett's Critique of the Military-Cultural Complex," *Topia*, nos. 23–4 (2010): 368.

84 Judith Copithorne, "A Personal and Informal Introduction and Checklist Regarding Some Larger Poetry Enterprises in Vancouver Primarily in the Earlier Part of the 1960s," in *Making Waves: Reading BC and Pacific Northwest Literature*, ed. Trevor Carolan (Vancouver: Anvil Press, 2010), 90.

85 Gregory Betts, *Avant-Garde Canadian Literature: The Early Manifestations* (Toronto: University of Toronto Press), 71.

86 Betts, quotations at 72 and 71, respectively.

87 Betts, 71.

88 Betts, 74.

89 Only a small fraction of this dimension has been accounted for in this chapter, and even with the additional context provided in the following chapters, this book still cannot do it justice.

90 Sophie Seita, *Provisional Avant-Gardes: Little Magazine Communities from Dada to Digital* (Stanford, CA: Stanford University Press, 2019), 16.

91 Seita, 3.

92 Charles Bernstein, "Provisional Institutions: Alternative Presses and Poetic Innovation," *Arizona Quarterly: A Journal of American Literature, Culture, and Theory* 51, no. 1 (Spring 1995): 134.

93 Bernstein, 143.

94 Bernstein, 144.

95 Nichol, "Statement," n.p.

96 David Antin, "what it means to be avant-garde," in *what it means to be avant-garde* (New York: New Directions, 1993), 46.

97 Antin, 46–7.

98 Antin, 53.

99 Though, as I detail in chapter 2, women artists like Copithorne faced their own gender-based obstacles and barriers, which often made them feel dislocated from the scene.

100 bpNichol, *Doors: To Oz & Other Landscapes* (Toronto: grOnk, 1979): n.p.

101 Hong, "Delusions of Whiteness," 248.

102 Maxine Gadd, *Lost Language: Selected Poems* (Toronto: Coach House, 1982), 179.

103 Gadd, 179.

104 This is an important point to consider when examining these poets' politics more broadly, which included anti-colonial and anti-imperial stances, suggesting, perhaps, a premature embrace of McLuhan's ideas about connectedness and the global village.

105 See Andy Weaver, "'The White Experience between the Words': Thoughts on Steve McCaffery's *Carnival, the Second Panel: 1970–75*," *Open Letter* 14, no. 7 (Fall 2011): 130–46.

NOTES TO CHAPTER 2

1. Beat poet, inventor, and painter Brion Gysin was also included in this anthology. Born in Taplow, England, to Canadian parents, Gysin largely renounced his connections to Canada and spent most his life as an expatriate living abroad in France, Morocco, and elsewhere.
2. Mary Ellen Solt, "Introduction," in *Concrete Poetry: A World View*, ed. Mary Ellen Solt (Bloomington: Indiana University Press, 1968), 7.
3. Richard Kostelanetz, *Dictionary of the Avant-Gardes* (Chicago: Chicago Review Press, 1993), 45.
4. Lori Emerson, *Reading Writing Interfaces: From the Digital to the Bookbound* (Minneapolis: University of Minnesota Press, 2014), 99.
5. Marjorie Perloff, *Unoriginal Genius: Poetry by Other Means in the New Century* (Chicago: University of Chicago Press, 2010), 50.
6. *Canadada* is also the title of a Four Horsemen album mentioned in chapter 3.
7. David UU, "Beyond Concrete Poetry," *British Columbia Monthly* 1, no. 3 (December 1972): n.p.
8. UU, n.p.
9. UU, n.p.
10. Notably, too, critics Caroline Bayard, Stephen Scobie, Frank Davey, and others have placed the work of Canadian concrete poets in dialogue with international currents, including continental philosophies and literary theories, historical avant-gardism, and the international concrete poetry movement. In this way, concrete poetry in Canada is provoked by its strained relationship to cultural nationalism and animated by its relationship to international currents of avant-gardism.
11. David Antin, "what it means to be avant-garde," in *What It Means to Be Avant-Garde* (New York: New Directions, 1993), 53.
12. Wai Chee Dimock, *Through Other Continents: American Literature across Deep Time* (Princeton, NJ: Princeton University Press, 2006), 3.
13. Stephen Bann, *Concrete Poetry: An International Anthology* (London: London Magazine Editions, 1967), 7.
14. Bann, 7.
15. Eugen Gomringer, "Concrete Poetry," in Solt, ed., *Concrete Poetry*, 67.
16. Haroldo de Campos, Augusto de Campos, and Decio Pignatari, "Pilot Plan for Concrete Poetry," in Solt, ed., *Concrete Poetry*, 71.
17. bill bissett, "bissett to bp 1972," MSC 12b.1.11.1, Ganglia Press Archive, Special Collections and Rare Books, Simon Fraser University Library.
18. bpNichol, "Interview: Stuart Ross," in *Meanwhile: The Critical Writings of bpNichol*, ed. Roy Miki (Vancouver: Talonbooks, 2002), 345.
19. David UU, "Press Release for *Microprosophus*," LMS-0217, Box 14 1996-01, David Harris Fonds, Library and Archives Canada.
20. Antin, "what it means to be avant-garde," 53.

21 Ed Varney, *Concrete Poetry: An Exhibition in Four Parts* (Vancouver: University of British Columbia, 1969), n.p.
22 UU, "Press Release for *Microprosophus*."
23 Marshall McLuhan, *The Mechanical Bride: Folklore of Industrial Man* (1951; London: Duckworth Overlook, 2011), v.
24 McLuhan, 22.
25 McLuhan, 115.
26 Michael Hardt and Antonio Negri, *Empire* (Cambridge, MA: Harvard University Press, 2000), 285.
27 Hardt and Negri, 289.
28 Arjun Appadurai, *Modernity at Large: Cultural Dimensions of Globalization* (Minneapolis: University of Minnesota Press, 1996), 4.
29 John Berger, *Ways of Seeing* (London: British Broadcasting Corporation and Penguin Books, 1972), 129.
30 Berger, 131.
31 Berger, 154.
32 Eugen Gomringer, "From Line to Constellation," in Solt, ed., *Concrete Poetry*, 67.
33 Marjorie Perloff, *Radical Artifice: Writing Poetry in the Age of Media* (Chicago: University of Chicago Press, 1994), 116.
34 Perloff, 111.
35 Perloff, 117–18.
36 Perloff, 118–19.
37 Perloff, 119.
38 Steve McCaffery, "Lyric's Larynx," in *North of Intention: Critical Writings, 1973–1986* (New York: Roof, 2000), 178.
39 Steve McCaffery, "Diminished Reference and the Model Reader," in *North of Intention*, 13.
40 Steve McCaffery, "Writing as a General Economy," in *North of Intention*, 201.
41 See Sianne Ngai, "Raw Matter: A Poetics of Disgust," *Open Letter* 10, no. 1 (1998): 98–122.
42 Derek Beaulieu, "an afterward after words: notes toward a concrete poetic," in *fractal economies* (Vancouver: Talonbooks, 2006), 80.
43 An equally compelling but divergent reading of "Blues" could locate the word's significance in the context of the 1960s counterculture and the diffuse application of the word as part of the anti-war and hippie movements.
44 bpNichol, "Captain Poetry in Love," in *The Captain Poetry Poems Complete* (Toronto: BookThug, 2011), n.p.
45 Stephen Voyce, "Love in Precarious Times: bpNichol's Poetry of Re-invention" (presentation, Avant-Canada Conference, Brock University, St. Catharines, ON, 4–6 November 2014).
46 bpNichol, "Journeying & the Returns," *Journeying & the returns* (Toronto: Coach House, 1967), n.p.

47 Voyce, "Love in Precarious Times."
48 Nichol, "Journeying," n.p.
49 David UU, *Touch* (Toronto: Ganglia Press, 1967), n.p.
50 UU, n.p.
51 This is an approach to book making that lives on with jwcurry's 1c series, for which he imprints poems onto the backs of soup can labels and used envelopes.
52 McLuhan, *The Mechanical Bride*, v.
53 Darren Wershler, *The Iron Whim: A Fragmented History of Typewriting* (Ithaca, NY: Cornell University Press, 2007), 85.
54 Wershler, 140.
55 Wershler, 141.
56 Emerson, *Reading Writing Interfaces*, 87.
57 Emerson, 100.
58 Emerson, 88.
59 Stephen Cain, "Introduction: Clinamen/Context/Concrete/Community/Continuum," in "Breakthrough Nostalgia: Reading Steve McCaffery Then and Now," ed. Stephen Cain, special issue, *Open Letter* 14, no. 7 (Fall 2011): 5.
60 Nichol, bp, "The Annotated, Anecdoted, Beginnings of a Critical Checklist of the Published Works of Steve McCaffery," *Open Letter* 6 no. 9 (1987): 72.
61 Emerson, *Reading Writing Interfaces*, 114.
62 Steve McCaffery, *Carnival: The Second Panel, 1970–75* (Toronto: Coach House Press, 1978), n.p.
63 McCaffery, n.p.
64 Andy Weaver, "'the white experience between the words': Thoughts on Steve McCaffery's *Carnival, the second panel: 1970–75*," *Open Letter* 14, no. 7 (Fall 2011): 135.
65 Weaver, 136.
66 McCaffery, *Carnival: The Second Panel*, n.p.
67 Steve McCaffery, "Voice in Extremis," in *Prior to Meaning: The Protosemantic and Poetics* (Evanston, IL: Northwestern University Press, 2001), 161.
68 McCaffery, *Carnival: The Second Panel*, n.p.
69 McCaffery, 6.
70 Charles Russell, *Poets, Prophets, and Revolutionaries: The Literary Avant-Garde from Rimbaud through Postmodernism* (Oxford: Oxford University Press, 1985), 35.
71 For more on McCaffery's consideration of these ideas, see his essay "Writing as a General Economy" in *North of Intention*.
72 Paul Dutton, *The Plastic Typewriter* (London: Writer's Forum; Toronto: Underwhich Editions, 1993), n.p.
73 In particular, the rendition of the hymn that Dutton knew at the time was "Certainly Lord" by the Five Blind Boys of Mississippi, an American gospel quartet active between the years 1936 and 1994.

74 Paul Dutton, "Flamenco Sequence/1977," in *Sound Poetry: A Catalogue*, ed. bpNichol and Steve McCaffery (Toronto: Underwhich Editions, 1978), 44.

75 Dutton, 46.

76 See "Interview: Carole Itter with Lorna Brown," *Ruins in Process: Vancouver Art in the Sixties*, ed. Lorna Brown, Morris and Helen Belkin Art Gallery and Grunt Gallery, 1 June 2009, vancouverartinthesixties.com/interviews/carol-itter.

77 Wershler, *The Iron Whim*, 86.

78 Wershler, 86.

79 Wershler, 91.

80 Wershler, 92–3.

81 Wershler, 93.

82 N. Katherine Hayles, *How We Became Posthuman: Virtual Bodies in Cybernetics, Literature, and Informatics* (Chicago: University of Chicago Press, 1999), xi.

83 Gregory Betts, "Postmodern Decadence in Canadian Sound and Visual Poetry," in *Re:Reading the Postmodern: Canadian Literature and Criticism after Modernism*, ed. Robert David Stacey (Ottawa: University of Ottawa Press), 167.

84 Caroline Bayard, *New Poetics in Canada and Quebec: From Concretism to Post-Modernism* (Toronto: University of Toronto Press, 1989), 142.

85 Judith Copithorne, *Release* (Vancouver: Bau-Xi Gallery, 1969), 7.

86 Copithorne, 7.

87 Copithorne, 7.

88 Copithorne, 3.

89 Basmajian, like many other poets discussed in this book, used various different spellings of his name, including Shant Basmajian and Sha(u)nt Basmajian.

90 bpNichol, "Tabling Content: writing a reading of Shant Basmajian's *Quote Unquote*," in Miki, ed., *Meanwhile*, 194.

91 bill bissett, "why ths stars," in *Stardust* (Vancouver: Talonbooks, 1975), 8.

92 Friedrich Kittler, *Gramophone, Film, Typewriter* (Stanford, CA: Stanford University Press, 1999), 145.

93 Kittler, 119.

94 bill bissett, "THE TUBE IS GASEOUS," in *Stardust*, 12.

95 bissett, 12.

96 bissett, 12.

97 Sam Rowe, "Panopticon—Steve McCaffery," *Full Stop*, 15 May 2012, http://www.full-stop.net/2012/05/15/reviews/sam/panopticon-steve-mccaffery/.

98 Charles Bernstein, *A Poetics* (Cambridge, MA: Harvard University Press, 1992), 62.

99 Rowe, "Panopticon—Steve McCaffery."

100 Steve McCaffery, *Panopticon* (Toronto: Bookthug, 2011), n.p.

101 Bernstein, *A Poetics*, 64.

102 McCaffery, *Panopticon*, n.p.

103 Ann Rosenberg, *The Bee Book* (Toronto: Coach House, 1981), 58–9.

104 Rosenberg, 59.
105 Rosenberg, 61.
106 Rosenberg, 61.
107 Rosenberg, 86.
108 Rosenberg, 188.
109 Rosenberg, 188.
110 Rosenberg, 189.
111 George Bowering, "Vancouver as Postmodern Poetry," *Colby Quarterly* 29, no. 2 (June 1993): 113.
112 Stephen Morton, "Multiculturalism and the Formation of a Diasporic Counterpublic in Roy Kiyooka's *StoneDGloves*," *Canadian Literature*, no. 201 (Summer 2009): 89.
113 Roy Kiyooka, *Stoned Gloves* (Toronto: Coach House Press, 1971), n.p.
114 Kiyooka, n.p.
115 Brian Dedora, "I Have a Remember When," *Journal of Canadian Studies* 54, nos. 2–3 (Spring/Fall 2020): 322.
116 Dedora, 321.
117 Dedora, 321.

NOTES TO CHAPTER 3

1 "Why Are These People Screaming?," *Globe and Mail*, 23 March 1970.
2 Don Delaplante, "A Scream for Canada: Poet's Salute to Spring," *Globe and Mail*, 17 March 1970.
3 Delaplante.
4 Swede quoted in Delaplante.
5 Joe Rosenblatt, "Live in the West" (liner notes to the album *Live in the West*), Electronic Poetry Center, University of Pennsylvania, accessed on 2 January 2023, https://writing.upenn.edu/epc/authors/horsemen/liner.html.
6 Marshall McLuhan, *Understanding Media* (New York: Signet, 1964), 82.
7 Michael Hardt and Antonio Negri, *Empire* (Cambridge, MA: Harvard University Press, 2000), 280.
8 Hardt and Negri, 285.
9 Hardt and Negri, 286.
10 Hardt and Negri, 285.
11 Hardt and Negri, 289.
12 bpNichol, "Statement," *Journeying & the returns* (Toronto: Coach House Press, 1967), n.p.
13 Melissa Gregg and Gregory J. Seigworth, "Introduction," in *The Affect Theory Reader*, ed. Melissa Gregg and Gregory J. Seigworth (Durham, NC: Duke University Press, 2010), 1.
14 Dennis Lee, "Cadence, Country, Silence: Writing in Colonial Space," *boundary 2* 3, no. 1 (1974): 153.

15 "Bill Bissett and BP Nichol - 1 - Interviewed by Phyllis Webb" [*Extension: Here, Now, and Then*; first aired 2 July 1967], YouTube, uploaded by bill bissett, 11 April 2009, 8:38, https://youtu.be/eBmxvfktZaM.

16 See Sara Ahmed, *The Promise of Happiness* (Durham, NC: Duke University Press, 2010); Ahmed, *The Cultural Politics of Emotion* (New York: Routledge, 2015); Sianne Ngai, *Ugly Feelings* (Cambridge, MA: Harvard University Press, 2009).

17 See Brian Massumi, *Parables of the Virtual: Movement, Affect, Sensation* (Durham, NC: Duke University Press, 2002), and Massumi, *Politics of Affect* (Cambridge: Polity, 2015).

18 Myrna Kostash, *Long Way from Home: The Story of the Sixties Generation in Canada* (Toronto: James Lorimer and Co., 1980), xvi.

19 Hardt and Negri, *Empire*, 293.

20 Charles Bernstein "Provisional Institutions: Alternative Presses and Poetic Innovation," *Arizona Quarterly: A Journal of American Literature, Culture, and Theory* 51, no. 1 (Spring 1995): 144.

21 Steve McCaffery, "Sound Poetry: A Survey," in *Sound Poetry: A Catalogue*, ed. bpNichol and Steve McCaffery (Toronto: Underwhich Editions, 1978), 6.

22 McCaffery, 16.

23 Jerome Rothenberg, "Preface," in *Technicians of the Sacred: A Range of Poetries from Africa, America, Asia, Europe, and Oceania*, 3rd ed. (Berkeley: University of California Press, 2017), xvii.

24 Rothenberg, xvii.

25 Rothenberg, xvii.

26 Stephen Scobie, "Bissett, Bill," *Oxford Companion to Canadian Literature*, ed. William Toye and Eugene Benson, 2nd ed. (New York: Oxford University Press, 1997), https://www.oxfordreference.com/view/10.1093/oi/authority.20110803095508815.

27 bpNichol and Lionel Kearns, "bpNichol and Lionel Kearns at SGWU, [November] 1968," SpokenWeb Montreal, accessed 18 May 2018, https://montreal.spokenweb.ca/sgw-poetry-readings/bpnichol-and-lionel-kearns-at-sgwu-1968/#1.

28 Stephen Cain, "*CaNADAda*: The Four Horsemen's Ambivalent Nationalism" (presentation, Modern Language Association Convention, Toronto, ON, 7–10 January 2021).

29 Nichol and Kearns, "bpNichol and Lionel Kearns at SGWU."

30 Warren Tallman, "Wonder Merchants: Modernist Poetry in Vancouver during the 1960's," *boundary 2* 3, no. 1 (Autumn 1974): 66.

31 Michael McClure, "Tantra 49," *Ghost Tantras* (1964; San Francisco: City Lights Books, 2013).

32 bpNichol, "Interview: Nicette Jukelevics," in *Meanwhile: The Critical Writings of bpNichol*, ed. Roy Miki (Vancouver: Talonbooks, 2002), 133.

33 Jim Brown and Wayne Carr, *See/Hear: A Record Magazine*, See/Hear Productions, 1970, 33⅓ rpm. I am quoting here from the back of the record sleeve.

34 Dedora was initially involved in these sonic explorations but did not become an official member of the group.

35 Douglas Barbour, "Interview with Douglas Barbour," by rob mclennan, *Jacket*, no. 18 (August 2002), http://jacketmagazine.com/18/c-barbour-iv.html.
36 bpNichol, "Improvising Sound: Ten Poets on the Poetics of Sound," *Music Works*, no. 38 (1987): 10.
37 See "Douglas Barbour," UAlberta.ca, accessed 1 May 2018, https://sites.ualberta.ca/~dbarbour/bio.html.
38 Sean O'Huigin sometimes also rendered his name in lowercase, as sean o'huigin.
39 Sean O'Huigin and Ann Southam, *Sky Sails*, MHIC, 1973, 33⅓ rpm.
40 Rachel Zolf, "Travailing Gerry Shikatani's Protean Poetics," *West Coast Line* 41, no. 4 (Winter 2008): 8.
41 "Penn Kemp: Publications," Canadian Poetry Online, University of Toronto, accessed 6 February 2023, https://canpoetry.library.utoronto.ca/kemp/pub.htm.
42 For more on the Writers' Weekend, see Zena Cherry, "Poetry Meet 'Liberating,'" *Globe and Mail*, 4 June 1982.
43 Susan McMaster, *The Gargoyle's Left Ear: Writing in Ottawa* (Windsor, ON: Black Moss Press, 2007), 23.
44 McMaster, 23.
45 Susan McMaster, "Epilogue," *Arc*, no. 22 (Spring 1989): 67.
46 McMaster, *The Gargoyle's Left Ear*, 26.
47 Charles Bernstein, "Provisional Institutions: Alternative Presses and Poetic Innovation," *Arizona Quarterly: A Journal of American Literature, Culture, and Theory* 51, no. 1 (Spring 1995): 132.
48 Pauline Butling, "bpNichol and a Gift Economy: 'The Play of Value and the Value of Play,'" chap. 4 in *Writing in Our Time: Canada's Radical Poetries in English* (Waterloo, ON: Wilfrid Laurier Press, 2005), 68.
49 "Around Toronto This Week," *Globe and Mail*, 19 January 1973.
50 bpNichol, *Underwhich Checklist, 1978–1984* (Toronto: Ganglia Press, 1984), n.p.
51 Underwhich maintained the energy and spirit of Nichol's and McCaffery's efforts to internationalize Canada's connections to a transnational network. Of the nearly fifty cassettes produced as part of the Audiographics Series, not only did Underwhich feature the work of Canadians, including many of the poets mentioned so far, but they also released the work of international contributors, including Paula Claire, P. C. Fencott, and Bob Cobbing (England); Susan Frykberg (New Zealand–born); and Larry Wendt (United States).
52 Rudy and Butling, "Chronology 1 (1957–1979): From the Canada Council to Writing in Our Time," in *Writing in Our Time*, 13.
53 Richard Cavell, *McLuhan in Space: A Cultural Geography* (Toronto: University of Toronto Press, 2003), 137.
54 Jamie Hilder, *Designed Words for a Designed World: The International Concrete Poetry Movement, 1955–1971* (Montreal: McGill-Queen's University Press, 2016), 194.
55 McLuhan, *Understanding Media*, 82.
56 McLuhan, 83.

57 R. Murray Schafer, *The Soundscape: Our Sonic Environment and the Tuning of the World* (Rochester, VT: Destiny Books, 1993), 3.
58 Schafer, 273.
59 Schafer, 91.
60 Schafer, 91.
61 McCaffery, "Sound Poetry," 10.
62 McCaffery, 11.
63 McCaffery, 10.
64 bpNichol, introduction to *The Prose Tattoo: Selected Performances*, by the Four Horsemen (Milwaukee, WI: Membrane Press, 1983), n.p.
65 Hardt and Negri, *Empire*, 33.
66 Steve McCaffery, "a poetry of blood." *Text-Sound Texts*, ed. Richard Kostelanetz (New York: William Morrow and Company, 1980), 275.
67 McCaffery, 275.
68 Nichol, "Statement," n.p.
69 Nichol, n.p.
70 Steve McCaffery, "Lyric's Larynx," in *North of Intention: Critical Writings, 1973–1986* (New York: Roof, 2000), 178.
71 Steve McCaffery, "Diminished Reference and the Model Reader," in *North of Intention*, 13. Emphasis in original.
72 Steve McCaffery, "Writing as General Economy," in *North of Intention*, 214–15.
73 Paul Dutton, "Preface to *Right Hemisphere, Left Ear*," in McCaffery and Nichol, eds., *Sound Poetry*, 44.
74 Owen Sound, "From Correspondences: A Pun on Baudelaire," in McCaffery and Nichol, eds., *Sound Poetry*, 50.
75 Owen Sound, 50.
76 Owen Sound, 50.
77 Patricia Keeney Smith, "Creating the World She Inhabits," *Cross-Canada Writers' Quarterly* 9, no. 2 (1987): 8.
78 Smith, 8.
79 Lydia Fensom, "Dark Galaxies: The Poetry of Susan McMaster," *Quarry*, December 1987, 80.
80 McMaster, *The Gargoyle's Left Ear*, 26.
81 Dorothy Smith, *The Everyday World as Problematic: A Feminist Sociology* (Toronto: University of Toronto Press, 1987), 19.
82 Nichol, introduction to *The Prose Tattoo*, n.p.
83 Melissa Gregg and Gregory J. Seigworth, "Introduction," in *The Affect Theory Reader*, ed. Melissa Gregg and Gregory J. Seigworth (Durham, NC: Duke University Press, 2010), 1.
84 Adriana Cavarero, *For More than One Voice: Toward a Philosophy of Vocal Expression*, trans. Paul A. Kottman (Stanford, CA: Stanford University Press, 2005), 12.

85 Gregg and Seigworth, "Introduction," 1.
86 Stephen Voyce, *Poetic Community: Avant-Garde Activism and Cold War Culture* (Toronto: University of Toronto Press, 2013), 234.
87 James Sanders and Mark Prejsnar, "The Four Horsemen Burn through Atlanta," *Open Letter* 13, no. 8 (2009): 56.
88 Marq de Villiers, "You, Too, Can Become a Great Canadian Poet," *Globe and Mail*, 20 October 1973.
89 Gregg and Seigworth, "Introduction," 1.
90 De Villiers, "You, Too, Can Become a Great Canadian Poet."
91 Steve Goodman, *Sonic Warfare: Sound, Affect, and the Ecology of Fear* (Cambridge, MA: MIT Press, 2012), 82.
92 Owen Sound, "Biography," in *Meaford Tank Range* (Toronto: Wild Press, 1977), n.p.
93 Owen Sound, "Kesawagas," side 2, track 1 on *Meaford Tank Range*, Wild Productions, 1977, 33⅓ rpm.
94 Rothenberg, *Technicians of the Sacred*, 598.
95 Owen Sound, "Kesawagas."
96 Owen Sound, "A Spiral of Forgotten Intimacies," side 1, track 6 on *Sleepwalkers*, Underwhich, 1987, audiocassette.
97 Owen Sound, "A Spiral of Forgotten Intimacies."
98 Owen Sound, "A Spiral of Forgotten Intimacies."
99 McMaster, *Gargoyle's Left Ear*, 26.
100 McMaster, 26.
101 First Draft, "ABCD," side 2, track 11 on *Wordmusic*, self-released, 1986, audiocassette.
102 bpNichol, "A Love Song for Gertrude Stein," side 1, track 1 on *bp Nichol*, High Barnet Company, 1971, audiocassette.
103 bpNichol, "Incest Song," side 1, track 1 on *Motherlove*, Allied Record Corporation, 1968, phonodisc.
104 bpNichol, "Son of Sonnet," side 1, track 3, *bp Nichol*.
105 "Bill Bissett and BP Nichol - 2 - Interviewed by Phyllis Webb" [*Extension: Here, Now, and Then*; first aired 2 July 1967], YouTube, uploaded up bill bissett, 11 April 2009, 9:59, https://youtu.be/Vv8BN2NA6nk.
106 Unfortunately, I have been unable to track down any public recordings of bissett's early experiments with tape machines or multi-sensory environments.
107 Richard Kostelanetz, "Text-Sound Art: A Survey (Concluded)," *Performing Arts Journal* 2, no. 3 (Winter 1978): 80.
108 The vocalization of a lyric poem, for example, follows the action and emotion implied by its content (if the reader even goes so far as to do so).
109 Penn is credited as "Penn(y) Kemp" on the cassette, rather than her now more common spelling, Penn Kemp.
110 Penn Kemp, "Re Solution," side 1, track 1 on *Ear Rings*, Underwhich, 1987, audiocassette.

111 Kemp, "All the Men Tall," side 1, track 2 on *Ear Rings*.
112 Kemp, "Her Mind Set," side 1, track 5 on *Ear Rings*.
113 Kemp, "Matter Matters," side 1, track 6 on *Ear Rings*.
114 Smith, *The Everyday World as Problematic*, 19.

NOTES TO CHAPTER 4

1 Caroline Bayard and Jack David, "Interview with bp Nichol, February 10, 1976," in *Outposts/Avant-Poste*, ed. Jack David and Caroline Bayard (Erin, ON: Press Procépic, 1978), 27.
2 bpNichol, "'Syntax Equals the Body Structure': bpNichol in Conversation with Daphne Marlatt and George Bowering," in *Meanwhile: The Critical Writings of bpNichol*, ed. Roy Miki (Vancouver: Talonbooks, 2002), 276.
3 Nichol, 276.
4 Bayard and David, "Interview with bp Nichol," 27.
5 bpNichol, "Statement," *Journeying & the returns* (Toronto: Coach House, 1967), n.p.
6 bpNichol, "Pome Poem," side 1, track 2 on *Ear Rational: Sound Poems, 1966–1980*, Membrane Press/New Fire Tapes, 1982, audiocassette.
7 *Merriam-Webster Online*, s.v. "kinetic," accessed 10 February 2023, https://www.merriam-webster.com/dictionary/kinetic.
8 Suzanne Zelazo, "Sport as Living Language: bpNichol and the Bodily Poetics of the Elite Triathlete," *Canadian Literature*, no. 202 (Autumn 2009): 33.
9 Marshall McLuhan, *Understanding Media* (New York: Signet, 1964), 105.
10 Sara Ahmed, *Strange Encounters: Embodied Others in Post-coloniality* (New York: Routledge, 2000), 45.
11 Ahmed, 45.
12 Sara Ahmed, *The Cultural Politics of Emotion* (New York: Routledge, 2015), 28.
13 Ahmed, *Cultural Politics of Emotion*, 28.
14 Massumi, *Parables of the Virtual*, 58.
15 Massumi, 179.
16 Charles Olson, "Projective Verse," Poetry Foundation, 13 October 2009, https://www.poetryfoundation.org/articles/69406/projective-verse.
17 Olson.
18 Olson.
19 Hélène Cixous, "The Laugh of the Medusa," trans. Keith Cohen and Paula Cohen, *Signs* 1, no. 4 (Summer 1976): 875.
20 Barbara Godard, "Excentriques, Ex-centric, Avant-Garde: Women and Modernism in the Literatures of Canada," *A Room of One's Own* 8, no. 4 (Fall 1984): 64.
21 McLuhan, *Understanding Media*, 105.
22 Warren Tallman, "Wonder Merchants: Modernist Poetry in Vancouver during the 1960's," *boundary 2* 3, no. 1 (Autumn 1974): 60–1.

23   Tallman, 61–2.
24   Charles Olson, "Proprioception," in *Collected Prose*, ed. Donald Allen and Benjamin Friedland (Berkeley: University of California Press, 1997), 181.
25   Olson, "Projective Verse."
26   Oslon.
27   Olson.
28   Olson, "Proprioception," 181.
29   Frank Davey (quoting Robert Duncan), "Introduction," in *TISH No. 1–19*, ed. Frank Davey (Vancouver: Talonbooks, 1975), 9.
30   George Bowering, Poet as Projector," in Davey, ed., *TISH No. 1–19*, 18.
31   bpNichol, "Interview: Nicette Jukelevics," in Miki, ed., *Meanwhile*, 133–4.
32   Steve McCaffery, "Sound Poetry: A Survey," in *Sound Poetry: A Catalogue*, ed. Steve McCaffery and bpNichol (Toronto: Underwhich Editions), 10.
33   Frank Davey, *From There to Here: A Guide to English-Canadian Literature since 1960* (Erin, ON: Press Porcépic), 14.
34   McLuhan, *Understanding Media*, 113.
35   Marshall McLuhan, *The Mechanical Bride: Folklore of Industrial Man* (1951; London: Duckworth Overlook, 2011), 33.
36   McLuhan, 34.
37   Marshall McLuhan and Quentin Fiore, *The Medium Is the Massage: An Inventory of Effects* (New York: Bantam Books, 1967), 31–2.
38   McLuhan and Fiore, 38–9.
39   McLuhan and Fiore, 40.
40   McLuhan, *Understanding Media*, 105.
41   McLuhan, 105.
42   McLuhan, 105.
43   Michael Turner, "Expanded Literary Practices," *Ruins in Process: Vancouver Art in the Sixties*, ed. Lorna Brown, Morris and Helen Belkin Art Gallery and Grunt Gallery, 1 March 2011, http://expandedliterarypractices.vancouverartinthesixties.com/.
44   Keith Wallace, bill bissett, Al Neil, and Vancouver Art Gallery, *Rezoning: Collage and Assemblage: Bill Bissett, George Herms, Jess, Al Neil: Vancouver Art Gallery, October 19, 1989 to January 1, 1990* (Vancouver: Vancouver Art Gallery, 1989), 15.
45   Wallace et al., 21.
46   "The Intermedia Catalogue," *Ruins in Process: Vancouver Art in the Sixties*, ed. Lorna Brown, Morris and Helen Belkin Art Gallery and Grunt Gallery, 1 June 2009, http://intermedia.vancouverartinthesixties.com/introduction/default.
47   "The Intermedia Catalogue."
48   "The Intermedia Catalogue."
49   "The Dome Show—Intermedia Builds Geodesic Domes, Vancouver Art Gallery, 1970," *OunoDesign* (blog), 5 October 2009, http://ounodesign.com/2009/10/25/the-dome-show-intermedia-geodesic-domes-vancouver-art-gallery-1970.

50 Ed Varney, "Performance au/in Canada 1970–1990: Chronologie-chronology," in *Performance au/in Canada, 1970–1990*, ed. Alain-Martin Richard and Clive Robertson (Quebec: Éditions Intervention, 1991), 95.

51 Pauline Butling and Susan Rudy, "Chronology 1 (1957–1979): From the Canada Council to Writing in Our Time," in *Writing in Our Time: Canada's Radical Poetries in English* (Waterloo, ON: Wilfrid Laurier Press, 2005), 5.

52 Dennis Reid quoted in Rudy and Butling, 5.

53 jwcurry, "5th Galumph: Underwhich Editions," 17 March 2017, rich text file.

54 Nichol, "Statement," n.p.

55 Nichol, "Cold Mountain," in *Journeying & the returns*, n.p.

56 Nichol, n.p.

57 Nichol, n.p.

58 Nichol, n.p.

59 jwcurry (jwc 3o2), "COLD MOUNTAIN, by bpNichol. Toronto, Ganglia Press, 1966," Flickr, 28 October 2015, https://www.flickr.com/photos/48593922@N04/22530764462/in/album-72157628170195319/.

60 Later editions of the booklet, like damian lopes's reissue, published by Fingerprinting Inkoperated in 1992, burned quite differently because the design was slightly altered: "doesn't quite reproduce it correctly," remarks curry; "Lopes having made the center sheet a french-fold that won't tuck in properly. i tried to get it to poof out a bit to form a tube but this is as far as i could get it to stay open &, when i dropped a match down it—having held it a bit to get it going good—it promptly went out & i had to carefully use a lighter to get it going from the bottom of that central loop." curry, "COLD MOUNTAIN."

61 Earle Birney, *pnomes jukollages and other stunzas* (Toronto: Ganglia Press, 1969), n.p.

62 Sherril Grace, "Inner Necessity," review of *The Scream* by First Draft, *Canadian Literature, no. 108* (Spring 1986): 153.

63 First Draft, *The Scream: First Draft, the Third Annual Group Show* (Ottawa: Ouroboros, 1984), n.p. The quotes cited here and in the next note come from the book's back cover.

64 First Draft, n.p.

65 First Draft, 72.

66 First Draft, 84.

67 First Draft, n.p.

68 Lori Emerson and Derek Beaulieu, "Introduction: Media Studies and Writing Surfaces," in *Writing Surfaces: Selected Fiction of John Riddell*, ed. Lori Emerson and Derek Beaulieu (Waterloo, ON: Wilfrid Laurier University Press, 2013), 4.

69 John Riddell. *WAR*, vol. 1 (Toronto: Underwhich Editions, 1981), n.p.

70 Riddell, n.p.

71 Riddell, n.p.

72 Riddell, n.p.

73 Riddell, n.p.

74 Riddell, n.p.

75 Riddell, n.p.
76 Riddell, n.p.
77 Riddell, n.p.
78 John Riddell, "Object D'art," in *How to Grow Your Own Lightbulbs* (Toronto: Mercury Press, 1997), n.p.
79 Riddell, n.p.
80 Four Horsemen, "Andoas," *Only Paper Today* 6, nos. 4–5 (May–June 1979): 29.
81 McLuhan, *Understanding Media*, 105.
82 Four Horsemen, "Andoas," 28.
83 Four Horsemen, 29.
84 Michael Dean, "An Approach to Linguistic Onto-Genetics," *Open Letter* 4, nos. 6–7 (Winter 1980–1): 83.
85 Michael Dean, "An Introduction from the Chair," in *Papers Delivered at the Symposium of the Institute of Linguistic Onto-Genetics*, ed. bpNichol (Toronto: grOnk, 1985), 6.
86 Steve McCaffery, "The Perseus Project: Paleogorganization and the Sexual Life of Fossils," in Nichol, ed., *Papers Delivered at the Symposium of the Institute of Linguistic Onto-Genetics*, 69.
87 Janine Mather, "The Alphabet Speaks," *Papers Delivered at the Symposium of the Institute of Linguistic Onto-Genetics*, 81.
88 Michael Dean, "The Imagination of Aldo Breun," in Nichol, ed., *Papers Delivered at the Symposium of the Institute of Linguistic Onto-Genetics*, 18.
89 Dean, 17.
90 Dean, 16.
91 Dean, 19.
92 jwcurry, "defying linear deification," *Cross Canada Writers' Quarterly* 9, nos. 3–4 (1987): 7.
93 curry, 7.
94 curry, 7.
95 curry, 7.
96 curry, 7.
97 Bayard and David, "Interview with bp Nichol," 27.
98 Nichol, "'Syntax Equals the Body Structure': bpNichol in Conversation with Daphne Marlatt and George Bowering," in Miki, ed., *Meanwhile*, 276.
99 Alain-Martin Richard and Clive Robertson, eds., *Performance au/in Canada, 1970–1990* (Quebec: Éditions Intervention, 1991), 210.
100 Gerry Shikatani, email message to author, 14 August 2017.
101 Shikatani, email message.
102 Gerry Shikatani, "Introduction," in *Paper Doors: An Anthology of Japanese-Canadian Poetry*, ed. Gerry Shikatani and David Aylward (Toronto: Coach House Press, 1981), 7.
103 Shikatani, 8.
104 Gerry Shikatani, email message to author, 14 August 2017.

105 Rachel Zolf, "Travailing Gerry Shikatani's Protean Poetics," *West Coast Line* 41, no. 4 (Winter 2008): 8, 9.
106 Shikatani, "Introduction," 10–11.
107 Shikatani, 11.
108 Shikatani, 13.

NOTES TO CODA

1 Marshall McLuhan, "Canada: The Borderline Case," in *The Canadian Imagination*, ed. Dave Staines (Cambridge, MA: Harvard University Press, 1977), 241.
2 McLuhan, 226.
3 Lillian Allen, "poem for bp," in *Psychic Unrest* (Toronto: Insomniac Press, 1999), 69.
4 Wayne Keon, "an opun ltur tu bill bissett," in *Native Poetry in Canada: A Contemporary Anthology*, ed. Jeannette Armstrong and Lally Grauer (Peterborough, ON: Broadview Press, 2001), 86–7.
5 Gregory Betts, "Becoming Clinamen: McCaffery and the (new) York School of Writing," *Open Letter* 14, no. 7 (Fall 2011): 44.
6 Betts, 44.
7 damian lopes, "requiem for the avant-garde," *Sensory Deprivation/Dream Poetics* (Toronto: Coach House Books, 2000), 23.
8 See Eric Schmaltz, "The Politics of Memory: Digital Repositories, Settler-Colonialism, and Jordan Abel's *Un/inhabited*," *English Studies in Canada* 45, no. 4 (2019): 123–42.
9 Dani Spinosa, "Introduction," in *OO: Typewriter Poems* (Picton, ON: Invisible Books, 2020), 1–2.
10 Spinosa, 2.
11 Spinosa and Kate Siklosi, "Afterword," in *OO: Typewriter Poems*, 70.

Bibliography

Abel, Jordan. *Injun*. Vancouver: Talonbooks, 2016.

———. *Nishga*. Toronto: Penguin Random House, 2020.

———. *The Place of Scraps*. Vancouver: Talonbooks, 2013.

———. *Un/inhabited*. Vancouver: Project Space Press/Talonbooks, 2014.

Acorn, Milton. "Avoid Bad Mountain." *Blackfish*, no. 3 (1972): n.p.

Adachi, Ken. "B.C.'s 'Porno' Poetry Controversy Was All So Depressingly Familiar." *Toronto Star*, 13 January 1978.

Aguiar, Fernando. "Poetry: Or, the Interaction of Signs." Translated by Harry Polkinhorn. In *Corrosive Signs: Essays on Experimental Poetry (Visual, Concrete, Alternative)*, edited by César Espinosa, 89–98. Washington, DC: Maisonneuve Press, 1990.

Ahmed, Sara. *The Cultural Politics of Emotion*. New York: Routledge, 2015.

———. *The Promise of Happiness*. Durham, NC: Duke University Press, 2010.

———. *Strange Encounters: Embodied Others in Post-coloniality*. New York: Routledge, 2000.

Allen, Donald, ed. *The New American Poetry*. New York: Grove Press, 1960.

Allen, Lillian. "poem from bp." In *Psychic Unrest*, 69–70. Toronto: Insomniac Press, 1999.

———. *Women Do This Every Day: Selected Poems of Lillian Allen*. Toronto: Women's Press, 1993.

Anderson, Benedict. *Imagined Communities: Reflections on the Origin and Spread of Nationalism*. London: Verso, 2006.

Andrews, Jim. "Seattle Drift." 1997. Vispo.com, accessed 1 May 2018. http://www.vispo.com/animisms/SeattleDrift.html.

Antin, David. "what it means to be avant-garde." In *what it means to be avant-garde*, 41–61. New York: New Directions, 1993.

Apollinaire, Guillaume. *Calligrammes: Poems of Peace and War (1913–1916)*. Berkeley: University of California Press, 2004.

Appadurai, Arjun. *Modernity at Large: Cultural Dimensions of Globalization*. Minneapolis: University of Minnesota Press, 1996.

Armstrong, Jeannette, and Lally Grauer, eds. *Native Poetry in Canada: A Contemporary Anthology*. Peterborough, ON: Broadview Press, 2001.

Arnold, Grant and Karen Henry, eds. *Traffic: Conceptual Art in Canada, 1965–1980*. Vancouver: Vancouver Art Gallery, 2012.

Attali, Jacques. *Noise: The Political Economy of Music*. Translated by Brian Massumi. Minneapolis: University of Minnesota Press, 1985.

Atwood, Margaret. *Survival: A Thematic Guide to Canadian Literature*. Toronto: House of Anansi, 1972.

Aylward, David. *Typescapes*. Toronto: Coach House Press, 1967.

Balgiu, Alex, and Mónica de la Torre, eds. *Women in Concrete Poetry, 1959–1979*. New York: Primary Information, 2020.

Balkind, Alvin, Helen Goodwin, Iain Baxter, David Orcutt, Cortland Hultberg, Abraham Rogatnick, Takao Tanabe, Sam Perry, Roy Kiyooka, and Helen Sonthoff. "The Medium Is the Message—Festival of the Contemporary Arts, 1965," press release. *Ruins in Process: Vancouver Art in the Sixties*, edited by Lorna Brown. Morris and Helen Belkin Art Gallery and Grunt Gallery, accessed 1 May 2018. http://vancouverartinthesixties.com/archive/19.

Ball, Hugo. *Flight Out of Time: A Dada Diary*. Edited by John Elderfield. Translated by Ann Raimes. Berkeley: University of California Press, 1996.

———. "Seepferdchen und Flugfische." UbuWeb: Sound, accessed 1 May 2018. http://www.ubu.com/sound/ball.html.

Bancroft, Marian Penner. "UBC in the Sixties: A Conversation with Audrey Capel Doary, Gathie Falk, Donald Gutstein, Karen Jamieson, Glenn Lewis, Jamie Reid, Abraham Rogatnick." *Ruins in Process: Vancouver Art in the Sixties*, edited by Lorna Brown. Morris and Helen Belkin Art Gallery and Grunt Gallery, accessed 1 May 2018. http://vancouverartinthesixties.com/essays/ubc-in-the-sixties.

Bann, Stephen. *Concrete Poetry: An International Anthology*. London: London Magazine Editions, 1967.

Barbour, Douglas. "Douglas Barbour." UAlberta.ca, accessed 1 May 2018. https://sites.ualberta.ca/~dbarbour/bio.html.

———. "Interview with Douglas Barbour." By rob mclennan. *Jacket*, no. 18 (August 2002). http://jacketmagazine.com/18/c-barbour-iv.html.

———. "The Young Poets and the Little Presses, 1969." *The Dalhousie Review*, no. 50 (1970): 112–26.

Barbour, Douglas, and Stephen Scobie, eds. *Carnivocal: A Celebration of Sound Poetry*. Red Deer Press, 1999. Compact disc.

Barrett, Paul. "The Wild Rise of CanLit." *The Walrus*, 12 October 2017. https://thewalrus.ca/the-wild-rise-of-canlit.

Barthes, Roland. *The Grain of the Voice: Interviews, 1962–1980*. Translated by Linda Coverdale. Evanston, IL: Northwestern University Press, 2009.

———. *Image Music Text*. Translated and selected by Stephen Heath. London: Fontana Press, 1977.

———. *The Pleasure of the Text.* Translated by Richard Miller. New York: Hill and Wang, 1975.

———. *S/Z: An Essay.* Translated by Richard Miller. New York: Hill and Wang, 1974.

Barwin, Gary. "Squaring the Vowels: On the Visual Poetry of Judith Copithorne." *Jacket2*, 23 October 2013. https://jacket2.org/commentary/squaring-vowels.

Basmajian, Sha[u]nt. *Boundaries Limits and Space.* Toronto: Underwhich Editions, 1980.

———. *Quote Unquote.* Toronto: Old Nun Publications, 1973.

Bataille, Georges. *Eroticism.* Translated by Mary Dalwood. London: Penguin, 2012.

Baudrillard, Jean. *The Ecstasy of Communication.* Translated by Bernard and Caroline Schütze. London: Semiotexte, 2012.

Bayard. Caroline. *New Poetics in Canada and Quebec: From Concretism to Postmodernism.* Toronto: University of Toronto Press, 1989.

Bayard, Caroline, and Jack David. "Interview with bp Nichol, February 10, 1976." In *Outposts/Avant-Poste*, edited by Jack David and Caroline Bayard, 17–40. Erin, ON: Press Procépic, 1978.

Beaulieu, Derek. *fractal economies.* Vancouver: Talonbooks, 2006.

Beaulieu, Derek, Jason Christie, and Angela Rawlings. *Shift & Switch: New Canadian Poetry.* Toronto: Mercury Press, 2005.

Beker, Marilyn. "Concrete Poetry: Sound, Not Sense." *Toronto Daily Star*, 12 August 1967.

Berger, John. *Ways of Seeing.* London: British Broadcasting Corporation and Penguin Books, 1972.

Bernstein, Charles. *Close Listening: Poetry and the Performed Word.* New York: Oxford University Press, 1998.

———. *A Poetics.* Cambridge, MA: Harvard University Press, 1992.

———. "Provisional Institutions: Alternative Presses and Poetic Innovation." *Arizona Quarterly: A Journal of American Literature, Culture, and Theory* 51, no. 1 (Spring 1995): 133–46.

Berton, Pierre. *1967: The Last Good Year.* Toronto: Doubleday Canada, 1997.

Betts, Gregory. *Avant-Garde Canadian Literature: The Early Manifestations.* Toronto: University of Toronto Press, 2013.

———. "Becoming Clinamen: McCaffery and the (New) York School of Writing." *Open Letter* 14, no. 7 (Fall 2011): 41–55.

———. *Finding Nothing: The Vangardes, 1959–1975.* Toronto: University of Toronto Press, 2021.

———. *If Language.* Toronto: BookThug, 2005.

———. *In Search of Blew: An Eventual Index of* Blewointment *Magazine, 1963–1977.* Buffalo: Among the Neighbours, 2016.

———. "Postmodern Decadence in Canadian Sound and Visual Poetry." In *Re:Reading the Postmodern: Canadian Literature and Criticism after Modernism*, edited by Robert David Stacey, 151–79. Ottawa: University of Ottawa Press, 2010.

Betts, Gregory, and Christian Bök, eds. *Avant-Canada: Poets, Prophets, Revolutionaries*. Waterloo, ON: Wilfrid Laurier Press, 2019.

"Bill Bissett and BP Nichol - 1 - Interviewed by Phyllis Webb" [*Extension: Here, Now, and Then*; first aired 2 July 1967]. YouTube, uploaded by bill bissett, 11 April 2009, 8:38. https://youtu.be/eBmxvfktZaM.

"Bill Bissett and BP Nichol - 2 - Interviewed by Phyllis Webb" [*Extension: Here, Now, and Then*; first aired 2 July 1967]. YouTube, uploaded by bill bissett, 11 April 2009, 9:59. https://youtu.be/Vv8BN2NA6nk.

Birney, Earle. *pnomes jukollages and other stunzas*. Toronto: Ganglia Press, 1969.

bissett, bill. *Awake in the Red Desert*. Vancouver: Talonbooks, and See/Hear Productions, 1968. Print/33⅓ rpm.

———. *Beyond Even Faithful Legends: Selected Poems*. Vancouver: Talonbooks, 1980.

———. "Bill bissett's Acceptance Speech for Woodcock Award." *BC Booklook*, last modified 2 April 2008. https://bcbooklook.com/105-bill-bissett/.

———. *Birds*. Vancouver: Blew Ointment Press, 1970.

———. *blew trewz*. Vancouver: Blew Ointment Press, 1971.

———, ed. *Th Combind Blewointment Open Picture Book nd the News*. Vancouver: Blew Ointment Press, 1972.

———. *Dragon fly*. Toronto: Weed/Flower Press, 1971.

———. *Drifting into War*. Vancouver: Talonbooks, 1971.

———. *Th fifth sun*. Vancouver: Blew Ointment Press, 1975.

———. *Th jinx ship nd othr trips, or, Fires in the temple: pomes, drawings, collage*. Vancouver: Very Stone House, 1966.

———. *Th first snow*. Vancouver: Blew Ointment Press, 1979.

———. *the first sufi line*. Vancouver: Blew Ointment Press, 1973.

———. *The gossamer bed pan*. Vancouver: Blew Ointment Press, 1967.

———. *Gregorian chant*. Vancouver: Blew Ointment Press, 1967.

———. *Heat makes th heart's window for Martina*. Toronto: Coach House Press, 1967.

———. *The high green hill*. Vancouver: Blew Ointment Press, 1972.

———. *IBM: saga uv th relees uv human spirit from compuewterr funckshuns*. Vancouver: Blew Ointment Press, 1972.

———. *Image Being*. Vancouver: Blew Ointment Press, 1975.

———. *Lebanon voices*. Toronto: Weed/Flower Press, 1967.

———. *Liberating skies*. Vancouver: Blew Ointment Press, 1972.

———. *Living with th vishyun*. Vancouver: New Star Books, 1974.

———. *The Lost Angel Mining Co.* Vancouver: Blew Ointment Press, 1969.

———. *MEDICINE MY MOUTH'S ON FIRE*. Ottawa: Oberon Press, 1974.

———. *NOBODY OWNS TH EARTH*. Toronto: House of Anansi Press, 1971.

———. *Northern birds in color*. Vancouver: Talonbooks, 1981.

———, ed. *occupation issew*. Vancouver: Blew Ointment Press, 1970.

———. *Of th land divine service: poems*. Toronto: Weed/Flower Press, 1968.

———. *Parlant*. Vancouver: Blew Ointment Press, 1982.

———. "Part 1 bill bissett documentary" [*Strange Grey Day This*; first aired 1965]. YouTube, uploaded by bill bissett, 25 January 2009, 8:33. https://youtu.be/cEbTzMgeD4k.

———. "Part 2 bill bissett documentary" [*Strange Grey Day This*; first aired 1965]. YouTube, uploaded by bill bissett, 25 January 2009, 7:42. https://youtu.be/cEbTzMgeD4k.

———. "Part 3 bill bissett documentary" [*Strange Grey Day This*; first aired 1965]. YouTube, uploaded by bill bissett, 25 January 2009, 10:26. https://youtu.be/cEbTzMgeD4k.

———. *pass th food release th spirit book*. Vancouver: Talonbooks, 1973.

———. *Plutonium Missing*. Vancouver: Intermedia Press, 1976.

———. *Polar bear hunt*. Vancouver: Blew Ointment Press, 1972.

———. *Pomes for Yoshi*. Vancouver: Blew Ointment Press, 1972.

———, ed. *Poverty isshew*. Vancouver: Blew Ointment Press, 1972.

———. *Ready for framing*. Vancouver: Blew Ointment Press, 1982.

———. *RUSH: what fuckan theory; a study of language*. Vancouver: Blew Ointment Press, 1972.

———. *Sailor*. Vancouver: Talonbooks, 1978.

———. *Sa n th monkey*. Vancouver: Blew Ointment Press, 1980.

———. *Seagull on Yonge Street*. Vancouver: Talonbooks, 1983.

———. *Soul Arrow*. Vancouver: Blew Ointment Press, 1980.

———. *Space travl*. Vancouver: AIR, 1974.

———. *Stardust*. Vancouver: Blew Ointment Press, 1975.

———. *S the story I to*. Vancouver: Blew Ointment Press, 1970.

———. *Sunday Work*. Vancouver: Blew Ointment Press, 1969.

———. *Venus*. Vancouver: Blew Ointment Press, 1975.

———. *We sleep inside each other all: poems, prose & drawings*. Toronto: Ganglia Press, 1966.

———. *Where Is Miss Florence Riddle*. Toronto: Fleye Press, 1967.

———. *Th wind up tongue*. Vancouver: Blew Ointment Press, 1976.

———. *Words in th fire*. Vancouver: Blew Ointment Press, 1972.

———. *Yu can eat it at the opening*. Vancouver: Blew Ointment Press, 1974.

Bök, Christian. *Crystallography*. Toronto: Coach House Books, 2003.

———. *Eunoia*. Toronto: Coach House Books, 2009.

Bowering, George. "A Lyrical Boom in Slim Volumes." *Globe and Mail*, 23 September 1967.

———. "Poet as Projector." In *TISH 1–19*, edited by Frank Davey, 18. Vancouver: Talonbooks, 1975.

Bradley, Nicholas., ed. *We Go Far Back in Time: The Letters of Earle Birney and Al Purdy, 1947–1984*. Madeira Park, BC: Harbour Publishing, 2014.

Brennan, Teresa. *Transmission of Affect*. Ithaca, NY: Cornell University Press, 2004.

Breton, André. "Manifesto of Surrealism" (1924). UbuWeb, accessed 15 December 2020. https://www.ubu.com/papers/breton_surrealism_manifesto.html.

Bronson, A. A. "Of Frogs, Music, Words and Sound in Poetry." *Globe and Mail*, 10 March 1979.

Brossard, Nicole. *Mauve Desert*. Translated by Susanne de Lotbinière-Harwood. Toronto: Coach House Books, 1987.

Broudy, Hart. *A Book of A*. Vancouver: Blew Ointment Press, 1974.

———. *Serpentine*. Vancouver: Blew Ointment Press, 1982.

———. *Soundings*. Erin, ON: Press Procépic, 1979.

Brown, Jim, and Wayne Carr, eds. *See/Hear: A Record Magazine*. See/Hear Productions, 1970, 33⅓ rpm.

Bürger, Peter. *Theory of the Avant-Garde*. Translated by Michael Shaw. Minneapolis: University of Minnesota Press, 1984.

Butling, Pauline. "Phyllis Webb as Public Intellectual." In *Wider Boundaries of Daring: The Modernist Impulse in Canadian Women's Poetry*, edited by Di Brandt and Barbara Godard, 237–52. Waterloo, ON: Wilfrid Laurier Press, 2009.

Butling, Pauline, and Susan Rudy. *Writing in Our Time: Canada's Radical Poetries in English (1957–2003)*. Waterloo, ON: Wilfrid Laurier University Press, 2005.

Butterfield, Chris. "Some Notes on the Sound Poetry Festival." *MusicWorks*, no. 6 (Winter 1979): 2–3.

Cain, Stephen. *American Standard/Canada Dry*: Toronto: Coach House Books, 2005.

———. "'As Many Entrances and Exits as Are Possible': An Interview with Stephen Cain, Editor of *bp: beginnings* by bpNichol." By Kristen Smith. BookThug, 27 June 2014. http://bookthug.ca/as-many-entrances-and-exits-as-are-possible-an-interview-with-stephen-cain-editor-of-bpbeginnings-by-bpnichol.

———, ed. *bp: Beginnings*. Toronto: BookThug, 2014.

———. *Dyslexicon*. Toronto: Coach House Books, 1998.

———. *False Friends*. Toronto: BookThug, 2017.

———. "Imprinting Identities: An Examination of the Emergence and Developing Identities of Coach House Press and House of Anansi Press (1967–1982)." PhD diss., York University, 2002.

———. "Introduction: Clinamen/Context/Concrete/Community/Continuum." In "Breakthrough Nostalgia: Reading Steve McCaffery Then and Now," edited by Stephen Cain, special issue of *Open Letter* 14, no. 7 (Fall 2011): 5–16.

———. *Torontology*. Toronto: ECW, 2001.

———. "'A Vision in the UofT Stacks': bpNichol in the Library." In *Avant-Canada: Poets, Prophets, Revolutionaries*, edited by Gregory Betts and Christian Bök, 59–75. Waterloo, ON: Wilfrid Laurier Press, 2019.

Cain, Stephen, and Jay Millar. *Double Helix*. Toronto: Mercury Press, 2006.

Călinescu, Matei. *Five Faces of Modernity: Modernism, Avant-garde, Decadence, Kitsch, Postmodernism*. Durham, NC: Duke University Press, 1997.

Carlson, Tim. "bill bissett." In *bill bissett: Essays on His Works*, edited by Linda Rogers, 33–49. Toronto: Guernica, 2002.

Cavarero, Adriana. *For More Than One Voice: Toward a Philosophy of Vocal Expression*. Translated by Paul A. Kottman. Stanford, CA: Stanford University Press, 2005.

Cavell, Richard. *McLuhan in Space: A Cultural Geography*. Toronto: University of Toronto Press, 2003.

———. "World Famous Across Canada, or Transnational Localities." In *Trans.Can.Lit*, edited by Smaro Kamboureli and Roy Miki, 85–92. Waterloo, ON: Wilfrid Laurier University Press, 2007.

Cherry, Zena. "Poetry Meet 'Liberating': Readings and Cabaret Are Weekend Highlights." *Globe and Mail*, 4 June 1982.

Cixous, Hélène. "The Laugh of the Medusa." Translated by Keith Cohen and Paula Cohen. *Signs* 1, no. 4 (Summer 1976): 875–93.

Claire, Paula. *Steppingstones*. Underwhich Editions, 1990. Audiocassette.

Clinton, Martina. *Something in*. Toronto: Ganglia Press, 1969.

———. *Yonder Glow*. Vancouver: Blew Ointment Press, 1971.

Clutesi, George. *Potlatch*. Sidney, BC: Gray's Publishing, 1969.

———. *Son of Raven, Son of Deer*. Sidney, BC: Gray's Publishing, 1967.

Cohen, Leonard. *Beautiful Losers*. New York: Viking Press, 1966.

Colombo, John Robert. *New Direction in Canadian Poetry*. Toronto: Holt, Rinehart and Winston of Canada, 1971.

Copithorne, Judith. *Albion's Rose Blooms to Calypso Beat*. Toronto: Ganglia Press, 1985.

———. *Arrangements*. Vancouver: Intermedia Press, 1973.

———. *Meandering*. Vancouver Returning Press, 1967.

———. *Miss Tree's Pillow Book*. Vancouver: Intermedia Press, 1971.

———. "A Personal and Informal Introduction and Checklist Regarding Some Larger Poetry Enterprises in Vancouver Primarily in the Earlier Part of the 1960s." In *Making Waves: Reading BC and Pacific Northwest Literature*, edited by Trevor Carolan, 89–101. Vancouver: Anvil Press, 2010.

———. *Rain*. Toronto: Ganglia Press, 1968.

———. *Release*. Vancouver: Bau-Xi Gallery, 1969.

———. *Returning*. Vancouver: Returning Press, 1965.

———. *Runes*. Toronto: Coach House Press; Vancouver: Intermedia Press, 1970.

———. [Untitled.] *blewointment* 2, no. 4 (September 1964): n.p.

———. *Where Have I Been?* Vancouver: Very Stone House, 1967.

Coupey, Pierre. "The Alphabet of Blood." *Delta*, no. 24 (December 1964): 13–20.

Cox, Ryan J. "HP Sauce and the Hate Literature of Pop Art: bill bissett in the House of Commons." *English Studies in Canada* 37, nos. 3–4 (2011): 147–62.

curry, jw. "defying linear deification." *Cross Canada Writers' Quarterly* 9, nos. 3–4 (1987): 6–8.

———. "5th Galumph: Underwhich Editions." 17 March 2017. Rich text file.

Daems, Jim. "i wish war wud fuck off": bill bissett's Critique of the Military-Cultural Complex." *Topia*, nos. 23–4 (2010): 368–80.

Davey, Frank. *Aka BpNichol: A Preliminary Biography*. Toronto: ECW, 2012.

———. *From There to Here: A Guide to English-Canadian Literature since 1960*. Erin, ON: Press Porcépic, 1974.

———. "Not Just Representation: The Sound and Concrete Poetries of The Four Horsemen." In *Crosstalk: Canadian and Global Imaginaries in Dialogue*, edited by Diana Brydon and Marta Dvorak, 135–50. Waterloo, ON: Wilfrid Laurier University Press, 2012.

———. *Post-national Arguments: The Politics of the Anglophone-Canadian Novel since 1967*. Toronto: University of Toronto Press, 1993.

———. *Reading Canadian Reading*. Winnipeg: Turnstone Press, 1988.

———. *Surviving the Paraphrase: Eleven Essays on Canadian Literature*. Winnipeg: Turnstone, 1983.

———, ed. *TISH No. 1–19*. Vancouver: Talonbooks, 1975.

———. *When TISH Happens: The Unlikely Story of Canada's Most Influential Literary Magazine*. Toronto: ECW, 2011.

David, Jack. "Visual Poetry in Canada: Birney, Bissett, and Bp." *Studies in Canadian Literature/Études En littérature Canadienne* 2, no. 2 (1977). https://journals.lib.unb.ca/index.php/SCL/article/view/7870.

Dean, Michael. "An Approach to Linguistic Onto-Genetics." *Open Letter* 4, nos. 6–7 (Winter 1980–1): 83.

———. *The Imagination of Aldo Breun*. 21–2 November 1981, Toronto, ON.

———. "The Imagination of Aldo Breun." In *Papers Delivered at the Symposium of the Institute of Linguistic Onto-Genetics*, edited by bpNichol, 11–20. Toronto: grOnk, 1985.

———. "An Introduction from the Chair." In *Papers Delivered at the Symposium of the Institute of Linguistic Onto-Genetics*, edited by bpNichol, 5–6. Toronto: grOnk, 1985.

De Campos, Augusto. "Poema Bomba." YouTube, uploaded by Sesc em São Paulo, 30 January 2018, 0:25. https://www.youtube.com/watch?v=h3gzuQ-3R94.

De Campos, Haroldo, Augusto de Campos, and Decio Pignatari. "Pilot Plan for Concrete Poetry." In *Concrete Poetry: A World View*, edited by Mary Ellen Solt, 71–2. Bloomington: Indiana University Press, 1968.

Dedora, Brian. *CRACK*. Toronto: self-published, 1978.

———. *Eye Where: A Book of Visuals*. [Toronto]: Teksteditions, 2014.

———. "I Have a Remember When." *Journal of Canadian Studies* 54, nos. 2–3 (Spring–Fall 2020): 320–33.

Dedora, Brian, and Michael Dean, "The Symposium of Linguistic Onto-Genetics: An Introduction." *Canadian Poetry*, nos. 84–5 (2019): 56–79.

Delaplante, Don. "A Scream for Canada: Poet's Salute to Spring." *Globe and Mail*, 17 March 1970.

De Villiers, Marq. "You, Too, Can Become a Great Canadian Poet." *Globe and Mail*, 20 October 1973.

Dimock, Wai Chee. "Theory of Resonance." *PMLA* 112, no. 5 (October 1997): 1060–71.

———. *Through Other Continents: American Literature across Deep Time*. Princeton, NJ: Princeton University Press, 2006.

Dobson, Kit. *Transnational Canadas: Anglo-Canadian Literature and Globalization*. Waterloo, ON: Wilfrid Laurier University Press, 2009.

Dolar, Mladen. *A Voice and Nothing More*. Cambridge, MA: MIT Press, 2006.

"The Dome Show—Intermedia Builds Geodesic Domes, Vancouver Art Gallery, 1970." *Ouno Design* (blog), 5 October 2009. http://ounodesign.com/2009/10/25/the-dome-show-intermedia-geodesic-domes-vancouver-art-gallery-1970.

Donen, Stanley, dir. *Royal Wedding*. Beverly Hills, CA: MGM, 1951.

Duchamp, Marcel. *With Hidden Noise*. 1916. Philadelphia Museum of Art, Philadelphia, PA. Mixed media.

Dutton, Paul. "A Preface to 'Right Hemisphere, Left Ear'." In *Sound Poetry: A Catalogue*, edited by bpNichol and Steve McCaffery, 44. Toronto: Underwhich Editions, 1978.

———. "From *The Plastic Typewriter:* Flamenco sequence/1977." In *Sound Poetry: A Catalogue*, edited by bpNichol and Steve McCaffery, 45–6. Toronto: Underwhich Editions, 1978.

———. *The Plastic Typewriter*. London: Writer's Forum; Toronto: Underwhich Editions, 1993.

———. *Sonosyntactics: Selected and New Poetry*. Edited by Gary Barwin. Waterloo, ON: Wilfrid Laurier University Press, 2015.

———. "Underwhich Editions and the Radical Tradition." Underwhich Editions, accessed 1 May 2018. http://freemarketrecords.com/underwhich/about.shtml.

Drucker, Johanna. *Figuring the Word: Essays on Books, Writing, and Visual Poetics*. New York: Granary Books, 1998.

Earl, Amanda. *Judith: Women Making Visual Poetry*. Malmo, SE: Timglaset, 2021.

Early, Len. "Bill Bissett: Poetics, Politics & Vision." In *Brave New Wave*, edited by Jack David, 143–71. Windsor, ON: Black Moss, 1978.

———. "Introduction." In *Beyond Even Faithful Legends*, 11–19. Vancouver: Talonbooks, 1980.

Emerson, Lori. *Reading Writing Interfaces: From the Digital to the Bookbound*. Minneapolis: University of Minnesota Press, 2014.

———. "Women Dirty Concrete Poets." Loriemerson.net, accessed 1 May 2018. https://loriemerson.net/2011/05/04/women-dirty-concrete-poets.

Fenollosa, Ernest. *The Chinese Written Character as a Medium for Poetry*. New York: Fordham University Press, 2008.

Fensom, Lydia. "Dark Galaxies: The Poetry of Susan McMaster." *Quarry* (December 1987): 78–82.

Fetherling, George. *Travels by Night: A Memoir*. Toronto: Quattro Books, 2014.

Finlay, Ian Hamilton. *Ian Hamilton Finlay: Selections*. Edited by Alec Finlay. Berkeley: University of California Press, 2012.

———. *Stony Path/Little Sparta*. 1966–present. Dunsyre, UK. Mixed media.

First Draft. *North/South: Wordmusic Performance Scores for One to Seven Speakers*. Toronto: Underwhich Editions, 1987.

———. *Pass This Way Again*. Underwhich Editions, 1983.

———. *The Scream: First Draft, the Third Annual Group Show*. Ottawa: Ouroboros, 1984.

———. *Wordmusic*. Self-released, 1986, audiocassette.

———. *Wordmusic 2: 1981 First Draft 2007*. Stove Top Studio, 2007, CD.

Forest, Léonard, dir. *In Search of Innocence*. National Film Board of Canada, 1964.

Four Horsemen. "Andoas." *Only Paper Today* 6, nos. 4–5 (May–June 1979): 29–31.

———. *Bootleg*. Underwhich Editions, 1981, audiocassette.

———. *Canadada*. Griffin House, 1974, 33⅓ rpm.

———. *Live in the West*. Starborne Productions, 1977, 33⅓ rpm.

———. *The Prose Tattoo: Selected Performance Scores*. Milwaukee: Membrane Press, 1983.

———. *2 Nights*. Underwhich Editions, 1988, audiocasette.

Freedman, Adele. "Sounds Unlikely: What Is Elating about Sound Poetry Is the Sense of Human Possibility It Conveys." *Globe and Mail*, 23 March 1978.

Freytag-Loringhoven, Elsa von. *Body Sweats: The Uncensored Writings of Elsa Von Freytag-Loringhoven*. Edited by Irene Gammel and Suzanne Zelazo. Cambridge, MA: MIT Press, 2016.

Friedman, Susan Stanford. "Planetarity: Musing Modernist Studies." *Modernism/Modernity* 17, no. 3 (2010): 471–99.

———. *Planetary Modernisms: Provocations on Modernity across Time*. New York: Columbia University Press, 2015.

Friskney, Janet B. *New Canadian Library: The Ross-McClelland Years, 1952–1978*. Toronto: University of Toronto Press, 2007.

Gadd, Maxine. *Guns of the West: Poems*. Vancouver: Blew Ointment Press, 1967.

———. *Hochelaga*. Vancouver: Blew Ointment Press, 1970.

———. *Lost Language: Selected Poems*. Edited by Daphne Marlatt and Ingrid Klassen. Toronto: Coach House Press, 1982.

———. *Westerns*. Vancouver: AIR, 1975.

Gammell, Irene and Suzanne Zelazo, eds. *Florine Stettheimer: New Directions in Multimodal Modernism*. Toronto: Book*hug, 2019.

Garnet, Eldon, Ed. *W)here: The Other Canadian Poetry*. Erin, ON: Press Procépic, 1974.

Gauvreau, Claude. *Entrails*. Translated by Ray Ellenwood. Toronto: Coach House Press, 1981.

Geddes, Gerry. *Twentieth Century Poetry and Poetics*. London: Oxford University Press, 1969.

George, Chief Dan. *My Heart Soars*. Toronto: Hancock House Publishers, 1974.

———. *My Spirit Soars*. Toronto: Hancock House Publishers, 1982.

Glassco, John. "At the Mermaid Inn—Poet as Performer." *Globe and Mail*, 12 November 1977.

Gnarowski, Michael, and Eli Dudek, eds. *The Making of Modern Poetry in Canada*. Toronto: Ryerson Press, 1970.

Godard, Barbara. "Excentriques, Ex-centric, Avant-Garde: Women and Modernism in the Literatures of Canada." *A Room of One's Own* 8, no. 4 (Fall 1984): 57–75.

Gomringer, Eugen. "Concrete Poetry." In *Concrete Poetry: A World View*, edited by Mary Ellen Solt, 68. Bloomington: Indiana University Press, 1968.

———. "From Line to Constellation." In *Concrete Poetry: A World View*, edited by Mary Ellen Solt, 67. Bloomington: Indiana University Press, 1968.

Goodman, Steve. *Sonic Warfare: Sound, Affect, and the Ecology of Fear*. Cambridge, MA: MIT Press, 2012.

Grace, Sherril. "Inner Necessity." Review of *The Scream* by First Draft. *Canadian Literature*, no. 108 (Spring 1986): 152–5.

Gregg, Melissa, and Gregory J. Seigworth, eds. *The Affect Theory Reader*. Durham, NC: Duke University Press, 2010.

Hardt, Michael, and Antonio Negri. *Commonwealth*. Cambridge, MA: Harvard University Press, 2009.

———. *Empire*. Cambridge, MA: Harvard University Press, 2000.

———. *Multitude: War and Democracy in the Age of Empire*. New York: Penguin, 2004.

Harvey, David. *A Brief History of Neoliberalism*. Oxford: Oxford University Press, 2005.

Havelda, John. "Against Preconditioning: Steve McCaffery's Sound Poetry." *West Coast Line* 46, no. 1 (2012): 96–110.

Hayles, N. Katherine. *How We Became Posthuman: Virtual Bodies in Cybernetics, Literature, and Informatics* Chicago: University of Chicago Press, 1999.

Higgins, Dick. *George Herbert's Pattern Poems: In Their Tradition*. West Glover, VT: Unpublished Editions, 1977.

———. "Statement on Intermedia." ArtPool, accessed 1 May 2018. http://www.artpool.hu/Fluxus/Higgins/intermedia2.html.

Higgins, Dick, with Hannah Higgins. "Intermedia." *Leonardo* 34, no. 1 (February 2001): 49–54.

Hilder, Jamie. "Concrete Poetry and Conceptual Art: A Misunderstanding." *Contemporary Literature* 54, no. 3 (Fall 2013): 578–614.

———. *Designed Words in a Designed World: The International Concrete Poetry Movement, 1955-1971*. Montreal: McGill-Queen's University Press, 2016.

Hindmarch, Gladys. *Wanting Everything: The Collected Works*. Edited by Deanna Fong and Karis Shearer. Vancouver: Talonbooks, 2020.

Hong, Cathy Park. "Delusions of Whiteness in the Avant-Garde." *Lana Turner Journal*, no. 7 (Winter 2014): 248–53.

Houédard, Dom Sylvester. "'Between Poetry/Painting': Letter from Dom Sylvester Houédard 07/10/1965." bpNichol.ca, accessed 18 September 2021. http://bpnichol.ca/archive/documents/between-poetrypainting-letter-dom-sylvester-hou%C3%A9dard-07101965.

———. *Notes from the Cosmic Typewriter: The Life and Work of Dom Sylvester Houédard*. Edited by Nicola Sampson. London: Occasional Papers, 2012.

"The Intermedia Catalogue." *Ruins in Process: Vancouver Art in the Sixties*, edited by Lorna Brown. Morris and Helen Belkin Art Gallery and Grunt Gallery, accessed 1 May 2018. http://intermedia.vancouverartinthesixties.com.

Itter, Carole. "Carole Itter with Lorna Brown." *Ruins in Process: Vancouver Art in the Sixties*, edited by Lorna Brown. Morris and Helen Belkin Art Gallery and Grunt Gallery, accessed 1 May 2018. vancouverartinthesixties.com/interviews/carol-itter.

Jaeger, Peter. *The ABC of Reading TRG*. Vancouver: Talonbooks, 1999.

Jameson, Frederic. *Postmodernism; or, The Culture of Late Capitalism*. Durham, NC: Duke University Press, 1991.

———. *A Singular Modernity: Essay on the Ontology of the Present*. London: Verso, 2002.

Jansen, Ann. "Poetry Event Rich in Variety." *Globe and Mail*, 9 July 1982.

Jirgens, Karl. *bill bissett and His Works*. Toronto: ECW, 1992.

———. "Chopping Wood, an Excerpt from a Talk with bill bissett in a Toronto Restaurant during the Spring of 1980." *Rampike* 1, nos. 2–3 (1980): 22.

———. "A Short History of 'Pataphysics.'" *Rampike* 5, no. 2 (1986): 8–12.

Jones, D. G. *Butterfly on Rock: A Study of Themes and Images in Canadian Literature*. Toronto: University of Toronto Press, 1970.

Kamboureli, Smaro. "Preface." In *Trans.Can.Lit: Resituating the Study of Canadian Literature*, edited by Smaro Kamboureli and Roy Miki, vii–xv. Waterloo, ON: Wilfrid Laurier University Press, 2007.

Kamboureli, Smaro, and Kit Dobson. *Producing Canadian Literature: Authors Speak on the Literary Marketplace*. Waterloo, ON: Wilfrid Laurier University Press, 2013.

Kamboureli, Smaro, and Roy Miki, eds. *Trans.Can.Lit: Resituating the Study of Canadian Literature*. Waterloo: Wilfrid Laurier University Press, 2007.

Kamboureli, Smaro, and Robert Zacharias, eds. *Shifting the Ground of Canadian Literary Studies*. Waterloo, ON: Wilfrid Laurier University Press, 2012.

Karasick, Adeena. "A Writing Outside of Writing." In *bill bissett: Essays on His Works*, edited by Linda Rogers, 50–71. Toronto: Guernica, 2002.

Kemp, Penn. "About Penn Kemp." Penn Kemp (blog), accessed 15 December 2022. http://pennkemp.weebly.com/about.html.

———. *Bearing Down*. Toronto: Coach House, 1972.

———. *Ear Rings*. Underwhich Editions, 1987, audiocassette.

Keon, Wayne. "an opn ltur tu bill bissett." In *Native Poetry in Canada: A Contemporary Anthology*, edited by Jeannette Armstrong and Lally Grauer, 86–7. Peterborough, ON: Broadview Press, 2001.

Kerouac, Jack. "Jack Kerouac, The Art of Fiction No. 41." Interviewed by Ted Berrigan. *Paris Review*, no. 43 (Summer 1968). https://www.theparisreview.org/interviews/4260/jack-kerouac-the-art-of-fiction-no-41-jack-kerouac.

Kittler, Friedrich. *Gramophone, Film, Typewriter*. Stanford, CA: Stanford University Press, 1999.

Kiyooka, Roy. *Pacific Windows: Collected Poems of Roy K. Kiyooka*. Edited by Roy Miki. Vancouver: Talonbooks, 1997.

———. *Stoned Gloves*. Toronto: Coach House Press, 1970.

Kostash, Myrna. *Long Way from Home: The Story of the Sixties Generation in Canada*. Toronto: James Lorimer & Company, 1980.

Kostelanetz, Richard. *Dictionary of the Avant-Gardes*. Chicago: Chicago Review Press, 1993.

———. "Text-Sound Art: A Survey." *Performing Arts* 2, no. 2 (Fall 1977): 61–70.

———. "Text-Sound Art: A Survey (Concluded)." *Performing Arts Journal* 2, no. 3 (Winter 1978): 71–84.

———, ed. *Text-Sound Texts*. New York: William Morrow and Company, 1980.

Kress, Gunther. *Multimodality: A Social Semiotic Approach to Contemporary Communication*. New York: Routledge, 2010.

Kress, Gunther, and Carey Jewitt, eds. *Multimodal Literacy*. New York: Peter Lang, 2003.

Kress, Gunther, and Theo Van Leeuwen. *Multimodal Discourse: The Modes and Media of Contemporary Communication*. London: Oxford University Press, 2001.

———. *Reading Images: The Grammar of Visual Design*. 2nd ed. New York: Routledge, 2006. First published 1996.

Kruchenykh, A. "Declaration of the Word as Such." In *Russian Futurism through Its Manifestoes, 1912–1928*. Edited and translated by Anna Lawton and Herbert Eagle, 67–8. Ithaca, NY: Cornell University Press, 1988.

Kruchenykh, A., and V. Klebnikov. "From *The Word as Such*." In *Russian Futurism through Its Manifestoes, 1912–1928*. Edited and translated Anna Lawton and Herbert Eagle, 57–62. Ithaca, NY: Cornell University Press, 1988.

Lagace, Naithan, Niigaanwewidam, and James Sinclair. "The White Paper Policy, 1969." *Canadian Encyclopedia*. Last modified 10 June 2020. https://www.thecanadianencyclopedia.ca/en/article/the-white-paper-1969

Lamberti, Elena. *Marshall McLuhan's Mosaic: Probing the Literary Origins of Media Studies*. Toronto: University of Toronto Press, 2012.

Lane, Patrick. "bill bissett circa 1967–1968." *Capilano Review* 2, no. 23 (1997): 85–8.

Lawton, Anna, and Herbert Eagle, eds. *Russian Futurism through Its Manifestoes, 1912–1928*. Ithaca. NY: Cornell University Press, 1988.

Lee, Dennis. "Cadence, Country, Silence: Writing in Colonial Space." *boundary 2* 3, no. 1 (1974): 151–68.

———. *Civil Elegies*. Toronto: House of Anansi Press, 1968.

———. *Kingdom of Absence*. Toronto: House of Anansi Press, 1967.

Lee, Sook Yin. *Where Have All the Poets Gone?* Canadian Broadcasting Corporation, 25 March 2016, 49:56. https://www.cbc.ca/player/play/2685434391.

Lefler, Peggy. *Anthology*. Toronto: a scenario press, 1989.

Lippard, Lucy R. *Six Years: The Dematerialization of the Art Object from 1966 to 1972.* 1st paperback ed. Berkeley: University of California Press, 1997. First published 1973.

lopes, damian. *sensory deprivation/dream poetics*. Toronto: Coach House Press, 2000.

Mac Low, Jackson. "Of the Black Tarantula Crossword Gathas." PennSound, accessed 1 May 2018. http://writing.upenn.edu/pennsound/x/Mac-Low.php.

———. "Phoeneme Dance for John Cage." PennSound, accessed 1 May 2018. http://writing.upenn.edu/pennsound/x/Mac-Low.php.

———. *Thing of Beauty: New and Selected Works*. Edited by Anne Tardos. Berkeley: University of California Press, 2008.

Mallarmé, Stéphane. *A Roll of the Dice*. Translated by Robert Bononno and Jeff Clark. Seattle: Wave Books, 2015.

Mandel, Eli, ed. *Poets of Contemporary Canada, 1960–1970*. Toronto: McClelland and Stewart, 1972.

Marinetti, F. T. "Destruction of Syntax–Wireless Imagination–Words-in-Freedom (May 1913)." In *Modernism: An Anthology*, edited by Lawrence S. Rainey, 27–34. Malden, MA: Blackwell, 2011.

———. "Founding Manifesto of Futurism." Italianfuturism.org, accessed 1 May 2018. https://www.italianfuturism.org/manifestos/foundingmanifesto.

———. "A Response to Objections (Aug. 1912)." In *Modernism: An Anthology*, edited by Lawrence S. Rainey, 20–3. Malden, MA: Blackwell, 2011.

Mars, Tanya, and Johanna Householder, eds. *Caught in the Act: An Anthology of Performance Art by Canadian Women*. Toronto: YYZ Books, 2004.

Massumi, Brian. *Parables of the Virtual: Movement, Affect, Sensation*. Durham, NC: Duke University Press, 2002.

———. *Politics of Affect*. Cambridge: Polity, 2015.

Mather, Janine. "The Alphabet Speaks." In *Papers Delivered at the Symposium of the Institute of Linguistic Onto-Genetics*, edited by bpNichol, 79–84. Toronto: grOnk, 1985.

McCaffery, Steve. *The Basho Variations*. Toronto: BookThug, 2007.

———. *The Black Debt*. London, ON: Nightwood Editions, 1989.

———. *Broken Mandala*. Toronto: Ganglia Press, 1974.

———. *Carnival: The First Panel, 1967–70*. Toronto: Coach House Press, 1973.

———. *Carnival: The Second Panel, 1970–75*. Toronto: Coach House Press, 1978.

———. *Dr. Sadhu's Muffins: A Book of Readings*. Erin, ON: Press Procépic, 1974.

———. *Every Way Oakly*. Toronto: BookThug, 2008.

———. *Evoba: The Investigations Meditations, 1976–78*. Toronto: Coach House Press, 1987.

———. "An Interview with Steve McCaffery on the TRG." Interview by Peter Jaeger. *Open Letter* 10, no. 4 (Fall 1998): 77–96.

———. *Knowledge Never Knew*. Montreal: Véhicule Press, 1983.

———. *North of Intention: Critical Writings, 1973–1986*. New York: Roof, 2000.

———. *'Ow's "Waif" and Other Poems*. Toronto: Coach House Press, 1975.

———. *Panopticon*. Toronto: BookThug, 2011.

———. "The Perseus Project: Paleogorganization and the Sexual Life of Fossils." In *Papers Delivered at the Symposium of the Institute of Linguistic Onto-Genetics*, edited by bpNichol, 67–78. Toronto: grOnk, 1985.

———. "a poetry of blood." In *Text-Sound Texts*, edited by Richard Kostelanetz, 275. New York: William Morrow and Company, 1980.

———. *Prior to Meaning: The Protosemantic and Poetics*. Evanston, IL: Northwestern University Press, 2001.

———. *Research on the Mouth*. Toronto: Underwhich Editions, 1978.

———. *Seven Missing Pages*. Vol. 1, *Selected Texts, 1969–1999*. Toronto: Coach House Books, 2000.

———. *Seven Missing Pages*. Vol. 2, *Previously Uncollected Texts, 1968–2000*. Toronto: Coach House Books, 2002.

———. *Theory of Sediment*. Vancouver: Talonbooks, 1991.

———. "Trans-Avant-Garde: An Interview with Steve McCaffery." Interviewed by Ryan Cox. *Rain Taxi*, Winter 2007–8. https://www.raintaxi.com/trans-avant-garde-an-interview-with-steve-mccaffery/.

———. "Voice in Extremis." In *Prior to Meaning: The Protosemantics and Poetics*, 161–86. Evanston, IL: Northwestern University Press, 2001.

McCaffery, Steve, and bpNichol. *Rational Geomancy: The Kids of the Book-Machine: The Collected Research Reports of the Toronto Research Group, 1973–1982*. Vancouver: Talonbooks, 1992.

———. *Sound Poetry: A Catalogue*. Toronto: Underwhich Editions, 1978.

McCarthy, Cavan, ed. "Special Canadian Issue." *Tlaloc*, no. 10 (1965).

McClure, Michael. *Ghost Tantras*. San Francisco: City Lights Books, 2013.

McLeod, Katherine. "Poetry on TV: Unarchiving Phyllis Webb's CBC-TV Program, *Extension* (1967)." In *CanLit across Media: Unarchiving the Literary Event*, edited by Jason Camlot and Katherine McLeod, 72–91. Montreal: McGill-Queens University Press, 2019.

McKinnon, Barry. "Blewointment." Interview by bill bissett. *Open Letter*, 7th ser., no. 2 (1988): 73–86.

McLuhan, Marshall. "Canada: The Borderline Case." In *The Canadian Imagination: Dimensions of Literary Culture*, edited by David Staines, 226–48. Cambridge, MA: Harvard University Press, 1977.

———. *Counterblast*. Toronto: McClelland and Stewart, 1969.

———. *The Gutenberg Galaxy: The Making of Typographic Man*. New York: Signet, 1962.

———. *The Mechanical Bride: Folklore of the Industrial Culture*. 50th ann. ed. London: Duckworth Overlook, 2011. First published in 1951.

———. *Understanding Media: The Extensions of Man*. New York: Signet, 1964.

McLuhan, Marshall, and Quentin Fiore. *The Medium Is the Massage: An Inventory of Effects*. New York: Bantam, 1967.

McMaster, Susan. "Epilogue." *Arc*, no. 22 (Spring 1989): 67–9.

———. *The Gargoyle's Left Ear*. Windsor, ON: Black Moss Press, 2007.

McMaster, Susan, Andrew McClure, and Claude Depuis. *Pass This Way Again*. Underwhich Editions, 1983.

McTavish, Robert, dir. *The Line Has Shattered*. Delta, BC: Non-Inferno Media, 2013.

———. "Undone Business: Charles Bernstein on the 1963 Vancouver Poetry Conference." *Capilano Review* 3, no. 21 (Fall 2013): 12–30.

Morris, Michael, and Alvin Balkind, curators. *Concrete Poetry: An Exhibition in Four Parts*, University of British of Columbia, Vancouver, 28 March–19 April 1969.

Mount, Nick. *Arrival: The Story of CanLit*. Toronto: House of Anansi, 2017.

New, W. H. "Canada." *Journal of Commonwealth Literature* 24, no. 2 (January 1989): 36–72.

Ngai, Sianne. "Raw Matter: A Poetics of Disgust." *Open Letter* 10, no. 1 (1998): 98–122.

———. *Ugly Feelings*. Cambridge, MA: Harvard University Press, 2009.

Nichol, bp. *ABC: The Aleph Beth Book*. Ottawa: Oberon Press, 1971.

———. *Aleph Unit*. Toronto: Seripress, 1973.

———. *The Alphabet Game: A bpNichol Reader*. Edited by Lori Emerson and Darren Wershler. Toronto: Coach House Books, 2007.

———. "The Annotated, Anecdoted, Beginnings of a Critical Checklist of the Published Works of Steve McCaffery." *Open Letter* 6 no. 9 (1987): 67–92.

———. *Beach Head*. Sacramento, CA: Runcible Spoon, 1970.

———, ed. *THE BIG MID-JULY grOnk mailout*. Toronto: Ganglia Press, 1969.

———. "Blues." In *As Elected: Selected Writing*, edited by bpNichol and Jack David, 36. Vancouver: Talonbooks, 1980.

———. *bp Nichol*. High Barnet Company, 1971, audiocassette.

———. *The Captain Poetry Poems Complete*. Toronto: BookThug, 2011.

———. "Cold Mountain." 3rd ed. Toronto: Fingerprinting Inkoperated, 1992.

———. *Continental Trance*. Lantzville, BC: Oolichan Books, 1982.

———, ed. *The Cosmic Chef: An Evening of Concrete*. Ottawa: Oberon, 1970.

———, ed. *COSMIC NEWS NOTES*. Toronto: Ganglia Press, 1969.

———. *Craft Dinner: Stories & Texts, 1966–1976*. Toronto: Aya Press, 1978.

———. *Doors: To Oz & Other Landscapes*. Toronto: Ganglia Press, 1979.

———. *Ear Rational: Sound Poems, 1966–1980*. Milwaukee, WI: Membrane Press/New Fire Tapes, 1982, audiocassette.

———. *As Elected: Selected Writing, 1962–1979*. Edited by bpNichol and Jack David. Vancouver: Talonbooks, 1980.

———, ed. *END OF AUGUST GIANT grOnk MAILOUT*. Toronto: Ganglia Press, 1969.

———. "eyes." In *An Anthology of Concrete Poetry*, edited by Emmett Williams, n.p. New York: Something Else Press, 1967.

———. *First Screening*. Toronto: Underwhich Editions, 1984.

———, ed. *Ganglia Press Index*. Toronto: Ganglia Press, 1972.

———, ed. *Ganglia Press Index 1964 to 1983*. Toronto: Ganglia Press, 1983.

———. *An H in the Heart: A Reader*. Edited by George Bowering, Michael Ondaatje, and Stan Dragland. Toronto: McClelland and Stewart, 1994.

———. "Improvising Sound: Ten Poets on the Poetics of Sound." *Music Works*, no. 38 (1987): 8–17.

———. "Introduction to *The Last Blew Ointment Anthology Volume 2*." In *Meanwhile: The Critical Writings of bpNichol*, edited by Roy Miki, 417–21. Vancouver: Talonbooks, 2002.

———. *Journeying & the Returns*. Toronto: Coach House Press, 1967.

———. "Letter to bissett, not dated." Box 1976-002/005, File 155, Correspondence, 1965–1970, Bill Bissett Fonds. Clara Thomas Archives and Special Collections, York University.

———. "Letter to bissett 2, not dated." Box 1976-002/005, File 158, Correspondence, 1970–1975, Bill Bissett Fonds. Clara Thomas Archives and Special Collections, York University.

———. *love: a book of remembrances*. Vancouver Talonbooks, 1974.

———. *The Martyrology Books 1 & 2*. Toronto: Coach House Press, 1972.

———. *The Martyrology Books 3 & 4*. Toronto: Coach House Press, 1976.

———. *The Martyrology Book 5*. Toronto: Coach House Press, 1982.

———. *Meanwhile: The Critical Writings of bpNichol*. Edited by Roy Miki. Vancouver: Talonbooks, 2002.

———. "The Medium Was the Message." *Journal of Canadian Poetry*, no. 4 (1989): 5–13.

———. *Motherlove*. Allied Record Corporation, 1968, 33⅓ rpm.

———, ed. *Papers Delivered at the Symposium for the Institute of Linguistic Onto-Genetics. grOnk* (March 1985).

———. "PASSWORDS: The Bissett Papers." *Brick*, no. 23 (Winter 1985): 5–18.

———. *THE RETURN OF GRONK*. Toronto: Ganglia Press, 1968.

———. *Selected Organs: Parts of an Autobiography*. Windsor, ON: Black Moss Press, 1988.

———. "Statement." In *Journeying & the returns*, n.p. Toronto: Coach House Press, 1967.

———. *Still Water*. Vancouver: Talonbooks, 1970.

———. "'Syntax Equals the Body Structure': bpNichol, in Conversation with Daphne Marlatt and George Bowering." In *Meanwhile: The Critical Writing of bpNichol*, edited by Roy Miki, 273–97. Vancouver: Talonbooks, 2002.

———. "Tabling Content: Writing a Reading of Shaunt Basmajian's *Quote Unquote*." In *Meanwhile: The Critical Writings of bpNichol*, edited by Roy Miki, 191–211. Vancouver: Talonbooks, 2002.

———. "this is the death of the poem." *grOnk*, no. 1 (January 1967): n.p.

———. *Translating Translating Apollinaire: A Preliminary Report from a Book of Research*. Milwaukee, WI: Membrane Press, 1979.

———. *The True Eventual Story of Billy the Kid*. Toronto: Weed/Flower Press, 1970.

———. *Underwhich Checklist, 1978–1984*. Toronto: grOnk, 1984.

———. "What Is Can Lit?" In *Meanwhile: The Critical Writings of bpNichol*, edited by Roy Miki, 118–19. Vancouver: Talonbooks, 2002.

———. *zygal: a book of mysteries & translations*. Toronto: Coach House, 1986.

Nichol, bp, and Lionel Kearns. "bpNichol and Lionel Kearns at SGWU, 1968." SpokenWeb Montreal, accessed 1 May 2018. http://spokenweb.ca/sgw-poetry-readings/bpnichol-and-lionel-kearns-at-sgwu-1968.

Nichol, bp and Steve McCaffery. *In England Now that Spring*. Toronto: Aya Press, 1979.

Norris, Ken. *The Little Magazine in Canada, 1925–80: Its Role in the Development of Modernism and Post-modernism in Canadian Poetry*. Toronto: ECW Press, 1984.

O'Connelly, Barbara. *There Were Dreams*. Toronto: Ganglia Press, 1967.

O'Huigin, Sean, ed. *Poe[tree]: A Simple Introduction to Experimental Poetry*. Windsor, ON: Black Moss Press, 1978. Print/45 rpm.

O'Huigin, Sean, and Ann Southam. *Sky Sails*. MHIC Company, 1973, 33⅓ rpm.

Olson, Charles. *Collected Prose*. Edited by Donald Allen and Benjamin Friedlander. Berkeley: University of California Press, 1997.

———. "Projective Verse." Poetry Foundation, 13 October 2009. https://www.poetryfoundation.org/articles/69406/projective-verse.

Ondaatje, Michael. *The Collected Works of Billy the Kid: Left-Handed Poems*. Toronto: Anansi Press, 1970.

Ono, Yoko. *Grapefruit: A Book of Instructions and Drawings*. New York: Simon and Schuster, 2000.

Owen Sound. *Beyond the Range: Owen Sound, 1976–1979*. Underwhich Editions, 1980, audiocassette.

———. *Meaford Tank Range*. Toronto: Wild Press, 1977.

———. *Meaford Tank Range*. Wild Productions, 1977, 33⅓ rpm.

"Owen Sound." PennSound, accessed 1 May 2018. http://writing.upenn.edu/pennsound/x/Owen-Sound.php.

Past Eroticism—Canadian Sound Poetry in the 1960s, Vol. 1. Underwhich, 1986, audiocassette.

Patchen, Kenneth. *The Journal of Albion Moonlight*. New York: New Directions, 1941.

Perloff, Marjorie. *Radical Artifice: Writing Poetry in the Age of Media*. Chicago: University of Chicago Press, 1991.

———. *Unoriginal Genius: Poetry by Other Means in the New Century*. Chicago: University of Chicago Press, 2010.

Perloff, Marjorie, and Craig Dworkin, eds. *The Sound of Poetry/The Poetry of Sound*. Chicago: University of Chicago Press, 2009.

Perrone, Charles A. *Seven Faces: Brazilian Poetry since Modernism*. Durham, NC: Duke University Press, 1996.

Phenomenθnsemble. *Phenomenθnsemble*. Toronto: Underwhich Editions, 1982.

Poggioli, Renato. *Theory of the Avant-Garde*. Translated by Gerald Fitzgerald. Cambridge, MA: Harvard University Press, 1968.

Polyck-O'Neill, Julia. "Words with(out) Syntax: Reconsidering Concrete Poetry: An Exhibition in Four Parts." In *Avant-Canada: Poets, Prophets, Revolutionaries*, edited by Gregory Betts and Christian Bök, 79–94. Waterloo, ON: Wilfrid Laurier Press, 2019.

Precosky, Don. "bill bissett: Controversies and Definitions." *Canadian Poetry*, no. 27 (Fall–Winter 1990). https://canadianpoetry.org/volumes/vol27/precosky.html.

———. "Self Selected/Selected Self: Bill Bissett's Beyond Even Faithful Legends." *Canadian Poetry*, no. 34 (Spring–Sumer 1994). https://canadianpoetry.org/volumes/vol34/precosky.html.

Ramazani, Jahan. "The Local Poem in the Global Age." *Critical Inquiry*, no. 43 (Spring 2017): 670–90.

———. *A Transnational Poetics*. Chicago: University of Chicago Press, 2009.

Rawlings, Angela. *Wide Slumber for Lepidopterists*. Toronto: Coach House, 2006.

Reid, Jaimie. *A Temporary Stranger*. Vancouver: Anvil Press, 2017.

Richard, Alain-Martin, and Clive Robertson, eds. *Performance au/in Canada, 1970–1990*. Quebec City: Éditions Intervention, 1991.

Riddell, John. *D'Art Board*. Toronto: Underwhich Editions, 1986.

———. *A Game of Cards*. Toronto: Underwhich Editions, 1985.

———. *How to Grow Your Own Lightbulbs*. Toronto: Mercury Press, 1997.

———. *WAR, Vol. 1: s/word/s Games*. Toronto: Underwhich Editions, 1981.

———. *Writing Surfaces: The Fiction of John Riddell*. Edited by Lori Emerson and Derek Beaulieu. Waterloo, ON: Wilfrid Laurier University Press, 2013.

Rogers, Linda, ed. *bill bissett: Essays on His Works*. Toronto: Guernica, 2002.

Rosenberg, Ann. *The Bee Book*. Toronto: Coach House Press, 1981.

———. *Movement in Slow Time*. Toronto: Coach House Press, 1988.

Ross, Malcolm. *Poets of the Confederation*. Toronto: McClelland and Stewart, 1960.

Rothenberg, Jerome. "The Anthology as Manifesto & as an Epic Including Poetry." In *Poetics & Polemics, 1980–2005*, 14–17. Tuscaloosa: University of Alabama Press, 2008.

———, ed. *Technicians of the Sacred: A Range of Poetries from Africa, America, Asia, Europe, and Oceania*. 3rd ed. Berkeley: University of California Press, 2017.

Rowe, Sam. "Panopticon—Steve McCaffery." *Full Stop*, 15 May 2012. http://www.full-stop.net/2012/05/15/reviews/sam/panopticon-steve-mccaffery/.

Russell, Charles. *Poets, Prophets, and Revolutionaries: The Literary Avant-Garde from Rimbaud through Postmodernism*. Oxford: Oxford University Press, 1985.

Sanders, James, and Mark Prejsnar. "The Four Horsemen Burn through Atlanta." *Open Letter* 13, no. 8 (2009): 54–63.

Saville, Victor, dir. *Kim*. Beverly Hills, CA: MGM, 1950.

Schafer, R. Murray. "Letter to David UU, dated 12 September 1992." LMS-0217, Box 15 1996-01, David Harris Fonds. Library and Archives Canada.

———. *My Life on Earth & Elsewhere*. Erin, ON: Porcupine's Quill, 2012.

———. *Patria: The Complete Cycle*. Toronto: Coach House Books, 2002.

———. *The Soundscape: Our Sonic Environment and the Tuning of the World*. Rochester, VT: Destiny Books, 1993.

Schmaltz, Eric. "Digital Repositories, Settler Colonialism, and Jordan Abel's *Un/inhabited*." *English Studies in Canada* 45, no. 4 (2019): 123–42.

———. "'to forget in a body': Mosaical Consciousness & Materialist Avant-Gardism in bill bissett & Milton Acorn's Unpublished *I Want to Tell You Love*." *Canadian Literature*, no. 222 (2014): 96–112.

———. "'the killing of speech': The Sonic Politics of the Four Horsemen." *FORUM*, no. 19 (2014): n.p.

———. "'my body of bliss': Judith Copithorne's Concrete Poetry in the 1960s and 1970s." *Canadian Poetry*, no. 83 (Fall–Winter 2018): 14–39.

———. "The Politics of Memory: Digital Repositories, Settler-Colonialism, and Jordan Abel's *Un/inhabited*." *English Studies in Canada* 45, no. 4 (2019): 123–42.

Scobie, Stephen. "Bissett, Bill." In *The Oxford Companion to Canadian Literature*, edited by William Toye and Eugene Benson. 2nd ed. New York: Oxford University Press, 1997. https://www.oxfordreference.com/view/10.1093/oi/authority.20110803095508815.

———. *bpNichol: What History Teaches*. Vancouver: Talonbooks, 1984.

———. "I Dreamed I Saw: bpNichol, Dada, and Sound Poetry." *boundary 2* 3, no. 1 (Autumn 1974): 213–26.

———. "Two Authors in Search of a Character." *Canadian Literature*, no. 54 (Autumn 1972): 37–55.

Scobie, Stephen, and Brian Busby. "John Glassco." *Canadian Encyclopedia*. Last modified 3 May 2014. http://www.thecanadianencyclopedia.ca/en/article/glassco-john.

Seita, Sophie. *Provisional Avant-Gardes: Little Magazine Communities from Dada to Digital*. Stanford, CA: Stanford University Press, 2019.

Sharpe, Graham. "Pushing International Concrete Canada: 'The Communication Link' of Ganglia Press." *Open Letter* 10, no. 6 (Summer 1999): 115–23.

Shikatani, Gerry. *Sans Titre*. Performed at Studio Gallery Nine, Toronto, ON, 24 October 1981.

———. "Introduction." In *Paper Doors: An Anthology of Japanese-Canadian Poetry*, edited by Gerry Shikatani and David Aylward, 7–13. Toronto: Coach House Press, 1981.

———. *A Sparrow's Food: Poems, 1971–82*. Toronto: Coach House Press, 1984.

Siklosi, Kate. *leavings*. Malmö, SE: Timglaset, 2021.

Simpson, Gregg. "The Sound Gallery: The Official History of the Sound Gallery, Motion Studio, the Trips Festival and the Founding of Intermedia." Greggsimpson.com, accessed 18 May 2018. http://www.greggsimpson.com/soundgallerymotionstudio.htm.

Smith, A. J. M. *Masks of Poetry: Canadian Critics on Canadian Verse*. Toronto: McClelland and Stewart, 1962.

Smith, Patricia Keeney. "Creating the World She Inhabits." *Cross-Canada Writers' Quarterly* 9, no. 2 (1987): 8–9, 29.

Solt, Mary Ellen, ed. *Concrete Poetry: A World View*. Bloomington: Indiana University Press, 1968.

"Sound & Syntax International Festival of Sound Poetry, Jeremy Adler, Steve McCaffery 1978." Vimeo, uploaded by CCA: Glasgow, 19 May 2014, 38:31. https://vimeo.com/95730712.

Spinosa, Dani. *OO: Typewriter Poems*. Picton, ON: Invisible Books, 2020.

Spivak, Gayatri. *Death of a Discipline*. New York: Columbia University Press, 2003.

Stacey, Robert David, ed. *Re:Reading the Postmodern: Canadian Literature and Criticism after Modernism*. Ottawa: University of Ottawa Press, 2010.

Stein, Gertrude. *Tender Buttons*. Toronto: BookThug, 2008.

Tallman, Warren. "Wonder Merchants: Modernist Poetry in Vancouver during the 1960's." *boundary 2* 3, no. 1 (Autumn 1974): 57–90.

Thibadeau. Colleen. *Lozenges: Poems in the Shape of Things*. London: Alphabet Press, 1965.

Thomas, Greg. *Borderblurs: Concrete Poetry in England and Scotland*. Liverpool: Liverpool University Press, 2019.

Tremblay, Jean-Thomas, and Andrew Strombeck, eds. *Avant-Gardes in Crisis: Art and Politics in the Long 1970s*. Albany: State University of New York Press, 2021.

Truhlar, Richard. *Five on Fiche*. Toronto: Underwhich Editions, 1980.

Truhlar, Richard, and Steve McCaffery. *Manicured Noise*. Underwhich Editions, 1981, audiocassette.

Turner, Michael. "Expanded Literary Practices." *Ruins in Process: Vancouver Art in the 1960s*, edited by Lorna Brown. Morris and Helen Belkin Art Gallery and Grunt Gallery, 1 March 2011. http://expandedliterarypractices.vancouverartinthesixties.com/.

Twigg, Alan. "B.C. Poets Faces Critics." *Quill and Quire* 44, no. 9 (1978): 27–8.

——. "#105 bill bissett." *B.C. BookLook*, 2 February 2016. https://bcbooklook.com/105-bill-bissett/.

Tzara, Tristan. "Dada Manifesto 1918." Center for Programs in Contemporary Writing, University of Pennsylvania, accessed 1 May 2018. http://writing.upenn.edu/library/Tzara_Dada-Manifesto_1918.pdf.

Uribe, Ana Maria. "Anipoems." Vispo.com, accessed 1 May 2018. http://www.vispo.com/uribe.

UU, David. "Beyond Concrete Poetry." *British Columbia Monthly* 1, no. 3 (December 1972): n.p.

——. *Gideon Music*. Vancouver: Blew Ointment Press, 1967.

——. *High C: Selected Sound and Visual Poems 1965–1983*. Toronto: Underwhich Editions, 1990.

——, curator. *Microprosophus: International Exhibition of Visual Poetry*. Avelles Gallery, Vancouver, BC, 9–28 September 1971. Exhibition.

——. *MOTION PICTURES*. Toronto: Ganglia Press, 1969.

——. "Press Release for *Microprosophus*." LMS-0217, Box 14 1996-01, David Harris Fonds. Library and Archives Canada.

——, ed. *Spanish Fleye: a perpetual anthology for living peepl*. Toronto: Fleye Press, 1966.

——. *Touch*. Toronto: Ganglia Press, 1967.

———. *Very Sound*. Underwhich Editions, 1984, audiocassette.

UU, David, and Gerry Gilbert. *Brazilia 73: An Exhibition of International Concrete Poetry*. The Mandan Ghetto, Vancouver, BC, 1–15 April 1967. Exhibition.

Valoch, Jiří, and bpNichol, eds. *The Pipe: Recent Czech Concrete Poetry*. Toronto: Coach House Press, 1973.

Vautier, Ben. *Total Art Matchbox*. 1965. Museum of Modern Art, New York. Mixed media.

Voyce, Stephen. "Love in Precarious Times: bpNichol's Poetry of Re-invention." Presentation, Avant-Canada Conference, Brock University, St. Catherines, ON, 4–6 November 2014.

———. *Poetic Community: Avant-Garde Activism and Cold War Culture*. Toronto: University of Toronto Press, 2013.

Wah, Fred. *Permissions: TISH Poetics 1963 and Thereafter*. Vancouver: Ronsdale Press, 2014.

———. *Pictograms from the Interior of B.C.* Vancouver: Talonbooks, 1975.

———. "Vancouver 1963 Poetry Conference & Miscellaneous Recordings." Slought.org, accessed 1 May 2018. https://slought.org/resources/vancouver_1963.

Wallace, Keith. S., bill bissett, Al Neil, and Vancouver Art Gallery. *Rezoning: Collage and Assemblage: Bill Bissett, George Herms, Jess, Al Neil: Vancouver Art Gallery, October 19, 1989 to January 1, 1990*. Vancouver: Vancouver Art Gallery, 1989.

Weaver, Andy. "'The White Experience between the Words': Thoughts on Steve McCaffery's *Carnival, the Second Panel: 1970–75*." *Open Letter* 14, no. 7 (Fall 2011): 130–47.

Wendt, Larry. "Sound Poetry: I. History of Electro-Acoustic Approaches II. Connections to Advanced Electronic Technologies." *Leonardo* 18, no. 1 (1985): 11–23.

———. "Vocal Neighborhoods: A Walk through the Post-Sound Poetry Landscape." *Leonardo*, no. 3 (1993): 65–71.

Wershler, Darren. *The Iron Whim: A Fragmented History of Typewriting*. Ithaca, NY: Cornell University Press, 2007.

———. "Vertical Excess: *what fuckan theory* and bill bissett's Concrete Poetics." *Capilano Review* 2nd ser., no. 23 (1997): 115–23.

"Why Are These People Screaming?" *Globe and Mail*, 23 March 1970.

Williams, Emmett, ed. *An Anthology of Concrete Poetry*. New York: Something Else Press, 1967.

Wilson, Milton. *Poets of Mid-century, 1940–1960*. Toronto: McClelland and Stewart, 1964.

Zelazo, Suzanne. "Sport as Living Language: bpNichol and the Bodily Poetics of the Elite Triathlete." *Canadian Literature*, no. 202 (Autumn 2009): 30–47, 154.

Zolf, Rachel. "Travailing Gerry Shikatani's Protean Poetics." *West Coast Line* 41, no. 4 (Winter 2008): 4–15.

Index

a scenario press, 77
A Space, 132, 136
Abel, Jordan, 4, 28, 222-224
Acorn, Milton, 14, 39
Adachi, Tomomi, 127
advertising, 70, 72, 80-82, 84-85, 87-89, 98, 103, 114, 122, 217. *See also* publicity
affect, 123, 147; affective labour, 25, 122-126, 139-140, 146, 162
Aguiar, Fernando, 77
Ahmed, Sara, 169, 171-172, 192
Albers, Joseph, 71
Albert-Birot, Pierre, 47
Allen, Donald, 75
Allen, Lillian, 27, 175, 219-220
Anansi, 9, 47, 123
Anderson, Benedict, 46, 124,
Anderson, Hugh A., 20
Andrews, Jim, 170, 220
Anglin, Anne, 135
Anonbeyond Press, 12
Antin, David, 59, 64-66, 78
Apollinaire, Guillaume, 40, 73
Appadurai, Arjun, 50, 53, 80, 124, 218
appropriation, 66-68, 128, 152, 222
Archer, Sacha, 222
Arensberg, Walter, 177
Armstrong, Jeanette, 175
asemic writing, 41, 75, 111
Astaire, Fred, 106-107
Atwood, Margaret, 9, 14, 23, 40, 47, 115, 218
Avalettes, 130-131
avant-garde, 1-7, 9-10, 12, 14, 22-24, 26-28, 31-35, 40, 43-44, 46-48, 57-66, 70-76, 94-95, 120, 126-127, 137, 147-148, 152, 163, 167, 175, 177, 217, 219, 221; avant-gardism and race, 58-59; historical avant-gardes, 43, 58, 60, 66; redefining, 59-66

Avasilichioaei, Oana, 4
Avelles Gallery, 76
Avison, Margaret, 14-15, 37, 44, 220
Aylward, David, 5, 10, 40, 44, 48, 50, 57, 71, 77, 212

Ball, Hugo, 73, 152
Ball, Nelson, 41, 48, 221
Bann, Stephen, 69, 73
Barbour, Douglas, 120, 132-133, 135, 137, 145-146
Baretto-Rivera, Rafael, 48, 132
Barrett, Paul, 9
Barrett, Ross, 130, 132
Barthes, Roland, 82
Barwin, Gary, 4, 24, 219
Basmajian, Shaunt, 5, 10, 71, 77, 103-105, 139
Bataille, Georges, 144
Bayard, Caroline, 26, 64, 84, 99, 132
Beaulieu, Derek, 4, 26, 82, 221
Belloli, Carlo, 76
Bennett, Deanna, 22
Bennett, John M., 77
Berger, John, 69, 80-81, 84, 103
Bergvall, Caroline, 127
Bernstein, Charles, 26, 59, 63-65, 110-111, 126, 136, 139
Berton, Pierre, 23
Betts, Gregory, 6, 10, 26, 57, 61-62, 64, 73, 88, 99, 221
Bevington, Stan, 46, 48, 189
Birney, Earle, 14-15, 39, 44-45, 189-190, 195-196, 220
bissett, bill, 1-6, 9-10, 12, 14-15, 18-23, 26, 31, 33-34, 36-41, 44-48, 50-51, 53, 55-57, 61, 64, 67, 70-71, 74-77, 87-91, 105-109, 114, 121, 124, 127-131, 136, 142, 144, 155, 159-161, 180, 185-187, 217-218, 220-221
Black Mountain (poetics), 75, 178, 180

273

blewointment (periodical), 10, 20, 23, 34, 37–40, 47, 87–88, 106, 180, 185–186, 188–189
Blew Ointment Press, 10, 20–21, 27, 37, 39, 108, 189
borderblur, 1–10, 12, 14–16, 18, 20–24, 26–29, 31–36, 38, 40–48, 50, 52, 54–72, 74, 76–78, 80–82, 84–86, 88, 90, 92, 94, 96, 98, 100, 102, 104, 106, 108, 110–112, 114, 116, 118, 120–126, 128–132, 134–140, 142–144, 146–148, 150, 152, 154–156, 158, 160, 162–163, 166–168, 170, 172–178, 180–182, 184–186, 188, 190, 192, 194–196, 198–200, 202, 204–206, 208, 210, 212, 214–225
Bök, Christian, 26, 57, 64, 133, 220–221
Bowering, George, 10, 14, 37, 44, 75–76, 114, 165–166, 180, 220
Brazilia 73: An Exhibition of International Concrete Poetry, 73, 76
breath, 87, 95, 145, 158, 174, 179
Breton, André, 35, 60
British Columbia Monthly (periodical), 71
Brossard, Nicole, 10, 146, 175
Broudy, Hart, 44, 48, 57, 77
Brown, Jim, 12, 44, 46, 131–132, 142,
Brown, Lorna, 96
Brown, Russell, 22
Bürger, Peter, 58, 60, 62
Butling, Pauline, 26, 57–59, 64, 66, 132, 138

Cain, Stephen, 4, 26, 92, 129, 133, 220–221
cadence, 123–124
Călinescu, Matei, 58, 60
Campbell, Maria, 9
Canada Council for the Arts, 9, 18–21, 52, 187
Canadada, 71
Canadada (album), 132
Canadian Broadcasting Corporation (CBC), 2, 18–19, 213, 218
Canadian Multiculturalism Act, 25
CanLit Boom, 9, 12, 33, 120, 126, 177
Capilano Review, The (periodical), 221
Carlson, Tim, 20
Carr, Wayne, 130, 132
Caruso, Barbara, 44, 48, 220
Cavarero, Adrianna, 148
CCMC, 142
Centennial, 1–2, 14, 23, 123
Cha, Theresa Hak Kyung, 58, 213
Chaplin, Charlie, 130

Chopin, Henri, 76, 127, 138–139
Christakos, Margaret, 24, 219
Cixous, Hélène, 175
Claire, Paula, 43, 127, 138
Clarke, Austin, 9
Clifford, Wayne, 48, 189
Clinton, Martina, 5, 23, 36–39, 44, 75, 130, 159
Clutesi, George, 27
Coach House Press, 12, 93, 114, 135, 189
Cobbing, Bob, 32, 47, 76–77, 127, 138, 186, 220
Cochrane, Maureen, 21
Cohen, Leonard, 14
Cold War, 50, 61, 201
Coleman, Victor, 44, 48, 130, 189
collage, 10, 36, 45, 72, 88, 90–91, 106, 111, 186, 205
Colombo, John Robert, 44, 57, 84
colonial, 123,127-128, 172, 218, 222–23; colonialism, 18
composition by field, 174–75
Compton, Wayde, 4
conceptual art, 178, 180–181
concrete poetry, 4, 6, 8, 10, 18, 22, 27–28, 31–34, 36, 48, 56–57, 69–79, 81–83, 85, 87–89, 91–93, 95, 97–99, 101–103, 105, 107, 109–111, 113, 115–117, 121, 126, 130, 135, 140, 159, 166–167, 169–170, 176–177, 180–181, 185, 217, 222–223; dirty concrete, 70, 92; first wave, 70–71, 73–74, 81–82, 92
Concrete Poetry: An Exhibition in Four Parts, 56, 76
conservative (politics), 18–24, 46
Copithorne, Judith, 5, 7, 9–10, 12–13, 15, 23, 27–28, 37–40, 44, 46, 48, 57, 61, 67, 70–71, 74–76, 96, 98–103, 113, 176, 187, 217, 221
Cormier, Nan, 198
Corriere Canadese (periodical), 119
Coutts, Mike, 129
Cox, Ryan J., 20
Creeley, Robert, 37
Cummings, E. E., 73
Curnoe, Greg, 44, 131

Dada (art movement), 71, 155, 178, 181, 222; Dadaism, 33, 60, 222
Daems, Jim, 61
Davey, Frank, 18, 26, 37, 54, 76, 130, 189, 220
Davey, Linda, 189
David, Jack, 26

Davies, Robertson, 14
Dawson, David, 37
de Campos, Augusto, 70
de Campos, Haroldo, 70
de Villiers, Marq, 150–151
Dean, Michael, 12, 31, 35, 41, 44, 106, 120, 132, 145, 169, 174, 176, 189, 207–211
Dedora, Brian, 5, 12, 31, 35, 41, 44, 71, 115–117, 132, 189, 208
Derwyddon Press, 12
Dewdney, Christopher, 189
di Prima, Diane, 47
digital poetry, 169
Dimock, Wai Chee, 73–77
Divine Order of the Lodge, 12
Dome Show (exhibiton), 187–188
downtown poets, 37, 47
Drucker, Johanna, 26
Dub poetry, 27, 219
Duchamp, Marcel, 177, 186
Duncan, Robert, 37, 75, 178–179
Dupuis, Claude, 41, 198
Dutton, Paul, 5, 12, 26, 41, 48, 71, 96–97, 120, 132, 144–145, 189, 220
Dylan, Bob, 2

electroacoustic, 121, 127, 131–132, 139, 141–142, 153–154, 158, 159, 181. *See also* sound poetry
embodied poetics, 169, 174–175
Emerson, Lori, 26, 70–71, 92, 96, 220
English, Carol, 198
Extension: Here, Now, and Then (television show), 2–5, 21, 23, 56

Farrell, Lance, 23, 36–39, 75, 159
feminism, 25, 28; feminist, 9, 28, 39, 135–136, 146, 154, 161–163, 175, 223
Fenollosa, Ernest, 66
Festival of Contemporary Arts, 55
film, 18, 37, 103, 105
Finlay, Ian Hamilton, 32, 47, 76, 177
Fiore, Quentin, 160
First Draft, 41, 120–121, 135–136, 146–147, 154–156, 163, 167, 169, 196–198, 215
Flahiff, Fred, 56
Flemmer, Kyle, 222
Fleye Press, 12, 41
Fluxus, 7, 33, 64, 177, 187, 193, 198
Forest, Léonard, 37, 106
Foucault, Michel, 89

Four Horsemen, 48, 119–120, 132–133, 135–139, 142, 144–145, 147–153, 155, 163, 176, 205, 207
Freytag-Loringhoven, Baroness Elsa von, 73
Friskney, Janet B., 14–15
Front de libération du Québec (FLQ), 25
Frye, Northrop, 23, 218
Frykberg, Susan, 43
Furnival, John, 32, 47, 76
Futurism (movement), 60; Futurist, 73, 126

Gadd, Maxine, 27, 37, 67, 176, 187–188, 221
Gammel, Irene, 33
Ganglia (periodical), 10–11, 23, 40, 47, 55, 75, 86, 189, 195
Ganglia Press, 10, 23, 40, 47, 55, 75, 86, 189, 195
Garnet, Eldon, 15
Garnier, Pierre, 47, 76
Gauvreau, Claude, 127
George, Chief Dan, 27
Gilbert, Gerry, 15, 37, 39, 44, 48, 57, 76, 187–188
Ginsberg, Allen, 2, 37, 75
Glass, Philip, 132, 153
Glassco, John, 20–21
Globe and Mail (periodical), 20, 119
Godard, Barbara, 26, 146, 175
Gomringer, Eugen, 69–70, 73–74, 76, 81, 84
Goodman, Steve, 151
Governor General's Award, 18–19
Grace, Sherril, 198
Grateful Dead, The, 130
Great Canadian Writers' Weekend, 135
grOnk (periodical), 1, 10, 12, 15, 23, 40–42, 47–49, 167, 188–189
Grove, Frederick Philip, 14
Gysin, Brion, 75

Hajnoczky, Helen, 222
happening (art form), 7, 167, 176, 187–188, 191
Happy Monks (press), 222
Harbourfront Centre, 137
Hardt, Michael, 25, 79–80, 121–122, 124–125, 143–144, 146
Hausmann, Raoul, 45
Heidsieck, Bernard, 50, 127
Herbert, George, 73
Hewitt, Al, 129
Higgins, Dick, 4, 7–8, 33–34, 40, 138, 186, 196, 220

Hilder, Jamie, 22, 26, 140
Hill, Crag, 77
Hindley-Smith, Rob, 40
Hindmarch, Maria (Gladys), 38
Hoch, Hannah, 73
Hong, Cathy Park, 58–59, 66
Houédard, Dom Sylvester, 3, 5, 31–34, 36, 44–46, 50, 76, 92, 224
House of Commons, 18, 20, 64
humanism, 54–55, 122

Imagination of Aldo Breun, The, 174, 176, 207–211
Imagist (literary movement), 73, 166
intermedia, 7–8, 18, 27, 31, 33–35, 43–44, 69, 75, 116, 131, 136, 143, 155, 180–181, 186–188, 196, 224–225; intermedial, 1, 3, 5–7, 9–10, 12, 14, 20–21, 26–28, 34, 36, 38–40, 46, 51, 54, 57, 62–65, 67–68, 70, 72, 74–75, 77–78, 92–96, 111, 116, 121, 125–126, 130, 135, 143, 146, 154, 163, 167–168, 177, 198, 217–225
Intermedia Society, 7, 186–187
International Sound Poetry Festival, 41, 133, 138–139, 151–152
Itter, Carole, 96

Jaeger, Peter, 26, 220
Jagger, Mick, 2
Jandl, Ernest, 47, 76, 127
Jankola, Beth, 39
Jantar, Maja, 127
Jarvis, Donald, 37
Jewitt, Carey, 7
Jones, Tom, 129
Joyce, James, 45
Jukelevics, Nicette, 180
jwcurry, 24, 41, 77, 193, 209, 219, 211

Karasick, Adeena, 4, 221
Kearns, Lionel, 44, 76, 131, 142
Kellough, Kaie, 4, 127
Kemp, Penn, 5, 10, 12, 27, 67, 119, 121, 134–136, 142, 145–146, 154, 161–163, 217
Keon, Wayne, 220
Kim (film), 106, 109
kinetic poetry, 6, 8–9, 23, 28, 34, 44, 72, 165, 167–171, 173–177, 179, 181–183, 185, 187–189, 191–193, 195, 197, 199, 201, 203, 205, 207, 209, 211, 213, 215, 217; digital kinetic poetry, 169–170

Kittler, Friedrich, 105, 108, 110
Kiyooka, Roy, 5, 37, 71, 114–115, 217, 219
Knowles, Alison, 33
Kontakte (periodical), 12
Kontakte Writers in Performance (reading series), 12, 153, 211
Kostelanetz, Richard, 47, 70, 77, 160
Kress, Gunther, 7

Lane, Patrick, 12, 38, 46
Lang, Kurt, 39
Laporte, Pierre, 25
Lawrence, Scott, 39, 48
Layton, Irving, 14
Leacock, Stephen, 14
Lee, David, 21
Lee, Dennis, 40, 47; sound 123–124
Lefler, Peggy, 77
Lennon, John, 186
Levertov, Denise, 37, 75
levy, d. a., 47, 76
Lim, Sing, 37
listening, 123–124, 141, 147, 161, 174, 187
Livesay, Dorothy, 39, 222
Long, Joy, 37, 136
Lopes, Damian, 221–223
Lynn, Vera, 129

Mac Low, Jackson, 127, 139
MacEwen, Gwendolyn, 14
Macpherson, Jay, 14
Mallarmé, Stéphane, 73
Mandan Ghetto, 76, 136
Mandan Massacre, 121, 130–131, 187
Mandel, Eli, 14
Marinetti, F. T., 73
Marlatt, Daphne, 27, 146, 165–166, 175, 220
Massey Report, *The*, 52
Massumi, Brian, 169, 171, 173
Mather, Janine, 208
Mayer, Hansjorg, 47, 76, 106, 108
Mayne, Seymour, 12, 44, 46,
McCaffery, Steve, 5, 12, 23, 26, 36, 41, 44, 47–48, 51–52, 57, 61, 64, 67, 70–71, 82, 88, 92–96, 99, 102, 108, 110–111, 113–114, 120, 126–127, 132, 137–138, 141–145, 149–150, 166, 169–170, 181, 189, 208, 217, 221
McCarthy, Cavan, 47–48, 76
McClelland and Stewart (publisher), 9, 12, 47, 51; M&S, 12, 14

McClelland, Jack, 14
McClure, Andrew, 41, 121, 135, 154–155
McClure, Michael, 127, 129–130
McCutcheon, Mac T., 18
McFadden, David, 44, 48, 189
McKinnon, Barry, 39, 48
McLeod, Katherine, 1
McLuhan, Marshall, 2–3, 7, 25, 32, 34, 43, 51–57, 64, 78–82, 92, 121, 131, 140, 144, 150, 160, 171–172, 178, 182–185, 187, 206, 217–218; *Counterblast,* 51–52; *The Gutenberg Galaxy,* 3, 52–53, 79; *The Mechanical Bride,* 79, 183; *Understanding Media,* 3, 53–57, 79, 140, 171, 172, 184–185; global village, 3, 53, 56, 184
McMaster, Susan, 5, 10, 27, 36, 41, 121, 135–136, 145–146, 154–156, 198, 219
McPherson, George, 18–19
McRobbie, Kenneth, 14
Metro-Goldwyn-Mayer, 106, 108
Michaux, Henri, 75
Microprosophus: International Exhibition of Concrete Poetry, 76, 78
Miki, Roy, 26
Moholy-Nagy, Laszlo, 71
Moodie, Susanna, 14
Morgan, Edwin, 47
Morrow, Charlie, 135
Morton, Colin, 41, 121, 135, 154–155, 198
Moss, Laura, 22
Motion Studio, 75
Mount, Nick, 9, 12, 23, 158
Mulroney, Brian, 24–25
Music Gallery, 132, 136
Music Works (periodical), 133
multimodal, 7; multimodality, 7

Nathan Phillips Square, 119, 125
National Film Board of Canada (NFB), 18, 37
nationalism, 4, 6, 22, 32, 51–52, 54, 78, 120, 123–124, 217–218; nationalist, 2–3, 6, 22, 44, 50, 54, 57, 72–74, 122, 139, 146, 163, 177, 218
Negri, Antonio, 25, 79–80, 121–122, 124–125, 143–144, 146
Neil, Al, 37, 39, 88, 130
Nesbitt, W. B., 18
New Canadian Library (NCL), 12, 14–15, 33, 47
New, W. H., 10
Newlove, John, 14, 37

Ngai, Sianne, 82
Nichol, bp, 1–10, 12, 15, 18–19, 21–24, 26–27, 31–35, 40–41, 43–48, 50–51, 54–57, 61, 63–64, 66, 69–71, 74–77, 84–87, 92, 102–103, 111–112, 122, 129–133, 135–138, 142–144, 147, 150, 155, 158–159, 165–170, 172–173, 177, 180, 183, 189, 192–196, 211–212, 215, 218–221, 223–224
Nightwood Editions, 21
Nihilist Spasm Band, 130, 152
Noigandres, 70, 74, 76, 81
Norris, Ken, 39
Nova, Gary Lee, 36, 76, 130
Nowlan, Alden, 14
Nowlan, J. P., 18

Ofo, Jerry, 44
O'Huigin, Sean, 41, 44, 133, 138, 142
Olson, Charles, 37, 75, 173–174, 178–180
Ondaatje, Michael, 9, 14, 44, 48, 189
Only Paper Today (periodical), 176
Ono, Yoko, 33, 178, 198
Open Letter (periodical), 106, 207, 220–221
Owen Sound, 120, 132–133, 139, 142, 145, 151–153, 155, 159, 163, 207

Page, P. K., 14, 39
Page, Robin, 76
Paperview Books, 222
paratradition, 6, 8–10, 12, 21–23, 26, 28, 35, 41, 46, 61–63, 66, 68, 72–73, 78–80, 120, 126, 132, 137, 139, 147, 163, 167, 169, 177, 217, 219, 222
Parsons, David, 198
pataphysics, 207
Patchen, Kenneth, 75
Penhale, David, 120, 132, 145
Pennsound (website), 147
Penteract Press, 222
performance art, 180–181
Perloff, Marjorie, 26, 61, 70, 81–82
Perry, Sam, 129–130
Peterson, Margaret, 37
Phenomenon Press, 12
Phenomenθnsemble, 142
Pignatari, Décio, 70, 73, 81
Piringer, Jorg, 121
poema processo, 177
Poggioli, Renato, 58, 60
Polyphonix Festival for International Poetry, 213

postmodern, 14, 61–62, 184
postmodern decadence, 61–62
Pound, Ezra, 73
Powell, Jane, 106–108
Precosky, Don, 20
Prentice, David, 135
proprioception, 98, 171, 173–175, 178, 182–184, 198, 205, 216; proprioceptive poetry, 173
Project Gutenberg (website), 223
provisional institutions, 126, 136, 147, 167, 182
publicity, 63, 80–81, 84, 89, 217
Purdy, Al, 14

race and borderblur, 50, 66–67, 114–115, 201, 222
Ramazani, Jahan, 6, 77, 218
Rappaport, Henry, 188
rawlings, a., 127, 221
Re: Sounding, 120, 133, 135, 142, 145
Reaney, James, 14–15
Regan, Ronald, 24
Reich, Steve, 132, 153
Reid, Jamie, 37, 61, 189, 221
Renaud, Thérèse, 127
Returning (periodical), 12–13, 46
Richler, Mordecai, 14
Riddell, John, 5, 12, 41, 44, 48, 167, 169–170, 189, 191, 199–205, 208, 215
Rosenberg, Ann, 5, 10, 12, 27–28, 67, 71, 111–114, 217
Rosenblatt, Joe, 14, 120
Ross, Malcolm, 14–15
Ross, Stuart, 24, 77, 219,
Rothenberg, Jerome, 44, 127–128, 138, 152
Rowe, Sam, 110
Royal Wedding (film), 106, 108
Rudy, Susan, 26, 132, 138
Russell, Charles, 22, 58, 60, 62, 95
Ryan, Ken, 129

Saroyan, Aram, 70, 103
Schafer, R. Murray, 24, 41, 123, 140–142, 160
schizophonia, 141–142, 148, 154
Schwitters, Kurt, 73
Scobie, Stephen, 26, 35, 43–44, 57, 70–71, 76, 120, 128, 132–133, 220
Scott, Jordan, 4
Scream-In, 119–123, 125, 142
See/Hear (periodical), 131–132
Seiichi, Niikuni, 76–77

Seita, Sophie, 59, 62–65
Selman, Dallas, 129
Shadbolt, Jack, 37
Sharpe, Graham, 48
Sheard, Sarah, 189
Shikatani, Gerry, 5, 10, 48, 50, 67, 77, 133, 135, 139, 167, 169, 174, 176, 211–215, 217, 219–220
Siklosi, Kate, 4, 222, 224
Silver Birch Press, 12, 115
Simpson, Gregg, 39, 76, 130, 136, 187
Smith, Dorothy, 146
Smith, Patricia Keeney, 145
Smith, Steven Ross, 12, 41, 120, 130, 132, 138, 153, 189, 220
Solt, Mary Ellen, 31, 69–70
Something Else Newsletter (periodical), 7
Something Else Press, 4
Sound Gallery, 75, 136, 159
sound poetry, 6–8, 27–28, 36, 41, 67, 92, 96, 119–123, 125–133, 135, 137–139, 141–149, 151–155, 157, 159, 161–163, 166–167, 176–177, 181, 185, 196, 207, 217
soundscapes, 123, 142
Souster, Raymond, 14
Southam, Ann, 133, 142
Spanish Fleye (periodical), 41
Spinosa, Dani, 4, 26, 29, 222–224
SpokenWeb, 147
spoken word, 27, 121, 131, 140, 155
Stein, Gertrude, 18, 45, 158
Stephens, Peter, 44
Stettheimer, Florine, 33
Stockwell, Dean, 106
Strombeck, Andrew, 59
Studio Gallery Nine, 207, 211
Sugars, Cynthia, 22
Suknaski, Andrew, 48, 57, 196
Sullivan, Françoise, 48, 127
Surrealism (art movement), 35, 52, 60, 127
Sutherland, W. Mark, 133
Suzuzki, Aiko, 133
Swede, George, 119–120, 122, 125, 142
Symposium of Linguistic Onto-Genetics, The, 176, 207

tactile, 173, 176, 178, 183–185, 215; tactility, 171, 173, 183, 206, 216. *See also* touch
Tallman, Warren, 18, 37, 75, 159, 178
Tekst, 142

television, 1, 3, 33–34, 40, 44–45, 50–51, 53, 65, 72, 80, 103, 111, 113–114, 187, 217–218
Thatcher, Margaret, 24
Thomas, Greg, 31–32
Timglaset (press), 222
TISH (periodical), 36–37, 45, 61, 173, 178–180, 185
Tlaloc (periodical), 76
To Call (periodical), 22
Toronto Star (periodical), 19
touch, 2, 33, 43, 54, 63–64, 86–87, 103, 131, 167, 171–175, 182–185, 192, 194, 198, 206, 215–216
Traill, Catherine Parr, 14
Trasov, Vincent 40; Mr. Peanut, 40, 76
Tremblay, Jean-Thomas, 59
Trips Festival, 129–130
Trudeau, Pierre Elliott, 25
Truhlar, Richard, 12, 41, 120, 132, 137–138, 142, 145, 152–153, 189, 191, 219
Turner, Michael, 23, 185
Twigg, Alan, 20–21, 47
typewriter, 36, 65, 72, 78, 89, 92–93, 96–100, 105–106, 110, 113, 159, 174, 179, 211–213, 223–224

UbuWeb (website), 147
Underwhich Editions, 12, 41, 129–130, 135, 138, 147, 153, 155, 161, 189, 191, 199, 205; Audiographic Series, 41, 161,
University of Alberta, 133, 137, 148
University of British Columbia (UBC), 18, 37–38, 56, 75, 76, 180, 188
Uribe, Ana Maria, 170
UU, David, 5, 12, 15, 23–24, 36, 40–41, 44, 48, 57, 71, 74, 76, 78, 80, 86–87, 103, 115, 130–131, 221–222

Valoch, Jiří, 47–48, 220
Vancouver Art Gallery, 187
Vancouver Poetry Conference, 37, 75
Varney, Ed, 44, 56, 76, 78, 80, 176, 187–188
Vautier, Ben, 177, 189, 193
Véhicule Gallery, 136
Very Stone House, 12, 46
vibratory nexus, 151, 153
video poetry, 169
Vietnam War, 25, 53
visual poetry, 8, 76, 209
Voyce, Stephen, 26, 51, 84–85, 149, 220
Vroom, Ivo, 47

wagner, d. r., 47–48
Wah, Fred, 37, 59, 66, 220
Waldrop, Rosemarie, 81
Walker, Gerry, 2
Wallace, Ian, 40, 76
Wallace, Keith, 186
Warhol, Andy, 130
Watson, Wilfred, 15, 56
Weaver, Andy, 67, 94–95
Weaver, Robert, 18, 213
Webb, Phyllis, 1–3, 23, 40, 44–45, 56, 218
Weigel, Matthew James, 4, 222
Wenman, Bob, 20
Wershler, Darren, 26, 89, 96, 98, 220–221
Western Front, 132, 136, 148
Whalen, Philip, 37
White Paper Policy, 25
Wild Press, 12
Williams, Emmett, 4, 31, 69–70, 129
Wilson, Milton, 14
wordmusic, 136, 154–155, 196

York University, 132, 137, 221
Yoshizawa, Shoji, 77

Zelazo, Suzanne, 33, 169, 221
Zolf, Rachel, 214–215

www.ingramcontent.com/pod-product-compliance
Lightning Source LLC
Chambersburg PA
CBHW041439300426
44114CB00026B/2936